Book

Murders spanning over a [ ]
Book contains History of the [ ] ～～～～ 1896 to 2007

Includes 50 murder cases

```
12 Hand Guns
10 Knives
6 Iron Pipes
5 Strangulation
4 Shotguns
2 Baseball Bats
1 Rifle
1 Axe
1 Cyanide Poisoning
1 Truck,
1 Car
1 Hanging
1 Hands
1 Electrocution
1 Exposure
1 Hammer
1 Unknown Means
```

FIVE OF THE FIFTY CASES!

Sixteen year old farm hand sneaks up behind farmer milking cow, with two blows from his axe, cuts off farmers head. Drags body and head to manure pit where he buried it.

Father murders six month old son by electrocution. Places son and wet diaper on metal tray, attaches wires to tray and plugs into outlet, electrocuting son.

Husband mixes cyanide poison to wife's medicine, killing her so he can pursue love affair with another women.

Mother blindfolds 9 year old son and 5 year old daughter in cemetery, putting cotton in their ears and tape over eyes then executes them with a .22 pistol, commits suicide with same gun.

Baby boy found dead in paper bag in dump off Crane Avenue with a 15 inch long blanket wrapped around his neck by two youths looking for stamps.

4 unsolved murders, one body never found.

MANY OTHER EVENTS IN THE DEPARTMENTS HISTORY

First U. S. Secret Service Agent killed in the line of duty in Pittsfield.

Details of Pittsfield Police Captain killed in the line of duty by troop train while saving mother and two daughters from death.

20 Bank robberies and shoot out with Bank robbers in high speed car chase.

By invitation only, witness executions by hanging at county jail. Last 2 in Pittsfield before the legislature enacted that the legal penalty of death should be paid thereafter at the state prison in Charlestown.

Prohibition and where to purchase illegal booze. Who made it and where.

Pittsfield Postmaster, disappears just as two inspectors from the US Post Office arrived for a routine check of local postal affairs.

Missing Bank President, unsolved mystery, lived only three houses away from Chief John L. Sullivan, who was a personal friend of FBI Director J. Edgar Hoover.

Runaway horse drawn wagon injures police officer trying to stop it.

Dedicated to
Detective Francis D. O'Neil

Members of the Pittsfield Police Department
Past-Present-Future

TABLE OF CONTENTS

CHAPTER ONE

Town of Pittsfield
1690-1879

On May 20, 1690, the Colonial legislature enacted an "Order that a watch be forthwith kept and maintained in every town and village of this colony of so many persons as Town Council in each town or village shall appoint". Prior to this enactment, arrests for crimes were always made by constables. Constables and watchmen who were the keepers of the town peace at night, sometimes shared their power with marshals, justices of the peace and sheriffs. All of these men exercised the same power throughout the colony in 1690 and probably at even earlier dates.

Pioneer settlers started to inhabit Pittsfield in 1743. The township was then known as "The Plantation of Pontoosuc." Col. William Williams secured the passage of the act by which the settlement was incorporated as a town. Sir Francis Bernard, the royal governor of Massachusetts, gave it the name of Pittsfield, in honor of William Pitt, Earl of Chatham and popularly known as "The Great Commoner." Pittsfield's incorporation papers were signed on April 26, 1761. On July 1, 1761, Berkshire County was established by separating it from Hampshire County. It was named by the governor after his home county in England. The town form of government was continued until 1891 when, by vote of the citizens, Pittsfield became a city. Pittsfield is situated in the center of the Berkshire Hills. In later years, the city was served by the Boston and Albany, New York, New Haven and Hartford railroads.

The records of the Town of Pittsfield were barren of any records of watchmen prior to November 17, 1847. At that time it was voted "that the selectman be authorized to employ a night watchman at the expense of the town if in their opinion such a watch is necessary". What was done to carry out this vote does not appear in the records.

The word "police" is not found anywhere in the indexes of the General Laws of either Colony or Commonwealth before 1851, except in the descriptive phrase "police court". In 1851, the position of policeman was formally created as an arm of the law. The enabling act permitted towns to appoint police officers with all the powers of constables in criminal matters.

The Annual Report of the selectmen of the Town of Pittsfield for the year ending April 1, 1852 shows the following expense account: Rent and expenses for the police officer and lockup was listed at $145.75. In addition the annual salaries of constables and night watchmen was $44.50, for a total cost of $190.25

Timid about this new extravagance assignable to their authority, the selectmen defended themselves on the following grounds: "We consider that the importance of our police and the manner in which the police office is conducted is of sufficient interest to the town to give it a distinct place in our report. The expense of the police may appear large to some, in fact, too large for our town, but as far as we are able to judge the establishment throughout meets the hearty approbation of the public". Imagine a police "establishment" as "too large" of an expense at $190.25 in a township peopled by 6,000 in the year of our Lord 1852. That year the Police Department made 121 arrests.

In 1855, salaries for the Police Department totaled $235.00, and the maintenance cost was $274.00, for a total cost of $509.00. In that year the number of arrests made had risen to 212.

In 1866 police work was still done only by part time use of several watchmen and special constables whose combined wages amounted to less than $600.00. The town's population by that time had increased to 9,676.

During 1869, the selectmen employed four night watchmen. This was equivalent to the services of two persons permanently and a special counsel who acted as sort of chief of police. This roster required a payroll of $1,977.55 and a maintenance cost of $164.28. The population was 11,112 persons by then and the Police Department made 190 arrests during that year.

On April 12, 1875 the town passed a by-law, approved by the Superior Court, which made it mandatory that the selectmen appoint police officers and designate one of them chief of police and a captain of the night watch. They were considered full-time officers on regular salaries. The pay of policemen was $1.75 a day under this by-law. Although George Hayes was appointed in charge of the day police and John M. Hatch in charge of the night police, these officers were still referred to, in 1866, as constables only.

From 1881 until the end of the town government in 1891, the voters added $.75 a day to the by-law wage for officers, thus bringing their salary to $2.50 a day. Each member of the police force was appointed annually by the Board of Selectmen and appointed verbally, in the presence of the entire board. This ceremony tended to impress upon the men a sense of responsibility to the public. It was also a reminder that at the end of each 12 month period, they might fail to be reappointed if they showed themselves to be ineffective.

CHIEF JOHN M. HATCH

Chief John M. Hatch gave the first report of a chief of police to the selectmen concerning the doings of the Police Department in the Town of Pittsfield in 1877. In part he said, "The force now consists of seven men; a chief of police and three patrolmen on duty from noon until midnight and a captain and two patrolmen on duty from midnight to noon". In his report the chief cited specific instances of frightful obscenities occurring in the presence of the female prisoners by male prisoners and strongly recommended a segregation of the sexes in jail. Chief Hatch served as chief for five years, from April 1876 to June 1881. Serving with Chief Hatch were Captain John H. Hadsell, Officers Daniel Barry, James W. Fuller, James Solon, L. R. Abbe and Patrick Cassidy. Each of seven men were on duty twelve hours out of twenty-four, and made a total of 256 arrests for the year.

CHIEF HATCH AND 5 OFFICERS - 1877

CAPTAIN DANIEL BARRY
1876-1882

In the fall of 1879, a new Police Station was erected on town land at the corner of School and Allen Street, presently the parking lot of Berkshire Bank, at a cost of $2,800. This land was formerly the Town of Pittsfield's Burial Ground. All the remains in the cemetery were moved to "The Hill" at the Pittsfield Cemetery on Wahconah Street. The new station was of brick construction 40 ft. and 4 in. by 24 ft. and 6 in.

Adjacent to the cemetery was the Berkshire Medical Institution, which operated for several years, training future physicians. The school taught anatomy, which required the dissection of bodies. This required a continuing supply of reasonably fresh bodies for the students. A person would be buried during the day; after dark the body could be exhumed by "Body Snatchers" and sold to the Institution.

Chief James McKenna

In June of 1881, James McKenna was appointed chief of police for the Town of Pittsfield, serving for over five years until November 13, 1886. Chief McKenna was a veteran of the Civil War serving several enlistments. He was a member of the Allen Guard and charter member of the Rockwell Grand Army Post. Three governors had previously appointed him Justice of the Peace.

Chief John Nicholson
New Chief

Chief John Nicholson was appointed chief of police for the Town of Pittsfield on November 13, 1886 and served until April 1, 1905 when he was appointed High Sheriff of Berkshire County by Governor Douglas. As the town completed the last year of its existence before becoming a city, in 1890, the Police Department consisted of a Chief of Police with a salary of $1,200.00; a captain with a salary of $1,016.12, ten patrolmen, sixteen part-time policemen, a police matron and a janitor.

City of Pittsfield
1891-1892

Acting under the requirements of the first city charter in 1891, Mayor Charles E. Hibbard appointed, and the Aldermen confirmed, a chief of police. John Nicholson became the first chief of police for the City of Pittsfield. Chief Nicholson was also the chief for the Town of Pittsfield beginning after the retirement of Chief McKenna on November 13, 1886. Chief Nicholson was the first captain of the F Company of the Massachusetts Volunteer Militia. He retired as a major. Also confirmed were a captain, eleven regular and four provisional patrolmen, sixteen special or part-time patrolmen and one police matron. This organization not only functioned under the charter but in accordance with the provisions of a city ordinance approved February 24, 1891, which stipulated, among other things, that each member of the force be duly sworn in; that the station house be kept open day and night; and that the chief keep an active account of all duties performed by the force, and all absences of any member. At that time, the chief's salary was fixed at $1,200.00 a year.

In the early days, many duties outside the fundamental activity of crime prevention, suppression and punishment, were exacted from this department by orders of the Mayor and Aldermen and from the Board of Health.

For example, in 1892 the department inspected 1,395 buildings and served 1,540 notices for the Board of Health, ordered 843 straps put into sink pipes, 901 privy vaults cleaned, 143 cesspools put in sanitary condition and 294 new cesspools installed. It required full time for one officer for four months to do this work. Incidentally, the year 1892 was a "No License Year" in Pittsfield. Consequently the police made 200 raids and found illegally kept liquor in 91 places.

1897-1905

CELL BLOCK

A much needed addition to the Police Station was completed in 1897 at the modest expense of $6,975.82. A second floor was added. There were now twenty-four cells and one padded cell in the station in three separate rooms.

There was also a room to lodge "knights of the road", better known as hobos or tramps. This room was 30 ft. by 20 ft. The beds were slats nailed to two uprights so that they were raised from the floor about six inches. They were two feet wide and about seven feet long. There were no mattresses, no bed clothes. The drifter would take off his coat and roll it up for a pillow and stretch out on the bare boards. The city strictly enforced the law against vagrancy and showed no pity to a knight of the road. As a railroad center, Pittsfield was visited by every tramp between Boston and Albany.

When a person arrived at the station for lodging on a Saturday night, it was not uncommon for the department to bring in a half-dozen drunks after the saloons were closed. Drunkenness accounted for most of the arrests made at night. The "lodger" was lined up against the sergeant's desk for registration. The person's (usually a male) height was taken, together with the color of his eyes and hair, and a thorough description of the clothing he was wearing. This comprehensive system was employed in case any "unknown hobo" was killed on the railroad or committed any crime while in Pittsfield. The department only had to go to their register log book to learn his name and place of residence. During the winter months this room was warm and when filled was even warmer. The ventilation was not the best, but it was better than an empty railroad car or a barn, where one could freeze to death and not be found for days. Lodgers were put out on the street at about 6:30 a.m. There was no breakfast served. Over 3,986 lodgers were accommodated for the year 1897.

OLD BRICK STATION WITH SECOND FLOOR

FRONT DESK OF OLD STATION
OFF. GEORGE CHAPMAN BADGE #13

CHAPTER TWO

Captain Michael T. Leonard
Killed in the Line of Duty

On the night of Tuesday, May 31, 1898, Chief John Nicholson, Captain Michael Leonard, and Officers Daniel Flynn, Henchel Stubbs and Daniel White were at the Union Railroad Station on West Street, awaiting the arrival of the 9th Massachusetts Regiment. (The Union Train Station has since been torn down. The Big Y Store is now on the site where the train station was, at the corner of West and Center Streets). This regiment was composed wholly of Irish-American troops and known as the "Fighting 9th". Several troop trains from as far away as Maine had passed through the city in the last few weeks, drawing large crowds. The troops were on their way to Cuba to fight the Spanish, in the Spanish-American War. The crowd awaiting the regiment numbered about 6,000 citizens. About 4,000 were assembled on the railroad platform which was about 400 ft. long and 40 ft. wide. There were another 2,000 citizens on the tracks and on the steep side banks of Jubilee Hill which looked down onto the tracks and roadways. Mayor William Whiting and members of the City Council were also on the platform. Music was provided by two drum corps and two bands. It was a cheerful occasion with the largest crowd yet coming out to cheer the troops. The troop train had left Springfield, Massachusetts at 8:00 PM for the hour and a half trip to Pittsfield. Unknown to anyone, a twenty-three car freight train was heading to Pittsfield from New York State on the adjacent track at the same time. At this time in history, freight trains had no set schedules. As soon as they were loaded, they were sent out. Station employees were not notified as to when they would pass through their station. Freight trains traveled at about 15 miles per hour. Hundreds of citizens were still on the tracks waiting the "Fighting 9th" when suddenly, this fast moving freight train was seen approaching. The chief of police, captain, and officers rushed to clear the tracks. The noise from the two drum corps and two bands added to the confusion and prevented the crowd from hearing the engineer's warning bell and whistle. At the west end of the station, Edward Lynch of 75 Third Street was struck by the train and the engineer put on his air brakes. Captain Leonard had just pulled a woman and a youngster who had fallen across the track away from the train. He then took hold of a man and tried to get him to a place of safety. The man escaped, but when the captain tried to spring from the track himself, he was too late. The engine struck him. He whirled around and fell by the side of the train where the back of his head struck the platform. His left hand rested on the track and the wheels of the train passed over it. The engine, in the meantime, had passed the station by some distance before the heavy train finally came to a full stop. A scene of great confusion then followed. Chief Nicholson ran directly back west to about where he thought the captain had been thrown. Chief Nicholson passed between the cars and found the captain lying face down. His left hand was severed and his head rested over the platform. Chief Nicholson picked the captain up and carried him directly across the platform to a wagon and took him to the station house, where he was attended by a physician. Later he was taken to the House of Mercy, on Francis Avenue, where he died at about 9:30 a.m. the following day. Captain Leonard's left arm had been torn completely off from the elbow and his skull fractured. He never regained consciousness. Officer Stubbs found his ring in two pieces where he had fallen, indicating that the wheels of the train had run over his hand. Captain Leonard's body was moved to his residence at 50 Wellington Avenue. The funeral was held on Friday June 3rd at St. Joseph's Church at 9:30 a.m. The entire city government attended along with many of his former associates. The entire community was profoundly moved by the bravery of the Captain. He was buried on the hill at St. Joseph Cemetery, about 500 ft. from the main entrance, which is closed now. A large crimson marble headstone marks his grave. He was fifty-five years old. Every year on Memorial Day a flag from the Pittsfield Police Association is placed at his grave, as well as the graves of all the deceased members of the department.

An Inquest into the incident was held at District Court Central Berkshire on June 19 and July 8, 1898, before the Honorable Joseph Tucker, Presiding Justice. Twenty-one witnesses testified. The findings were that it was a tragic accident with many factors involved. Edward Lynch, the first man who had originally been hit suffered a deep gash in the left shoulder, where his bone was crushed. In addition his left hip was injured, and he had many cuts and bruises.

The troop train came in at 10:00 p.m. Although the largest crowd assembled was still present to greet the troops, the accident had put a damper on the spirits of all. Still, the troops were showered with boxes of food and three barrels of coffee which was made at the court house.

CITY SCALES

The Police Station was also the site of the city scales where loads of coal, lumber, etc. were weighed for taxation. A team of horses pulling a wagon would pull up onto the scales and be weighed. The weight would be recorded and a ticket with the amount owed was passed out the window or the driver would come inside and pay the fee. There were a total of 4,679 transactions during the year 1898: 2,005 loads at 10 cents each, 1,902 were at 5 cents each, and 772 loads for the city which was not charged.

DOGS

Dogs seemed to be a big problem for the city. There were 854 dogs that should have been licensed in 1898 according to the assessors. The department had to track down where these dogs were. The department found that six were sold to persons in other cities, twenty had died, three were lost and five accidentally killed. There were fifteen shot by officers. Twenty-nine could not be found. Two persons were prosecuted and convicted for keeping unlicensed dogs. The city received $2,188.10 for dog licenses, but had to pay out $660.60 for damage to domestic animals caused by dogs.

CHAPTER THREE

MURDERER NEVER CONVICTED

On August 20, 1900, Miss May L. Fosburgh, 20, beautiful and friendly, was shot to death in her home at 287 Tyler St. The murder was investigated by Chief John Nicholson. In January 1901, Robert S. Fosburgh, her brother was arrested on an indictment from a grand jury, charging him with manslaughter.

The Fosburgh family at the time of the tragedy consisted of Robert L. Fosburgh, millionaire building contractor, his wife, Amy, two sons, Robert S. and James, and three daughters, May, Esther and Beatrice. The General Electric Company (previously the Stanley Electric Co.) had given the elder Fosburgh a contract to erect one of its giant structures in the Morningside area in an extensive building-expansion program. They had rented the house on Tyler Street to be near the work.

In the house on the night of the homicide were the parents May, Robert, and Beatrice, James and Miss Bertha Sheldon of Providence, Rhode Island., a friend of the family. Esther was visiting a friend in Adams. The time was between 1:00 a.m. and 2:00 a.m. Shots were heard in the hall upstairs and rushing out from their rooms, May was found lying prostrate at the threshold of her room. She had been mortally wounded by a bullet which pierced her heart. One other shot had been fired. The father and defendant, Robert (Bert), claimed they were awakened by two masked burglars with whom they had engaged in a desperate struggle. Hearing the commotion, May Fosburgh had left her bed and stepped out into the hall and was shot by the burglars.

News of the shooting reached police headquarters at 1:30 a.m. and Capt. William G. White telephoned Chief Nicholson, who ordered every man in the department, including reserves, to report at the Police Station. Within an hour the old fire alarm number 42, whose piercing shrieks could be heard from Dalton to the Lenox town lines, was sounded. This was done to arouse all able-bodied men to join in the search for the slayers.

Firearms were obtained from the Pearson Hardware Company for those who didn't have their own. Chief Nicholson believed the men were still in the city, which he had surrounded. This was the greatest manhunt in the history of Pittsfield at this time. The armed citizens searched the woods and mountains of Pittsfield for the burglars, without any luck.

Horses and wagons were provided by the Fire Department for the transportation of the officers and citizens engaged in the patrol duty which was being constantly performed by between 500 and 800 citizens. Upwards of two thousand citizens were waiting in the streets at the station for an opportunity to render some assistance to help find the murderers. Patrols searched for two days as far north as Williamstown, west to the New York state line, east to Cummington and south to Lenox, with no luck.

PEARSON HARDWARE STORE

After further investigation, Chief Nicholson believed that the burglar story was a myth made up by members of the family to prevent exposure that Robert shot his sister. None of the valuable jewelry or cash on the bureau in the room the "mythical" burglars first entered was touched. Chief Nicholson had learned that Robert had been downtown early, the night of the shooting, and had returned home drunk. He had engaged in a violent quarrel with his father, and May was trying to separate them when she was accidentally shot by her brother, who carried a .22 revolver in his hip pocket.

.44 REVOLVER FOUND UNDER BED

The search for additional clues yielded a mixed bag. A .44 revolver presumably wrestled from a burglar was found under Mr. Fosburgh's bed. Since the murder weapon was a .22, was never found, it was presumed that the heavier pistol had been wrestled from the burglar. On the back stairs were matches and a strange shoe. Outside, the investigators found a pair of worn stockings, apparently worn over shoes to muffle footsteps, and a badly worn pair of trousers belonging to Robert. Beneath the escape window were four footprints.

The footprints seemed to corroborate the story, and yet they didn't. A man jumping from a height naturally lands on his toes to take up the shock of landing. Here, however, the heel prints were much more distinct, as though someone had stamped his feet on the ground. The yard was covered with grass, and the dew was heavy that night. The fleeing burglars should have left a distinct trail through the grass, but not a drop of dew was disturbed. Mr. Fosburgh saw two masked burglars and Beatrice saw three unmasked. Beatrice said the shot had been fired by a man standing several feet away, yet May's nightgown carried powder burns indicating that the muzzle was less than a foot away from her when the fatal shot was fired. The burglars had not been in Beatrice's room, yet there were signs of a struggle there, and police found Amy's nightgown, ripped from throat to hem, in a corner. The family doctor reported that James had summoned him to the scene with the message; "There's been a ruckus at our house and my sister is mortally wounded."

A grand jury indicted Robert for murder. The case came to trial in July, 1901. Robert's defense attorney was Charles E. Hibbard who became the first Mayor of Pittsfield. Dr. Frank Paddock, me, one of the principal Commonwealth witnesses at the trial, questioned Robert on how he received bruises on his face. Robert told him he could not remember. Dr. Paddock was stricken ill soon after he testified at the trail, dying that night, unable to rebut any of Robert's testimony. After a stormy eight-day trail, the presiding justice, William B. Stevenson, directed a verdict of innocent and discharged the defendant. Judge Stevenson said the government had not provided sufficient evidence to show Robert shot his sister.

A $1,500.00 reward was offered by the Fosburgh family for the capture of May Fosburgh's murderer, which was never collected. Governor Murray Crane along with an unknown prominent citizen of the city hired the Pinkerton Detective Agency to help with the case, with no results.

The Fosburgh family moved out of the house and rented rooms at the Wendell Hotel. Upon the acquittal of Robert a large party was held at the Wendell Hotel.

May Fosburgh was buried in Portsmouth, New Hampshire, in July 1901. The Fosburgh's completed their contract with the General Electric Company and moved back Buffalo, N. Y., where they owned a contracting company. Chief Nicholson marked the case closed.

1901

Pursuant to an order by the mayor of July 1, 1901, a regular police officer was detailed to enforce the sanitary laws and ordinances of the city and the rules and regulations of the Board of Health under the direction of the board. Two hundred and fifty-four premises were inspected, 114 persons were notified to clean yards and vaults, and 25 orders to connect tenements and public sewer were served.

Seven new cesspools were constructed, eleven cesspools were found in an unsanitary condition and were ordered cleaned, and 21 surface drain nuisances were abated. Chief Nicholson recommended that an ordinance be enacted so the chief of police could detail an officer to report to the board at such times as the services of an agent may be required, as the present authority is provided for by an annual order.

Chief Nicholson also recommended that the department be provided with a police signal system, saying that at the present time the posts of police patrol extended from Lake Pontoosuc to the Junction (outer Holmes Road) with no means whatever for prompt communication with Police Headquarters.

The chief also believed that the homes of the every police officer should be connected with the Police Station by electrical appliances so that every member of the police force could be summoned promptly in case of an emergency. The cost for construction of the signal system was estimated to be about $4,500.

Chief Nicholson also requested the city purchase a patrol wagon at a cost of about $400. The cost for the care of the signal system and the service of the patrol wagon with the co-operation of the Fire Department was estimated to be less than the estimated $300.

The police report for 1901 indicated a payroll of $17,321.38 with one chief, one captain, sixteen patrolmen and one police matron, with operating expenses of $2,596.27. That year, there were 1,093 arrests.

CHAPTER FOUR

INMATE MURDERS JAIL-GUARD

On the morning of July 17, 1901, at 7:15 a.m., Daniel Leary, 38, an inmate at the Berkshire County Jail and House of Correction, struck overseer (guard) James W. Fuller, 70, on the head with a six and one half pound mallet and fractured his skull. The mallet was used to make heels for shoes in the leather shop, at the jail on Second Street.

Leary was also known as Ed or Michael Walsh. He was serving a 68 day sentence for drunkenness and assault, which took place in West Stockbridge on June 17. Leary was found sleeping in a lime kiln building by Morris Bossidy, foreman of the lime kiln plant. Bossidy ordered Leary out of the building. Still in a drunken condition, after a night of drinking, Leary put up a fight and assaulted Bossidy. Leary was arrested at the scene. After testifying in court, Bossidy was attacked by Leary, striking him several times before being restrained.

While being transported to the Berkshire County Jail and House of Correction, Leary was very combative with the officers. This was his second incarceration at Second Street. During his first time there, he spent 30 days for illegal riding on a freight train in Great Barrington. He also previously spent time in an Albany, New York jail, in 1883, for public drunkenness. During that jail time, Leary struck a guard on the head with a mallet and stabbed him with a shoe knife. It was after finishing his Albany sentence that he drifted to the Berkshires.

While serving this sentence, Leary was placed in solitary confinement for refusing to do the work he was assigned. He was placed there as a discipline action, by Guard Frank W. Fuller. Frank was the son of James W. Fuller and brother of Sheriff Charles W. Fuller.

After being released from solitary confinement, Leary returned to his station number 30, in the leather shop. Here, Leary confessed to a fellow inmate, Charles Carroll, that he planned "to do this man" (kill) guard James W. Fuller. Carroll had served time with Leary in the Albany jail, several years before. Carroll told Leary that he was making a mistake, but Leary would not listen.

On the morning of the attack, prisoners were released from their cells. Around 7:00 a.m. Guard James W. Fuller counted thirty-two males as they walked by him into the leather shop. Fuller had an office on the second floor, on the west end of the workshop. Upon leaving his office, he walked down to the main workshop area, walking by Leary, and went to a sink at the east end of the shop.

Fuller stopped at the sink and was looking out the window. Leary left his work bench with a six and one half pound mallet. Coming up behind Fuller, he struck him in the head, just below the right ear. Fuller fell to the floor with fractured skull and a three inch circular cut.

Two inmates rushed to Fuller's aid. They grabbed and held Leary down, but he had already grabbed Fuller's billy club and was searching his trousers' pocket for his revolver. Thirty other inmates just stood by and watched. Leary later stated if he had found the revolver, there would have been one dead guard. Two guards rushed in and forcefully restrained Leary, putting him in a solitary confinement cell. Fuller was carried to the sheriff's residence, which was attached to the jail. Dr. S. C. Burton, the jail physician, dressed the injured guard's wounds, using stiches to close the gash in his head. At that time, Fuller was in a semi-conscious condition. However, later that day, he slipped into an unconscious state and one week later, never regaining consciousness, he died.

A special sitting of the grand jury was called and sat in superior court, hearing evidence of the attack. The grand jury was made up of all males from around Berkshire County; one from Great Barrington; one from Dalton; one from Stockbridge; one from Richmond; two from Williamstown; one from Windsor; four from North Adams; one from Mt. Washington; one from Sheffield; two from Adams; one from New Marlboro; one from Lenox; one from Lee; one from Lanesboro; and four from Pittsfield. A true bill was found against Daniel Leary, alias Michael Walsh, charging him with murder of James W. Fuller.

Leary was arraigned the same day that the grand jury returned the true bill. He pleaded not guilty. At the arraignment, Leary asked that a new attorney be assigned to him. The Chief Justice of the Superior Court set a date of December 2, 1901 for the trial.

The trial began with several doctors testifying that Leary was insane. They stated they had examined him over a period of time and all agreed he was insane. The District Attorney said that there was no doubt in his mind that the mental condition of Leary was such that a trial would be improper. There were two Superior Court judges hearing the case, Judge Sherman and Judge Aiken. Judge Sherman told the clerk to dismiss all the jurors and take a fifteen minutes recess. After returning, Judge Sherman stated it was apparent that Leary was insane and ordered him committed to the Asylum for Insane Criminals at Bridgewater. On November 8, 1903, Leary died in this prison from the infectious disease of tuberculosis.

James W. Fuller was a member of the Town of Pittsfield Police Force for six years, from 1876 to 1882. He served five years under Chief John Hatch and one year under Chief James McKenna, typically working the noon to midnight shift. Fuller was a deputy sheriff under three sheriffs, Sheriff Root, Sheriff Wellington, and Fuller's son, Sheriff Charles W. Fuller. It was his son that appointed James W. Fuller as a deputy sheriff and overseer of the leather shop at the jail.

CHAPTER FIVE

1902

Secret Service Agent William Craig
Killed in the Line of Duty

On September 3, 1902, the department investigated the death of the first United States Secret Service agent ever to die in the line of duty. Secret Service agent William Craig, 47, was guarding President Theodore Roosevelt, who was on a speaking tour of New England. The president had just given a speech to 10,000 people gathered in downtown Pittsfield. The store fronts were draped and decorated with American flags and horse-drawn carriages lined the street. When the speech ended, the crowd dispersed, and 35 people hopped onto Trolley No. 29 heading down South Street to the Pittsfield Country Club.

President Roosevelt, along with Massachusetts Governor Murray Crane of Dalton, Agent Craig and the coachman of the open-air horse-drawn carriage, were on their way to the Pittsfield County Club for a planned reception for the president. The trolley and the carriage drawn by four horses collided, throwing Agent Craig onto the trolley tracks. Agent Craig was run over by trolley number 29, killing him. One of the four horses was also killed. President Roosevelt and Governor Crane received minor injuries. The president was thrown about 30 feet; bruised and limping, he issued a blistering oath toward the trolley motorman. The trolley motorman, Euclid Maddan, was charged with manslaughter for the death of Agent Craig. On January 21, 1903, Maddan pleaded guilty and was sentenced to six months at the Berkshire County House of Correction and Jail and paid a fine of $300. Euclid did his jail time during the day, and returned home at night. The Pittsfield Electric Street Railway paid his fine. They also paid his weekly salary to his family while he was in jail. He was released on July 14 and returned to former job as a motorman.

Several months after the accident, three lions were reported to have escaped from their cages while being transferred to a theater. The lions roamed the city at will, terrorizing residents. Legend has it that Mayor Daniel England, recalling Roosevelt's prowess in Africa, sent him a wire: "Three lions running loose here. Can you come and help us?" The president wired back: "No need of my coming. The street cars will get them."

RESERVE OFFICER

In 1902 the title of reserve officer was added to the roster. Sergeants had been created within the department earlier.

Chief John Nicholson recommended that two additional police officers be appointed to the department, for more efficient performance of the constantly increasing demands for police service in all parts of the city. The chief said that numerous miscellaneous duties required the services of two regular officers for the greater part of the year, and the two places of amusement, needed the attention of the department. The trolley cars running out of the city, especially on Saturday nights, also required the services of the officers to accompany the cars to the city limits. He noted that no additions had been made to the personnel of the department since 1895.

The chief noted that it was necessary to increase the number of posts of patrol duty, and also to extend the limits of the posts in the business and residential sections of the city. This was done by dividing the force into three details: the first detail was from 9:00 a.m. to 7:00 p.m., the second from 7:00 p.m. to 4:00 a.m., and the third from 12:00a.m. to 9:00 a.m. Two special details were also made, of one officer each, from12:00 a.m. till 11:00 p.m. and from 1:00 p.m. till 12:00 a.m.

In ending his report Chief Nicholson noted that the Police Station was in good sanitary condition. The interior was painted during the year, the closets, cells and lodging rooms were kept thoroughly clean and well disinfected. The total number of persons cared for at the station was 3,336, the city scales were thoroughly repaired and in excellent condition.

1903

PADDY WAGON
BLACK MARIA

The first patrol wagon used for making arrests and for transporting prisoners to and from the courthouse was placed in operation on April 1, 1903 by Chief Nicholson. The new wagon was housed in the first stall in the Central Fire Station. When the wagon was needed, the desk officer pushed a button and a bell rang at the fire station. The driver used the swinging harnesses that were installed in the station to harness up a pair of horses and proceed to where the wagon was needed.

Later the town converted the old storehouse opposite the Police Station on School Street (this is the present sight of the Police Station now, 39 Allen Street) into a patrol stable with three stalls for horses, a work stand and driver's sleeping quarters. This unit now included one pair of horses, Dan and Grace, a patrol wagon, a buggy, a sleigh and the necessary harnesses.

Two men were employed to drive the wagon, one for day duty and the other for nights. They were on duty for 12 hours giving the department continuous service, day and night. Also installed was a private telephone service which placed the station and officers on the beat in constant communication with the wagon drivers.

With the new patrol wagon the department didn't have to pay horse stables or livery for transporting prisoners from the Station House to court or jail. In previous years it cost the department several hundred dollars which was taken out of the department budget. The District Court paid the City Treasurer one hundred and thirty dollars for the use of the wagon to transport prisoners from the court house to the county jail. The pair of horses, Dan and Grace that was used to pull the wagon were retired in 1914 to a Southfield farm, surrendering to an automobile patrol.

OFFICER KIRTLAND-CHIEF FLYNN-
OFFICER BASTION-DAN AND GRACE

From April 1st to December 31, the wagon made 884 calls. Arrests were made without the usual fuss and disturbance caused by drunken and disorderly persons being paraded through the public streets; 65 tramps found in camps and barns in the outlying districts were arrested and brought to the station by the wagon. "Yegg men" (burglars) occasionally adopted the methods and customs of tramps, to better enable them to pursue their profession. The station house was a busy place, providing housing for 3,428 persons during the year. Also arrested for various crimes were 1,358 people; of this number 933 were for drunkenness. The desk officer was very busy along with his other duties, with the city scale, recording 5,107 transactions. Officers were present at all public assemblies, and were in attendance at 73 weddings and entertainments. Two officers were added to the force bringing the total of patrolmen to eighteen.

1904

Chief John Nicholson recommended the addition of two patrolmen to the force due to the increased work load. Officers put in 1,224 hours of service in six days canvassing the city for sewer connections for the Board of Health along with the other duties required of them from the Board of Health.

During the year 1,130 persons were arrested, including 818 for drunkenness. Chief Nicholson recommended that the police matron, Mrs. Sarah M. Dean, be paid the same as regular patrolmen. Her duties required long hours in the station and court. Her constant attention was required when female persons were in custody.

1904
OFFICER LASH-FIREFIGHTER
MACDONALD-OFFICER DUNN

1905

CHIEF RESIGNS

Chief John Nicholson resigned as chief of police on April 1, 1905 when he was appointed High Sheriff of Berkshire County by Governor Douglas.

The High Sheriff of Berkshire County, Charles W. Fuller had died in office. The High Sheriff was in charge of the County Jail on Second Street, built in 1870 for $190,000 two years after a voter referendum finally affirmed a legislative petition, first filed in 1812, to make Pittsfield, rather than Lenox, the county seat. A condition of the designation was that Pittsfield would provide both a courthouse and jail. Nicholson remained High Sheriff for 27 years until his death on June 23, 1932. Sheriff Nicholson had just returned from an automobile ride which he took every Sunday with his family. He returned home and died of a heart attack at 5:00 p.m.

CHAPTER SIX

COUNTY JAIL

The County Jail on Second Street was twice the scene of execution by hanging, before the legislature enacted that the legal penalty of death should be paid thereafter at the state prison in Charlestown. Public outcry about the cruelty of the gallows required the state to change to the electric chair for its executions. John Ten Eych was hung on August 16, 1878, for a double murder committed in Sheffield, of David Stillman and his wife, under circumstances of peculiar atrocity, on the evening of Thanksgiving Day in the previous year. For the hanging of Eych, Sheriff Graham A. Root sent out formal invitations which required an RSVP to secure a ticket of admission. John Whalen of the village of Washington was killed by a wood chopper, William Coy. Using his axe, Coy inflicted a head wound four inches long an inch wide and half an inch deep. The motive was revenge. A verdict murder in the first degree was returned on March 21, 1892 and on October 28 of that year Coy was sentenced to be hanged. The hanging took place on March 3, 1893.

Both hangings took place in the courtyard outside of the jail. Tickets or cards of admission were required for a person to attend. The person that was to be hung was led up to the gallows, a rope placed around his neck and a hood was placed over his face. Ankles and knees were bound. A doctor was present to pronounce death. Large crowds gathered on Second Street in front of the jail attempting to see the hanging. Families brought picnic lunches for the day long event. Kids ran around playing games. On the day of the hanging a detail of police officers would be sent to the jail for crowd control by the chief of police.

There was a gallows set up inside of the jail on the third floor but never used. The person to be hanged would walk out on a plank. Shackles would be attached to their legs. Attached to the shackles were heavy weights. The person on the end of the rope would fall through the opening in the floor ending up in midair, snapping his neck. On the second floor there was a gallery where the spectators or witnesses watched. Due to the change in the law the gallows was never used. The shackles and weights are still at the jail.

NEW CHIEF OF POLICE
William G. White

Chief William G. White was appointed as chief of the department on April 1, 1905, replacing Chief Nicholson. Chief White served as chief for 8 years until he retired on January 6, 1913. Chief White had a total of 32 years on the department. Chief White was the captain in the department before he was promoted to chief. Patrolmen James F. Dean was promoted to captain and Daniel P. Flynn was promoted to the rank of sergeant. Three men were appointed to the regular force, one to fill the vacancy caused by the resignation of the Chief John Nicholson.

William E. Dunn and William P. Lasch were appointed from the reserve force, and Stephen W. Monks was appointed from the Civil Service list to the regular force. Patrick J. Colbert, Daniel McColgan, Dennis Condon, Jedidiah N. Shepardson, Zadock G. Williams and Henry W. Zeph, were appointed to the reserve force.

OFFICER PATRICK J. COLBERT- BADGE #20

1906 to 1912

Two things of more than ordinary importance occurred in 1906. The first Gamewell Police Signal System, intended to serve the city for the next thirty-four years, was installed. As then set up, it consisted of a central switchboard and telephone at headquarters to which were connected fifteen street call boxes and twenty-two emergency call bells. This system proved to be a valuable addition to the department. By means of the central phone and the street call boxes, the officer in charge at headquarters was in communication with the patrolmen on their post at least once every hour, and by the emergency bells, one of which was located in the home of each officer, which enabled the whole department to be called to headquarters in a very short time. This signal system soon turned out to be inadequate. Three years after its installation it was enlarged and entirely rebuilt. In 1908 a Superintendent of the combined police signal and fire alarm systems was appointed.

AERO PARK

Chief William G. White assigned officers to Aero Park, at the corners of Newell and East Streets. On weekends, large crowds gathered to watch and ride in hot air balloons, an exciting way to view Pittsfield. The Pittsfield Coal & Gas Company would inflate the balloons with gas.

Patrolmen Stephen W. Monk's electrical knowledge saved the department from calling in outside assistance to keep the department's signal system of boxes and call bells in working condition. In his annual report of 1907, Chief White recognized Officer Monks for this.

1908 saw some needed repairs to the station. A portion of the women's cell room on the second floor was utilized to extend the locker room for patrolmen, providing adequate locker facilities for each officer. Existing lockers were moved from the waiting room into the new quarters, giving men an enlarged and more pleasant room in which to spend their time during the meal hour or while waiting to go on duty. The change was needed for the growth of the force.

1909 the force now consisted of twenty-five patrolmen. Chief White asked for the addition of two more, saying under the present system of allowing the patrolmen one day off in thirty, they were needed to cover the beats. The department was always short the services of one man. Two theaters required the services of patrolmen, one requiring the time of one man every evening during the week for a considerable portion of the year. The department constantly received requests for the services of patrolmen, and the present number of the force hardly allowed it. The population of the city was constantly and rapidly increasing and the number of officers on the force was hardly adequate to meet the demands of the city.

1909 MEMORIAL DAY

In Chief William G. White's Annual Report for 1910, he states that Officer Charles W. Thompson retired after more than thirty-two years of service. Officer Thompson would receive a pension of half pay at his own request for the rest of his days. Another officer was hired to replace Thompson. Retired Officer Thompson died in May, collecting his pension only for a few months. The chief also announced that a horse was now at the disposal of the chief for emergency calls along with the wagon.

He recommended that a suitable automobile be purchased for the department for use in answering calls from the outskirts of the city and for general use in the business of the department. He referred to a recent incident in West Pittsfield where a fourteen year old boy was stabbed and died. Had there been an automobile available in the department, response to the call for help would have been a great deal quicker and while life might not have been saved, "the machine would have been of material assistance."

RUN-AWAY HORSES

One June morning in 1910, while on patrol at the corner of North and School Streets, Officer Peter Lamore witnessed two horses with a wagon attached trotting around in a circle. They were from Aspinwall in Lenox. The ring in one of the horse bits got caught on the end of the wagon, and the animals began to plunge downward. On reaching a point near the sidewalk the horses started to trot around in a circle. They made two revolutions and became more and more excited, threatening to do serious damage not only to the wagon and harness but to property in the vicinity as well as to the terrified driver of the team. Officer Lamore rushed from the sidewalk and very skillfully grasped the horses by the bit and in an instant brought them to a full stop. Though the horses were high spirited and were plunging recklessly, Officer Lamore was uninjured.

A few weeks later on June 9th, 1910 Officer Lamore had another bout with runaway horses. While on patrol near Orchard and North Streets, Officer Lamore tried to stop a pair of runaway horses attached to a heavily loaded wagon. The horses bolted and the driver was thrown from his seat. Officer Lamore rushed out to meet the pair and had partially succeeded in bring them to a stop, when one of them knocked him over. His head struck the curb inflicting a gash and he rolled under the wheels of the wagon, which passed over him. Officer Lamore sustained two sprained ankles, a deep cut in his forehead about five inches in length which required eight stitches to close, and was badly bruised about the body. Several bystanders carried the unconscious officer to Mathewson's Drug Store. Dr. George Reynolds was summoned, and went with Officer Lamore to his home on First Street in an ambulance, where he attended the injuries. Lamore recovered consciousness during the ride, but was out of work for a month.

MEMORIAL DAY 1910 SOUTH ST.

CHAPTER SEVEN

14 YEAR OLD BOY MURDERS 14 YEAR OLD BOY WITH KNIFE

It was a cold Sunday morning, January 22, 1911. A group of friends were walking home from church. They had attended Mass at St. John's Chapel, a branch of St. Joseph's Church, located on Lebanon Avenue in the Barkerville section of the city. Catholics from West Pittsfield attended services there until the mid-1950's. It's now the Town Players Hall.

The group of boys walked down to Tillotson's Mill which was across from Oswald Avenue on West Housatonic Street. There was a large pond on the property which was fed by the West Branch of the Housatonic River. Kids used to fish in the pond which was stocked with trout by the Massachusetts Fish and Game until 1960 when it was drained. Eight boys were present: Francis Donovan, 14; James McKeever, 14; Edward Redmond, 13; John Ryan, 15; William Cote, 14; Joseph Gallagher, 12; Daniel Tierney, 13; and David Tierney, 14, Daniel's cousin.

James McKeever and Francis Donovan had some sort of a quarrel between them. McKeever said that Donovan had hit him on the left side of his face. McKeever had an open pocket knife with him. McKeever said he had the knife opened because he was going to whittle a stick. McKeever stabbed Donovan in the throat near the breast bone and Donovan fell to the ground; this was a fatal blow. Two neighbors on the corner of Oswald Avenue carried Donovan into their house. He died within a few seconds. Neighbors called police who arrived shortly in the department's sleigh, pulled by one of the department's horses.

McKeever left the scene and walked to his house on Gale Avenue a short distance away. Officers John Hudner and William J. Keegan arrived shortly and placed McKeever under arrest for murder. The officers retrieved the knife, a very cheap one with a three inch blade. McKeever was arraigned in District Court on Monday on the murder charge and was held without bail. The Grand Jury indicted McKeever for manslaughter. At his trial in Superior Court, 16 witnesses were sworn in. Chief William G. White in court said he had interviewed McKeever and he saw a red mark on McKeever's face near his ear and blood spots. The chief said McKeever told him that Donovan struck him twice. Dr. W.A. Millett and Dr. Henry Colt who did the autopsy told about their findings. All the boys at the scene testified. After a long talk at the bench between presiding Justice Crosby, DA Callahan and McKeever's Attorney James Fallon, McKeever changed his plea from not guilty to guilty of manslaughter. Justice Crosby continued the case for sentencing; as long as McKeever stayed out of trouble, there would be no sentence.

INSPECTOR OF POLICE

As a result of another ordinance passed on June 19, 1911 a new type of officer, namely an Inspector of Police, was created, Sergeant Daniel P. Flynn was appointed inspector. Officer John Hunder was appointed sergeant. The rank of sergeants had been created earlier within the department. These two officers worked in civilian clothes.

Patrolmen William H. Tobin retired from active duty after 27 years of service and placed on the pension roll because of physical incapacity. Tobin was only the second officer to take advantage of the police pension law and the only officer on the retirement list.

Chief White made several recommendations to the City Council. He wanted more officers for traffic duty and patrol noting that the rearrangement of the street railway lines at the corner of North and West Streets had resulted in creating a dangerous district not only for pedestrians but for drivers who had occasion to use the highway at this point. The chief wanted to station an officer in the street opposite the park to regulate and direct traffic in order to minimize the danger that the rearrangement had caused. The chief stated that a new patrol wagon was an absolute necessity as the present wagon was dilapidated and unsuitable. It was patched and repaired as much as possible and had outlived its usefulness. Chief White also recommended that a new station be acquired as the present building was small, the cell rooms are inadequate and unsanitary and the quarters for patrolmen are not large enough.

DOGS

Tracking of dogs was almost a full time job for one officer. Each year the mayor sent to the department a list from the assessors of dog owners. In 1911 there were 1,054 dogs in Pittsfield. Each of these dogs had to have a dog license and be accounted for. Officer Hogan was assigned to this task. Of this number, Officer Hogan found that 265 dog owners didn't have a license, 18 left the city; police officers shot 96 and 30 had died. Officer Hogan collected $420 dollars for the city. Each year the department had to go through this process.

DUTIES PERFORMED FOR THE BOARD OF HEALTH

The department had to service 1,139 orders from the Board of Health and made sure that they were complied with, which took many man hours. Listed below are some of the orders:

Order to bury horses-14
Order to move pigs-25
Order to clean cesspools-33
Order to stop dumping-72
Order to get garbage cans-64
Order to clean outhouses-192
Order to keep quarantine-57
Order to clean yards-380
Order to clean cellars-40

WHISTLE STOP FOR PRESIDENT

Chief William G. White and a detail of officers worked at the old Union Train Station for crowd control in 1911. President William H. Taft had made a whistle stop and a short speech on his way out West.

PRESIDENT WILLIAM H. TAFT

150 ANNIVERSARY OF PITTSFIELD

On July 4, 1911, there was a huge celebration at the Allen's Farm where Pittsfield's Aviation Field was located. Many of the crowd took the Pittsfield Electric Street Railway to the event, which ran along Dalton Avenue. This marked the 150 anniversary of Pittsfield. There was a crowd of 30,000 watching "Curtiss Aeroplane Flights." Chief White and a detail 50 officers were present. Sheriff John Nicholson also known as Captain John Nicholson of company F was on hand with his mounted horsemen to help out with crowd control. One accident occurred when a pilot had to terminate his take off and his plane hit the ground.

PHOTO BY MRS. MARY KELLY

CHIEF WHITE PUTS IN RETIREMENT PAPERS

Chief William White submitted his 1912 Annual Report to the City Council. It consisted of wages, a table of arrests and requests. Also in his Annual Report he announced that after thirty-two years of service as a member of the department, nearly eight years of which were spent as chief, he asked for retirement as provided for by the police pension law. He would step down on January 6, 1913. The Board of Aldermen granted his request.

The force consisted of a chief, captain, inspector, sergeant, matron, twenty-eight patrolmen and six reserve officers. Total wages for the department were $29,106.00. The average wage for patrolmen was $1,000. The chief asked for a raise of $50 a year, which would boost his salary to $1,550 annually.

Chief White's major grievance was not having an automobile. The chief said the horse drawn vehicle was not quick enough to respond to calls of any emergency. Calls from the outskirts of the city were frequent and in the winter time especially could not be responded to quickly enough by a horse drawn vehicle. He also stated that it frequently was necessary to send men to surrounding towns in the course of police work, and livery and garage bills were the end result. An automobile would be more efficient in many ways and would mean a considerable savings to the city. Mayor Kelton B. Miller noted that having one nag in the stable and one at home was too much for the chief to bear.

The chief, before closing his report, added a strong desire for more men and a new station house. At present, he said the only patrolled streets during the day were in the business section. The services of one man were given up almost wholly to the Board of Health for orders to clean out houses, abolish privies, and bury dead horses, move pigs and other duties. Two men were needed at headquarters, one during the day and one at night. He noted there were so many commitments to State Institutions: Northampton State Hospital, Shirley Reform School, Sherborn Prison for Women, Bridgewater State Farm and Charlestown State Prison, the oldest prison in the nation. One officer's time was taken up several days a month conveying prisoners to them, and another officer had to chase unlicensed dogs down.

POLICE BRIEFS

LEFT GOLD WATCH UNDER PILLOW

Chief of Police White received a letter, dated July 1912, from an Atlantic City man, Henry Dondi, who when touring through the Berkshires spent a night in this city, and left his gold watch under a pillow in his hotel room. He could not remember the name of the street, but said there was a dog hospital near it. Chief White thought it might be Bradford Street, where The Animal Hospital was located. He went to the Kenney Hotel on North Street next to Bradford Street and located the watch, for Mr. Dondi.

POLICEMAN'S BALL

The 1st Annual Policemen's Ball will be held this evening, October 12, 1912, at the Wendell Hotel. The public is invited to attend the after dinner party from 8:00 p.m. to 11:00 p.m. Tickets are available at the police station for $.50. There will be live entertainment by the Nightingale Sisters singing everyone's favorite popular tunes of the day.

1913 to 1915
Chief Daniel P. Flynn

Chief Daniel P. Flynn took over as the head of the department on March 10, 1913, until his untimely death while still serving as chief on May 8, 1915. Chief Flynn was appointed a patrolman on May 15, 1887, sergeant on April 18, 1905 and inspector July 6, 1911. He was only fifty-five years old when he died.

In his first Annual Report the chief called for six more officers as the city was growing and the demands on the department were abundant. The beats in many instances were too long to patrol. He also called for the purchase of a suitable automobile, saying that Dan and Grace, the team of horses used on the patrol had outlived their usefulness. They had worked 24 hours a day for the last eight years and had reached the stage where they couldn't render the service which should be given in a city of such extensive territory as Pittsfield. To buy another team of horses and repair the wagon would cost in the neighborhood of $800. Chief Flynn also called for a new station house saying it would be better to build a new one than to spend a large sum in repairing the present structure. In Chief Flynn's second Annual Report of 1914 he called for four more police signal boxes so officers could keep in better contact with the station house.

CHAPTER EIGHT

CHIEF JOHN L. SULLIVAN

The department was without a chief for four months until the Aldermen appointed John L. Sullivan as chief on September 13, 1915. Sullivan was appointed chief after a lengthy Aldermen's meeting. The Aldermen couldn't come to an agreement on who was to be chief. At about 11:45p.m., one of the Aldermen was looking out of the second floor window of City Hall. (This building is now a branch office of Berkshire Bank on Park Square). The Alderman saw Officer Sullivan ringing the call box at Park Square and nominated Sullivan as chief. Sullivan was approved and became chief of police of Pittsfield for the next 32 years.

Just prior to his appointment Sullivan had captured an alleged arsonist running away from his burning tailor shop. He saw the man running down a side street, stopped him, smelled gasoline on his clothes, returned to the shop and aided in extinguishing the blaze in the block that housed 20 persons. The man was arrested on a charge of arson, convicted and given a three year sentence.

At this time the roster of the department showed that it consisted of a chief, an inspector, a sergeant, thirty-three patrolmen, a part-time matron and two patrol drivers. The total maintenance cost of that year was $9,761.72, bringing the total expenses of the Police Department to $49,761.72. The department reported 1,871 arrests in the year of 1915. During the same year a motorcycle officer was added to the service. Safety zones were established on certain busy streets. A Safety First Week, a pioneer idea, was celebrated for the first time.

1915 to 1925

The Annual Reports of the Police Department from 1915 to 1925 show persistent attention to matters of public safety, traffic control, protection of school children and street crossings, liquor law enforcement, public morals and general improvement of the efficiency of the department.

1916 FIRST TRAFFIC SQUAD

1917 OFFICERS ON STEPS OF CITY HALL

Almost simultaneous with his appointment as Chief of Police, John L. Sullivan began his insistent demand for a new Police Station. On page 12 of his Annual Report of 1917 he states as follows: "I notice when the City Council or Board of Trade have visitors they do not bring them to see the Pittsfield Police Department. I wonder why? Are they ashamed of the Police Station? The City Council asked forty-five men to make it their headquarters, they ask that 3,000 men and women be housed here as prisoners, that 500 tramps be taken care of by the department, that young women charged with minor crimes be confined in the same room with lewd and lascivious women overnight". Twenty-three years later the department moved into a new station, where females, males and juveniles had separate retaining areas.

Among the chief's recommendations were "that the City Council make a special appropriation for sign boards to be placed one mile from the center of the city on all main roads warning automobiles not to exceed fifteen miles per hour and not to use open mufflers through the streets of the city." He also recommended the purchase of new revolvers for the entire Police Department, sayings that the revolvers in use were mostly cheap makes of all kinds. Some of them were twenty years old, and practically worthless as firearms.

CHAPTER NINE

1917
MURDERED BY AXE
BURIED IN MANURE PIT

KILLED WITH TWO BLOWS
DISCONNECTING HEAD FROM BODY

Miles Hewitt, 38, a farmer vanished from his farm on Hancock Road. His body was later found in the manure pit in his barn. He had been missing for three months. His body was discovered on April 19, 1917 by Armand and Emil Charffe, brothers who had taken over the Hewitt farm. The manure pit was in the basement of the farm's barn. The brothers had started to use this manure for fertilizer on the farm. When they came upon the body buried under three feet of manure, it was in a badly decomposed state, the head separated from the body. The skull was badly crushed and most of the flesh had left the remainder of the body. The skeleton was encased in a suit of clothes and a blue sweater. Neighbors stated that Hewitt wore a red, and not a blue sweater. They also told of quarrels that had occurred at the Hewitt farm when Hewitt and Lincoln McKinley Grant, a sixteen year old, who lived there. The farm, located on the north side of Hancock Road, was better known as the Farrell Farm.

Chief of Police John L. Sullivan, Inspector Daniel McColgan and Officer Jedediah Shepardson went to the farm in the department's automobile after receiving word of the finding of the body. Dr. Henry Colt, Medical Examiner viewed the body and had it removed to the John R. Feeley Funeral Home. Lincoln Grant was arrested on suspicion that he might be able to shed some light on the mystery. Grant maintained that he knew nothing of the crime, but after being questioned for some time confessed to killing Hewitt. Grant was charged with murder in the first degree.

In his confession Grant said that he killed Hewitt with two blows over the head with an axe as Hewitt was milking a cow. After felling Hewitt,

Grant picked up the body and carried it a short distance to the manure pit and buried it. In his confession Grant implicated Mrs. Margaret Hewitt, 28, wife of Miles, and her sister Cella Noistering, 24. Grant also stated in his confession that he had improper relations with Margaret Hewitt.

After the murder, Margaret continued to live on the farm until the middle of March, when she sold the stock remaining to the Charffe brothers and moved to Springfield, where her sister lived. Grant lived with Margaret for two days after the murder and then left her because of her changed demeanor, saying that he began to fear her. Grant left the state for a while, but returned after the sisters were arrested. Margaret Hewitt was charged with first degree murder and being an accessory before the fact in inciting Grant to commit the crime. Mrs. Noistering was charged with being an accessory after the fact, as she was staying in the house and knew about the murder. The complaints charged that the murder was committed on Monday, February 26, 1917.

Following the confession of Grant, Captain John Hudner, Inspector McColgan and Officers John Hines and Jedidiah Shepardson went to Springfield by automobile to locate Mrs. Hewitt and her sister. The officers visited several places before finding the women as they had moved since going to Springfield. They were arrested early in the morning. When informed that Mr. Hewitt was found dead, neither of the women expressed surprise. They were returned to Pittsfield by train.

Grant was found guilty of second degree murder and sentenced to life in prison; he was released on parole in 1935 after serving 16 years in prison. DA Joseph B. Ely who prosecuted the case didn't believe Mrs. Margaret Hewitt or her sister Cella Noistering had anything to do with the murder and filed their cases. They were charged with accessory before the fact to murder.

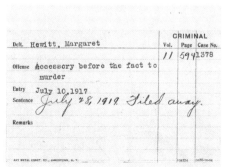

RECORD SHOWING MARGARET
HEWITT'S CASE FILLED

1918

In Chief Sullivan's Annual Report for 1918, he stated he would have all officers pay strict attention to the conditions in the rear of stores, also more attention to the Italian and Polish sections of the city. The department drilled once a week; more often if drill master Officer William Marshall thought necessary.

Chief Sullivan also noted the attack on Officer B. Horton stating, "An Italian gangster made a dastardly attack on Officer Horton's life, cutting his throat with a razor, so as to expose his jugular vein. The officer pursued his assailant for a distance of four hundred feet and placed him under arrest. The officer showed great courage and I have highly commended him for his bravery."

1919
MORAL MATTERS

Sunday sports, even amateur sports, were still banned by state law, under Puritan statutes that prohibited not only pleasure but all work on the Sabbath. In 1919 the legislature relaxed these laws a bit, making it legal for people to work on Sundays in their war gardens.

Women's clothes were a matter of mounting concern. Younger women were charged with carrying war economy to an extreme, in their shorter skirts and especially in their bathing suits. The chief didn't approve of bare skin showing. Chief John L. Sullivan did not like the trend, and announced that if any women appeared "indecent" at local beaches, they would be ordered "in to get some clothes on." Chief John L. didn't like the latest dances; he closed down a dance pavilion at Pontoosuc Lake when he found some young people there doing the "shimmy." In one incident, Chief Sullivan had gone into the lobby of a respectable hotel and arrested four young women for appearing in public with their stockings rolled below the knees and their bloomers rolled above, warning that Pittsfield would not tolerate bare knees or "any of that stuff." Chief Sullivan in his Annual Reports made many recommendations to the City Council. In his 1919 report he recommended that the City Council of 1920 appoint a special committee in reference to parking of automobiles on North, Fenn and Dunham Streets. He requested that the city provide some parking spaces where automobiles could park. Automobile owners were using North Street for a garage and the chief wanted a stop to this. He said it was unreasonable for automobile owners to leave their machines on main streets, and even though twenty years ago it was legal to hitch horses on them, automobiles were a different matter.

He recommended that motorcycle officers be assigned to West Pittsfield and the Lakewood area. He requested that two new patrol cars be bought, trading in the department's three cars, whose upkeep was unreasonable.

Chief Sullivan believed automobile traffic was going to be a major problem for the city, that with new paved streets, traffic would move along at faster speeds, causing accidents. With the opening of state roads from Albany to Pittsfield and from Springfield through Hinsdale to Pittsfield, traffic would be enormous.

CHAPTER TEN

LOVERS MURDER

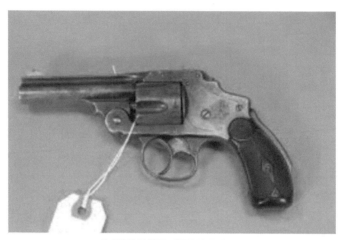

MURDER WEAPON

On the night of August 13, 1919, Anna Philomena was crocheting in her living room. Her sweetheart Jimmy Deslito was playing his guitar near the window. The time was 9:45 p.m. All of a sudden three gun shots were heard and three bullets came through the window, striking and killing Jimmy. Looking out the window Anna saw Bruno Mazzatto running from the house.

Bruno was in love with Anna and had asked her to marry him several times, but she had refused. Bruno and Jimmy had been the best of friends until Anna came between them; both were in love with her. Learning that Bruno Mazzatto was the shooter, Officer Daniel W. Dunn arrested him within an hour at the corner of Eagle and North Streets, finding a revolver in Mazzatto's pocket.

At his trial in Superior Court, witnesses testified that at a christening party just the week before, Bruno said he would kill Jimmy. He then took a revolver out of his pocket and shot two shots from the neighbor's house where he was, into his own house. The Commonwealth also introduced testimony from the late William Jaked that he saw Bruno put a gun in his pocket while he was standing in front of the shoe shop on Eagle Street. A fifteen year boy also testified that he saw Bruno put the gun in his pocket.

The Commonwealth said that the motive for the murder was lost love and jealousy. The jury found Bruno Mazzatto guilty of 2nd degree murder on January 21, 1921. He was sentenced to life in prison; his first day was in solitary confinement and the rest of his sentence at hard labor. On December 9, 1936 he was paroled.

	CRIMINAL		
Deft. **Mazzatto, Bruno**	Vol.	Page	Case No.
	12	*3 7*	**1671**

Offense **Murder**

Entry **January 14, 1920**
Sentence *Jan. 21, 1921. Life imprisonment*
State Prison, 1st day sol
Remarks *residue, hard labor*
December 9, 1936. Pardon on parole condition filed.

ART METAL CONST. CO., JAMESTOWN, N. Y.   P94354   10M-10-04

SUPERIOR COURT RECORD OF MAZZATTO

CHAPTER ELEVEN

Prohibition
1919 to 1933

On October 28, 1919, Congress passed the Eighteenth Amendment to the United States Constitution, the "Volstead Act". This act banned the sale, manufacture, and transportation of alcohol for consumption anywhere in the country. A person who sells illegal whiskey is called a bootlegger, and a person who makes the whiskey illegally is called a moonshiner. Moonshine goes by many names such as white lightning, corn liquor, sugar whiskey, skull cracker, bush whiskey, stump, stump hole, mule kick and hillbilly pop.

Chief John L. Sullivan, a teetotaler himself, was an ardent supporter of prohibition, though he confessed that enforcement gave him "aggravating troubles." It was very difficult to get evidence sufficient to convict bootleggers, but worse than the bootleggers were the respectable people who patronized them. The chief said there were "more stills than ever in private homes, which make liquor for their own use and are even ready to give some to their friends. Many hundreds make their own beer and wine. Our aliens hold permits to make their wine up to 200 gallons, from the Internal Revenue Department. The alien population was the ones that are most troublesome, as they are able to manufacture it in one place, conceal it in another place and sell it in small quantities from their own homes or their pockets or the wife carries it concealed in her dress. Those patronizing bootleggers or making booze at home were corrupting both the community and their own families."

NO ONE EVER WENT THIRSTY IN PITTSFIELD

During the "Prohibition Era", William Jetty, 99, of Pittsfield, worked as an assistant manager in several theaters in Pittsfield: the Majestic, the Kameo, and the Capital. Bill, in his early twenties at this time, said, "No one ever went thirsty in Pittsfield." He explained that the bootleggers would bring their booze from Albany, New York, by truck, dropping half a truck load off in Canaan, New York. The other half of the truck load would be brought to Pittsfield. The barrels of booze would be stored in the dressing rooms of the Majestic Theater. The Majestic was known for its vaudeville acts, which consisted of a variety of singing, dancing, and comic acts. Both the Capital and Majestic Theaters could hold 1,500 people and were filled almost every night. Each Saturday morning Bill would have to go to City Hall and have the mayor sign a special permit to open on Sunday. The theaters would rotate each Sunday, as to what one would be open that week. Certain acts could not be performed on Sundays. Dancing was never allowed. Each week Massachusetts would publish and distribute a list of what could be performed at a vaudeville show.

Bill became friendly with many of the officers. Each night an officer in an unmarked cruiser would escort Bill to the bank to drop off the day's receipts. The officers on the beats would stop in the theater, either to shoot the breeze or catch a vaudeville act on a slow night. Bill was transferred to the Paramount Theater in Springfield in 1938. One night, one of the officers, Officer Camille Marcel, who had escorted Bill nightly to the bank, stopped in after delivering some paper work to the Springfield Police Department and took Bill out for a drink. Prohibition was long over with.

ALL WHISKEY CAME
OUT OF THE SAME BARREL

All the whiskey came from the same barrels, but labels were printed up with every whiskey name there was. Two of the favorite names were Golden Wedding and Old Crow. When asked for a certain brand, if that brand wasn't already on the shelf, one of the stage hands would go into another dressing room, slap that name on the bottle and it bring back. You would hand him a five dollars bill in payment for the bottle, but the price varied, depending on who you were. If in the right circle you could get a bottle for three dollars. The bottles were kept in burlap bags.

Jack Diamond was the main bootlegger in this area. "Legs" as he was known, received this nickname from either his being a good dancer or from how fast he could escape his enemies. Diamond had a house in nearby Lebanon, New York, on the hill between routes 20 and 22. Legs entrained many a gangster friend with female companionship and alcohol in this house. Several unsuccessful attempts were made on Legs' life in prior years with no success by gunmen. On December 18, 1931, Legs' enemies caught up with him, shooting him in the head, killing him after he was found passed out in Albany after a night party.

NYPD mugshot of Jack Diamond

JACK DIAMOND

GRANDMOTHER O'NEIL-MOONSHINER- BOOTLEGGER

Lieutenant Jedediah N. Shepardson, Officers John D. McNaughton and John J. Blair, raided the home of Mrs. John J. O'Neil at 302 Linden Street. In the morning raid, police sized four cases of porter, five cases of ale, three and one-half gallons of moonshine liquor, 50 gallons of moonshine mash, 16 gallons of porter mash, 10 gallons of beer mash and one complete still in operation. Mrs. O'Neil was notified by the officers to appear in court for illegal keeping of liquor, maintaining a liquor nuisance and illegal manufacture of liquor. It took several trips by the officers to remove all the moonshine from the house.

Mrs. O'Neil, a widow, raised a family of nine children. She had learned the art of making moonshine when she was a girl in Ireland before coming to the United States. She had a steady clientele for her liquor. Each Sunday after Mass at a church on West Street, a steady stream of customers would follow the winding path from the church to her house at the top of the hill on Linden Street. She would sell the moonshine for fifty cents for a small "Ball" pint jar.

TOURING CAR TO CANADA

Whiskey could be bought in Canada legally but not transported back into the United States. Joe R., relates the story on how his father and three of his friends, one an officer on the force, would drive up to Quebec in a Ford Model T Touring Car, with the roof down for a weekend. The touring car was an open-air vehicle that was very popular during the early 1920s.

The Model T had a large spare tire mounted to the trunk of the car. At the end of the weekend they would take the spare tire off the trunk and remove the tube. They would place bottles of whiskey in the inside of the tire and replace the tube in the tire. The tube was then inflated to cushion the bottles; once this was done the tire was placed back on the trunk. They had a leisurely drive back to Pittsfield with their whiskey.

KNEW OF RAID IN ADVANCE

Sam B., 90, tells of how his father always knew in advance when to hide his extra wine. Sam never knew of how his father knew until he was 21 years old and going out with a girl from Albany. Talking with his girlfriend's father, he learned his father and an officer on the force were best of friends. When a raid was going to take place the officer would call his father with a heads up. His father had a permit from the Internal Revenue Department to make up to 200 gallons of wine, but he always made a lot more to sell to friends. Before the raid, his father would have Sam and his sister take all the extra bottled wine down to where they kept their horse, in the barn and hide it in the hay. When the officers showed up, there would be less than 200 gallons of wine in the house. Sam said a lot of nights he would hear a knock at the back door. A friend of his father's would be there with fifty cents for a small "Ball" jar of wine.

PITTSFIELD SO DRY FEDERAL AGENTS NOT NEEDED

On Sunday, March 26, 1922, Attorney General J. Weston Allen, at the Tremont Temple, said Chief John L. Sullivan "made Pittsfield so dry federal agents are not needed." Allen was cheered as "our next governor" by those in attendance. Allen paid high compliments to Chief Sullivan and the Pittsfield Police Department for the manner in which they enforced the liquor laws, saying that Pittsfield had enforced the liquor laws impartially and there was no need for federal agents to be in Pittsfield. With a wave of crime riding on a sea of illicit booze sweeping the country, Pittsfield is "high and dry as the Rock of Ages," according to state prohibition enforcement officers. Pittsfield has enforced the laws so strictly and successfully that drunkenness has decreased 85 percent since prohibition began. The arrest for drunkenness formerly averaged from 290 to 312 a month. Now they average from 20 to 25 a month. In 1918, Saturday night generally found from 12 to 25 men under arrest before midnight and half a dozen more after that hour.

Chief Sullivan designated two officers, Inspector J. D. Shepardson and Duncan McNaughton, to spend practically all their time on enforcing liquor laws. The chief said that didn't mean that the rest of the department could lay down on prohibition enforcement. He expected the officer on each post to be able to present evidence in the Police Court as to conditions concerning an alleged liquor nuisance for some time preceding a raid by the liquor squad. Sullivan said "I have personally visited homes of foreign-born residents, warned them to obey the liquor laws, destroyed settings of mash and told them not to make more. I let them know that the law was to be enforced in Pittsfield and gave them fair warning before making any arrests."

Sullivan said "It has been our policy to clean up liquor nuisances, disorderly houses, gambling joints and kitchen barrooms. And Pittsfield will never have house of ill-fame if the Police Department can prevent it. It is my belief that disorderly houses are the breeding places of gangsters and criminals." The chief said "the men who drink moonshine, jakey or the other home-made decoctions are not the same men they were when they drink pure whiskey and beer. They are dangerous, vicious animals. It has been my aim to make rumrunners and bootleggers feel that Pittsfield isn't a safe place for them, that they cannot use our garages as distributing depots or even park their cars with impunity in a Pittsfield garage. I have tried to make bootleggers feel that every time they sold booze in Pittsfield they were knocking at the jail door."

"Pittsfield was one of the cities on the rum-running route from Canada two years ago," the chief said, "the booze cars were coming through Albany, over Lebanon Mountain highway into Pittsfield and then east." I am told by Federal Revenue Agents that run-runners avoid Pittsfield like poison now. They detour around the city and go over the Mohawk Trail. We have made too many captures of booze-laden automobiles to suit the runners. Only six of the 38 cafes and saloons that were open previous to prohibition remained opened.

Pittsfield had a few speakeasies, but kept them very low keyed, so Chief Sullivan and his liquor squad would not raid them. One of Pittsfield's senior citizens relates a story he heard while growing up during that period. "A new officer, assigned to a business district beat, stationed himself in front of a popular speakeasy night after night. The owner of the speakeasy, upon seeing a uniformed policeman outside his business, turning away thirsty customers and cutting into his profits, called up a police official he was supposedly paying off to avoid being raided. He told this officer, "If we are going to make a living, you've got to take that "Statue of Liberty" away from my place." The next night the rookie cop, at roll call, was assigned to a beat in the Morningside area." Was someone in the department taking a payoff, or was this just a story that has been passed down from speakeasy to barroom? Prohibition did lead to corruption.

ORDERS FROM THE CHIEF

Chief Sullivan was very straightforward in his orders and pulled no punches; he received information daily from citizens reporting violation of the liquor laws. He would leave orders to his officers with this information and what he wanted done. (Out of the thousands of orders that Chief Sullivan issued, Capt. O'Neil has about 100 hard copies of these orders, given to him by the family of a retired detective.) The following are excerpts of some of these orders:

To: Sgt. Rock:
I saw this Brown, that lives up on Onota St. the stage hand, I think he is running some kind of a joint down on South St. over the Chinaman's. I have seen him looking out the window and seen him come out around 6 p.m. and at 9 p.m.

I understand that there is some kind of a bell when you ring it a certain number of times, you can come into this place.

I wish that you would check this fellow up, as I believe you have received complaints from me on this fellow before.

Respectfully yours,
Chief of Police

To Sgt. Rock:

There is quite a lot of comment again that Our Place on Wendell Ave. the Butler, is doing a land office business. I wish that you could send someone in there and made a buy, perhaps Barry could make one or some of the young fellows.

Respectfully yours,
Chief of Police

To: Sgt. Rock:

No. 35 Mill St. is selling liquor to one Frank Potts. Mrs. Potts has gone there and told them to stop and they have not. 101 Woodlawn Ave. is selling to him also and they will not stop selling to him either. Understand he swaps vegetables for the liquor. Mrs. Potts is coming to see me and so is he. She made this complaint to Jim Kelly to see it he could get relief. Check the Nick's family on Pitt St. for a disorderly house, for drunks. I think it is a bed house. They raise hell there.

Respectfully yours,
Chief of Police

To: Sgt. Rock:

Jones on New Road is the man who is making and selling beer for a period of two years and never been touched.

Respectfully yours,
Chief of Police

To: Sgt. Rock:

Mayor Moore reported to me Max Jones; corner of Francis Ave. and Summer St. house or tenements upstairs; corner of Bradford & Francis Ave. over Samuels Store, Carlos Taxi office; Mrs. Keegan, Wahconah St. Place in the Bigley Building, on Columbus Ave.

McCormick of the Eagle stated that Coleman said there were some slot machines in Pittsfield. I told him that I would be pleased to go with Coleman personally, anyplace where he thought there was one and I didn't care whether they were in the Eagles or in the Moose or in the Elks. That I would kick in the front door of any dam fraternal organization where there is one.

Of course we must get the money in them to prove that they have been used as gambling machines. Remember mere possession of a slot machine is not sufficient evidence to make them gambling implement. Be sure to get a statement from them that they played it and find out how much they played it, so we can use it to convict them in Court.

Sergeant on these complaints, I want you to be sure to have evidence so as to be able to secure a warrant and if you should go in on them cold be sure and get a statement in the presence of Barry or bring them into my office and we will try to get a statement that can be used in court to convict, your only chance for traffic in liquor or rather a liquor nuisance.

Respectfully yours,
Chief of Police

Inspector: McColgan:
You will bring in your four men to report to you 6:30 p.m. Monday night. I want them to be at Roll Call at 6:50 p.m. upstairs yourself included. These men are to tour the city in two separate cars. Make arrangements with Lieut. Shepardson to assign these cars.

These officers are to call you or the desk every thirty minutes. They are not to report back to the station house until 10:45 p.m. This is effect until further orders.

Respectfully yours,
Chief of Police

To: Sgt. Rock:
Check up on a Lincoln car, it least looks like a Lincoln. Has Grey Hound head on front, Mass. 154736. I understand this car delivers liquor. There are always young fellows in it.

Respectfully yours,
Chief of Police

To: Sgt. Rock:
Please secure warrant and raid either on Friday or Saturday night, Carlo's place. At this place I would advise you to take the Captain and two or three

good men. Carlo has a strange bunch of Italians with him and I don't like their looks at all.

I received another complaint Seller's Store on Wahconah Street is selling. Mrs. Seller is no dam good, the boy is the same. I don't want any widow woman and boy of that type selling liquor.

I am very anxious that you raid 220 Robbins Ave which is John Doe. Has a still. He had ten people in this place last Sunday afternoon. I would rather have you raid it at night if possible.

Whatever you do Sergeant, get that 220 Robbins Ave. clean everything in it, take his wine and take everything. You can us members of the squad or any officers that you want to, to be ordered back to you. I would made arrangements to take one squad and go from one place to another and clean them all up.

I would give a list of the places to Talbot and have him get the warrants all ready. I will sign with you and let him turn the warrants over to men and I will bring them over with me for you.

Respectfully yours,
Chief of Police

To: Sgt. Rock:
There is a man in Pittsfield who is running a Treasury Balance. He has got quite a clever scheme. He has ten Agents employed by him selling chances from a penny to 2 cents I want to secure the arrest of this man in the very worst way. It is just really a Policy Game. He has retained attorneys to represent him to aid and advise him. I will give him all the damn attorneys that he wants.

They are working in stores, pool rooms and on the street. I was unable to secure the man's name or where he worked.

Respectfully yours,
Chief of Police

1924 STEPS OF SUPERIOR COURTHOUSE

OFFICER SUSPENDED-30 DAYS

It was February 22, 1928. The event was the 16th Annual Policemen's Ball. A veteran officer of 28 years on the force was escorted from the event by Captain John H. Hine on the order of Chief John L. Sullivan. The officer was suspended for 30 days on a charge of conduct unbecoming an officer. The officer came to the ball with a bottle of liquor (moonshine) in his back hip pocket. He was seen drinking from the bottle during the event. This was brought to the attention of Chief Sullivan who ordered him removed. Earlier in the week federal agents had made a raid on Pecks Road. This was the officer's beat and it was believed that he should have known that a still was operating on his beat. After a hearing before the chief, he was exonerated on the charges that he knew the still was in operation. The 30 day suspension was the first black mark on the officer's record in his 28 years of service.

CHIEF SULLIVAN WANTED THE CITY "BONE DRY"

On February 24, 1928, because of the embarrassment from the Pecks Road raid by Federal Agents, Chief Sullivan formed two special liquor squads. Mayor J. Barnes supported the chief on this move. These two squads were separate and distinct units from the rest of the department.

Chief Sullivan said in an effort to make Pittsfield "bone dry" he declared war on bootleggers and rum runners. He placed Lieutenant J. Shepardson and Sergeant Richard Rock in charge of these squads. These squads were to obtain evidence and to make raids at all hours of the day. They could go directly to district court and obtain search warrants; no raids were to be made without a warrant. They could use as many officers as they needed. The chief made it clear that no one was to know in advance where a raid was to take place. The captain in charge was to assemble officers only 10 minutes before a raid if they needed more officers than assigned to the squads.

No Federal Agents ever stepped foot in Pittsfield to make any raids or arrests after the Pecks Road raid in 1928.

ADAMS VISITORS TREATED TO RAID

The Pittsfield Turnverein Hall at 117 Seymour Street was the scene of a liquor raid staged Saturday night, March 16, 1933, by Pittsfield Police, led personally by Police Chief John L. Sullivan, which resulted in the arrest of three men and the seizure of a quantity of alleged beer and whiskey. The raid interrupted a party which the Pittsfield Turners were giving in honor of members of a bowling team from Adams and their wives and was the cause of considerable comment in Pittsfield. Those arrested were Casper K., President of the Turnverein Society, Frank Z., manager of the building, and Charles C. bartender. They were charged with illegal sales of alleged intoxicating liquor, illegal keeping and maintaining a liquor nuisance, and were released on bail of $200 each.

Attorney George A. Prediger of Pittsfield was retained by the three men to represent them at the court hearing. According to police, they found an old-fashioned bar in the basement of the clubhouse over which the beer and liquor was being sold. A number of persons were standing at the bar and others were interested in a bowling match on the alleys located in the basement. About 40 persons were in the clubhouse at the time of the raid, including the party from Adams. It was customary for Turnverein societies to hold interclub matches and socials usually followed the matches. In picking out officers to accompany him on the raid, Chief Sullivan entirely ignored the new "dry" squad which he appointed the first part of the week at the reported direction of Mayor P. J. Moore. City hall and the Police Department had been at odds since the inaugural of Mayor Moore. The Saturday evening raid was the first one staged on the Turnverein Club since its organization 50 years ago. Officers and members of the society were highly indignant over the raid and attributed it to jealousy between the mayor and the chief.

END OF PROHIBITION

In 1933 President Franklin Roosevelt called a special session of Congress which amended the Volstead Act to legalize beer and wine up to 3.2 percent alcoholic content. Pittsfield welcomed this legislation and on April 10, 1933 the Licensing Board granted 15 temporary licenses for the sale of beer and wine. On December 5, 1933, President Roosevelt signed the 21st Amendment which repealed the 18th Amendment (prohibition) and said "What American needs now is a drink." On December 7, 1933, legal hard liquor went on sale at noon in the Wendell Hotel, but only to patrons of the dining room. Package stores were busy selling whiskey, gin and wine. Chief John L. Sullivan reassigned the departments Liquor Squad to other duties.

1920's
$140,000 DIAMONDS ROBBERY

A North Street jeweler, Philip E. Schwartz, reported to the department the disappearance of $140,000 of diamonds on consignment to him from a business friend, a New York jeweler, who was visiting the city. Investigation of the Schwarz store failed to reveal the diamonds or any clue as to how they might have been stolen.

During their inquiries, officers found that in Schwarz's private office on the second floor of his store there was a secret stairway leading to a luxurious room on the third floor, a so-called "Throne Room". At one end was a "royal" chair on a dais, with a canopy overhead. On the carpet which stretched from wall to wall were two polar bear rugs. The furniture included a large handsome lounge and a day bed. There were artificial flowers hanging from the richly decorated ceiling. Heavy brocade curtains covered the walls and also the windows, so that no light could get in or out.

Schwarz modestly described this secret chamber as his "rest room." In it the officers found a large cache of bonded whiskey, a violation of the prohibition law. A week after the "robbery," while making another thorough search of the premises, the officers found the missing diamonds in a bag stuffed behind a steam pipe in the basement, evidently just "planted" there. "An inside job" Chief John L. Sullivan declared from the start, and charged Schwarz with larceny. Schwarz was acquitted of the charge in court.

MURDER ON EAST MOUNTAIN

CAPTAIN HUDNER

On August 15, 1915 the body of unknown male was found on East Mountain, just over the Pittsfield line in Dalton, by two berry pickers. A bullet wound was found in his skull and the head was cracked open; there was no flesh on the face. The body was wearing a blue suit, black overcoat and yellow shoes. His right hip pocket was turned out. Before reporting their findings, the berry pickers went home to supper. After eating they went to the Pittsfield Police Department to report what they had found.

Dr. Stephen Burto, ME, Inspector Daniel McColgan and Officer Jedediah Sheparson accompanied the berry pickers back to the body. Chief Sullivan and Captain John Hudner were notified.

Captain Hudner and Inspector McColgan found a letter in the male's pocket, addressed to a Vincenzo Cresci from his father with Francis Avenue address on it, and some cashed money orders. Going to the rooming house on Francis Avenue, they found the names of the four males who rented the apartment: Vincenzo Cresci, Joseph Balzarano, Matteo Patrello and Vincenzo Napolitano. Cresci and Balzarano came to the United States from the same town in Italy, and played together while growing up there. The body on the mountain was Vincenzo Cresci.

After the murder and robbery, Balzarano, Patrello and Napolitano hopped a train to Albany. From there they went of Jacksonville, Florida, next to Key West, then to Galveston, Texas. Here Balzarano split up with Matteo and Vincenzo. Balzarano who now went by the name of Norman Cole paid all their bills with the dead man's money. After their separation Cole kept on the move. Matteo and Vincenzo were arrested in Galveston and spent 30 days in jail. The twosome were in a back alley when Officer Flurnoy F. Smith, making his nightly check, saw them at the other end of the alley. He followed them as they stepped out from behind obstructions and walked up to them as they squatted behind a hedge. He shined his flashlight on them, walking over to them with his .45 pistol in hand. Matteo tried to pull a .38 revolver from his back pocket, but Officer Smith hit him over the head with his .45, and both were placed under arrest. The .38 revolver was loaded with five cartridges. Matteo also had a blackjack and straight edged razor on him. Napolitano had a .32 revolver loaded with six cartridges and a black jack on his person. After getting out of jail Matteo and Vincenzo traveled back to the North east. One was arrested in Brooklyn, New York, the other in Bridgeport, Connecticut, for carrying a gun. They were transported back to Pittsfield in July, 1916, found guilty in Superior Court of the 2nd degree murder of Vincenzo Cresci, and sentenced to life in prison.

After nearly four years of traveling out West, Balzarano (Cole) headed back East. He worked for a while in Alabama and Savannah, Georgia and finally ended up in a boarding house on Wall Street, Bridgeport, Connecticut a neighbor called police after spotting Balzarano at the boarding house, seeing his picture on a wanted poster in the Bridgeport Post Office. Inspector McColgan traveled to Bridgeport to make the arrest along with Massachusetts State Detective Thomas E. Bligh and officers from the Bridgeport Police. Inspector McColgan and Det. Bligh transported Balzarano back to Pittsfield for his trial. When arrested, Balzarano had a .38 revolver on his person, which was taken by Inspector McColgan.

Balzarano was charged with 4 counts of murder. The 1st count read that Balzarano did assault and beat with intent to murder Vincenzo Cresci and did murder him. The 2nd said the Balzarano did assault by shooting Cresci with a bullet and did murder him. The 3rd said the Balzarano did assault and beat Cresci by striking him upon his head with an unknown object and did murder Cresci. The 4th and last said that Balzarano did assault and beat Cresci with intent to murder by shooting him in the head with a revolver and did murder him. It was determined that murder occurred on March 27, 1915, but the body was never found until August 15, 1915.

In July of 1920, Balzarano's trail began in Superior Court before Judge Christopher T. Callahan of Holyoke and an all-male jury. The Commonwealth maintained that Cresci was lured to the mountain by the three other

Italians, who beat, shot and robbed him of $200. On the stand in court, Balzarano denied he had anything to do with the murder; he said he was in a cabin at the foot of the mountain while the trio, Cresci, Patrello and Napolitano went farther up the mountain. After a while he left the cabin and went back to his boarding house on Francis Avenue in Pittsfield, where he later met up with his two friends.

The Commonwealth brought in two witnesses, his friends, Patrello and Napolitano who were serving life terms in prison at Charlestown for the same murder. They testified that Balzarano actually did the shooting. For their testimony, the DA was going to talk to the parole board. Both gave the same details of what happened, saying all four left their boarding house on Francis Avenue and caught the trolley to outer East Street. Here they hitched a ride with a man driving a sleigh with two horses. He dropped them off at the bottom of East Mountain. They walked part way up the mountain and stopped to have lunch under a tree where there was no snow. While walking up the mountain, Joe was target practicing; he shot about fifteen or twenty shots at stumps. Cresci was sitting on a stump and Joe came up behind him and hit him in the head with his gun. Cresci started running and Joe started shooting at him, hitting and knocking him to the ground. Then he stood over him, shooting him in the head. Joe then kicked him several times and took his money out of his pocket. They then went to the boarding house on Francis Avenue, getting a ride from a man driving a sleigh. They packed all of their clothes along with Cresci's, which they left at the train station in Albany. They spent Cresci's money while traveling around the country.

Balzarano's lawyers tried to prove Cresci committed suicide. DA Joseph Ely had two distinguished doctors with 20 years' experience each testify that it wouldn't be possible for a person to shoot himself in the back of the head at the angle the bullet had entered. Dr. Stephen Burton, who viewed the body on the mountain, said the position of the body and clothing indicated that Cresci didn't shoot himself. He thought it probable the wound was inflicted by some other person. Dr. Burton also stated that he had searched the area for a gun, finding none.

CRACK IN FRONTAL BONE

.38 REVOLVER

Inspector McColgan brought Cresci's skull into court and showed the jury where the bullet entered the skull on the right hand side, and the crack in the frontal bone. The bullet was entered into evidence. Inspector Mc-Colgan told how he was present when the bullet was taken from Cresci's skull by Dr.Colt and Dr. Burton at the undertakers where the autopsy was done. He explained to the jury how he and Captain John Hudner searched the mountain for evidence. DA Ely had Officer Smith of Galveston testify that he took a .38 revolver from Patrello when he arrested him. The .38 was entered into evidence. Next DA Ely called on Captain William H. Proctor, a member of the Massachusetts State Police who for 20 years made a special study of firearms. He said the grooves in the bullet found in Cresci's skull came from the .38 Patrello had on him when arrested.

To show the jury that Balzarano was lying when he said he went back to the boarding house on Francis Avenue by himself, DA Ely put Harry Adamson on the stand, who testified that he picked up Balzarano, Patrello and Napolitano in his sleigh and gave them a ride down the mountain. He said that Balzarano had a weird look on his face and it frightened him. Over 80 pieces of evidence were shown to the jury.

On July 20, 1920, Balzarano was found guilty of the 2nd degree murder of Vincenzo Cresci. Judge Callahan sentenced Balzarano to life in prison; his first day was in solitary confinement and the rest of his sentence at hard labor. On December 1, 1936, he was paroled.

ANNUAL REPORT OF 1920
ONE DAY OFF IN EIGHT

PADDY WAGON ABOUT 1920

In Chief Sullivan's Annual Report of 1920 he thanked the citizens for allowing the officers of the department to have one day off in eight. He recommended that the department's Kissel Kar and Hudson car be exchanged for one real car, a car with speed and endurance and a car that will be as good as a bandit's car, or if necessary to overtake a gang in a stolen car. It was very easy for a gang of criminals to make their getaway because as a whole police cars are mostly junk compared with cars operated by thieves.

The chief also acknowledged the appointment of John H. Hines as captain and Richard A. Rock as a sergeant in the department.

MURDER CHARGES AGAINST GENERAL ELECTRIC WORKER

In a late night arrest made by Chief John J. Sullivan, Captain John Hudner, Inspector Daniel J. McColgan and Officer John H. Hines, Dominick May was arrested for murder. According to police in Easton, Pennsylvania, May was a member of the "Black Hand Gang" who murdered several men in their city. May was accused of two or more of the murders. In the last murder, in the later part of June, 1920, Easton Police found the body of a man in 50 feet of water in a quarry with a 100 pound weight attached to his legs. This was one of several that the "Black Hand Gang" had committed.

Dominick May had moved to Pittsfield and was living with his brother William. He had gotten a job with General Electric Co. soon after he arrived in Pittsfield, living only a short distance from the GE building. Dominick was arraigned in District Court on a charge of being a fugitive from Northampton County, Pennsylvania, where he was alleged to have committed the murders. He pled not guilty and was held without bail. Easton Police Department was notified and sent two officers to take him back to stand trial. Everyone had been under the impression that May would waive extradition and return to Easton; however May's intention was to fight extradition. He wanted the Easton authorities to come to Pittsfield and show the reasons why they wanted to have him taken back to answer to the murder charges. May fought extradition all the way up to the governor's office; he lost his battle and was returned to Easton to stand trial. Chief John L. Sullivan had received word that May was one of the last of the "Black Hand" gang to be arrested. The "Black Hand" was a criminal organization that extorted money from Italian immigrants. It was known to use explosives in carrying out its extortion threats.

With the increase of automobiles, Chief Sullivan made hundreds of recommendations for traffic control and parking ordinances, saying that the most trying and important functions of a Police Department were the regulation of traffic. He requested that the City Council enact laws for traffic control, many of which are still in effect today.

At this time patrolmen had to wear dark blue, single-breasted, skeleton sack coats, which were buttoned up to their chins. Directing traffic in one of these coats in the hot sun was unbearable. The chief recommended a change in the regulations to allow the patrolmen to wear "from June 15th to September 15th, a light flannel shirt, color gray, single breasted, two bellow pockets, and collar white. Regulation police trousers, badge to be worn on shirt, gun to be carried in holster on a belt." With the sack coats guns were worn under the coat, not showing. The City Council went along with the chief's recommendation, with the change of the uniform and patrolmen no longer had to wear the heavy blue skeleton sack jacket buttoned up to their chins.

TRAFFIC ACCIDENTS

With traffic accidents mounting, many ascribed the maiming and "slaughter of the innocents" to the fact that many more women were driving, now that cars were equipped with self-starters. It was alleged that women were not as good drivers as men. Chief Sullivan did not subscribe to this view, but he had noted, that when milady put on her finery and got behind the wheel of a "nice car" for a tour along crowded North Street, she was less concerned about the weaving traffic than "watching the sidewalks for friends, and enemies."

Moveable Traffic Lights

In 1922, Chief Sullivan bought six moveable semaphore standards for better control of traffic. Equipped with red and green lamps for night use, those were set up in the center of main intersections. In summer, each was shaded by a large green umbrella. One of Chief Sullivan's recommendations was for a new Recall Gamewell System with colored lights attached on the top, which would enable headquarters to notify the entire department in a few moments of any serious crime, accident, by simply turning a switch, which would light these call box lights and to warn all officers to get in touch with the station at once. These call boxes were still used into the late 1970s. Walking beats had to ring in every hour or when the blue light flashed on and off on top of the call box. Officers had to ring in within ten minutes before or after the approved ring time. The communications officer would record what time the officer rang in on a log sheet, which was turned in after each shift. If an officer failed to ring in within the ten minutes time period, the station would have the officer on the next beat or the street sergeant check on his welfare. The beat officer on the midnight shift would have to stand by his call box at 4:00 a.m. for the street sergeant's nightly check.

REFLECTIONS ON ARRESTS

Each year Chief John L. Sullivan in his Annual Reports would highlight some important arrests that the department made. The following are from 1921 and 1922:

"Fred S., Italian gun man and Catherine P., of Boston, Mass., came here with the intentions of running a disorderly house. Evidence secured and place raided before it had been running a week. They were arrested by Chief of Police, John L. Sullivan, Captain John H. Hines and Sergeant Richard B. Rock."

"Raymond W., a dangerous man and automobile thief, wanted in eight different cities in two states. Arrested and indicted by Grand Jury. He was sentenced to four years State Prison. Chief Sullivan said sentences of this description will soon stop the larceny of automobiles by automobile thieves. Officer William J. Keegan and Sergeant Sheehan of Boston made the arrest."

"On November 26, 1922, Officer Martin Fahey, apprehended Joseph G., Alias W. Lee of Pawtucket, R.I. and Edward C., alias Edward Cutler of Boston, Mass. When arrested they had a Ford Sedan stolen from taxi driver of Saratoga Springs, N. Y., whom they hired and robbed. They bound and gagged chauffeur, and carried him from Saratoga Springs, N.Y., to Stephentown, N.Y., and left him bound and gagged in a building in rear of a church. These men were turned over to Saratoga Police as fugitives from justice. They were charged with assault and attempt to kill, highway robbery and larceny of automobile."

"Charles H., Albany, N.Y., pick pocket, known all over the United States as "Big Albany", arrested for larceny from person by Officer Herbert Violin."

"Edward L., Plattsburg, N.Y. apprehended by Officer Richard L. Naughton, with automobile full of liquor and carrying a loaded automatic 45 caliber."

CHAPTER TWELVE

MISSING POSTMASTER

On the morning of September 2, 1922, just as two inspectors from the U.S. Post Office arrived for a routine check of local postal affairs, Postmaster Clifford H. Dickson walked out of his office as if he intended to be gone only a few minutes on some business in town. That evening he was seen in New York City by two young Pittsfield women. Chief Sullivan and the department were notified several days later that Dickson failed to return and no word from him had come either to his office or his worried wife, who had the care of five children. Their suspicions aroused, the postal inspectors began a closer check and found that he had absconded with at least $16,662 and perhaps more.

No clue or trace of him was found since his reported sighting in New York. A nation-wide search was made for him. He became, in a sense, the most photographed man in the city's history, for in all post offices and other public buildings from coast to coast, his picture was posted among those "Wanted."

WANTED POSTER OF POSTMASTER DICKSON

After wandering for five years, Dickson decided to surrender, giving up in Fort Smith, Arkansas. Brought back to Massachusetts, he pleaded guilty and was given three years in prison. Dickson declined to talk about his wanderings saying that none of the money taken had been spent on himself.

Dickson had been the city's Tax Collector from February 1, 1915 to August 31, 1921. Some evidence at his trial suggested that the funds stolen from the post office had been used to cover an unexplained deficit of almost the same amount which had been found in the city Tax Collector's Office soon after Dickson had left it. If so, he had been juggling public funds for some time.

1923

REVOKE ICE CREAM LICENSES

In 1923 Chief Sullivan recommended that 65 percent of the city's ice cream licenses be revoked. The chief said that "there were so many small stores that are open on Sundays and holidays and they have no the proper facilities for selling ice cream and soft drinks. It was very unfair to our merchants. That so many small stores owned by aliens, are allowed this privilege of opening on Sundays. It means the sale of merchandise as well. Less than one percent of these stores have hot water, to wash and clean glasses and receptacles properly. This is absolutely unsanitary."

PEDESTRIANS

Chief Sullivan wanted the city to build more sidewalks on paved roads so citizens could walk safely. He cited that too many serious accidents had happened from one-man electric cars, caused by passengers entering or being discharged, in the roadway. He wanted the Pittsfield Electric Street Railway to make some kinds of arrangements for passengers to enter or leave the car by the door nearest a sidewalk.

TWO OF THE DEPARTMENTS
MOTORCYCLE OFFICERS

A progressive chief, in his Annual Report of 1924, Chief Sullivan recommended that cruiser patrolmen supplement the foot patrolmen in the outlying districts. He said "I recommend that the patrolmen in the outlying districts be equipped with a car owned by themselves and the city allow them a certain amount for the use of their machines. What good is a patrolman on foot? Today is the motor age; good roads, fast automobiles, bootleggers, speeders, automobile thefts, and reckless drivers have increased the difficulties of Law enforcement. The criminal of today has the best of automobiles".

CHAPTER THIRTEEN

MURDER BY CYANIDE POISONING

CYANIDE MIXED IN
PAREGORIC BOTTLE

On February 13, 1924, a young French woman, Eugenie Mercier, 25, died. Eugenie and her husband, Louis, lived in a two room apartment on Turner Avenue. When police arrived, she was dressed in a red kimono, a night dress, a pair of slippers, and stockings. Louis told police that she had risen about 6:00 a.m. to light the fire, and then returned to bed. Just before 8:00 a.m. Eugenie again got up and went to the kitchen where she took her morning medicine, paregoric.

Returning to the bedroom, she told Louis, "I am dizzy" and then fell to the floor. Louis ran into the kitchen, poured some milk, returned, and attempted to give it to Eugenie. She was unable to drink it; within a matter of minutes she was dead. Louis lifted his wife to the bed, and then ran out across the snowy street to a neighbor's house where a doctor was called.

Police found that Louis was always well-dressed and passed himself off as a single man among a group of girls, to one of whom, before his wife's death, he became engaged. When she learned he was married she broke off the engagement. Louis explained to her that his wife was in Canada, and as she could neither read nor write, she could not return to the United States and he would get a divorce.

At the burial, Louis showed no emotion over the curious death of his wife when her casket was lowered into the gravel. Fifteen minutes after the family departed from the cemetery, police arrived and Mrs. Mercier was ordered exhumed from her resting place. She was taken immediately to the Robert Fairchild Funeral Home where an autopsy was performed. The autopsy disclosed no signs of death by violence or heart trouble, but traces of cyanide poison were found in her stomach. Police had acted swiftly and secretly. Louis did not know that an autopsy had been conducted when he was called into Chief John L. Sullivan's office that same afternoon. The chief wanted to know whether her death was accidental, suicide or murder.

"If I told you that there was poison in your wife's stomach, what would you say to that?" Asked the chief, standing over Mercier.

"I don't know", Mercier told the chief and stood by this story of ignorance through hour after hour of questioning. Police were baffled on how the cyanide came into the Mercier household.

At a later date Mercier admitted that he had stolen the poison from the Morse Plating Works, where he had been formerly employed. While no one was looking, he dipped a four-ounce bottle labeled paregoric into a cyanide tank holding it by a wire fastened to the neck of the bottle. Later he threw the wire away and put the bottle into his right inside overcoat pocket. Upon reaching home he placed the bottle where his wife always kept it.

During the questioning Mercier gave several different stories of why he had the cyanide. One was that he took the potassium of cyanide to clean rust off a small bank. The police went to the Turner Avenue apartment. After examining the bank, they found no traces of rust on it, nor did it appear that it had even been rust-encrusted.

The case was sent to the Grand Jury and on July 18, 1924, an indictment was returned charging Mercier with murder. Mercier later repudiated his confession. At Mercier's trail, Dr. William F. Boos, an eminent Boston Toxicologist, found that something had indeed destroyed the black dye on the right inside pocket of Mercier's overcoat, leaving a patch of dirty brown. This is just what a strong cyanide solution would do.

Mercier was convicted beyond reasonable doubt by the stain on the inside pocket of his overcoat. He was found guilty of second degree murder and was sentenced to life imprisonment in the state prison. Mercier was paroled after serving about ten years of his prison term, moving to Canada.

1925 to 1940

In the summer of 1925, Pittsfield installed its first traffic lights, four in total. They were located in the center of the city. At South Street and East and West Housatonic Streets, at the corner of West Street and North Street, on North Street at Fenn Street, and on Fenn Street at First Street. These light were turned off from December 31 to May 1. With these lights installed it freed up officers from doing traffic at these intersections and enabled them to walk their beats.

PEACE MEMORIAL DEDICATION
SOLDIERS AND SAILORS MONUMENT

MARCH TO SOLDIERS AND SAILORS MONUMENT

With white gloves on and carrying his dress baton with bright gold tassels, Chief John L. Sullivan, marched down South Street. It was Monday morning, July 8, 1926. Beside the chief were Governor Alvan T. Fuller, Mayor Fred T. Francis and U.S. Attorney General John G. Sargent, who represented President Calvin Collidge. Following them, were more than 2,000 marchers and five bands. There was a crowd of 25,000 citizens lining the street, waving American flags. The procession was on its way to the dedication of the Peace Memorial, built to commemorate the end of World War I. The bronze monument, sculptured by Augustus Lukeman, shows an aviator, infantry officer, foot soldier and sailor.

There were 2,978 men and women who served in World War 1 from Pittsfield; 88 of this number never came back from the war. During the two and one half hour ceremony a band played "America the Beautiful" and other patriotic songs. Veterans from the Civil War and World War I were in attendance. A great number of World War I veterans later became members of the Pittsfield Police Department.

Judge John C. Crosby, former Mayor of Pittsfield, and now a member of the Massachusetts Supreme Court, presided at the ceremony. The city's oldest Civil War veteran, Commodore William F. Hunt, unveiled the monument.

Pittsfield Police Officer Charles "Spike" Kelly, who was wounded in World War I was the second name to be read off at the ceremony. Officer Kelly's name is the first name on the town of Dalton's monument, as he was a resident of Dalton, where he grew up. Chief Sullivan ordered every off-duty officer on the force in for parade duty.

CHIEF OF POLICE HEARING IS HELD

City committee exonerates Chief
John L. Sullivan on Abusive Language

On December 14, 1927, the Police Committee of Pittsfield gave a hearing in the case of Harrie G., of Livingston Avenue, Pittsfield, on his complaint against Police Chief John L. Sullivan. Harrie G. alleged that the chief was guilty of abusive and unseemly language against him on October 17, in the office of Clerk of Court Leland C. Talbot. The committee was composed of Mayor Harry G. West and Aldermen Goetz and Murphy. The defendant failed to appear and the committee, after hearing Mr. Talbot and his assistant, Miss Laura E. O'Hearn, exonerated the police chief.

TEN MEN ARE INJURED WHEN TRUCK SKIDS OFF HIGHWAY

On August 14, 1929, a one ton truck carrying 13 workmen from Albany to Woronoco, Massachusetts, rolled down Lebanon Mountain embankment, turning over twice. The truck was on route to a dam being built by the Springfield Water Company.

Sergeant Stephen W. Monks, Officer Peter O. Ano and Officer Camille L. Marcel of department were sent to the scene to investigate the accident and help out with injured. Four were in serious condition and taken to House of Mercy Hospital in Pittsfield. At the hospital the driver who was pinned beneath the wheel had his hand amputated, another had a fractured skull and broken ribs.

Sergeant Monks learned from a witness that she saw the truck leave the road at a curve, turn over, sliding on its side for 70 ft., then go down the embankment, scattering the occupants in all directions. The investigation was turned over to the state police, who after the driver was released from the hospital, arrested him and charged with dangerous driving.

EARLY 1930'S
FRONT OF OLD POLICE STATION
1929 OR 1930 MODEL T's
L to R OFFICER CHARLES A. BARRY, UNKNOWN, INSPECTOR DANIEL J. McCOLGAN,
UNKNOWN, OFFICER CAMILE MARCEL AND CHIEF JOHN L. SULLIVAN

1929 or 1930- MODEL T'S

TWEAKING THE DEPARTMENT'S AMBULANCE

DOG OFFICER

In 1931, the Mayor Jay P. Barnes appointed the Chief of Police, John L. Sullivan, as the city's Dog Officer. This was in compliance with the state law requiring the appointment of an officer to enforce the laws relating to dogs. Before this a dog constable was appointed annually by the mayor.

CHAPTER FOURTEEN

MISSING BANK PRESIDENT
UNSOLVED MYSTERY

William L. Adam, 78, President of Berkshire Savings Bank, disappeared from his home on West Housatonic Street late Sunday night, April 9, 1933. Upon receiving a report from one of his maids that he was missing, Inspector Daniel McColgan immediately went to his home. In talking with the maids, the inspector learned that both maids had gone out on that afternoon. Mr. Adam was there when they left and when they returned. He attended church in the morning, as his custom, but didn't attend a concert at the First Church on Sunday night as he usually did. He ate a good dinner and supper. He sat reading until about 10:30 p.m., when the maids went to bed.

One of the maids, Mrs. Mary McGinns, who had been in Adam's employment for eleven years, woke up at about 2:30 a.m. and could not go back to sleep. She did not know what woke her up, but did not hear any noise.

When one of the maids came down in the morning she noticed the bath room door open. She thought it was strange that the door was not closed, as Mr. Adam always shaved the first thing in the morning. She waited until about 8:30 a.m. and then went to his room and found that he was not there. She noticed that the bed had been lain upon. She did not hear any noise at any time, and said that he must have been very quiet. No clothes or clothes bags were missing. He left his keys and some money and his watch in his room. No one saw him after 10:20 p.m.

Mr. Adam was a 1877 graduate of Williams College, and graduated from Columbia Law School in 1880. He was admitted to the Berkshire Bar in 1882, and had been identified with the Berkshire County Savings Bank since 1894. He was a director of the Agricultural National Bank, Berkshire Mutual Fire Insurance Company, Hampshire Mutual Fire Insurance Company and Russell Manufacturing Company.

The West branch of the Housatonic River was dragged the next day by a squad of officers, with no results. Chief Sullivan called in 500 boy scouts, police officers, fishermen, hunters, and private parties, to help search. Onota Lake and Richmond Pond were drudged. The grounds of the Pittsfield Country Club, Morewood Lake and Tillotson Pond were searched. Chief Sullivan had to call the search off for one day due to a twelve inch snow storm. Arrangements were made with Fire Chief Thomas F. Burke to make a sudden blast of the fire whistles throughout the city to indicate the discovery of the body of William L. Adam but the signal was never sounded.

The Police Department offered a $200 dollar reward for any information about the disappearance of William L. Adam, without any response, and then raised it to $300 for his return, dead or alive; this offer ran only for 30 days with no one claiming it. A while later, through Judge Charles L. Hibbard, one of Mr. Adam's closest friends, a $1,000 reward was offered by his two nearest relatives.

REWARD POSTER FOR
MISSING BANKER

Two Pinkerton detectives were called in by the bank, but they discovered not a single clue as to Adam's disappearance. A world-wide search was conducted for the bank president. Posters were sent to over 200 cities, towns, and detectives agencies. Paid ads were taken out in major cities newspapers across the country, and even as far as London, England.

To this day, neither the body nor any evidence of what happened to President William L. Adam has been found. The case of the missing bank president remains unsolved.

JEDEDIAH N. SHEPARDSON

LIEUTENANT JEDEDIAH N. SHEPARDSON
RETIRES AFTER 25 YEARS SERVICE

On February 1, 1933, Lieutenant Jedediah N. Shepardson retired after 25 years of service. He was a member of the Fire Department for many years, before being appointed an officer, by Mayor William H. MacInnis, on May 19, 1908. Several times he declined an appointment to the active force, while serving as a reserve officer.

In 1914 he was made a plain clothes officer. When the department was equipped with motor vehicles, he had the entire charge of the repairing and maintaining them. In 1919, was appointed inspector. For some years he was designated lieutenant although inspector and lieutenant carried the same ranking in the department. He headed the Liquor Enforcement Squad for several years. Lieutenant Shepardson died on September 11, 1937 at the age of 61.

ROAD BLOCK AT CITY LINE

In the fall of 1934, Pittsfield's button factory workers, at one of local mills, walked out in protest against wages of $8.00 a week or less. Pittsfield workers were not unionized. North Adams mill workers were unionized and decided to help their fellow workers in Pittsfield, sending representatives to Pittsfield to help them organize.

Upon reaching the Pittsfield city line they found a roadblock set up and manned by Chief John L. Sullivan, who ordered them to turn around an never to return. Individually or in small groups, they returned and established a local in Pittsfield of the United Textile Workers of America.

M/C OFFICERS JOSEPH KIRVIN-
HERBERT VOLIN – RICHARD NAUGHTON
INDIANS 1200 CC MOTORCYCLES

KILLED WITHOUT WARNING SHOT ON NORTH STREET

PARISI

Rocco Yetz, 32, a foreman for the C.B. Lindholm Company, was shot to death without warning on North Street. This shooting took place on Friday, September 13, 1935. The Lindholm Construction Company was working on the Pittsfield Electric Company's steam installation job in front of the Sweeney-Farrell and Pender Blocks on North Street. Yetz was considered a key man in the Lindholm Construction Company. He had worked for the company for four years. He had a wife and seven year old son.

Yetz went down almost too instant death, the bullet blasting through his heart. The shooter, Carmeno Parisi, 53, of Whipple Street, an unemployed laborer, who declared he had been refused a job by Yetz, said he shot the foreman "because he no give me a job."

Chief John L. Sullivan said Yetz didn't have a chance, according to witnesses. Parisi gun in hand came along the street walked up to Yetz, and pulled the trigger. Parisi then fired a second shot as Yetz staggered, bleeding to death in the doorway of the Rochford Hat Shop in the Pender Block. The first bullet hit Yetz about one inch above the left breast, picrcing the heart. The second bullet failed to hit Yetz and landed up in the window of the hat shop. The weapon used was a .32 caliber pearl-handled Harrington & Richards Revolver.

Joseph Palmer of West Street another employee of Lindholm, told police he was carrying a board two-feet long, looking toward Yetz. When he saw Parisi take a gun out of his right pants pocket, and fired twice at Yetz, falling to the floor of the doorway of Nick's Poolroom. Parisi took off running toward the Bridge Lunch. A man grabbed for him but he got away. Palmer ran toward Parisi with the two-foot board in his hand; he was going to hit Parisi with it, but changed his mind and dropped the board and made a drive for Parisi. Parisi turned to pull his gun on Palmer, but Palmer got his hand in Parisi's right pants pocket and got the gun. As he pulled the gun out of Parisi's pocket, Patrolmen Leon Darey, who was across the street, heard the yelling and ran to the scene. Officer Darey retrieved the gun from Palmer who now had possession of it.

With the capture of Parisi, Sergeant Richard B. Rock with Officers Medos Discoe, Andrew Miller, arrived at the scene in the patrol wagon. Officers Discoe and Miller picked up the wounded man and started for the House of Mercy Hospital. Although Yetz was believed to be alive when he was loaded into the police ambulance (patrol wagon), he was dead when he reached the hospital. Yetz was taken in an operating room and Dr. Albert C. England, ME, viewed the body. Later Chief Sullivan ordered an autopsy, which showed that the bullet passed into the chest in the region of the heart, pierced that organ, passed across the chest, through the windpipe to lodge in the right shoulder.

Parisi had a knife clinched in his hand and after Discoe grabbed it, Sergeant Rock ordered the wagon to delay a moment and Officer Darey commandeered a passing car in which Parisi was brought to the Police Station. The knife that Parisi pulled, a jackknife, remained closed. Officers Darey and Discoe saw to that.

Chief Sullivan, Captain John H. Hines and ADA Harold R. Goeway directed the investigation. Parisi told them he had been drinking before the shooting. He had no money but had an axe which he sold to a junk dealer for 30 cents. He used this money for a beer. Starting on West Street he had a drink or two then walked to North Street. He arrived at the Pittsfield Café about 6:30 p.m. and had some beer there, then went south on North Street. He also stated to the officers that he was nervous, feeling bad because he was off relief. When he saw Yetz, he just shot him. He said he didn't know why he had the revolver with him, but he had been carrying it since last Friday. That night Captain Hines went to Parisi's rooming house and looked over his belongings. In a trunk he found a stiletto and a box containing 14 bullets of the same caliber used in the murder weapon.

After a jury trial in Berkshire Superior Court, Parisi was found not guilty by the reason of insanity. He was committed to the Bridgewater State Hospital for the insane.

DIAGRAM OF MURDER SCENE

BABY STRANGLED TO DEATH

WORN BLANKET AROUND NECK

On April 23,1936, Joseph King, 13, of 1059 North Street, and Martin McNamara, 13, of 197 Montgomery Avenue were stamp hunting at a dump on Bryan Street which runs off Crane Avenue. While going through old papers looking for stamps for their collection, they spotted a partly opened brown paper bag. Hoping it would contain stamps, they made the dreadful discovery of a small deceased male baby. The baby had a 15 inch long piece of what at the time, was thought to be a towel wrapped around its neck. The cloth turned out to be a well-worn blanket. A copy of the Berkshire Evening

Eagle, dated Friday, March 13, was also found in the bag.

Both boys ran to Joseph's house and told his father what they had found. Mr. King returned with the boys to the dump. After seeing for himself, he called Captain John H. Hines at Police Headquarters. Capt. Hines, Detectives William P. McCormick and Charles A. Barry soon arrived at the Bryan Street dump. Where they found the body of a well–developed, and only slightly decomposed baby boy.

Dr. Albert England, Medical Examiner and Dr. T. W. Jones did an autopsy on the baby and determined the cause of death was strangulation. The baby had been murdered about April 1st. The umbilical cord had not been tied.

Detectives canvassed the neighborhood asking if anyone had seen any strange cars. Captain Hines believed that the baby was probably illegitimate and the mother unmarried. The mother of the baby has never been found.

PADDY WAGON MADE BY WHITE MOTOR COMPANY

SEVEN NEW OFFICERS

On October 22, 1937, the city appointed seven new officers. They were Howard J. Heneau, badge number 48; Patrick D. Ryan, 49; James Manger, 50; William J. Noon, 51; James P. McCarthy, 52; Raymond Marcel, 53; and Daniel A. McGill,54.

All were assigned to the midnight shift. The new officers were given special instructions on Massachusetts General Laws and Department Rules and Regulations by Captain John H. Hines, Inspector Daniel J. McColgan, and Sergeants Richard B. Rock, William J. Keegan and Camille L. Marcel. Motorcycle patrolmen were also added to the patrol force.

1935 FORD V8 FLEET

DEPARTMENT'S AMBULANCE 1936

On December 30, 1938, Officer Raymond Coakley was appointed a reserve officer by Mayor James Fallon. He was made permanent patrolman on August 17, 1941, was elevated to a sergeant three years later and was appointed a captain in 1948. Before heading the Detective Bureau, he was in charge of the Vice Squad and in that capacity headed all horse bookie raids. He participated in the investigation of four murder cases. On July 5, 1969, with 31 years of service, Captain Coakley retired.

COURT DUTIES

In 1939, Chief Sullivan had been chief for twenty-four years. An important part of his duties as chief was representing the Commonwealth in District Court each morning. During this twenty-four year period the chief handled approximately 35,000 cases for "The People."

The position of captain was made vacant by the death of Captain John H. Hines on July 16, 1939, and had not been filled by the mayor.

CAPTAIN JOHN H. HINES

Neither was a lieutenant appointment made to take the place of the late Lt. Jedediah N. Shepardson. Captain Hines was appointed a reserve officer in 1902, and to the regular force on April 14, 1903; he was promoted to sergeant on February 10, 1919. For four years before that he was in the Detective Bureau doing plain clothes work. He was made a captain a year later. Captain Hines was in charge of the Vice Squad and during one year on that assignment he made 141 arrests. Captain Hines had on his 35th anniversary as a police officer an estimated 4000 arrests to his credit. In addition to his police work in the city, Captain Hines was for more than 15 years a familiar figure at the Great Barrington Fair where each year he did plain clothes duty during fair week. His duty for the most part was at night when he was in charge of the departments activities.

CHIEF SULLIVAN'S "HALT YOUR SPEEDING" CAMPAIGN

1940

Police activity during these years consisted of combating the rising problem relating to traffic and public safety. The Annual Report for 1940 showed the city population at 50,000 and the department personnel consisted of a chief of police, a captain, and inspector, three sergeants, fifty-one patrolmen and a matron. The report includes a long list of miscellaneous duties performed, protective and preventive in their nature relating to persons, property, health, and general public welfare.

During the 1940 national elections Wendell Willkie, who was running against President Roosevelt for the presidency, stopped in Pittsfield. A long walkway was erected from the railroad tracks near the bridge on First Street to the Common. Willkie spoke to an enthusiastic crowd of 8,000. Mayor Fallon declined to serve as a member of the committee named to welcome Willkie. The mayor said it was not part of his duty as a non-partisan mayor to welcome, or in any way favor, the candidate of one party or the other. Chief Sullivan assigned a squad of officers to be on hand for crowd control and public safety.

VETERAN OFFICER SUCCUMBS TO HEART ATTACK WHILE INVESTIGATING CASE IN NORTH ADAMS.

DETECTIVE JOSEPH J. KIRVIN

On January 23, 1940, while investigating a stolen motor vehicle case in North Adams, Detective Joseph J. Kirvin succumbed to an acute heart attack. Detective Kirvin and Inspector Daniel J. McColgan were returning to Pittsfield after completing their investigation.

Detective Kirvin, who was driving, stopped his cruiser and told Inspector McColgan that he didn't feel well. "My arm feels numb. I'm going to have a shock, but don't get alarmed", he said and then he collapsed. North Adams patrolmen aided in removing Detective Kirvin to the O'Brien Clinic, where last rites were administered to him. Chief Sullivan was notified, and with Sergeant Richard Rock, drove Mrs. Kirvin and her sister to North Adams, but Detective Kirvin died just before their arrival. He was 52 years old.

On Saturday, January 26, forty patrolmen headed by Chief Sullivan marched in procession to St. Joseph's Church, where a solemn high mass of requiem was held. Mayor James Fallon, members of the city council, and a delegation of state police attended.

OFFICERS GET NEW POSTS

Officer Martin L. Fahey, who was assigned to desk duty at Police Headquarters for several years, was promoted to detective by Chief Sullivan. Officer Fahey filled the vacancy created by the death of Detective Kirvin. Officer William H. Ford transferred from detail service to desk duty to succeed Officer Fahey. Officer Fahey was appointed a reserve officer on March 13, 1919, and to the regular force as a patrolman on December 10, 1919. He served in the Detective Bureau for a short time in 1925. Also in the transfers, Officer Peter O. Ano was placed on detail from Post 5 and 6. Officer Joseph P. Kondey was transferred from Squad B, 4:00 p.m. to mid-night, to Squad A, days, 8:00 a.m. to 4:00 p.m.

1940
NEW POLICE HEADQUARTERS

On January 1, 1940 the Police Department moved from its antiquated quarters on School Street to a new building at 39 Allen Street. It was on the site of the former Municipal Building at the corner of Allen and Dunham Streets. The new station was within one hundred feet of the old station. The new headquarters was funded by the Public Works Administration, a Great Depression-era agency, to the tune of 45 percent of the $211,000 cost. This station was the fifth lockup in Pittsfield's history, and housed one of the most modern and adequate Police Stations in the entire state. Special features consisted of separate quarters for juvenile offenders, a women's cell block, matron's quarters, a shooting gallery, an assembly hall and adequate locker room for the officers. On the Dunham Street side of the building was the entrance to the Welfare Offices, which shared some space in the new building. (1970 Dunham Street was closed and made into a mall.) During the construction of the new station, while excavating the site, the remains of one more original settler of the Town of Pittsfield was found and transferred to the Pittsfield Cemetery.

THE PISTOL RANGE. The department maintains membership in a number of rifle and pistol leagues and has a goodly number of men who can hold their own in competitive matches. Here all men of the department are required to qualify as to marksmanship.

PISTOL RANGE

THE GUN RACK. The equipment shown here is ready 24 hours a day in case of civil commotion or whenever anti-riot weapons are needed. Seldom used, it is maintained at 100 p.c. efficiency at all times.

GUN RACK

COMMUNICATION ROOM

NERVE CENTER. The police desk is the contact point between the citizens and the Police Department. Hundreds of calls come to the telephone desk and numerous citizens come here to report accidents, lost wallets, lost children or to seek information. Specially trained sympathetic police officers are on duty at the desk 24 hours a day.

FRONT DESK

CHAPTER FIFTEEN

TWENTY-FIVE YEARS AS CHIEF
TESTIMONIAL BANQUET

J. EDGAR

On September 14, 1940, Chief John L. Sullivan was honored at a banquet at the Wendell Hotel. This marked his twenty-fifth anniversary as chief of police for the City of Pittsfield. In attendance were: John Edgar Hoover, better known as J. Edgar Hoover (He did not like to be called John), Director of the Federal Bureau of Investigation, U.S. Department of Justice; Hugh Clegg, assistant director of the FBI; Edward J. Kelly, Executive Secretary, International Association Chiefs of Police, Chicago, Illinois; Ernest W. Brown, Supt. and Major, Metropolitan Police, Washington, D.C., President of the International Association Chiefs of Police; Archibald Bullock, President New England Chief of Police Association, Chief of Police, Arlington, Massachusetts. Also in attendance were the Commissioner of Police, Boston, Massachusetts; Commissioner of Police, New York City; Supt. of Police, Bridgeport, Connecticut and D .A. Thomas Moriarty of Springfield. Many distinguished citizens of the area were also present, among them the president and vice president of Crane and Company. Just about every Police Department in Massachusetts was represented along with judges from every court in Berkshire County. John J. O'Connell, Commissioner of New York City Police Department, was toastmaster. Broiled fillet mignon and French fried potatoes was the main dinner course. Entertainment was provided by Pittsfield High School Glee Club.

ORDINANCE BANS TICKET SALES BY POLICE, FIREMEN

Mayor James Fallon, only two days after the Testimonial Banquet for Chief Sullivan, filed an ordinance forbidding members of the Police and Fire Departments from selling or soliciting the sale of tickets for any "ball, dance, show, dinner, testimonial, game, exhibition, display or contest." Mayor Fallon had received an invitation to the testimonial dinner, but returned it to the committee, saying he would not attend. Chief Sullivan and Mayor Fallon had a lengthy conference in which the chief denied point blank that any police officers delivered any tickets to his testimonial while on duty.

WORLD WAR II

When war became imminent in 1941, the Police Department was augmented by a force of Auxiliary Police Officers which consisted of nearly 200 members. These members were from all walks of life and contributed their services without compensation. They were trained by a group of instructors, including the chief of police, on the laws, ordinances and the rules and regulation of the police department. They were used principally on traffic duty and at other strategic points during black-outs.

AIR RAID DRILLS

PITTSFIELD'S CHIEF AIR RAID
Warden was Charles Hodecker,
Public Welfare Commissioner.

There were air raid sirens throughout city to warn the citizens of an enemy attack. One long blast on the siren meant that cars could continue driving but had to put their headlights on low beams and pedestrians could continue to move about; all buildings must start to blackout. Short, quick blasts meant that the street lights would be turned off. Cars must stop, turn their lights off and pedestrians must take cover. Auxiliary Police and Air Raid Wardens would bang on doors and windows yelling "Blackout." The all clear signal would be indicated by turning the streets lights back on.

During the year, over 1,200 investigations and 100 raids or searches were conducted in cooperation with the FBI for national security. Officers were looking for guns, ammunition, binoculars, cameras, and shortwave radios that could be used by enemy agents, who had taken up residency in the United States. Also investigated were 156 cases of lights burning during blackouts and over 4,000 people were fingerprinted as a contribution to national defense.

WAR DUTY
Suggestions for
POLICE

1942

FEDERAL BUREAU OF INVESTIGATION
UNITED STATES DEPARTMENT OF JUSTICE

1942 POLICE WAR DUTIES BY FBI

During a test drill, a woman on Park Street refused to turn off her lights. An Air Raid Warden asked her to turn off her lights, but she refused. The warden then went to Police Officer Michael A. Barry, who went to the house and made the same request. The woman flatly refused to turn off her light, saying "I have some work to do." Next morning Chief John L. Sullivan went to District Court to obtain a warrant for Pittsfield's first accused viola-tor of the black-out regulations.

FOUR ARRESTED AT GUN POINT
Smiles Have Different Meaning

Smiling after their arrest by Officer Francis O'Neil, right, who heroically held them at bay with his service revolver until police help arrived, this quartet told police they staged a holdup in East Nassau "just to raise hell." Sgt. Camille L. Mazel, who went to Officer O'Neil's assistance is at left. They are, left to right, Joseph A. Pongiteri, 19, and Wilfred Treadwell, 28, of Boston; Dorothy Shanb, alias Dottie Blake, 19, of Troy and Guy J. Guilmette, 21, of Boston, former resident of Pittsfield.

Chief John L. Sullivan described the capture of the armed trio and girl as one of the most courageous in local police history. February 4, 1942 was a snowy night; there were very few cars on the road. Officer Francis D. O'Neil was on patrol in the West Pittsfield section of the city. He had just made his hourly ring on the call box at 10:15 p.m.

Desk Officer Francis E. Dwyer had received a report of a holdup in East Nassau, New York, from New York State Police. Officer Dwyer notified, through the recall system, all officers on their posts and policemen in cruisers, about the holdup. He gave the description of three men and the registration of a stolen Buick sedan from Boston, with Massachusetts plates 504-311.

Officer O'Neil decided to drive out West Housatonic Street, to the Richmond town line. At the corner of West Housatonic Street and Lebanon Avenue, he spotted a car traveling east. Catching only the last three numbers of the plate, -311, due to the visibility of the snow storm, he made a U-turn, and he start pursuing the Buick at speeds reaching 60 to 65 miles per hour. At the corner of West Housatonic and Merriam Streets, the Buick slowed down to make the corner. O'Neil gained speed. Just over the railroad bridge on Merriam Street, heading to West Street, O'Neil pulled his cruiser across the path of the fleeing bandits, blocking their path. Jumping out of his cruiser with his revolver in hand, he ordered the three men and girl to "come out with your hands up." Threatening to shoot the first of them to move their hands, he ordered them to walk to the side of the Yellow Cab garage. They obeyed. Lining them up against the wall of the garage, he held them at bay with their hands in the air. A taxi cab driver, who was passing by, called Police Headquarters and excitedly reported that "Red O'Neil" has four people up against the wall down here on Merriam Street at the cab company, and hung up the receiver.

Sgt. Camille L. Marcel and his brother, Officer William C. Marcel, drove immediately to the scene and found Officer O'Neil covering the quartet with his revolver. Clamping handcuffs on them, the sergeant searched the four and found one had a .32 revolver in his coat. On inspecting their car Sgt. Marcel also came across an automatic pistol in the glove compartment. Chief Sullivan was notified, and went to the scene.

When they were taken to Police Headquarters and searched more thoroughly, Officer Marcel found a dirk knife in an inside coat pocket of one man. At headquarters the chief, Sgt. Marcel and Officer O'Neil questioned the quartet.

Asked why they held up the general store, one of the men said "just for the hell of it." They only got change from the cash register, a total of $5.60. If they had held up the store a few hours earlier, they would have gotten a few hundred dollars.

All four were from the Boston area, one formerly lived in Pittsfield. They waived extradition and were returned to Troy, New York, to face charges of armed robbery. Officer O'Neil received a citation from the Troy, New York, grand jury for his arrest of the quartet.

VISIT FROM QUEEN WIHELMINA

On June 27, 1942, Chief Sullivan, along with a detail of plain clothes officers and two motorcycle officers, provided an escort to Queen Wilhelmina of the Netherlands. Queen Wilhelmina liked shopping at England Brothers Store on North Street. Chief Sullivan was notified in advance by the queen's body guards when she would be in Pittsfield. She made several shopping trips to Pittsfield. She spent the summers in Lenox, with her daughter Princess Juliana. Queen Wilhelmina reigned over the Kingdom of the Netherlands from 1890 to 1948, longer than any other Dutch monarch. Outside the Netherlands she is primarily remembered for her role in World War II, in which she proved to be a great inspiration to the Dutch resistance. On May 10, 1940, Nazi Germany invaded the Netherlands, and Queen Wilhelmina and her family were evacuated to the United Kingdom three days later and were unable to return until the war was over.

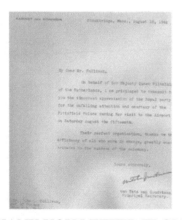

THANK YOU LETTER FROM
QUEEN WILHELMINA

M/C OFFICER VINCENT-CHIEF
JOHN L. WILHELMINA

POLICE GIVE EMPTY SHELLS TO SALVAGERS

On December 4, 1942, Chairman Edward J. Russell of the War Salvage Committee announced that Chief John L. Sullivan, on behalf of the Police Department, turned over 101 pounds of empty cartridge shells to the Salvage Committee. The shells had been collected over a long period of time at the police shooting range in the basement of the station. Russell also commended the department and its motorcycle officers for helping out at Wahconah Park during salvage drives. Citizens brought all kinds of metal to Wahconah Park to be melted down to build guns, tanks and ships for the war.

1943

CAPTAIN MARCEL-CAPTAIN CALNAN
TAKEN OATH OF OFFICE

On January 1, 1943 two captains were appointed to the vacancy created by the death of Captain John H. Hines who died in 1939. They were Captain Camille L. Marcel and Captain Thomas H. Calnan. These captains alternated on day and night shifts, changing on the first of each month.

3O YEAR VETERAN DIES

DETECTIVE CHARLES A. BARRY

Detective Charles A. Barry, 60, a member of the department for 30 years, passed away on July 19, 1943, after a two weeks' sickness at St. Luke's Hospital. At the time of his death he was an active member of the Detective Bureau which he had been connected to for18 years. He was born in 1882 at his house on Church Street where he lived his entire life. He was appointed a reserve officer by Mayor Kelton B .Miller, on December 7, 1912, and the following year, May 5, 1913, he was named a permanent member of the department by Mayor Patrick J. Moore. Detective Barry served for several years as desk officer and clerk to Chief John L. Sullivan. In 1924 he was named to the Detective Bureau.

For 25 years Det. Barry served as Treasurer of Pittsfield Branch, Massachusetts Police Mutual Aid Association. One of his three sons, Charles F. Barry, was a member of the Federal Bureau of Investigation. Two others sons at the time, were serving in the Armed Forces, William and John. John A. later became a well-known judge in Pittsfield and Chairman of the Board of Directors of Hillcrest Hospital.

Chief John L. Sullivan, who was in Washington D.C. attending a conference of the International Chiefs of Police Association executive committee when he heard the news of the death, sent back to Pittsfield this tribute: "Charles A. Barry was fine type of officer. For many years he was my secretary. He served the Vice Squad for 20 years he was assigned to the Detective Bureau. Pittsfield has lost the services of a valuable officer. He was a conscientious, painstaking police officer. He will be missed by his associates in the department."The flag on the station was placed at half-staff out of respect for Detective Barry.

Detective Charles A. Barry's grandson, Captain Patrick F. Barry is presently the commander of the Detective Bureau and Drug Unit. As commander for the last several years he has overseen every major investigation that has taken place in Pittsfield with great success.

CHAPTER SIXTEEN

NOXON MURDER TRAIL
MURDER OR MERCY KILLING?

Attorney John F. Noxon, Jr., 46, father of six month old Lawrence S. Noxon, was arrested and charged with his son's murder by electrocution, on September 22, 1943. Death was due to acute heart failure induced by the passage of an electrical current through the chest from forearm to forearm. The prominent Pittsfield corporation lawyer was arrested at 10:30 a.m. at his law office at 28 North St., September 27, 1943

Noxon was taken into custody by Inspector Daniel J. McColgan and Captain Camille L. Marcel and was held at the Police Station overnight for his arraignment in District Court. Inspector Daniel J. McColgan, Detectives R. Lawrence Naughton and Martin L. Fahey took Noxon to court in the police patrol wagon the next day for his arraignment.

The baby was found dead shortly after 5:00 p.m. on the floor of the living room of the Noxon home on West Street. Upon finding the baby, John F. Noxon immediately called the family pediatrician, Dr. George P. Hunt, who called in Dr. Albert C. England, M.E. The doctors attributed death to electrocution from exposed wires on a "trouble light" which Noxon said he was using to repair a radio.

The next morning at 11:00 a.m. the day after baby was electrocuted; Chief John L. Sullivan, Inspector Daniel J. McColgan, and Captain Camille L. Marcel went to the Noxon home and talked to Noxon in the presence of his wife, Margaret Swift Noxon. Noxon was sitting on the lawn at the south side of the house. Chief Sullivan told him he was sorry over what had happen and asked if he could have a talk with him. The chief asked Noxon to recount the events of the night before. Noxon told them he had returned to his home in the afternoon and had found his wife not home. He inquired of the maid and she informed him that Mrs. Noxon had taken the baby to Dr. Hunt's office.

Page 95

Noxon said he had noticed a few days before that his radio wasn't working properly and decided to try to fix it. He went into the garage to get the light cord, termed the trouble cord, which he had taken down the Sunday before from where it had been strung because the light bulb end which hung down had hit him in the head. He brought the cord into the book room and plugged it into the socket in the north side of the room. This was the socket which is below the bay window about in the middle of the bay window. He snapped on the light and it lighted, he then turned it off.

Noxon then said he went to the pantry and got the radio tubes, six in number, and placed them on a tray. Noxon used trays to transport items because he walked with two canes, the results of crippling polio. He brought the tray into the book room. Mrs. Noxon had returned home, came in and said she was going out to the garden to pick some corn for supper and placed the baby in a chair at the right of the radio set in the northeast corner of the room. Noxon moved the radio out so as to get at it better. He said he needed some pliers and a screw driver to assist in the work on the radio. They were in the garage.

He said he took the baby from where it had been placed by his wife in the chair, fearing that while he was in the garage the infant might fall off, and placed him on the metal tray on the floor. When he picked the baby up from the chair, he noticed that the baby's diapers were wet. That was the reason for placing the baby on the tray and not on the Oriental rug. He believed that when he left for the garage the light cord was extended out into the room on the right side of the baby, about a foot from the infant. When he moved the radio set out from the wall to get at it better, he found the black cable, comprising the antenna or aerial and ground wires, were loose in the socket and he pulled it out. He was not sure where this cable was when he left for the garage, possibly on the left side of the baby near the tray.

When he returned from the garage he smelled something and saw blood trickling down the baby's mouth. Also he saw the light wire across its chest and apparently wrapped around his left arm. He grabbed the wire and pulled on it. As he did so he noted the baby's arm raised. He jerked the wire sharply to free it from the child and it came loose. Then he called Mrs. Noxon. When she came in she asked him to pick up the baby from the tray and put it in the chair. He did so and then called Dr. Hunt.

Chief Sullivan asked Noxon what had become of this wire and Noxon said he had put it in the gas incinerator along with the baby's diaper and shirt, which had blood on it. He had decided to get rid of it because he did not want to have anyone else get hurt by it. After removing the plug and light bulb and cage he burned the wire in the incinerator. Noxon told the officers that he had first tried to tape over the breaks in the cord where it had been wrapped around the baby's arm.

The officers and Noxon went to the incinerator and took from it the remaining unburned portion of the wire. When the officers left the house they took the wire, a light socket, wide bulb, cage and some pieces of copper wire. Noxon also gave them a metal serving tray, and pink and green pillow. This is the pillow Noxon said he put under the baby's head.

Noxon asked the chief "What do you think, chief?" Chief Sullivan replied, "I think you have been very, very, careless, to say the least." Noxon replied "I suppose there could have been a motive."

When asked if he know anything about electricity, he said he did not. While the officers were in the basement they check up to see if any of the fuses in the fuse box, which was located in the south side of the basement, were blown out.

After the chief and witnesses had viewed the Noxon baby's body at the Wellington Funeral Home they returned to the Noxon home. Chief Sullivan asked Noxon who he had been studying electricity with and Noxon said a Mr. Bailey of Providence in which he was the plaintiff counsel. But in the morning he had previously told the officers he didn't know anything about electricity. The chief asked if he had any other conversations with anyone over electricity, and Noxon replied that he had with William A. Whittlesey at the trustees' meeting at the Berkshire County Savings Bank. Noxon had asked Whittlesey about some newspaper article that he read, if a person could get electrocuted by a household light circuit of 110 volts. The chief then asked Noxon about the burn on the baby's left arm and remarked that the bottom of the arm looked as if it had had a clamp on it. Noxon said he had not noticed the burns on the left arm.

Noxon said, "You talk as though you think I killed the child." The chief said, "I suspect you did." Noxon made no reply to this. Then after a few moments, "If I had I would have done it today as the maid is off duty."

Noxon was indicted by the Grand Jury on first degree murder. A Superior Court trial started on February 23, 1944, Judge Abraham E. Pinanski presiding. District Attorney Charles R. Alberti was the prosecuting attorney. Former Governor of Massachusetts, Joseph B. Ely was one of the defense counsels along with Michael L. Eisner and Walter J. Donovan. Out of 150 prospective jurors, 12 men were chosen for the jury. (Jurors were paid $6.00

a day and mileage of five cents a mile until a full jury was empanelled.) Once a full jury was empanelled the jurors were sequestered until the end of the trial. The jurors were housed at the Wendell-Sheraton Hotel all on one corridor. Fifteen rooms were reserved, twelve for the jurors and three for the deputy sheriffs. Two deputies guarded the prisoner while in court, and four were with the jurors when they were off duty, at the hotel, or engaged in recreation.

By ancient Massachusetts custom, the defendant in a murder case sits in a cage of iron grillwork in the center of the courtroom. The padlock of Noxon's cage often dangled, open, but there he sat, in an oak armchair, his repose that of an assured lawyer in the courtroom where he himself had practiced for two decades and where his father achieved distinction as the District Attorney.

On Thursday, March 9, 1944, Judge Abraham E. Pinanski declared a mistrial due to the fact that juror No. 9, James E. Cullen, became sick and was unable to continue to serve on the jury. Three competent physicians and surgeons examined Cullen and reported to Judge Pinanski he was too sick to continue to service as a juror. Judge Pinanski said under the present law the trial couldn't continue with only 11 jurors.

As a result of this mistrial a bill was filed by Senator James P. McAndrews of Adams to provide that two alternate jurors in a capital crime case would be seated and be prepared to substitute in the event one or two jurors were forced to withdraw. If the services of the alternates were not needed they would have no voting power and would be dismissed at the end of the trial. This bill was enacted by the legislature and became law.

A new trail started on the last day of May, 1944, and lasted for five weeks. The prosecution took 18 days of the trial, called 31 direct witnesses, and placed 73 exhibits in evidence. The defense required eight days and called as many witnesses. Both the Commonwealth and defense relied heavily on scientific testimony. Chemists, doctors with special expertise in treating burns, electricians, and wire engineers from General Electric, were all called for expert opinion and often clashed angrily in court. Numerous reconstructions of the death of the baby were presented by several experts. They argued at length as to the strength of electrical current necessary to kill humans. Detail by detail, the State attempted to disprove Noxon's own story.

Dr. George Pratt Hunt was one of the State's key prosecution witnesses. Dr. Hunt was the city's leading pediatrician. He had noticed something strange about the baby and suggested that the parents take their baby to Children's Hospital in Boston for examination by Dr. Richard Mason Smith, one of the nation's foremost pediatricians, professor of pediatrics at Harvard, and physician-in-chief at Children's Hospital. The Noxon's drove to hospital and left the baby with Dr. Smith for 48 hours. At the conclusion of the test it was agreed that the baby suffered from Mongolism or Down syndrome. The parents learned that their child could not be cured. The baby's care would require the full time of one adult and his presence in the home would be unwholesome for the older, normal brother. The baby's life span would probably not exceed 20 years.

At the trial, Dr. Hunt firmly declared that the baby did not have the strength to grasp a wire and pull it to him. Dr. Hunt also did a Shick Test on the baby the afternoon of his death. Dr. Hunt positively placed the Shick test marks on the baby's right arm. He denied there were identical with important "dumbbell shaped" marks which the State ascribed to a "clamp" which it said held a second wire to the baby to produce death, and which the defense said might easily have been made by the baby's diaper pin.

A plumber was brought in to expound the science of insulation because the trouble cord was supposed to have hung over an asbestos-insulated water pipe in the garage for many months.

Next the State called Hector Molleur, radio repair man of 18 years' experience. He said that he went to the Noxon home with police and tested the radio. He tuned it to station WBRK and the program came in well. He made an examination of its tubes. Seven of the eight tubes were found all right, Tube No. 42, a power or output tube, was found weak but not dead.

Dr. Alan R. Moritz, professor of legal medicine at Harvard Medical School, expert assistant in pathology to the department of public safety and an associate ME for the county of Suffolk and pro tempore ME for the county of Norfolk, along with his assistants, performed an autopsy on the baby. The autopsy report was signed by Dr. England as ME. Dr. Moritz went into a gruesome description of the rainbow of burns on the baby's arms, and his elaboration of the procedure of autopsy.

On July 6, after deliberating for six hours, the jury of 12 men, of which 10 were fathers, returned their verdict, "Guilty of murder in the first degree." Judge Abraham E. Pinanski imposed the mandatory sentence of death in the electric chair.

As Noxon sat on death row for over two years, his defense team filed over 115 motions to get the case overturned. Hundreds of letters calling for clemency, many from the state's leading citizens, poured into the office of Governor Maurice Tobin the month before Noxon's scheduled execution, July 1946. Margaret Noxon met with the governor and pleaded for her husband's life.

On August 7, just eight days before Noxon was to die in the chair, Governor Tobin turned the death sentence into a life sentence. Two years later, the new governor, Robert Bradford, decided "nothing further would be gained" by keeping Noxon behind bars, even though Bradford did not believe he was innocent. On January 7, 1949, John Noxon, leaning heavily on his two canes, walked through the prison's steel doors to freedom and his wife's waiting arms, moving from Massachusetts to another state.

RADIO THAT WASN'T WORKING   TRAY FROM PANTRY

SHOOTING LEAVES TWO DEAD AND ONE WOUNDED

On Saturday night, November 6, 1943, Horace D. Eddy, 62, of 44 Brown Street, a foreman at May's Machine Shop, shot Mrs. Effie Plumb, 60, his sister-in-law. Eddy also severely wounded his niece, Mrs. Charles R. Hume, 35, Effie's daughter. Mrs. Hume was hit once in her right shoulder; the bullet shattered her collarbone and passed through the upper portion of her lung, leaving her in serious condition. Effie was shot four or five times in the chest and stomach. The shooting took place in the kitchen of the Plumb's house, several doors down from the Eddy's house. At 11:15 p.m., a neighbor of the Plumbs, who lived on the next street, Franco Terrace, called Police Headquarters reporting that someone had just been shot at 44 Brown Street. Sgt. Richard B. Rock and Officer Frank R. Carlon drove the police ambulance to the scene, where they found both women in the kitchen bleeding profusely. They applied compresses to control the bleeding. On their way to the House of Mercy Hospital, Mrs. Hume told the officers that her uncle had shot them. Chief John L. Sullivan was notified by Sgt. Rock and ordered all the 4:00 p.m. to mid-night shift held over. He gave orders for the monitoring of all bus and railroad lines going out of the city and to notify the state police.

Returning to Eddy's house on Brown Street, Officer Carlon found Horace in the back seat of his car in the back yard. He had shot himself in the right temple; the bullet passed through the head and come out the left temple. The .32 caliber Colt automatic was still clutched in his right hand. There were still two rounds left in the magazine, which could hold eight.

.32 COLT AUTOMATIC

Sgt. Rock learned from family that Horace had been in poor health for the last year and that in recent weeks acted queerly and complained frequently of severe pains in his head. Horace and his wife, along with his sister-in-law, Effie, and Mrs. Hume had driven to Springfield on business that afternoon. After returning home, they had supper at about 6:45 p.m. and Horace said he was going to the shop. Later investigation revealed that instead he had drove downtown and had several drinks. On the way home he saw Effie and Mrs. Hume, offering them a ride, but they refused as he had been drinking. They later took a bus home where they found Horace's car parked in front of their house. Effie's husband was a work. Horace drove the car back to his house and parked it in the back yard, walking back to Effie's house. Banging at the kitchen door, he demanded to be let in. Effie refused as he was drunk and her two daughters were upstairs sleeping. Eddy forced his way into the kitchen, shooting Effie once at the door. He then fired three or four more rounds at Effie, one round striking Mrs. Hume in the shoulder. Officers couldn't determine if this round was intended for Mrs. Hume or if it was for her mother. Horace walked back to his house and shot himself. After viewing the body, Chief Sullivan, Dr. Albert C. England, Medical Examiner, and District Attorney Charles R. Alberti, determined there would be no autopsy. Effie passed away on Tuesday, November 9, four days after being shot. Also taking part in the investigation were Captain Camille L. Marcel, Inspector Daniel J. McColgan, Detectives R. Lawrence Naughton, Martin L. Fahey, and Officer Leon Darey.

CHRISTMAS EVE BOOKIE RAID

On December 24, 1943, at 4:15 p.m. squads of officers simultaneously arrested five bookies. Captain Thomas Calnan and Sergeant Michael P. Barry headed the investigation.

At their arraignment in District Court, Judge Charles L. Hibbard fined the defendants a total of $1,500. Chief Sullivan described the five as "some of the big shot horse bookies of Berkshire County." All five pleaded guilty to charges of registering bets. In disposing of the cases, Judge Hibbard said if the statutes did not specify that the penalty for such an offense must be either a jail sentence or a fine but not both, would have ordered suspended sentences for the five, in addition to the fines, "in the hope that it might discourage this vicious practice."

1944

RADIOS IN CRUISERS FOR FIRST TIME

On May 17, 1944 a long awaited radio system was installed in the department which greatly facilitated communications. This was an important day for the department. On this day radios in police cruisers first went into action. The system cost $9,000 and had a yearly upkeep of between $300 and $400. Communication had come a long way since the men made a duty call to headquarters every hour. Now, in an emergency or when the station needed an officer to call the station from his beat the green beacon light on top of the call box was flashed on and off from the switch board in the communication room.

The years shows a decline in department activity, as far as arrests were concerned, due in part to the restriction placed on the motorist by the president's thirty-five mile per hour speed limit and gas consumption program during WW II. One feature of gas conservation was the banning of pleasure drivers. It was strange and an unusual sight to see the streets of Pittsfield barren of cars during that period. Stranger still, was the duty of the police to call on motorists who were visiting clubs, bars and other places of assembly and remind them they must take their cars off the streets. It was surprising to see the compliance and cooperation shown to the police by the public at this time.

MORALS ARREST AT CRACK OF DAWN

On Wednesday, May 24, 1944, at 7:45 a.m., Inspector Daniel J. McColgan, Sgt. Richard B. Rock and State Trooper Kenneth T. Brown, arrived at a Lanesboro cottage with a non-support warrant for a Mrs. X. Upon entering the cottage they found a Mr. J., also living there. Both were arrested on morals charges and the outstanding warrant. Also arrested was the owner of the cottage, Mrs. A., who rented it out to the couple. She admitted housing the couple, but saw nothing wrong with it and stated when people like each other, (they share all expenses).

In District Court that morning before Judge Charles L. Hibbard, Mrs. A., said, "A disorderly house is a place where many men come, in and out, like many apartments in Pittsfield." She was given a suspended sentence of three months in the House of Correction and put on probation for two years, for running a Disorderly House (polite term for a house of prostitution). Judge Hibbard also ordered Mrs. A., a part-time local waitress, to leave the city and stay away.

Mrs. X., was sentenced to the Reformatory for Women on the morals charge. On the Welfare Department complaint of non-support of her two minor children, this case was continued. She appealed the decision of morals charge to Superior Court as did Mrs. A., Mr. J. pled guilty to the morals charge.

CHIEF PRAISES SGT. WILLIAM J. KEEGAN

Police Chief Sullivan paid tribute to 69 year old veteran Sgt. William J. Keegan, whose retirement petition was adopted unanimously by the City Council for August 1, 1944. The chief said Sgt. Keegan was one of the old guard, a good police officer who displays initiative, loyalty and willingness to work. He said we shall all miss him for he was well liked and did numerous favors for officers and citizens alike. Chief Sullivan said, Sgt. Keegan, when he first started, had "to pull in drunks" by hack, wheelbarrow or on his back as the rest of the police department has done as well. Sgt. Keegan helped investigate five murders cases, during his years of service. His host of friends wished him enjoyment of all the pleasures of life in the next few years.

CHIEF ASKS FOR CLOSER SUPERVISION OF WORK
TWO NEW SERGEANTS APPOINTED

At roll call on Monday, October 30, 1944 Chief Sullivan announced that starting November 1, newly appointed Sergeant Michael P. Barry would be assigned to Squad B (from 4 p.m. to midnight). At the age of 17, Barry went into the Marines. During his hitch he saw duty at 14 stations in this country and two years at Guantanamo Bay, Cuba. He made corporal in the Marines before he was discharged. Mayor Allen H. Bagg named Barry reserve patrolmen in 1937. Barry was appointed permanent patrolmen on August 26, 1941 by Mayor James Fallon and within a few years as a rounds man (acting sergeant) for Squad C, midnight to 8:00 a.m. Newly appointed Sergeant Raymond D. Coakley was assigned to Squad C (midnight to 8 a.m.). The two new sergeants rotated monthly. Senior Sergeant Richard B. Rock took over the day shift permanently for supervisory and special details.

The chief, in a "straight from the shoulder" meeting of the entire department, went over "carefully and severely" certain phases of police work he wanted emphasized, and insisted upon closer supervision of the work so to better service the city. There were also several changes to the beats, among them Patrolmen Francis B. Hughes was made Squad B. desk officer, while Patrolmen Martin King, formerly on that job, moved into the communications room. The three officers assigned to the communications room, Martin King, Fred Harrington and Thomas Maxwell, rotated on shifts monthly. Desk officers had permanent shift assignment, with Francis E. Dwyer on days and Daniel A. McGill on the graveyard spot. Several of the walking and cruiser beats were also changed. Captains Camille L. Marcel and Thomas H. Calnan continued to rotate shifts.

LETTERS TO CHIEF JOHN L. SULLIVAN

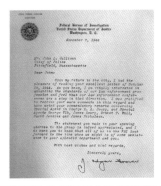

SIGNED J. EDGAR HOOVER   SIGNED EDGAR

1944
PRESIDENTIAL CAMPAIGN

In October, 1944 a squad of officers was detailed to Union Station on West Street for crowd control. The Republican candidate for president, Governor of New York, Thomas E. Dewey, spoke to a large, cheering crowd from the train's rear platform. Governor Dewey said that on January 20 of next year, anticipating his occupancy of the White House, he would "start the largest housecleaning in the history of Washington, sweeping out the New Dealers and most of their works". On April 12, 1945, having served less than three months of his new term, President Roosevelt died, and was succeeded by Vice President Harry S. Truman.

1945

CHIEF SULLIVAN CLAMPS DOWN
ON PROPOSED V-E DAY PARADE

"No V-E Day parade will be held in Pittsfield," declared Chief Sullivan, designated grand marshal of the parade by the City Council on April 14, 1945. Chief Sullivan came out publicly for the first time with his opinion that the parade should not and would not be held. The victory over Germany may come at any time now, Sullivan said, but he felt the public would rather to go to their homes and churches than put on a demonstration of joy. A million boys from the European front, after V-E Day, will have to face death in the war with Japan. The thousands of seriously wounded Americans and the death of the president have brought about a reversal of feeling, said the chief. There was no parade in Pittsfield and members of the City Council stood behind the chief, as he was a very influential public official.

1946

POOL TICKETS PRINTED AT GE-
LOTTERY DEFENDANT DECLARES

On January 1, 1946, Richard Y., a machine operator in the screw machine department of the GE, was arrested for drunkenness. When relieved of his personal belongings at Police Headquarters before being placed in a cell, police found in his pockets 49 lottery tickets which were stapled together. This was brought to the attention of Sgt. Raymond F. Coakley, who questioned Richard Y., a few hours after his arrest. Coakley found out that 100 tickets were made up weekly from paper used in different departments at the GE. Prizes of $15 daily and $25 on Saturday were paid to winners of the pool. The last two figures of the daily treasury balance determined the winner and the Boston Post was the official newspaper for the winning numbers. Richard Y. pleaded guilty to a charge of being concerned in setting up and promoting a lottery for money and was fined $50 by Judge Charles L. Hibbard. He also pleaded guilty to a drunkenness complaint and was fined $15.

ONE DAY OFF IN SIX

Chief Sullivan and President of the City Council George Purnell, on May 14, 1946, endorsed the petition submitted by the Pittsfield Branch of the Massachusetts Police Association to give local officers a day off in six. The petition specifically requested adoption by Pittsfield of Section 16B of Charter 147 of Mass. General laws, which provides for the one-in-six day off schedule. Previous to this, officers were on the one-in-eight schedule. Under the one-in-eight schedule, officers only received 52 days off a year and under the one-in-six schedule they would receive 61 days off. Fifty-two cities and towns in the state had already adopted the one-in-six system, with only eight still on the one-in-eight. This petition was accepted by the City Council, after it was vetoed by Mayor James Fallon. Chief Sullivan pointed out that police officers get no holidays off or extra pay for overtime. Industry employees get a total of ten holidays, exclusive of vacations; employees get 114 days off a year and paid time and a half for overtime.

RETURN HOME FROM WAR

On February 14, 1946, Patrolman Charles (Spike) C. Kelley returned to his police duties after serving five years in the army. Kelley received the nick name of "Spike" from his years in the ring as an amateur boxer. He was discharged as a lieutenant colonel and placed on terminal leave by the Army. Kelley joined the army when he was 16 years old in 1916 and was sent to the Mexican Border with his outfit the 4th Infantry Division. General John (Black Jack) Pershing of Fort Bliss, Texas commander of the 8th Cavalry Regiment, led forces into Mexico in search for Pancho Villa the bandit who was raiding the ranchers along the U.S. - Mexican border. In 1917 Kelley was shipped with 4th Division to France and was attached to Company C, 12th Machine-Gun Battalion. Kelley was in the battle of Meuse-Argonne and received a Purple Heart, Distinguished Service Cross and Silver Star.

The citation reads:

The Distinguished Service Cross is presented to Charles Kelly, Sergeant, U.S. Army, for extraordinary heroism in action during the Meuse-Argonne offensive, France, September 29, 1918. Sergeant Kelly led his platoon in the attack with great bravery against strongly held enemy trench-

es. Shortly after reaching his objective he was wounded in the throat. He refused to be evacuated, but continued to actively command his men until the night of October 1, by which time, due to his wound, he had lost the power of speech. General Orders No. 19, W.D. 1920.

Kelly stayed in the army until was he appointed a patrolman on December 19, 1924. Now a major, joined the Army Reserves. He was one of the first officers to be activated for World War II and the Korea War in 1950. He was promoted in World War II to the rank of Lieutenant Colonel and received several Oak Leaf Clusters.

On August 1, 1962 Kelley, resigned from the department after being hospitalized from a paralytic stroke, holder of badge "No.1". He died on April 20, 1973, and was buried in Arlington National Cemetery with full military honors. Kelley added the "e" in his last name in the 1920's.

Six other patrolmen who served in the army with great distinction also returned: Carmel W. Russo, Joseph F. Para, Mieczyslaw S. Wojtkowski, John J. Killeen, Edward M. Demick, and Raymond T. Killeen.

POLICE LEAD FIRST POST-WAR MEMORIAL DAY PARADE

Chief Sullivan ordered the entire department in for the first post-war Memorial Day Parade on Thursday, May 30, 1946, for traffic duties. Captain Camille L. Marcel and a detail of officers led the parade carrying their dress batons with bright blue sash cords for officers and red for superior officers. Marching in the parade were Veterans of Foreign Wars along with different social groups.

Three bands, the Eagles, Pittsfield High School and the Musicians all played the Star Spangled Banner. On the way back from the Pittsfield Cemetery marchers stopped at the Holy Family Church on Seymour Street for the dedication of the shrine of "Our Lady of Victory" in honor of Pittsfield citizens killed in World War II.

MEMORIAL DAY 1946
SEYMOUR STREET
CAPTAIN CAMILE L. MARCEL
1ST ROW-L-R-CHARLES C. KELLY-ROYAL A. McGUIRT- MIECZYSLAW WOJTKOWSKI-
FRANK CARLON-JOSEPH PARA-EUGENE CATALANO- ADRIAN P. COTY-CARMEL RUSSO
2ND ROW-L-R-FRANCIS D. O'NEIL-JAMES F. MAGNER-DONALD KELLY-PATRICK D. RYAN-
THOMAS P. FLYNN-MARTIN J. KING-WILLIAM NOON

1946 MEMORIAL DAY PARADE

FOUR VERTAIN OFFICERS RETIRE

On October 9, 1946, the City Council unanimously adopted the compulsory retirement of Police Officers and Fire Fighters at the age of 65. Until then a Police Officer or Fire Fighter could work to the age of 80. Chief Sullivan was not in favor of this law as he didn't want to retire. Under the law he would have to retire on his 65th birthday which was February 16, leaving him with less than four months to work. He would receive an annual pension of $2,600. Chief Sullivan was hoping that the council would create the position of Public Safety Commissioner and appoint him to it, but it never happened.

As a result, on November 13, 1946, after turning in their police equipment and wearing civilian clothes, four retiring officers stopped in see Chief Sullivan. They were Inspector Daniel J. McColgan, 69, Officers Robert F. Boyd, 65, William B. Kirtland, 72, and Herbert F. Volin, 68. Chief Sullivan described them as "the finest bunch of officers I have ever had the pleasure of serving with". He invited them to "visit us whenever you are around headquarters."

Chief Sullivan paid individual tributes to the men. In describing Inspector McColgan, the chief said he was one "of Pittsfield's most faithful and distinguished public servants." He credited the head of the Detective Bureau with solving many of the big crimes committed in this city. Well known in police circles throughout the country." He commended "Bob Boyd for the kindness and courtesy you have always shown to the public, especially to school children." The chief described Chauffeur Kirtland, "as a faithful and diligent member of the department," commending Kirtland for his work as a patrol driver, particularly at accidents. Chief Sullivan said he "was always ready and willing to assist in any situation." In speaking of Officer Volin, his assignments have been "in the busy traffic areas." "Officer Volin has always been neat in appearance and no person can state that they even found him leaning against a building or a motor vehicle."

THE WHITE HOUSE–AUGUST 15, 1946

CHIEF ROFF-PRESIDENT TRUMAN-CHIEF JOHN L. SULLIVAN

CHAPTER SEVENTEEN

1947

BRIBERY OF POLICE SERGEANT

In February of 1947, Nicholas Daligian, 27, counterman at the Majestic Restaurant on North Street went on trial on the charge of bribery of Sergeant Raymond F. Coakley and two counts of bookmaking. The jury consisted of 12 men. At his trial in Superior Court, Daligian said that $15,000 a day is bet in Pittsfield, and that $6,000 of this money comes out of the General Electric. Bookmaking was a big business. Bookmakers need some advance notice if police were going to make a raid.

District Attorney Charles R. Alberti prosecuted the case for the Commonwealth and defense attorneys were Santino Cornello, Harold R. Goeway and James Noonan. At the outset of the trail Judge William A. Burns told the jurors that "if you are satisfied beyond a reasonable doubt and find money was passed with "intent" as alleged in the indictments, it is your sworn duty to return a guilty verdict. You weigh the evidence of police officers just the same as any other testimony from any other witness."

On the stand, Sgt. Coakley said he had known Daligian for four or five years and that a man by the name of "Potatoes" had approached him and said Daligian wanted to set up a meeting to talk to him. On December 8, 1946, Daligian showed up at Coakley's apartment on Gordon Street at 12:30 a.m. He brought a bottle of liquor and some soda and ginger ale for highballs. Coakley said he drank golden ginger ale to make it look like a rye highball, while Daligian had five or six highballs before he left at 5:30 a.m. During their discussion, Daligian said he believed that one of the "captains would get the job," meaning the chief's job, as Chief Sullivan was retiring. Daligian then said "hoped Captain Calnan wouldn't get the job because he would be tough on all of us." He was the one that raided us on Christmas Eve". Coakley stated during the night Daligian propositioned him to tip him off if either of the two captains were going to raid him, and quoted the defendant as saying "it is worth $200 a month to me." When leaving, Daligian left three $100 bills on a footstool, saying that it was a consideration for a tip if the police intended to raid him and for the sergeant to "lay off tailing him."

Coakley said he contacted Officer William J. Potter and talked over the transaction and they made plans for a subsequent visit from Daligian. Coakley typed out a report to Chief Sullivan on the happenings of what took place at his home. Before roll call that night he showed the report to Officer Potter and they both signed it and locked it in his desk drawer.

Coakley said that Daligian called him and said he wanted to see him around Christmas. Coakley said he told Daligian that he worked Christmas Eve but did not work Christmas Day. When he returned home at 2:00 a.m. on Christmas morning from work he found a package, wrapped in Christmas paper, without a card. In it he found two bottles of Lord Calvert whisky and a box of cigars, stating that Daligian later said he left the Christmas package for him.

Sergeant Coakley informed Officer Potter of the Christmas present and said Daligian wanted to know when he would be home. Coakley then went to Officer Potter's home, talked to him and made arrangements for Potter not to work that night. He gave Potter the keys to his home so he could go there and wait for him. Coakley testified that he arrived home shortly after midnight and gave Potter his service gun and handcuffs, and had him sit in a chair with the door partly open. At 12:55 a.m., Daligian arrived and was seated in a chair in full view of Potter. During their conversation Daligian said that the $200 he offered to pay for protection would run until May when his probation time would expire. Coakley at about 1:35 a.m., told Daligian he was getting tired and had to get up in the morning for court. Daligian then took out a roll of bills "and handed me one $100 bill and two $50 bills." Coakley took them and asked would this be for January and Daligian said yes. Coakley then went into his bedroom and had Officer Potter come out and place Daligian under arrest for bribery.

Officer Potter testified to all the same facts. District Attorney Alberti placed the $500 into evidence.

LOAN NOT BRIBERY

Daligian called the payments to Sgt. Coakley a "Loan" not bribery. On the stand in his own defense, Daligian said that the sergeant asked him on December 31, for a loan of $600, but that he could spare only $200, having already "loaned $300" on December 8th. Daligian said Coakley wanted to borrow the money to go over to Albany to buy his girlfriend a diamond ring and could pay him back in a month.

Daligian denied that either payment was in the nature of a gift or gratuity to influence Coakley's activities as a police officer. He said he lived with his in-laws and worked as a counterman and received a salary of only $52 a week. Prior to April, 1946, Daligian had admitted he was engaged in bookmaking and told of being arrested on December 24, 1943 and fined $500 and again arrested in April 1946, fined $2,000 for registering bets and given a year's suspended sentence and probation for operating and maintaining a lottery. He denied being engaged in bookmaking, lottery or any other sort of illegal activity since he was raided last April.

Daligian was acquitted by the Superior County jury of charges of bribing a police officer and bookmaking, but was committed to the House of Correction by Judge Hibbard for violating the terms of his probation on a previous offense. After serving six months of the one-year sentence, Daligian was paroled by the County Commissioners.

OFFICER WILLIAM POTTER

SGT. COAKLEY

CHAPTER EIGHTEEN

CHIEF JOHN L. RETIRES

On February 16, 1947, Chief John L. Sullivan having reached the age of compulsory retirement at 65 left the Police Department. Chief Sullivan was one of the city's most colorful public figures, well-known and outspoken. Chief Sullivan had served as chief for 32 consecutive years with a total of thirty-seven years on the force. Chief Sullivan was perhaps best remembered for his management style. He was fair, tough, and demanding, but he commanded the respect of his men and would back them up when they were in the right. In the middle of the night he would show-up at the station, after walking up North Street to check on his troops.

Chief Sullivan was a personal friend of FBI Director J. Edgar Hoover and was one of three police chiefs in the country to confer with Director Hoover on making plans for the establishment of the FBI National Training Academy in Washington D.C. On July 29, 1935, the academy opened. Its purpose was the standardization and professionalization of law enforcement departments across the U.S. through centralized training. Courses at that time included scientific aids in crime detection, preparation of reports, criminal investigation techniques, and administration and organization. With the advent of World War II, courses were added in espionage and sabotage. Hoover began his 48 year reign as Director of the FBI in 1924, nine years after Chief Sullivan was appointed chief.

Chief Sullivan was also the Treasurer of the International Association of Chiefs of Police. Director J. Edgar Hoover was scheduled to be the main speaker at Chief Sullivan's retirement party, but due to schedule conflicts was unable to attend, sending his next in command to address the retirement party, Inspector Lawrence A. Hince. Also attending were Edward S. Kelly, Executive Secretary, International Police Chiefs' Association of Washington D. C. and John F. Murray Secretary, International Police Chief's Association of Perth Amboy, New Jersey. The testimonial banquet was sponsored by the Chamber Commerce and held at the Sheraton Hotel, on Monday evening, March 17, 1947.

Appointed Patrolman December 31, 1913
Appointed Chief September 13, 1915
Retired February 18, 1947

John L. Sullivan

Testimonial Banquet for Chief John L. Sullivan
on the occasion of his retirement

•

THE SHERATON
PITTSFIELD, MASSACHUSETTS
Monday Evening, March 17, 1947
at 6.30 o'clock
Sponsored by the Chamber of Commerce

EXCERPT FROM THE LETTER OF J. EDGAR HOOVER

"As Director of the Federal Bureau of Investigation, I owe a personal debt of gratitude to Chief John L. Sullivan for the friendly advice and thoughtful guidance extended to me for many years from his wealth of experience in police work. As a law enforcement officer, I am deeply grateful to him for his unstinting efforts towards establishing our profession as an honorable one which is respected by law-abiding citizens for its high standards and uncompromising ideals. It has been a privilege to be associated with Chief Sullivan in striving toward the common goal of providing our nation with intelligent, effective police protection, and although he is now leaving the active ranks of law enforcement I know his contributions to his chosen profession will not soon be forgotten."

FBI HEADQUARTERS-CAPTAIN
CAMILLE L. MARCEL-CHIEFJOHN L. SULLIVAN
FBI DIRECTOR J. EDGAR HOOVER IN WHITE SUIT IN MIDDLE

NO CHIEF FOR TEN DAYS

The department was without a chief for ten days. During this time the responsibility of running the department was divided between Captain Camille L. Marcel and Captain Thomas H. Calnan. This division of command presented a mild problem because the retired chief likewise left the offices of Keeper of the Lockup, Smoke Inspector and Dog Officer vacant. The question arose as to how these various offices could be filled. The problem was solved on February 26, when Mayor James Fallon appointed Captain Thomas H. Calnan as provisional chief of police.

An examination for chief was held the following July and on August 26, 1947, Captain Thomas H. Calnan became the fifth Police Chief for the City of Pittsfield. Two chiefs had served the Town of Pittsfield, Chief John Hatch and Chief James McKenna.

CHAPTER NINETEEN

CHIEF THOMAS H. CALNAN

When Chief Calnan took office the organization of the department consisted of one chief of police, one captain, one inspector, two sergeants, fifty-two regular patrolmen and five provisional patrolmen. $174,125.00 was appropriated to run the Police Department for the year. Pittsfield ranked very low in crimes per capita compared to cities with corresponding populations. Despite the relative small size of the department its effectiveness was indicated by the fact that local crimes of all types reported during 1947 totaled only 7.3 per 1,000 inhabitants as compared to the national figure of 16.9. It was likewise noted that there was an enormous increase in the number of motor vehicle accidents over the previous year which was attributed to a great increase in motor vehicle registration. The same year an intensive drive on illegal parking was inaugurated resulting in issuance of 5,428 parking tickets as against only 1,947 in the previous year. The Traffic Bureau investigated six fatal accidents during the years.

DIES AT HIS POST

WALTER J. BUTTERLY

On July 24, 1947, Officer Walter J. Butterly, 51, badge number 11, reported for 8:00 a.m. roll call. After roll call, Officer Butterly reported to his beat on South Street, between Park Square and West and East Housatonic Streets. In front of the Masonic Temple, he told a friend he wasn't feeling well. At about 8:30 a.m., Officer Butterly went into Foley's Restaurant to get a cup of coffee. He started to discuss American Legion Baseball with John (Buck) Foley; Butterly was the athletic officer of the Pittsfield post of the Legion. He was the central figure in a heated controversy which had raged since the opening of the Pittsfield-Holyoke Western Massachusetts Legion semifinal series. He was showing Foley and several restaurant patrons' papers concerning the protest which he had filed on Holyoke's alleged violation of state junior baseball regulations when he was stricken with a heart attack. Rushed to St. Luke's Hospital in the department ambulance, he died several minutes later.

Officer Butterly was born in Pittsfield on March 29, 1896. Shortly after returning from army duty in World War I, he was named a reserve officer by Mayor William C. Moulton on March 13, 1919. He was appointed regular patrolmen on December 9, 1919 by Mayor Moulton. Butterly was the past Commander of the American Legion in 1940. Chief Thomas Calnan said Walter was "good officer, loyal, punctual and trustworthy."

Due to Officer Butterly's death Chief Calnan named Officer Merton Vincent as a temporary replacement on Squad A. Back then the saying was that someone had to die before you could get moved to the next shift, that sometimes it took years before you could see the sunshine.

Retired Officer Francis (Honk) Connors said "I would ride a jackass, backwards down North Street to move down a shift and give you a week to gather a crowd." Everything went by seniority; there was no shift bidding. The badge number identified where an officer ranked in seniority. As an officer retired or left the force, badges would be exchanged, the lower the number the more seniority you had on the force. In the 1953, this practice stopped. The old boiler plate badges were replaced with the present style badge and each officer was assigned a permit badge number for his career.

OFFICER FRANCIS (HONK) CONNORS

BURIED IN COAL UP TO CHIN

June 2, 1948, was a lucky day for nine-year-old Jimmy Scutt because his brother Francis heard his high cries from inside the coal gondola at Murphy's Coal & Grain Company. Otherwise Jimmy would have died of suffocation. Imprisoned and sinking deeper into the Anthracite Rice Coal. Jimmy was the son of Mr. and Mrs. Francis Scutt of 390 Cloverdale Street, just across the street from the coal company.

George F. Murphy, owner of the coal company, did not know Jimmy was "shoveling" in the gondola when he opened the chute, creating the suction that drew the boy down until the shiny black flakes were almost level with his mouth and nose. Mr. Murphy had been careful for a long time, because Jimmy had developed the habit of running from his home to the siding in front of the storehouse each time the coal car was uncoupled.

While Francis held his brother's left hand, Mrs. Scutt telephoned police and the fire department. Within minutes Detective Lieutenant Michael P. Barry was pulling at the boy's right arm, which was being painfully pulled downward by the increasing pressure. After building a wall of boards on each side of the hole to keep more coal from sliding into the center, six to eight men worked hard and silently for better than half an hour to free Jimmy. Among the shovelers were Patrolmen Francis D. O'Neil, R. Lawrence Haughton and Francis R. Hughes; Fire Captain Daniel McLaughlin, and Firemen Walter Winnard, Walter L. Morey, and Lansing Clow.

"Two tons had already been drawn when Francis heard Jimmy shout. That was why the coal was beginning to slip toward center, pushing him downward" George Murphy later told the officers. Murphy predicted that if the rescue work had started five minutes later, there would have been no chance to save the child.

Once safely carried from the gondola to the ground, Dr. Raymond G. Colby checked Jimmy over. Everything was found all right, except that hundreds of pieces of coal were wedged into the little boy's skin. Mrs. Scutt took Jimmy home for a good washing.

SERGEANT COAKLEY PROMOTED TO CAPTAINCY

On May 1, 1948, Mayor Robert T. Capeless appointed Sergeant Coakley to the rank of captain and was confirmed by the City Council. Sergeant Coakley was first in the civil service examination for the captaincy, with a grade of 94.13. Second was Patrolmen Howard J. Heneau with 93.14.

Coakley attended local schools and was employed in the radio department of Meyers North Street Store for 16 years. In 1943 he graduated from the third FBI National Police Academy in Washington, D.C., after completing a 14-week training program. Coakley was the second officer from the department to graduate from the National Academy. He was assigned by former Chief Sullivan to direct installation of the department's FM, two-way radio police system

1948

In 1948, recognizing the need for increased traffic enforcement; a special Traffic Bureau was formed with Captain Camille L. Marcel in charge. Marcel worked the day shift from 8:00 a.m. to 4:00 p.m. and Sergeant James Magner was in charge during the night from 4:00 p.m. to midnight. Their duties were to see that all motor vehicle laws were strictly enforced and that all conditions involving traffic hazards were investigated and recommendations made. They were likewise responsible for investigation of all accidents including the preparation of evidence for court. The traffic officers were likewise equipped for the first time with traffic safety belts and gloves. More intensive training programs were initiated to acquaint the members of the department with the changes necessary for effective enforcement.

The year 1948 closed with the department making 2,664 arrests, the largest number ever; the Traffic Bureau accounted for 1,166 of these arrests. Speeding arrests rose to 580, with the result that the city experienced not one fatal accident for 290 days. At this time, speeders were arrested on the spot if they had no license or were from out of state; they were transported to the station house, booked, and bailed for court.

Parking meters were installed in the city and the Police Department was made responsible for the collecting and counting of all monies, the keeping of the records and the repairing of all meters. One officer and one clerk were assigned to these duties. In 1950 these duties were transferred to the office of the City Treasurer and in the same year an officer in a jeep was assigned to cover the parking meter areas to enforce violations. This change resulted in the issuance of 11,549 parking tickets as compared with only 7,966 the previous years.

OFFICER VINCENT WITH
PARKING ENFORCEMENT JEEP

A Juvenile Prevention Bureau was created the same year for the purpose of combating delinquency and working in the close harmony with the churches, schools and social agencies in this respect.

The same year a motor vehicle maintenance man was put in charge of the department's fleet of cars and the three chauffeurs were assigned to the communications room.

Also, the hours of the Detective Bureau were extended to 2:00 a.m. so that this division now had both day and night detectives. A special records bureau was set up in the Detective Bureau; modernizing the old system used and an entirely new dark room with all photographic equipment that was necessary was purchased to bring the crime laboratory up to modern standards.

At the same time the Uniform Division was placed in charge of two captains and three sergeants who alternated day and night. Thus were created four special divisions each headed by a superior officer whose duty it was to report directly to the chief of police.

WHISTLE-STOPS

Chief Thomas H. Calnan and Captain Camille L. Marcel along with a contingent of 25 officers were kept busy for two days at the Union Train Station, West Street. On Wednesday, October 27, 1948, President Harry Truman made a whistle-stop talking to a crowd of about 7, 000. From Pittsfield he made a stop in Springfield and Boston.

The Secret Service, in a meeting with Mayor Robert T. Capeless and

Chief Calnan, requested that a wooden platform be built atop of the marble parapets of Union Station. The Secret Service didn't want President Truman to walk from the Union Station to City Hall. They thought it was too risky. This was done and the two hopefuls for president gave their speeches from this platform decorated with American flags. The platform had about fifty chairs on it for invited guests to sit in so they were within twenty feet of the speaker. This platform stood so the crowds, thousands of school children and white collar workers could see the speakers. President Truman gave his whistle-stop speech at 8:00 a.m. in the morning and Governor Dewey at 10:00 a.m., the next day, October 28, before a crowd of 8,000.

CHIEF CALNAN CAPTAIN
MARCEL GOV DEWEY

PRESIDENT TRUMAN HOLDS PAPER
DEWEY DEFEATS TRUMAN

The next day President Truman was in New York City and before a crowd of 25,000 Democrats he said, "Tom Dewey can follow me into Pittsfield, but he can't follow me into the White House." with the president were his wife Bess and their daughter Margaret.

It was just a week before Election Day. Experts said President Truman didn't have a chance of winning the election that Governor Dewey would win by a landslide. The Chicago Tribune Newspaper embarrassed itself with its morning edition, with the front page headlines saying Dewey defeats Truman.

Governor Robert Bradford was one of the guests on the platform and backed Governor Dewey. This cost him the governorship of Massachusetts. Also on the platform was Congressman John F. Kennedy, who became president 12 years later.

MURDER BY EXPOSURE TO THE COLD
SEARCH FOR MOTHER OF MURDERED NEWBORN BABY

Shortly after 11:00 a.m., on December 18, 1948, a bitter cold Saturday morning, contractor Jacob Lefkowitz entered 117 Allengate Avenue, one of the houses he was building on Allengate. There he found a new-born baby girl, dead, wrapped in a woolen cardigan jacket owned by one of his workmen.

Detectives were called to the scene and found entrance into the house was made by tearing one of the temporary tar paper coverings from a window. Also found were footprints, of a medium-sized man leading to 121 Allengate Avenue. Evidence showed the child was first taken to 121, that her clothes were changed.

Chief Thomas H. Calnan reported this was the first such death reported to police in the past 18 months. On the previous occasion, a boy was found abandoned with a rope around his neck.

Chief Calnan reconstructed the tragedy with Captain Camille L. Marcel, Detective Lieutenant Michael P. Parry, Detective R. Lawrence Haughton, Detective Francis D. O'Neil, and Patrolmen Frank W. Carlon and Merton J. Vincent of the crime prevention bureau. After 48 hours of continuous search, no clues were found as to the whereabouts of the person or persons who left the just-born baby girl to die late Friday night at the under-construction house.

Teams of detectives left Pittsfield to tour Berkshire hospitals and to interrogate Berkshire doctors, to learn whether a woman had been reported anywhere asking for postnatal care. Chief Calnan asked residents to consider whether any of their women acquaintances, pregnant last week, were now unable to account for their newborn child.

Albert C. England, Medical Examiner said the child was born alive and in perfect health Friday afternoon, and that she died from exposure to the cold sometime after 4:30 p.m. that day. He also determined that this wasn't the mother's first child. Burial was paid for by the Public Welfare Department.

The mother of the murdered dead girl and the person who abandoned her inside the house to die are still at large.

1949 To 1952

Mayor Robert T. Capeless, on Thursday, April 7, 1949 promoted Patrolmen Mieczyslaw S. Wojtkowski to sergeant. A member of the force since 1942, he headed the Civil Service list. Before his appointment as a patrolman he severed nearly four years as a Massachusetts State Police Officer.

The sergeant's vacancy was created three months before by a police ordinance amendment adding a sergeant and captain to the authorized complement of the force. On the sergeant's list was Patrolmen John J. Killeen, who was number one on the captain's list. The mayor delayed appointing Killeen to captain as it might have invalidated the sergeant list. Once before, in 1946, Wojtkowski qualified for appointment as sergeant. At that time former Mayor James Fallon passed him over along with Raymond Marcel, now a sergeant also, in favor of Sergeant James Magner, who stood third on the list.

During the years 1949 to 1952 the organization then consisted of one chief of police, three captains, one lieutenant-inspector, five sergeants, six detectives, one police matron, sixty-five patrolmen, a head clerk, and a motor vehicle equipment repairman. $310,531 was appropriated to run the Police Department and the population was 53,950 in 1952. Corresponding to the increase in expense, the arrests increased to 2,937, another record. Major crime was kept at a low level. Incidental to these arrests and other activities, the police department was responsible for the collection of $40,661.30, which monies were paid over to the city and county treasurers, thus reducing the overall cost of running the police department.

For the sixth consecutive year, Chief Calnan recommended that 15 addition patrolmen and 3 motor vehicles be added to the department. He also suggested that a municipal auditorium capable of seating 5,000 people be erected where big-name bands could be brought in for dancing, and events such as roller skating, ice hockey, basketball, wrestling and boxing could take place. He stated that according to the youngsters of the city, there was very little entertainment to keep them in the city. By youngsters he meant not only teenagers but those just out of their teenage group. He said when they are provided with the type of entertainment they want, they would not seek it elsewhere.

1950

OFF TO WAR

OFFICER JAMES FARRY

Officer James Farry was the first policeman on the force to be recalled to active duty for the Korean War. In the Naval Reserves, Officer Farry served as Chief Store Keeper. Also called back to active duty was Lieutenant Colonel Charles "Spike" Kelley of the army.

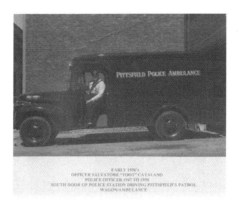

USED AS WAGON AND AMBULANCE

TAKES OWN LIFE IN CELL

On February 10, 1952, George M., was arrested in Springfield on a warrant out of the Pittsfield District Court for violating probation on a nonsupport conviction. George had been in court several times since 1948 on similar charges. He faced six months in the House of Correction. George was transported to Pittsfield in the afternoon and was to appear in court the next morning. According to Captain John J. Killeen, the desk officer checked all the prisoners at 6:40 p.m. At 7:00 p.m., when officers were bringing supper to the prisoners, they found George hanging by his belt from the top crossbar of the cell door. Officers immediately applied artificial respiration with the oxygen inhalator. Doctors Irving F. Rubin, Medical Examiner, Antonio P. Desautals, Assistance Medical Examiner worked over one and one half hours on George, to no avail.

CELL NUMBER 6 WHERE HANGING TOOK PLACE

HOME OWNER ROBBED AT GUNPOINT-
BOUND IN THEIR HOME

On Sunday night, April 8, 1952, at 11:05 p.m., Mr. and Mrs. Elmer E. Dawson Jr. of Crofut Street heard a knock at their front door. The Dawson's were in bed upstairs and Mr. Dawson went downstairs to answer the door. Opening the door he was confronted by two masked men pointing pistols at him announcing, "This is a stick up." He was forced into the library and Mrs. Dawson was called to come downstairs. A third unarmed robber then came into the house. The Dawson's were both tied up. The three then ransacked the house and stole $5,000 in jewelry. Taken from a safe in the upstairs bedroom were a diamond-studded woman's wrist watch, three diamond rings, and an emerald and diamond ring. Also taken were three pearl necklaces, two wrist watches, one topaz pin, one sapphire pin, one amethyst pearl bracelet, and miscellaneous pins.

Mr. Dawson was able to untie himself in a short time and immediately called Police Headquarters. Officer Nicholas Hess, in a cruiser, saw two men resembling the descriptions broadcast at 11:30 p.m., and gave chase. Officer Hess ordered the pair to halt; one did, but the other fled. Hess fired one warning shot, to no effect. The fleeing man was picked up later at his home. Both were taken back to the Dawson house where they were identified as the robbers. After questioning they confessed to the holdup and where they hid the jewelry. They also admitted to three previous burglaries and the stealing of three motor vehicles

After further investigation it was found that one of the three was 19 years old and he was charged as an adult; the other two were juveniles. Later that day most of the jewelry was recovered behind a house where they hid it. An eight state alarm was put out for the third youth who was later arrested and charged. A maid, sleeping in an upstairs room, remained undisturbed throughout the entire holdup. Chief Thomas H. Calnan commanded Officer Hess and his fellow officers who worked on the case. They were Sergeant James F. Magner, Sergeant Raymond D. Marcel, Patrolman Carmel W. Russo, Detectives Daniel A. McGill, and Edwin J. Blair.

TRAGEDY AT PONTOOSUC LAKE

CHIEF APPOINTS VICE SQUAD
TO LEAD DRIVE ON GAMBLING

On July 2, 1952, Chief Thomas H. Calnan, after a meeting with Mayor Robert T. Capeless, announced that he established a "Vice Squad" designed for action against gambling. Captains Raymond F. Coakley and John J. Killeen shared the command of the squad. Chief Calnan declined to identify its other members or how many officers would be involved, saying the two captains would choose their men from the uniformed division and will be responsible "to secure evidence and arrest violators whenever possible and to use every practical method to suppress and control gambling, particularly in license places." Mayor Capeless said he learned there was "organized gambling," in Pittsfield from a Licensing Board hearing on pinball machine distributing applications. Considerable testimony came out concerning alleged bookmaking activities in places where the pinball machines were to be placed. The Licensing Board had also received information from a ABCC inspector, that while in different establishments, he witnessed gambling taking place.

FIRST ARREST FOR VICE SQUAD

The first arrest for bookmaking for the new vice squad came within one week after it was established. James A., 22, was arrested and charged with vagrancy. In a trial before Judge Charles R. Alberti, James A., was found innocent of vagrancy, but Judge Alberti characterized him as a "bookie" and ordered police to "keep close tabs" on his activities. The judge said there was "no doubt" James A., had been operating as a bookmaker, but that the charge of vagrancy had not been sustained by the prosecution. Technically, the defendant was innocent even though his means of income was illegal, the judge ruled.

Sgt. Mieczyslaw Wojtkowski, one of the members of the team, testified that he saw James A., come in and out of a store that he was watching on Linden Street,"about six times." When arrested, he had a roll of bills totaling $258 in his pocket along with "two pieces of paper" containing various notations. James A., said he was unemployed. Captain Raymond Coakley then testified about the notations found on the pieces of paper. Coakley described himself as an expert on methods employed by bookies and lottery operators. He said the papers showed the total amount of play for the week, plus the number of hits made by bettors. That the figures showed a gross profit for the week of $202 and indicated a commission of 40 per cent or $81, for James A. On the back of one of the slips, Coakley stated, four "payoffs" were listed as follows: "Jack," $380; "Joe;" $260; "Frank," $55.60; and "Rose," $1

1952 To 1954

From, 1952 to 1954 the following changes and innovations in police personnel were noted: one hundred and fifty Auxiliary Police were appointed by the Mayor Robert T. Capeless and trained by the Police Department.

AUXILIARY OFFICERS WITH CHIEF CALNAN

They assisted the police greatly in controlling traffic at all major public functions. In 1952 the Auxiliary Police helped the regular force out at Union Station when both General Dwight Eisenhower and Adlai Stevenson made whistle-stops there while running for president. A total of fifteen School Crossing Guards, eleven of them women, were appointed by the mayor. They were trained by the department and made a unit of the Traffic Bureau. They were assigned to school crossings and did an excellent job. They were assisted by one hundred and fifty Schoolboy Patrol members.

On January 1, 1952, the department went from a 48 hour to a forty-hour work week which necessitated the addition of one sergeant and eleven extra patrolmen. Although the department was numerically stronger there was actually no increase in the number of officers available for duty at any given time. Rules and Regulations governing the conduct of the members of the Police Department were completely revised and approved by the mayor and the City Council on May 14, 1953. Three civilian clerks had been added to the roster of the department. The head clerk was responsible for all personnel records, payrolls, arrest records, and was generally regarded to be an administrative assistant to the chief.

In Chief Calnan's seventh year as chief, the emphasis was placed on the value of modernization and training. Three of the superior officers were graduates of the National Police Academy in Washington, D.C., and two other officers were sent each year to the Massachusetts State Police Training Academy at Framingham. Schools of instruction had become a regular part of the program with judges, district attorneys and members of the F.B.I. in the role of instructors. In addition to that, regular instructions and refresher courses were given to the men by the officers of the department.

PARKING TICKET RECORD

Chief Calnan announced another record for the department. Officer Royal A. McGuirt, who was assigned to the unpopular task of issuing parking tickets, tagged 11,549 cars in 1952. The previous record was 7,965.

1953
OFFICER ROYAL McGUIRT, BADGE 14, FIRST METER ENFORCEMENT OFFICER IN TRAFFIC BUREAU. NOTE ROOF OF DEPARTMENT'S JEEP IN FRONT OF 1951 CHEVROLET. PARKING 1 CENT

FIRST METER ENFORCEMENT OFFICER
ROYAL McGUIRT-PARKING -1 CENT

NEW BADGES

New badges were issued to the department on October 25, 1953, replacing the greatly outmoded badges which were at least fifty years old. It was the practice of the Police Department to exchange badges, to show which officer had the most seniority in the department. Badge #1, was given to the officer with the most years of service on the job. The next senior officer would receive badge #2, until every officer exchanged badges, showing seniority. This was a cumbersome job, which took a few weeks to complete. In later years this practice changed. When a patrolman started to work he was given one badge number, which he keeps until he retires or was promoted in rank. The badge numbers started with one-hundred. There was no badge #1 anymore. Every officer knew where he stood in the chain of seniority.

OCTOBER 23, 1953

FOR THE FIRST TIME IN MORE THAN 50 YEARS, NEW BADGES WERE ISSUED. THE FIRST ONE WENT TO DETECTIVE MARTIN L. FAHEY LEFT, WHO WEARS NO. 1 BECAUSE HE HAD THE LONGEST SERVICE—35 YEARS. STILL WEARING THE OLD, STERLING SILVER BADGE IS OFFICER FRANK CARLON. THE NEW BADGES, SMALLER AND MADE OF CAST CHROMIUM, WERE PURCHASED BECAUSE THE OLD ONES WERE WEARING OUT.

FIRST NEW BADGES IN FIFTY YEARS

With the year 1954 drawing to a close the department set another record in the way of arrests, well over 3,000. The budget cost for 1954 was $333,089.00. During these years Pittsfield was still maintaining the very fortunate record of being free from major crime. The juvenile delinquency problem was likewise very low in comparison with the average of other cities of Pittsfields size. Syndicated crime or commercialized prostitution has never invaded the city, although Pittsfield had its share of localized gambling.

DROVE POLICE HORSE

Officer William R. Kirland, who drove the Police Horse Patrol, died at the age of 80 on November 21, 1954. He was appointed patrol driver April 9, 1909, and named a patrolmen June 14, 1937. Officer Kirtland took the job as a temporary appointee, substituting for the regular driver, Robert Jacobs, who had bought a livery stable in Illinois and was moving there. Bill took over then and for five years he drove Dan and Grace, the police horses, until they were retired in 1914 to a Southfield farm, surrendering to an automobile patrol. Officer Kirland served for more than thirty-five years.

CHAPTER TWENTY

FIRST BRUTAL MURDER IN ELEVEN YEARS
IRON-POKER MURDER

IRON STOVE POKER

On the night of Sunday, December 19, 1954, William Todd, 64, beat to death William Rodgers, 41, with a heavy iron poker following an argument at their apartment on Deering Street.

Chief Thomas Calnan personally took charge of the investigation as this was the first murder during his tenure in office.

After his arrest, Todd signed a full confession to killing Rodgers with an iron poker following an argument over Rodgers telling Todd to get out of the house. Todd, Rodgers, and a third resident of the city had been drinking in the apartment earlier in the evening, but the two were alone when the fatal beating took place. Todd said that Rodgers had ordered him to get out of the apartment immediately, but he objected because of the lateness of the hour and because he had no place to go.

Rodgers, in his underwear, was preparing to go to bed. Todd went from his own bedroom into the kitchen, got the iron-poker from a hook behind the stove, and went into Rodgers' bedroom. Rodgers was sitting on the edge of the bed and jumped up as Todd struck him several times in the face. Death was not instantaneous. Rodgers stunned but not unconscious, staggered or crawled from the bedroom into the kitchen, leaving a trail of blood spots on the floor and objects he touched. Blood smears were found on the kitchen table, door, walls, and refrigerator. Rodgers then went back into the bedroom and succumbed while lying on his back across the bed. Death was caused by multiple fractures of the skull.

Todd replaced the poker, put on his coat, and left the house immediately after striking the blows. He went to several neighbors and asked for shelter for the rest of the night, but was refused admittance, wandering around the West Street area during the morning while police were at the scene investigating the killing. Todd was arrested at the Union Train Station on West Street at about noon by Detective Francis D. O'Neil and Patrolman Joseph J. Monteleone, about 8 to 10 hours after the fatal beating. Todd offered no resistance and readily admitted striking his roommate with the poker; he was brought back to the apartment in the afternoon and re-created the crime.

At his trial in Superior Court on February 2, 1955, Todd was allowed to plead guilty to manslaughter and was sentenced to serve 10 to 12 years in the State Prison at Charlestown.

1955

MURDER OF MOTHER-IN-LAW BY SHOTGUN

On the Sunday evening, July 10, 1955, Edward A. Geerholt, 31, shot and killed his mother-in-law, Hazel Tatro. Geerholt bashed his way into his mother-in-law's second floor apartment on Cherry Street and blasted away with a 16-gauge, pump-action shotgun. Two shots went wild. One blast caught Mrs. Tatro in the throat. She died about five hours later at St. Luke's Hospital. Another blast of buckshot pellets struck his wife, Virginia Tatro Geerholt, in the left side hip and arm and sent her to Pittsfield General Hospital.

The shooting climaxed a series of domestic disturbances for Geerholt. A court order had separated the family on June 25, 1955. Geerholt had been ordered by Judge Charles R. Alberti to stay away from his wife and two children. He found the defendant guilty of assault and battery on his mother-in-law.

The court and police heard no more of Geerholt until the evening of July 10 when Mrs. Tatro called police headquarters and reported her son-in-law had appeared in front of her house and threatened to kill her. That was at 6:40 p.m. The department immediately sent a radio call to all cruisers ordering that Geerholt be picked up on sight. Nothing further was heard from him, however, until calls started to flood the communication room, reporting a shooting in the Morningside section of the city at 7:34 p.m.

Cruisers converged on the scene and found Mrs. Tatro and the gun on the front porch. Pellet holes were found in a bedroom and in a venetian blind. Four expended shells were found near the shotgun. A few minutes later, Geerholt was arrested on Tyler Street in front of St. Mary's Church, about a half-mile from the scene of the shooting. One of his shoes had fallen off during his flight. Officers Roy J. Kitterman and Kenneth J. McDonough arrested Geerholt without a struggle.

On the way to the Police Station, Geerholt was asked why he had shot his mother-in-law. Officer Kitterman said Geerholt replied that she had taken his wife, children, car and all that he owned away from him.

Lt. Inspector Michael P. Barry, head of the department's Detective Bureau, at Geerholt's arraignment in District Court stated that Geerholt admitted having an argument with his wife one day. The mother-in-law butted in, so he struck her. He walked around the streets all night and was summonsed into court for assault & battery the next day and the order to stay away from his family was given.

Geerholt stated on the night of the shooting he had been drinking, took a cab to his father's house, got the shotgun, and headed back to Cherry Street. Seeing Mrs. Tatro coming through the screen door, he started shooting at her. At about the same moment, Geerholt's wife screamed from behind her mother, "Don't, there are kids out there."

In all, four shots were fired, all that the gun held. Geerholt tried to fire a fifth shot at his wife who was lying on the floor after being felled by one of the shots. He then dropped the gun on the porch and ran down the stairs. He continued running for about a half-mile, when he saw a cruiser going by and held up his hands to surrender. In Superior Court before Judge Edward J. Voke, Dr. Albert C. England, Medical Examiner reported that an autopsy showed a single pellet from the shotgun struck Mrs. Tatro in the subclavian vein which leads directly to the heart. This resulted in her death. District Attorney Stephen A. Moynahan prosecuted the case for the Commonwealth and defense attorney was Peter Genovese. Geerholt pleaded guilty to second-degree murder. He had been indicted for first-degree murder. Judge Edward J. Voke sentenced Geerholt to life in prison for the murder; for assault with a dangerous weapon on his wife, Geerholt received six to eight years, concurrent with his life term in the State Prison at Walpole.

CHAPTER TWENTY ONE

FUNERAL NOTICE LEADS TO
ARREST IN 29 YEAR OLD MURDER CASE

1926 SLAYING

On November 15, 1955, Philip Mancuso, 66, alias Michael Bertolino, was arrested at his home in Easton, Pennsylvania, by Lt. Michael Barry, Massachusetts State Police Lt. Det. John F. Horgan, and members of the Easton Detective Bureau.

A first degree murder indictment was brought by a Grand Jury in 1926 following the death of Frank Litano, 44, on the night of June 20, 1926. Litano was killed while trying to stop a fight in front of his house on Whipple Street. Mancuso fled from the city after the shooting, lived in New York City and Detroit, and later moved to Easton, where he was considered a model husband and father.

The murder case was reopened when Albert Litano, son of the dead man, read of a funeral notice in the Eagle Newspaper in which two of Mancuso's nephews were bearers. It was first thought that the missing man had attended the services, but, this later proved erroneous. Albert Litano contacted Chief Thomas Calnan, who turned the case over to Lt. Michael Barry, head of the Detective Bureau, and Lt. John Horgan of the state police. Lt. Barry and Lt. Horgan began an exhaustive search through dusty files, old newspaper accounts and began tracking down every possible source of new information that might lead them to Mancuso.

A set of Mancuso's fingerprints, obtained from the Alien Registration Service in Boston, which had them on file since Mancuso entered this country from Italy many years ago, was sent to the FBI in Washington to see if they matched any in their files. The prints corresponded to those of a Michael Bertolino who fingerprints were taken when he went to work in a defense plant in Easton, in 1940.

The detectives discovered that Mancuso had a brother in Waterbury, Connecticut. In checking the long-distance calls from his house, they found some to Easton, Pennsylvania. Thus, the Easton toll calls from Waterbury plus the matching of Mancuso's prints with those of Bertolino in Easton led to the conclusion that both men were one in the same. Lt. Michael Barry, State Police Lt. Det. John F. Horgan, and members of Easton Detective Bureau, went to his house and placed him under arrest.

Mancuso signed a two-page statement admitting that he shot Litano in self-defense as Litano came at him with a razor. Mancuso, Litano, and a third man had been drinking prohibition-time red wine on Sunday evening, when they got into an argument in an alley near Litano's house. Mancuso, according to his statement, tried to separate the two men when Litano slashed at him with a straight razor. The razor cut through his clothing and inflicted a seven-inch gash on the back of his neck. Mancuso said he then reached into his pocket, pulled out a .32 caliber gun, and shot at Litano. Five shots were fired in all; three of them entered Litano's body. The one which caused his death pierced his heart and one lung. One of the other two bullets went into the ground and the fifth went wild. Litano was rushed to the House of Mercy Hospital and was pronounced dead on arrival.

Mancuso said he panicked and hopped aboard a freight train and went to New York City, finally ending up in Easton, Pennsylvania. Mancuso moved his wife and three kids to Easton, and had another son while living there. Under his assumed name, he lived across the street from an Easton police officer for years.

When first arraigned, he was charged with first-degree murder and pleaded innocent. The District Attorney later let Mancuso plead guilty to manslaughter, due to the fact that most of the witnesses after 30 years had passed away. Mancuso was sentenced to two years of hard labor at the Berkshire County House of Correction and credited with six months' time, for time he had spent in jail.

According to William Thompson, whose father, Charles F. Thompson was Deputy Master at the House of Correction and worked at the jail for over 30 years, hard labor was picking the weeds out of the garden or flowers beds, polishing cars or cleaning out the pig sties, located in the rear of the jail.

ROLL CALL BY CAPTAIN COAKLEY
NOTICE WHITE STRIPS ON OFFICERS PANTS

TENTH ANNUAL REPORT

In Chief Thomas H. Calnan's tenth Annual Report, he stated the department was only one patrolman short due to one resignation. Fatal accidents had been reduced from 9 in 1955 to only 2 in 1956, a reduction attributed in a large measure to the increased pressure put on the motoring public by law enforcement agencies and accident prevention programs.

FATAL ACCIDENT WEST HOUSATONIC STREET

JUVENILE TO FACE COURT IN "UNLOADED GUN" DEATH

On July 2, 1956, vendors were setting up their concessions at the annual Fireman's Muster Carnival at Wahconah Park. One of the concessions, operated by William E. Thomas of Washington, D.C., was to test shooting skills with a .22 caliber rifle. Thomas was chaining the rifles to the counter so they couldn't be pointed away from the target area. A 15-year- old juvenile who was employed by Thomas was unpacking the .22s when he squeezed the trigger of one rifle; nothing happened.

He pumped the gun and pulled the trigger again; this time the rifle fired, striking a ten year old boy in the forehead. He was rushed to Pittsfield General Hospital in a Park Department truck. He was operated on by Drs. Peter Dillard and J. Ryder Neary, but died at 9 o'clock the following night, 32 hours after the shooting. After an investigation by the department, the shooting gallery was ordered closed by Chief Thomas H. Calnan. Charges of delinquency by the reason of manslaughter were brought against the 15-year- old boy. In a closed Juvenile Hearing, held on July 6, Judge Charles R. Alberti dismissed the charge, declaring it was an accidental shooting.

CHAPTER TWENTY-TWO

IN MEMORIAL

In 1956, three long- time officers with a total of 97 years' service to the department, passed away:

Detective Richard L. Naughton, who retired on March 11, 1953, passed away, on May 2, 1956.

Officer Leo T. Sullivan, succumbed to a heart attack after arresting a drunk at the Berkshire Restaurant, on June 18, 1956. Officer Sullivan was working a over-time detail, in uniform. He was called to the front of the diner where a drunk was causing a disturbance. Sullivan placed the drunk under arrest, and while awaiting the patrol wagon a struggle ensued and Sullivan was stricken with a heart attack. Officer Sullivan was rushed to St. Luke's Hospital, but was dead upon arrival. Forty-two years later, Officer Sullivan was officially acknowledged as "DIED IN THE LINE OF DUTY". Officer Sullivan's name has been placed on the memorial monument on south side of the Police Station. He was 54 years old.

OFFICER LEO T. SULLIVAN

Officer John Gogan was the desk officer that night. At 10:06 p.m., he received a phone call from the Berkshire Restaurant, requesting the wagon for a drunk that had been arrested. Two minutes later another call came into the station, from the restaurant, requesting the ambulance. The caller stated that Officer Sullivan had passed out on the floor, after fighting with the drunk. Officer Gogan recalled car 10, which was the wagon and sent car 9, the ambulance. Sergeant Raymond Marcel, Officers Donald Green, Edward Fields and Thomas Fitzgerald, responded to the restaurant. Sergeant Marcel requested the wagon, car 10. The patrons were holding the drunk down, awaiting the officers. Officers Dauro Baccoli, Earl Borden and Francis LeBlance responded with the wagon and transported the drunk to the station. Officers Daniel McGill and Carmel Russo drove Mrs. Sullivan to St. Luke's Hospital. Officer Gogan remembers the night perfectly, as he was next in line to go on the day shift.

BLOTTER OF JUNE 18, 1956

Officer Albert E. Haskins, who retired on July 1, 1948, passed away on September 12, 1956.

DEPARTMENT'S 1957 FORD AMBULANCE

SAILOR KILLS MARINE SERGEANT

Sailor Michael N. Slosky, 28, shot and killed Marine Sergeant Henry P. Gripenberg, 27, on August 3, 1958, when he found the sergeant sleeping with his wife.

Seaman Michael N. Slosky was assigned to a minesweeper that had just docked at a naval base in Charleston, South Carolina. Upon docking he received a letter that brought news of his family situation in Pittsfield that disturbed him. He called his sister on August 2 and got more bad news about the home situation.

He went to a Charleston pawn shop and purchased a .25 caliber revolver and a box of 50 shells. He then went to a hotel and made a plane reservation, and while he waited for the flight, loaded the clip with several shells.

He took off from Charleston, landed in Albany at about 2:30 a.m. on August 3, and took a cab to the intersection of Routes 9 and 20. He started to walk along the road and fired one shot from the revolver to try it out. A motorist stopped to give him a ride, and asked him whether he had heard an explosion. Slosky told him he had just fired his gun and that he was a gun collector. He asked permission to fire another shot from the car window and did so.

The driver left Slosky off in Nassau, New York where another car picked him up and brought him to the Checker Cab Co. on South Street. There he took a cab to the corner of Mohawk and Wahconah Streets and walked the remaining distance to his home on Mohawk Street. Slosky tried to get onto the front steps roof and in through a second-floor window, but couldn't make it, so he went to the back of the house and stacked two garbage cans on top of one another and entered through a kitchen window.

TWO GARBAGE CANS STACKED UP
PHOTO BY CAPT. BARRY

He left his suit jacket with the revolver in the pocket in the living room and went upstairs. He heard snoring, checked two bedrooms, and found that his two children were not at home. He went to the third bedroom, switched on the light, and saw his wife sleeping alongside Sgt. Gripenberg. The pair did not wake up, so Slosky turned off the light and went back downstairs. He tried to find a rolling pin but could not locate one. He then went to get the revolver from his coat pocket, went back upstairs, and slapped his wife's face, waking both her and her companion. .

Ten or twelve minutes of conversation followed. Slosky gave Gripenberg a cigarette at his request. Slosky's wife pleaded with him for another chance. Gripenberg got out of bed and was on his knees in front of Slosky, holding onto him, when the shooting started. Five shots were fired. Slosky went downstairs and found his wife there trying to telephone for help. He took the phone from her, called police, and asked for a doctor, an ambulance, and police officers.

Sergeant Raymond D. Marcel along with Officers Arthur R. Wood, Thomas J. Fitzgerald, Richard Barzottini, and Norman J. Bessette soon arrived at the house. Slosky handed Sgt. Marcel the gun and said he had shot and killed the Marine Sergeant.

Captain Raymond Coakley, who was in charge of the investigation, testified in Superior Court said the defendant was "vague" on what might have prompted Gripenberg to get out of bed. Slosky could only remember that the sergeant was on the floor in front of him and he was shooting at him.

Dr. Anthony Desautels, Medical Examiner, testified that a bullet wound caused a "massive internal hemorrhage." The fatal bullet had penetrated the chest and heart, perforated the diaphragm in two places, injured the liver and right lung, and was located in the left side of the abdominal wall.

The second-degree murder indictment by the Grand Jury was reduced to manslaughter to which Slosky pled guilty. He was sentenced to one year in the House of Correction. He was eligible for parole in six months and was released from the House of Correction in February 1960. Slosky received an honorable discharge from the navy.

NUMBER ONE BADGE HOLDER RETIRES

Number One badge of the department: Martin L. Fahey, detective

DETECTIVE MARTIN L. FAHEY

Detective Martin L. Fahey, the holder of "Badge #1", retired on February 21, 1959. Upon his last day of work, Chief Thomas H. Calnan presented Detective Fahey with a miniature gold badge from his colleagues in the Detective Bureau. The badge was of pocket size and inscribed with the policeman's name and dates of service on the back. When presenting the badge, Chief Calnan described it as "a token of the friendship and esteem of Capt. Michael P. Barry and the other detectives." Retired Detective Fahey passed away at the age of sixty-nine, in June of 1963.

CHAPTER TWENTY-THREE

MURDER FOR HIRE PLOT
ONE WOMAN+TWO MEN=HOMICIDE

On Monday, October 12, 1959, Columbus Day, the badly beaten body of Michael Koza, 71, a retired General Electric Company worker was found in his apartment. The body was discovered by the 12 year old daughter of Shirley Gilbert, Koza's housekeeper and a good friend of the family. Shirley, 35, was an attractive divorcee. Koza usually had Sunday dinner with Shirley and her daughter. This Sunday, Koza didn't show for dinner but Shirley didn't think too much of it as it was raining out and Koza didn't like to go out in the rain. The next morning, Shirley had sent her daughter over to Koza's apartment, which was on second floor in the Yon Building, on Summer Street just above the Summer Café.

YON BUILDING ON
SUMMER STREET

This is gentle Michael Koza who was beaten to death in his room in building at left. Housekeeper's daughter discovered corpse.

MICHAEL KOZA

Looking into the apartment, after knocking on the door, she saw Mike Koza lying on the floor in his long winter underwear, face down in a pool of blood, blood smeared everywhere. Koza was massive six-footer with a powerful frame. Running home, the girl told her mother, that Mike was dead. Mrs. Gilbert ran directly to Police Headquarters on Allen Street telling the desk officer what her daughter told her. The desk officer sent Officers William Mickle and John Gogan to the Yon Building. Shortly after, Sergeant Michael Wojtkowski and Dr. Antonio P. Desautels, Medical Examiner, arrived at the murder scene.

REMOVING KOZA BODY

Arrangements were made for an autopsy at Hillcrest Hospital with Dr. George Katzas, state pathologist from the Harvard School of Legal Medicine. The results of the autopsy showed that Koza's death was caused by multiple blunt injuries to the face, head, neck, chest and back; 11 fractured ribs; a laceration of the right lung, caused by fractured ribs; ruptures of the liver and the tissues holding the intestines in place; a massive hemorrhage of the abdominal cavity, blood in the chest cavity and a fracture of the Adam's apple. There were more than 52 separate injuries on the surface of the body. Cause of death had been the ruptured liver and lacerated lung. Dr. Katzas said Koza died within minutes of the beating, no more than half an hour.

Police Captain Camille L. Marcel, acting head of the department in the absence of Chief Thomas H. Calnan, who was on vacation, immediately put all available men to work on the case. Police learned that there had been an altercation on June 23 between Anthony Polcaro and Koza. Polcaro, 76,was are retired butcher who lived near the top of a short hill on Columbus Avenue only a few blocks from Koza's apartment.

The altercation between Koza and Polcaro was over Mrs. Gilbert. Polcaro had pulled a knife and stabbed Koza in the chest. Mrs. Gilbert, too, had suffered a knife slash on the leg and her right hand been broken when Polcaro hit her with a billiard cue. Polcaro had been arrested and placed on probation with a six-month suspended sentence to the House of Correction on a charge of assault and battery. He was also fined $1,000 on a second charge of assault and battery.

Captain Marcel gave orders to Detectives Francis D. O'Neil and Daniel McGill to bring in Tony Polcaro for routine questioning. They found the wizened old man, pale from a two-week siege in the hospital from stomach ulcers, limping along Columbus Avenue with the help of a heavy cane. He was brought to headquarters for questioning. Despite his protestations of innocence, he was held for further questioning, at least long enough to check out both his alibi and his room.

In a brief preliminary survey of Polcaro's recent activities, Detectives O'Neil and McGill learned that on certain occasions Polcaro had displayed a metal bar which he presumably carried for protection in case he became involved in a brawl. During the search of Polcaro's room, a three-foot round steel bar with blood on it was found hidden in his closet. This matched the one described to the detectives.

BLACKSMITH SHOP WHERE POLCARO
BOUGHT STEEL BAR FOR 85 CENTS

There was also a pink shirt and towel with blood on it. The steel bar was the key which unlocked the murder case.

The next morning, Polcaro was arraigned before District Court Judge Harold Goeway on a charge of violating the conditions of his probation for possession of a deadly weapon. The case was continued, and Polcaro was ordered held in jail without bail.

Detectives Edwin J. Blair, James McCarty and Dauro Baccoli worked in relays with Detectives O'Neil and McGill. Nearly 40 witnesses were involved in questioning. Detectives finally located a frightened Pittsfield resident who claimed to have firsthand knowledge of the murder. Calvin C. Corl, 36, told detectives that late in September, 1959, he was sitting in a booth at the Union Lunch, when Polcaro came over and sat down and said he wanted Mike Koza's arms and legs broken, enough to put him in the hospital. Polcaro wanted to pay to have the job done. Polcaro claimed that Mike Koza had cost him his girl and $2,500 in legal fees. Two days after this initial conversation, Polcaro accosted Corl again, this time handing him an iron pipe, which Corl threw in an alley near a bar on Columbus Avenue. Four days after this incident, Polcaro wanted the pipe back, saying he paid 85 cents for it. Corl also claimed that a friend of his, Eugene Benoit, 30, also of Pittsfield, was approached by Polcaro. They were in the Summer Street Café when Polcaro pulled a steel bar out of his trousers and tried to urge Benoit to us it on Koza.

Calvin Corl was afraid when police brought him in for questioning. Eugene Benoit, similarly, seemed terror-stricken. They stated that they weren't afraid of Polcaro but of the two young punks that he hired, who were as deadly as cobras. Their names were Joseph Dougherty and Bernie Kiley. Benoit stated that Dougherty and Kiley stated to him, "Eugene, if anybody else finds out about this, I'm going to put you alongside of the old man. You'll be in the grave next to him". This conversation took place in Benoit's apartment on the day before the body was found. Benoit was the one that introduced Joe Dougherty to Polcaro at a meeting in the Wahconah Café, on October 9, 1959. At this meeting Polcaro and Dougherty had a discussion about money. Benoit also said he saw Polcaro pointing out Koza's, apartment window in the Yon Building, on Summer Street, to Kiley. Both Dougherty and Kiley wore stocking masks during the murder.

A complaint was signed by Captain Marcel, it charged: "Bernard J. Kiley and Joseph T. Dougherty, Jr., did assault and beat Michael Koza with intent to murder, by striking him with an iron pipe and stomping, punching and kicking, and by such assault and beating did murder Michael Koza." Two complaints were issued against Polcaro which stated "That Anthony Polcaro, before the said felony was committed, did incite, procure, hire or command, the said Joseph T. Dougherty, Jr. the said felony to do and commit." The other complaint against Polcaro was the same except that the name of Bernard J. Kiley was substituted for that of Dougherty.

Both men were arrested in their respective houses and a quantity of suspiciously stained clothing was taken as evidence. Among the items were shoes belonging to Kiley and a black shirt of Dougherty's. Both men were locked up together in a cell in which a microphone had previously been hidden. In the photography room on the second floor of the station, Officers Edward J. Skowron and Richard P. Reddy took turns writing down their conversation between 4: 00 p.m. and 9:00 p.m. At their trail, their attorney's attempted to prevent the record of "bugged" conversation from being introduced as evidence, but the court overruled the objections.

After the arrest of Kiley and Dougherty, Polcaro was again questioned and told Detective James McCarty and Captain Marcel "I no kill, I know who did. A fellow named Joey."

Page 146

On the night of October 26, 1960, a burglary took place in the office of Dr. Antonio Desautels, Medical Examiner. The entire Koza case files were taken. The files were returned, a month later, by someone who shoved them under the door with the morning mail.

There had been a number of brutal beatings administered around town to persons who had expressed themselves about the Koza case. Shirley Gilbert had died two months before the trail but an autopsy performed on her remains substantiated that she died of natural causes.

The trial took place during December, 1960. The Commonwealth wanted verdicts of first-degree murder because the crime was committed with extreme atrocity and cruelty. District Attorney Matthew J. Ryan Jr. and Assistant District Attorney John A. Barry prosecuted the case for the Commonwealth. Defense attorney for Kiley was Maurice I. Lerner and Peter J. Genovese, for Dougherty, John N. Alberti, Andrea F. Nuciforo, and Andrew T. Campoli for Polcaro. The Commonwealth put on 48 witnesses, which were all cross-examined by the defense attorneys. Three material witnesses at their own request were held in protective custody, in jail, as they had received several threats on their lives.

On the afternoon of Tuesday, December 20, the jury left the court room, shortly after 5:00 p.m., to begin their deliberations, returning shortly before midnight. All three men were found guilty; Kiley and Dougherty of second-degree murder and conspiracy, Polcaro of two counts of accessory before the fact of second-degree and one count conspiracy.

Judge Francis J. Quirico ordered Kiley and Dougherty to be committed to Walpole State Penitentiary, "to suffer in prison for the term of your lives."

DOUGHERTY & KILEY

Polcaro was given two life sentences, to be served concurrently. He was given an additional sentence, as were Kiley and Dougherty, of from two and one-half to three years on the conspiracy counts. After serving ten years of their prison terms, Kiley and Dougherty were released on a technicality. This was based on a 1968, U.S. Supreme Court ruling in the case of Burton versus the United States, which found that out-of-court statements made by codefendants could not be used during a trial. Polcaro never testified to his pre-trial statements in court. Polcaro died in prison. Dougherty died within a year of his release of kidney failure, at the age of 33, in October 1971. Kiley moved to the Boston area.

1960
G. E. AND IUE Strike Shirley

In 1960, IUE, Local 255, went on strike against G.E., in fifty plants. This strike lasted three weeks. The entire police force was required to work the strike. Chief Thomas Calnan had laid down ground rules he hoped to be able to enforce impartially to both sides before the strike began, saying "we recognize the rights of the company to keep its plants open to all those who want to work, and that the union has no right to close it by means of mass picketing." Entrance to the GE plant proved possible only at two of the nine gates which the company sought to keep open, and even in the case of these two, entrance was often extremely difficult. At the other gates mass, picketing was in force without control, even though this practice was illegal. The Woodlawn Avenue main gate was a trouble spot at the beginning of the strike; six men were arrested and charged with assault and battery against each other.

G.E. STRIKE WOODLAWN AVE.

Employees milled about the gate entrance while picketers circled in front of the gate. Many workers turned back when they saw the formidable picket line set up by union members. Chief Calnan issued instructions to both sides from a police cruiser with a mounted loudspeaker. At the South Gate on East Street, two were arrested, one a picketer. Roofing nails were often thrown in the road to puncture employees' tires who attempted to-drive through the picket lines to get into work.

KILLED BY A 16- GAUGE SHOTGUN

On the afternoon of Saturday, November 26, 1960, James Pringle, 74, superintendent of buildings and grounds at Miss Hall's School, was shot by James A. Roy Wallace, 16.

Pringle and his wife were in their car on the grounds when they heard shots being fired. Pringle got out of his car to investigate the gun shots. He went into a wooded area of the grounds in the direction of the shots and yelled to shooter. Investigating officers said he encountered Wallace and was shot. Pringle was rushed to the Pittsfield General Hospital where an emergency operation was performed by Dr. Ralph Zupanec and 50 number six birdshot pellets were removed from his abdomen. Pringle was reported to be steadily improving at the hospital and was walking around his room when he went suddenly to his bed, collapsed and died.

Dr. A. P. Desautels, Medical Examiner, said Pringle died of a lung embolism. The embolism was caused by blood clotting, which in turn was caused by the "extensive bleeding area" of the gunshot wound. The embolism shut off Pringle's windpipe abruptly and he died within minutes.

Wallace, now 17, was tried in Superior Court for second-degree murder. District Attorney Matthew J. Ryan Jr. and Assistant District Attorney Clement A. Ferris prosecuted the case for the Commonwealth.

Wallace testified that the shooting was an accident and occurred as he was crouched on a knoll while attempting to retrieve a hat belonging to his companion, age 15. As he crouched, Wallace said "I heard a car stop on the road, I heard somebody yell coming through the woods toward me."

MURDER WEAPON

"The stock of the gun was resting on my hip, and the gun was pointing toward the sky. The gun was in my right hand. I told the person to stay where he was so I could break the action of the gun and I jumped up, wheeled to my right because of some bramble bushes in front of me, the gun muzzle dropped and the gun went off."

After the gun went off I ran from the knoll not realizing anyone had been hurt. I heard a scream and realized something was wrong. "

Ferris told the jury that "this boy is a cold-blooded killer. Not once has there been an expression of sorrow." He noted that if the jurors were to believe the defendant's testimony, all the witnesses for the prosecutions could not be believed. He said the Wallace's story contradicts "substantially" the testimony given by his 15 year old buddy. Ferris cited the testimony of Mrs. Pringle, who said she had heard Wallace tell her husband, "Don't move." The natural inference to be drawn from this is "Don't move or I'll shoot you."

The all-male jury returned a manslaughter verdict after deliberating for 6 hours. Ferris asked that the maximum sentence be imposed on Wallace since "our belief is that all the elements of first-degree murder" were present in the case. The jury's verdict was the "second break" Wallace had received. Ferris said the first break had occurred when the boy was indicted for second-degree, rather than first-degree, murder. Judge John M. Noonan sentenced Wallace to 6 to 10 term at Walpole State Prison.

1961

According to the fifteenth Annual Report of Chief Thomas H. Calnan, for the year ending December 31, 1961, the population of Pittsfield was 58,579. The total strength of the department was 87: 1 chief, 4 captains, 5 sergeants, 7 detectives, 5 traffic officers, 1 matron, 59 patrolmen, 4 clerks and 1 motor equipment repairman. $515,306.00 was the total cost to run the department. There were 3,326 arrests during the year. The Auxiliary Police put in 5,961 man hours, comprised of Thursday night details, Sunday Church details, parades, and special events. The School Crossing Guard program was in its tenth year, with 29 guards and 150 Schoolboy Patrol members.

Chief Calnan recommended that the present red and amber pedestrian light system on North Street be changed to the more modern "Walk-Don't Walk" system so that jaywalking could be brought under control. Chief Calnan also recommended that the department explore the use of radar to control speed along the principal routes in and out of the city. The chief requested that a commission be appointed to study the manpower needs of the department, recommending the appointment of six additional patrolmen to cover shortages occurring by the increased vacation period, sickness, and other absenteeism.

1962

The highlight of Chief Calnan Annual Report for 1962 was that a special detail for investigating gambling had been set up. This division was composed of two captains and four sergeants who alternated on days and nights. An estimated 1600 to 1700 man hours were spent on investigations of gambling and licensed places during the year.

GAMBLING SQUAD

1963

On December 31, 1963, Chief Calnan wrote his seventeenth and final Annual Report for the City of Pittsfield. The population of Pittsfield was 58,561. There were 2,982 persons arrested in 1963, which was an increase of 50 from the previous year 1962.

The city authorized the position of police woman and Thelma Thomas became the first police woman and was assigned to the Crime Prevention Bureau.

For the first time since the Police Department has been keeping records, Pittsfield had gone through an entire calendar year without experiencing a fatal traffic accident. A great deal of safety work was performed by the 200 Schoolboy Patrol members and 25 School Crossing Guards. The department had won eight awards for pedestrian safety and seven other awards for excellence in other branches of traffic safety.

Chief Calnan recommended that the strength of the department be increased by adding at least 20 more patrolmen and two extra cruisers, and the installation of a Central Records Bureau so that all personnel and operational reports could be centrally located. He recommended that higher wages be paid to attract the best possible personnel available.

1964

On June 8, 1964, Chief Thomas H. Calnan retired, having been chief of the department for over seventeen years. At the time of Chief Calnan's retirement, Captain Camille L. Marcel, a veteran of over thirty years, was appointed acting chief of police by Mayor Robert B. Dillon. In April, Marcel announced that he would not be an applicant for the position of chief of police. On June 13, 1964, a civil service examination was held for the position.

CHIEF THOMAS H. CALNAN

CHIEF JOHN J. KILLEEN

On November 30, 1964, Captain John J. Killeen, a Captain in the Provost Marshalls office during World War II, was appointed chief of police by Mayor Robert Dillon. Chief Killeen served in the United States Army Military Police from 1941 to 1946. He was inducted into the army with the second daft contingent from Pittsfield. While a lieutenant in the Military Police stationed at the prisoner of war camp at Camp Forest, Memphis, Tennessee, he aided in the breaking of two military murder cases. In one case a soldier shot and killed another soldier, while in the second case a civilian fatally stabbed a GI. Killeen was promoted to captain and was assigned to the Provost Marshal Court for War Crimes at Wiesbaden, Germany. He was appointed a reserve officer in 1938 by Mayor James Fallon and regular patrolmen on September 1, 1941. In 1949 he was elevated to captain. He was a graduate of the F.B.I. Police Academy and Northeastern University. Killeen served as chief for 14 years retiring on his 65th birthday, December 25, 1978. Chief Killeen died on Sunday February 1, 1998, at the age of 84.

NINE NEW OFFICERS

During the year, Mayor Dillon also appointed nine permanent patrolmen which brought the ranks up to full strength of seventy-four officers. In 1964, there were changes in the positions of Head Clerk, two changes in the Senior Clerk in the Detective Division and two changes in the Senior Clerk in the Traffic Division.

Early in 1964, five cruisers were turned in and five 1964 Dodge cruisers were purchased. As of December 31, 1964, the motor vehicles of the department were one 1957 ambulance, one 1964 patrol wagon, one 1963 Pontiac sedan, three 1963 Ford cruisers and five 1964 Dodge cruisers. These vehicles logged over 325,583 miles during the year. The department also had a motor boat which was used for patrol duty on the likes in Pittsfield.

During 1964 a radar set was purchased, an unquestionsble asset to the department for the detection of speeders. There were 4860 persons arrested during the year.

1965

In Chief Killeen's first full year Annual Report ending December 31, 1965 there were several changes in the department. The Table of Organization was changed to add 2 lieutenants, 5 more sergeants; one patrolman assigned as safety officer, and reduced the rank of patrolmen from 67 to 59. Under the new Table of Organization, the department was short one captain, two lieutenants, five sergeants, one senior clerk, and one matron, and was over by 7 patrolmen. This was brought into alignment when the two lieutenants and five sergeants were appointed. Civil Service examinations were given for the positions of captain, lieutenant and sergeants, during the year. Members of the department took it upon themselves to obtain the services of a Boston attorney to come to Pittsfield and conduct classes in preparation for these examinations.

During the year, a new ambulance was purchased for the department, and in 1965, 976 ambulance runs were made. Purchased also were 8 cruisers. The department's motor boat became disabled while recovering a drowning victim.

1965 saw the first year that full uniform allowances were received by members of the department, before this, officers had to purchase their own uniforms or received uniforms passed down from fellow or retired officers. It would take five years before all members were properly outfitted.

Chief Killeen pointed out that in a survey conducted by the Massachusetts Police Association of 235 cities and towns of Massachusetts, of whom 201 replied, Pittsfield ranked 79th in compensation. The chief recommended that officers should receive higher wages, that the top salary in Pittsfield was only $5,304 after five years. That many cities were recruiting police officers from low-paying cities by offering salaries at the $7,000 level, which salaries do not include generous fringe benefits.

Thirty-four members of the department received instructions and fired the moving target course at the General Electric Athletic Association target range.

1966

In his 1966 budget request, Chief Killeen recommended that the department start equipping the foot officers with walkie-talkie radios. During 1965, nine persons had been apprehended at the scenes of their crimes of breaking and entering into buildings in the city. Apprehending officers had no back-up without radio communications with the Police Headquarters.

There were a total of 5,148 persons arrested during the year. Among these were 505 arrested for drunkenness and three for being abroad at night-time not giving a good account of oneself.

CAPTAIN MARCEL GIVING OUT APB

The year 1966 saw a great many changes in the department. Authorized by the changed Table of Organization, retirements and the sudden death of Sergeant James F. Manger, there were 13 new supervisors appointed to the department out of a total of 19 authorized supervisors. These 13 new supervisors all came from the patrolman rank. Two more sergeants were added to the department to bring the total to twelve. The total budget for the department was $688,417.00. There was one murder during the year.

During the year some members of the department took advantage of and received various types of training. Members were sent to F.B.I. seminars, courses at the New York City Police Academy, and the Massachusetts State Police Academy in Framingham. All but four members of the Department held at least Standard First Aid Certificates. All officers received firearms training and thirteen members received gas training.

Several new cruisers and three motor scooters and a new motor boat were purchased. The new motor scooters with walkie-talkie radios and first aid equipment were a valuable addition to the department because of their mobility. The Police Department ran the city ambulance and made 1,163 runs during the year. The ambulance was manned by one communication officer (who was called a chauffeur) and two officers from a North Street beats, usual post 3 and 4.

There were six walking beats on North Street, one on Fenn Street and one on Tyler Street...

- Post 1: On the day shift there was a Post 1 walking beat. This beat was from North Street down West Street to the old train station. The Post 1 officer also did court duty; bring the prisoners from the Police Station to District Court, sitting in the prisoners docket with them until court was over. Post 1 would then call the station for the wagon to transport any prisoner that was going to the Berkshire County House of Correction. There were no court officers at this time as there are now.
- Post 2: ran from Park Square to Fenn Street, with five banks located on this post.
- Post 3: ran from Fenn Street to Eagle Street, this was an ambulance and wagon beat.
- Post 4: ran from Eagle Street to Melville Street, and was also an ambulance and wagon beat.
- Post 5: ran from Melville Street to Maplewood Avenue. Officers on this

beat would be picked up if a cruiser officer needed a back-up.

- Post 6: ran from Maplewood Avenue to Pittsfield General Hospital. (Now Berkshire Medical Center).
- Post 7 & 8: was the Fenn Street beat, from City Hall down Fenn Street to East Street.
- Post 9 & 10: ran the length of Tyler Street to Woodlawn Avenue.

The North Street officers were notified by radio or by the flashing blue light on the call box on their beat or by the siren on the vehicle. The department now had four hand walkie-talkies which were assigned to the North Street beats. The department also made 1,346 wagon calls for the year. When an officer made an arrest the wagon was sent to transport the prisoner. No cruiser had a cage built-in to transport prisoners at this time. The wagon was also manned by the chauffeur and two officers from their North Street beats. If there was a wagon and ambulance call at the same time, Post 2 would come into the station and drive either the wagon or ambulance and pick up Post 5 and 6.

There was a new record for traffic deaths in 1966. There were eleven total deaths, seven passengers and four pedestrians, the highest record number since the department started to record the statists in 1940. The Traffic Division had thirty regular School Crossing Guards and four substitutes at selected crossings and one hundred and sixty School Boy Patrol Guards.

CAPTAIN CAMILLE L. MARCEL

There were three significant changes in the Traffic Bureau in 1966. Captain Camille L. Marcel head of the Traffic Bureau since its inception in 1948, retired on May 1, after serving the department for over thirty years.

The responsibility of the Traffic Bureau was transferred to Captain Edgar

D. Almstead in June. In October, with over thirty years' service, Officer Merton Vincent retired. Officer Vincent had also been in the Traffic Bureau since it was established. Since 1965 he had been the department Safety Officer. The third change was a loss suffered not only by the Traffic Bureau, but the entire police force, the sudden death of Sergeant James F. Magner. Sergeant Magner had been a policeman for over thirty years and also served in the Traffic Bureau since its inception. Also retiring with over thirty years of service was Sergeant Raymond D. Marcel from the uniform division.

Chief Killeen created the Intelligence Unit, which was under his direct supervision and conducted special investigation. It was manned by Sergeant Eugene W. Catalano and Officer John E. Gogan.

The City of Pittsfield received from the District Court of Central Berkshire $31,445.00 in cash fines for parking violations. The police chief prosecuted all cases in District Court.

CD POLICE
PRESENTED FLAG

On July 1, 1966, the Pittsfield Civil Defense Auxiliary Police were presented a CD flag in a ceremony in the Police Station squad room. The flag was donated by the Pittsfield Downtown Association, and was presented by Edward Ediff, executive secretary of the downtown association, saying "Seldom does such a volunteer group ever receive appreciation until a catastrophe occurs." Ediff was referring to the directing of traffic on Thursday evenings on North Street and at eleven local churches on Sundays. On Halloween they guarded the city schools for three nights. Present were Mayor Raymond Del Gallo, Civil Defense Director William H. Cooney, John E. Joyce, administrative assistant to Cooney, Chief John J. Killeen, and 18 members of the Auxiliary Police. The auxiliaries had 48 active members.

MURDERDED BY TWO SHOT-GUN BLASTS

On Veterans' Day, Friday, November 11, 1966, at about 10:30 a.m., Vincent Velez, 18, was murdered by his great-uncle, Vincenzo Giudice, 74, at their home at 14 Oliver Street. The department received a phone call at 10:34 a.m. from Donald Durfee of Holmes Road, a next- door neighbor, who said that while looking out his second floor window, he witnessed the shooting of a young male. Upon arriving at the murder scene, Officers John W. Gogan and Thomas J. Flynn found the lifeless body of Velez lying in his yard, his head and shirt soaked with his blood. Central Berkshire Medical Examiner Dr. Irving I. Rubin was called to the scene and said that the wounds were not self-inflicted; his initial ruling was "probable homicide".

Chief John J. Killeen took charge of the investigation, assisted by Capt. Michael P. Barry, head of the Detective Bureau, Uniform Captain Raymond Coakley, Administrative Captain Edgar D. Almstead, Sgt. William E. Tuohy, and Detectives Carmel W. Russo and James E. McCarthy.

The body was removed to the Bencivenga Funeral Home, where an autopsy was performed by State Pathologist Dr. George Katsas of Boston, with the assistance of Dr. Rubin. Dr. Rubin said death was due to shotgun wounds to the head and chest and lacerations of the brain.

Giudice a white-haired, GE retiree who walked with a cane and had a stroke in January, was taken by cruiser to the station, where Sgt. Eugene W. Catalano, who spoke Italian, advised him his rights. Extra precautions were taken due to recent court decisions (Miranda Warnings) on handling prisoners and advising them of their rights. Giudice wanted an attorney, and within half an hour, Attorney Paul A. Tamburello was in the Detective Bureau conferring with him. Central District Court Clerk Edmund F. McBride was called and issued a warrant for murder. Giudice was taken down stairs, booked, and placed in a cell. Later that evening he spoke to a priest from Mount Carmel Church. The next morning, Saturday, he was taken to District Court and sat in the prisoners' docket with Officer Joseph Para. District Court Clerk McBride read the complaint signed by Chief Killeen, stating that on November 11, Giudice "did assault and beat Vincent Velez with intent to murder him by shooting him with a shotgun and by such assault and beating did murder Vincent Velez." Giudice pled not guilty and Special Justice Clement A. Ferris continued the case for eleven days until November 23. Defense Attorney Tamburello stood by his client.

Giudice was brought to court on Wednesday, November, 23, by Officer Edward Skowron and Detective James McCarthy. Assistant District Attorney William R. Flynn called only one witness for the Commonwealth, Donald Durfee, the next door neighbor, eyewitness to the shooting. He testified that on November 11, he was sitting in his living room with his wife and daughter. His daughter heard a gunshot and said, "Someone is shooting squirrels." Durfee said he then heard "a loud bang." He got up and looked out his apartment window which was opposite the Giudice yard with no obstructions in the way. He saw the boy lying in the yard, next to the garage. He watched as Giudice came out of the house, walked to within 10 ft. of the boy, pulled up the gun, aimed and fired. Durfee said he could see the boy's body "wrench from the impact." Giudice then walked back into the house. Durfee then ran to the phone and called the Police Department, reporting what he had just seen. After hearing the testimony, Judge Ferris ordered Giudice bound over to the Grand Jury.

LOOKING OUT APARTMENT
WINDOW TO MURDER SCENE

In late December, Superior Court Judge Francis J. Quirico committed Giudice to Northampton State Hospital for 35-day observation. It was decided that Giudice didn't have to go to Bridgewater State Hospital, where security was more rigid, because he posed no escape threat. Later it was ruled that Giudice was mentally ill and unable to stand trial in his own defense. In July of 1968, Giudice died at the hospital.

1967

Chief John J. Killeen in his Annual Report commended the officers on reducing the number of fatal traffic accidents, from eleven in 1966 to only three in 1967. He hoped that the trend would continue in 1968, stating the department now had 30 regular School Crossing Guards and 240 School Safety Patrol members. There were a total of 86 officers in the department,

19 superior officers, 7 detectives, 58 patrolmen, 1 policewoman, and 1 safety officer.

The department logged in 396,868 miles in various vehicles. There were 115 arrests for operating under the influence of liquor. In-service schools were conducted in which an average of 60 members attended classes for six days for a total of 26 hours each. A two day firearms class was conducted under the direction of Capt. Raymond Coakley and Lt. Robert Jordan at the G.E.A.A. Range. Forty-two officers attended, sharpening their skills in the use of shot guns and 38 revolvers. There were no murders during the year.

1968

WESTFIELD POLICE ACADEMY-1968

Chief John J. Killeen announced that Mayor Donald Butler appointed three new officers on March 27, 1968: Joseph D. Collias, John T. O'Neil and, Raymond Shogry.

The old brick Police Station, built in 1879 at 52 School Street, was torn down on April 16, 1968. It had served as the headquarters for the department for 61 years.

MURDER-INNOCENT BY REASON OF INSANITY

On July 27, 1968, Richard H. Ogle Jr., 54, and his two sons, Richard H. Ogle III, 27, and James, 22, had an argument in the family kitchen in their Williams Street home. During the argument Mrs. Ogle left the house to call the police. Upon responding to the scene, officers found the elder Richard Ogle's body in his front yard, several feet from Williams Street. After an investigation, an arrest warrant was issued for Richard H. Ogle III, for murder. One and half days later a New York State Trooper arrested Richard in nearby New Lebanon, New York.

In October, 1968, a Grand Jury indicted Richard on the charge of murder as well as the charges of assault and battery with a dangerous weapon and attempted murder upon his younger brother, James. In November, 1968, Richard was confined to Bridgewater State Hospital for 35 days for observation. He remained at the state institution for the criminally insane past the end of the 35 days.

In July, 1969, Judge Francis J. Quirico in Superior Court ordered Richard confined to Bridgewater indefinitely after the judge determined that he showed evidence of being schizophrenic with paranoid tendencies. Richard was adjudged competent to stand trial in December, 1970 and returned to Pittsfield to stand trial after 831 days in Bridgewater. The trial was held in Berkshire Superior Court before Judge Donald M. Macaulay. Assistant District Attorney William R. Flynn prosecuted the case for the Commonwealth. Attorney Kent B. Smith of Springfield was the defense lawyer. The trial lasted five days. Flynn put several witnesses on the stand. Dr. George Katsas, a forensic pathologist from Jamaica Plain who participated in the autopsy of the deceased, testified that there were 18 stab wounds in the body and that cause of death was perforation of the aorta and pulmonary artery.

Testifying from the Pittsfield Police Department were Detective Captain Raymond F. Coakley, Sgt. Lorenzo M. Briggs and Sgt. Robert J. Rozon. Testifying from the Massachusetts State Police were Detective Lt. Milo F. Brown, Jr., Detective Sgt. Richard J. Clemens from the district attorney's office, and Sgt. Edward J. Haughey who took pictures at the scene and autopsy. Psychiatrists from Bridgewater State Hospital and a private psychiatrist from Northampton also testified. The Superior Court jury took only 35 minutes to find Richard Ogle III not guilty of all charges by reason of insanity. After dismissing the jury, Judge Donald M. Macaulay ordered Richard committed to Bridgewater State Hospital "for the term of his natural life."

The commitment is not a sentence but is mandatory under state statutes in cases in which a person is found not guilty of murder or manslaughter by reason of insanity. Under the statutes, the governor, with the advice and consent of the Governor's Council, may discharge such a person from Bridgewater when he is satisfied after an investigation by the state Department of Mental Health that such a discharge will not cause danger to others.

REWARD OF $1,200 FOR MISSING MAN
PRESUMED -MURDERED
BODY NEVER FOUND

EDWIN THOMPSON

On October 20, 1968, Mrs. Virginia Thompson of Canaan, Connecticut reported that her son, Edwin Thompson, 24, was missing. Her son always visited her or at least got in touch with her on weekends but she hadn't heard from him in more than a week.

Detective Captain Raymond Coakley was put in charge of the investigation. At the time of his disappearance, Thompson was described as 5 feet 10 inches tall, 135 pounds, with brown hair and blue eyes. He normally wore glasses. He drove a 1961, white, Plymouth Valiant with black fenders, and red rally stripe along the sides. It was registered in Connecticut, with plate number 720-223. He served two years with the U.S. Navy, and was the first veteran of the Vietnam conflict to join the Couch Pipa Post of the VFW in Canaan, Connecticut. He was rooming at an apartment on Church Street, and was working both at Windsor Mountain School in Lenox and the Dalton Woolen Mills. He had worked at the mills only one day and was last seen at 11:00 p.m. on October 11, leaving the mills with a companion who also was employed there.

At the suggestion of Capt. Coakley, Mrs. Thompson posted a $500 reward for information of her son's whereabouts. The terms of the reward were that "information must be supplied leading to Edwin's whereabouts if living, or recovery of his body, if dead." Mayor Donald G. Butler, Assistant District Attorney William R. Flynn and Chief John J. Killeen were named by Mrs. Thompson as a committee to handle the details of the reward. On December 9, local auto dealer George Haddad added $200 to the reward money in the hope that it might lead to the discovery of Thompson. Then Mrs. Thompson offered an additional $500 to make it a total of $1,200 for the recovery of her son's body.

Three weeks after Thompson was reported missing, Chief John J. Killeen reported that Lanesboro Police found a 1961, white Plymouth Valiant with black fenders, and red rally stripe along the sides in a Lanesboro junkyard. Blood was found in the trunk of the car. The car was towed to the Massachusetts State Police Barracks on Dalton Avenue, where it was stored in a garage out of the weather. From the outset, the search for Thompson had been rigorous, with most officers working on the case believing he had been murdered. State Police Detectives from the District Attorney's office were now involved in the investigation, as the car was found in Lanesboro. Captain Raymond F. Coakley and Detective Lt. Richard J. Clemons of the State Police flew to Detroit, Michigan, to interview a man who had previously lived in Pittsfield but could shed no light on the investigation.

On the day last seen, Thompson worked as a bus boy until 2:00 p.m. at Windsor Mountain School in Lenox, and then went to work at the Dalton Woolen Mill at 3:00 p.m. until 11:00 p.m. This was his first day and last day of work at the mill. Officers believed that after work he visited a drinking spot in Massachusetts or nearby New York State. Thompson's picture was shown to employees of all licensed drinking establishments, with no luck.

Upon visiting her son's apartment, Mrs. Thompson reported that several items were missing, including some of his clothes, keys, and a TV set. Investigators received information that these items could be at an apartment on Tyler Street. The person who rented the apartment was in jail charged with assault and battery with a dangerous weapon for stabbing a woman. While incarcerated at the Berkshire County House of Correction, he talked to a fellow inmate about the disappearance of Thompson. The fellow inmate had made a deal with the investigators; if he could get information on where the body was concealed they would see about getting his sentence reduced. The inmate talked about several locations, but no specific one. Crime Scene Investigator William Mason borrowed a metal detector from Officer David Viner, as the department didn't own one. Mason and officers searched the areas talked about, but with no luck. In order for the metal detector to work, either a metal belt buckle or coins on the body would have to set it off. A search warrant was issued for his apartment where only the TV was found.

Captain Coakley, Lt. Clemens, Officers Eugene Catalano, John Perrone and Ronald Dean, with a contingent of New York State Police, also searched areas of New York State where Thompson once lived. They searched the areas of Gurley Farm, Canaan, New York, Mt. Greylock, Lanesboro's town dump, quarries and the terrain surrounding Ashmere Lake in Hinsdale. These are the areas that the officers contemplated that Thompson body may have been found, after talking with their informant at the House of Correction.

Detective Lt. Milo F. Brown said "In most homicide cases we have a body and have to find a killer but in this case were still looking for a victim." Thompson's body was never found and he is presumed dead.

On October 9, 1969, one year after he disappeared under mysterious circumstance, memorial rites were held at the Pilgrim Congregational Church in Canaan, Connecticut.

1969

CAPTAIN BARRY CUTTING HIS RETIREMENT CAKE

During 1969, seven members of the department retired and 4 members resigned. Those who retired were Detective Captain Michael P. Barry and Uniform Captain Raymond F. Coakley, Sergeant Lorenzo M. Briggs, Detectives Carmen W. Russo and Nicholas Hess, Patrol Officers Maurice C. Isenhart and Orlando F. Pezanelli.

In-service Training became a requirement of Massachusetts General Laws. Nine supervisory officers attended the Command Training School at Babson Institute, Wellesley, Massachusetts for a 3 week period. Six new officers were added to the force and attended a six week basic police school. The new officers were Robert C. Karpeck, David J. Mackey, David M. Viner, John H. White, Louis W. Marcel, Jr. and Anthony P. Wondoloski.

On January 1, 1969, the department was short nine members. On September 1, 1969, the department was short nineteen members. On December 31, 1969, this shortage had been reduced to ten members.

There were twenty-seven members of the department enrolled at Berkshire Community College under the provision of Public Law 90-351 Omnibus Crime Control and Safe Streets Act of 1968.

A total appropriation of $890,508.00 was used to run the department; of this amount, $4,394 was expended to maintain the department's motor vehicles which consisted of eleven cruisers, one wagon, one ambulance, two parking meter cars, three three-wheeled motorcycles and two motor boats. They traveled a total of 373,124 miles during the year. There were 1,293 wagon runs and 1,197 ambulance runs for the year.

During the year there were eleven deaths by motor vehicles. Since 1940, there had been only one other year, 1966, that the department had recorded such a number of deaths by motor vehicles. There were 240 School Patrol members that helped their fellow school children to and from school.

Under the new Firearm Identification Law, which required all residents of the city who owned or possessed firearms to register, $2,998.00 in collected fees was turned over to the City Treasurer.

POLICE OFFICER FIRED ON AT "BIG N" FROM RAILROAD TRACKS

OFFICER EDWARD A. SHERMAN

February 9, 1969, Sunday was a cold, snowy night. Officer Edward A. Sherman, 34, 2 year veteran of the department, was on cruiser patrol in West Pittsfield. Sherman was making one of his nightly checks of the stores in the "BIG N" Shopping Center on West Housatonic Street, shortly after 3:00 a.m., when he noticed a car turn its lights out and go behind the stores. Sherman drove into the parking lot to check out what the car was doing.

This car pulled up in back of the Big N Department Store and stopped next to another parked car. As the parked car pulled away four shots from a high-powered rifle rang out. The shots came from the railroad tracks, where the lookout David Dus, 19, stood. Dus used a stolen high- powered rifle taken from the Big N. One shot entered the hood of the cruiser about two feet from where Sherman was sitting. Two others hit the motor, and the last one penetrated a fender and came to rest in the tire, immobilizing the cruiser.

Sherman radioed the station that he had been shot at and his cruiser was down, that there was a break at the Big N, and that the shooter and partners were heading in a car to West Housatonic Street. Because of the late hour and heavy snow coming down, no cars were on the road. Officer Ralph Pivero spotted a car on Merriam Street, a rifle barrel sticking out of the back window. Officer Pivero and Sgt. Robert J. Rozon were able to stop the car in back of St. Mark's Church on Albro Street, arresting David Dus without a struggle. Dus's wife Heather, 19, Kenneth Vosburgh, 20, and his wife Monya, 19, were all able to jump from the car and ran up West Street to Backman Avenue.

The patrol wagon was called to transport the Dus to the station. Officer John O'Neil, communication officer and wagon driver, picked up Post 3 and 4 wagon officers to transport the prisoner to the station for booking.

PATROL WAGON

As three suspects were still at large, the wagon drove up and down the side streets, across from St. Mark's Church, looking for the trio, shining its spotlight as it drove around., with Dus handcuffed in the back. Just as the wagon passed a house with heavy bushes in front, two people ran across Backman Avenue and hid behind some bushes. Not knowing that a cruiser was sitting in a driveway, down the street watching, radioing their location, the Vosburgh's were arrested. A little while later Mrs. Dus gave herself up to an officer on Backman Avenue. Cruiser officers taking part in the search and arrest were Ralph Pisani, Richard Henault, Bruce Mendel, and Joseph Collias.

Back at the Big N, officers found about $5,000 worth of merchandise piled up by the back door. Among the items were three dozen shotguns and rifles, rifle cases, several thousand rounds of ammunition, assorted luggage, about two dozen watches, some TVs, and cameras.

Detectives found out that before the quartet broke in, they had driven in back of the Big N and knocked out two panels in a door to see if any alarms would go off. Waiting a while and not seeing any police or hearing any alarms, they returned and knocked out enough panels to get inside and gather their goods. David Dus climbed up to the railroad tracks as their lookout.

After additional investigation, it was found out that both males had broken into several homes in Lenox, Richmond and West Stockbridge. In District Court, Judge Clement A. Ferris bound the defendants over to the Grand Jury. Judge Ferris told Chief John J. Killeen that his officers presented excellent testimony and did a fine job. In Superior Court before Judge Francis J. Quirico, on April 15, 1969, Dus and Vosburgh pleaded guilty to the Big N break and several others, also to the shooting at Officer Edward Sherman. Assistant District Attorney William R. Flynn recommended prison terms, saying the breaks were well-planned and the defendants had a ready outlet for any items they could steal.

Dus was sentenced to an indeterminate term at Concord on three of 12 counts and an additional two years at the Berkshire County House of Correction on eight other counts. The last count of violation of the FID law was placed on file. Vosburgh received a sentenced of 2 years at the House of Correction for each of his 11 counts, which were served concurrently. Monya and Heather were sentenced to the Women's Reformatory at Framingham for indeterminate terms; their sentences were suspended and they were placed on three years' probation each.

CITY SAVINGS BRANCH BANK BROKEN INTO AT NIGHT

At 4:30 a.m. on August 22, 1969, Officer Joseph Collias discovered a break into the City Savings Bank branch office in the Adams Supermarket on Williams Street. The nighttime burglary was done by attaching an electrical device to wires connecting the bank's burglary alarm, preventing the alarm from sounding. The alarm was connected directly to the alarm panel in the communication room in the station. Sergeant Robert J. Rozon and Communication Officer John T. O'Neil were in the room. Sergeant Rozon was checking to make sure beat officers made their hourly call box rings. After they disabled the alarm, they broke down a back door leading into the supermarket. Once inside the supermarket they smashed through a wall leading into the bank. The safe was broken into and $12,115 in cash, Travelers checks, and blank checks were taken.

Detectives Edwin Blair and Richard Reddy were the department's lead investigators. The FBI from the Springfield office was also called in to help in the investigation, as the money was insured by the Federal Government. One week after the break at bank, four men were arrested in New York City on related charges. After an intensive investigation, connecting the Pittsfield and the New York City case together with the arrest in Springfield of a man for cashing one of the stolen City Savings Bank Travelers checks, evidence was presented to the Grand Jury. On October 8, 1969, the Grand Jury handed down six indictments for breaking and entering in the night time, larceny of $12,115, and larceny of Travelers Checks from City Savings Bank.

In Superior Court on November 18, 1974, three of the six who were arrested on the indictments pled guilty and were sentence to state prison terms. Donald Hykel, 32, of Springfield was sentenced to six to eight years which were to run concurrently with a 10 to 15 years term he was serving for participating in the $297,000 hold-up of the Holyoke National Bank on February 7, 1973. Paul George Callahan, 38, of Chicopee, was also given six to eight years and Anthony Liquori,34 , of Springfield was given a year in prison and two years' probation. At their trails later, Harry Schweitzer, 34, James Pepe, 30, and Calvia Roots, were found guilty for their part in the robbery.

CHAPTER TWENTY-FOUR

SOCIALIZING-PADDY WAGON AND THE CHIEF
HUMOR IN THE DEPARTMENT

It was the practice of some members of the midnight shift, after leaving work at 8:00 a.m., to gather at one of their favorite watering holes. This was to discuss the events of the night and world politics in general. This bar was at the corner of Fenn and Fourth Streets. Chief Killeen had received several complaints from different sources, about seeing officers coming out of this bar, five or six hours after their shift, unsteady on their feet. Killeen was a no nonsense chief. He worked endlessly behind the scenes for the officers and the department. He had the pulse of everything in the department. Killeen sent word by daily roll-call that he didn't want any more complaints about officers drinking or he would personally take care of the problem. Every officer knew him to be a man of his word.

During this time period the day shift, 8:00 a.m. to 4:00 p.m., was extremely short of officers. If no one volunteered to work on a day there was a shortage, a midnight officer would be mandated to work over. A few weeks had passed since Chief Killeen had given his warning about drinking. The midnight shift figured the pressure was off and gradually started to gather back at their favorite watering hole. One day, one of members of the "social club", Officer Dave Viner, was ordered to work the day shift. Officer Viner was quite perturbed and tried to get someone to take his place without any luck. He was assigned to walk North Street. At about 10:00 a.m., he came into the Communication Room and said, "You want to have some fun?" Officer Viner picked up the phone and dialed the number of the bar on Fenn and Fourth Streets, saying "Tell the guys the chief is on his way down there with the wagon" and hung up the phone. Pandemonium struck the bar, everyone knowing the chief to be a man of his word and his warning. Three or four officers ran out the back door crawling into a car and taking off, leaving two of their personal cars in the parking lot. Three officers ran up the back stairs to a storage room and hid there for a few hours until they figured the coast was clear. Officer Viner had only had to work until noon and went down to the bar to see how his joke was taken. According to the bartender, it was a big success; in fact the three officers hiding in the storage space were still there fast asleep.

At roll-call that night a few of the officers that were at the bar didn't think it was such a funny joke, while the rest of the shift did. That ended the social club actives for a while.

MAYOR ORDERS CHIEF KILLEEN TO
CHANGE STRIKE RULES 101 GE DAY STRIKE

On Monday, October 27, 1969, members of GE Union, Pittsfield's IUE Local 255 went on strike for 101 days, finally ending on February 5, 1970. Chief John J. Killeen at all roll calls passed out his 15 point instructions to officers duties at strikes. They started out by saying officer would not take sides. They were published in the Eagle so both sides knew the ground rules.

Local business agent for Local 255, Albert F. Litano, said Killeen's 15 point set of instructions discriminated against union pickets and favored management. Litano complained to Mayor Donald Butler, who said he "will insist" the rules are reworded to "spell out" equal application to both sides. Meetings were set up with the mayor, Chief Killeen and business agent Litano. Some of these sessions became very stormy. Chief Killeen maintained the instructions were the same ones used in the 1966, during a 62 day strike, and were neutral.

The points in the rules that seemed to draw the most anger from the union officers were Points 4 and 5. Point 4 in part said that picketers shall be notified of any wrong doing and if they persist shall be immediately arrested. Point 5 said to size up the situation early and determine who the real leaders are. In the event arrests are necessary, arrest the leaders at the first opportunity and remove them from the scene. Litano maintained that this referred to union leaders. The chief said it referred to leaders of both sides, union and management. Mayor Donald Butler told both sides he would remain neutral throughout the strike.

The Pittsfield GE plant remained open during the strike so that employees who wanted to work could. All except four gates remained open these four were closed so that police could provide adequate protection to the opened gates.

The strike began on Monday morning a miserable day, cold with light rain. Chief Killeen in uniform was at the North Gate with a detail of officers, including Captain Edgar Almstead. Many these officers worked the last strike. The entire force was ordered in, days off cancelled.

On the second day of the strike, three were arrested, one union member and two from management. Officer Daniel Grady who was assigned to the communication room drove the wagon. (Dan at the age of eighteen joined the Marines and fought in World War II at the battle of Iwo Jima.) He picked Officer O'Neil up in front of the Palace Theater. Traffic was heavy, so Officer Grady had the light and siren on. The chief's orders were for the wagon to arrive at the scene of an arrest and remove that person as soon as possible so the incident would not escalate.

PICKET LINE AT MERRILL ROAD GATE

Two were arrested on the first wagon run and transported back to the station. Once the prisoners were booked, another call was received by radio requesting the wagon. Despite the three arrests, the local scene was peaceful, compared to other GE plants like Schenectady, New York. Picket lines were heavily manned and employees in some cases had to wait 10 minutes before getting into work.

On the fifth day of the strike, eight were arrested, transported to the station in the wagon and booked. On two occasions, Officer O'Neil had to drive the wagon to the scene of an arrest as there were no other officers free.

The department was down about nine officers at the time of the strike. It was a long 101 days before the strike ended and employees started to filtrate slowly back to work.

CHAPTER TWENTY-FIVE

FIRST BANK ROBBERY IN THE HISTORY OF PITTSFIELD

On Tuesday, December 23, 1969, the First Agricultural National Bank's branch office located in a trailer on West Street, due to Jubilee urban renewal, was held up; this was the first bank robbery in the history of Pittsfield.

Two days before Christmas, Joseph David Williams III, 21, of Wood Avenue, received an application for a credit card from teller Nancy Boyer of the FANB. Williams was told to have his wife sign and return the application, as it was going to be a joint account.

Williams returned to bank at 1:15 p.m., telling Mrs. Boyer he had lost the application and needed another one. After receiving it, he went to a counter, pretending to fill out the form. After Mrs. Boyer finished waiting on another customer, he returned to her teller station handing her a note, which read, "Put all of your money in (paper) bag, act natural and no one will get hurt." Joseph kept one hand in his coat pocket, as if he had a weapon in it. Mrs. Boyer followed his instructions and was turning the bag over to Joseph when a second teller arrived. The second teller noted a hysterical note in Mrs. Boyer's voice when she spoke to her. The second teller sensed that something was wrong and hit the button on the silent alarm. This alarm rang in the communication room at the station. Responding to the bank were Detective Capt. Edgar Almstead, as well as eight other officers, on foot and in cruisers. They found that Williams had fled the scene, with $3,850 in cash.

Detectives Edwin Blair, William Paris, and Richard Reddy were able to retrieve a photograph from the bank's surveillance camera, which was set to take pictures every 30-seconds. The FBI was called into the case because the bank was a member of the Federal Reserve Bank System and deposits were insured by the Federal Deposit Insurance Corp.

Copies of the picture were made up and showed at all roll-calls. After an intensive investigation, Joseph's name was put to his picture. At 4:30 a.m. the next day, after receiving a federal warrant, Detectives Ronald Dean, and John Perrone, along with three FBI agents, led by Chief John J. Killeen, arrested Williams at his house. All but $100 of the hold-up money was found under the Christmas tree, in his house.

At his arraignment before U.S. Commissioner Paul A. Tamburello, Williams was held on $30,000 bail and Attorney Leonard Cohen was appointed to represent him. On March 26, 1970, in Federal District Court in Boston,

Federal Judge Francis J. W. Ford let Williams change his plea from not guilty to guilty, telling Judge Ford he was acting voluntarily.

Defense attorney Cohen said Williams was at first charged under the federal code with bank robbery "by force, intimidation or violence." However the federal grand jury indicted him for bank robbery only. On October 8, 1970, in Federal District Court, Judge Ford sentenced Williams to 5 years in a Federal Prison. The FBI was unable to ascertain whether or not he was armed.

1970

During 1970, two members of the department retired: Edward M. Demick, Safety Officer, and Officer Richard Duclos from the Uniform Division. One member resigned. This left the ranks of the department twelve officers short until seven additional officers were hired during the year, bringing the shortage down to five officers.

On February 27, 1970, Chief Killeen made some personnel changes. Patrolmen Edward Sherman, 34, and Richard Henault, 35, were promoted to detective. They were assigned to the Detective Bureau on the second shift; Squad B. Sherman joined the force on November 20, 1966, and Henault on September 28, 1961. Detective Ronald Dean, 34, who joined the force on February 25, 1959, was transferred to the Detective Bureau on days; Squad A. Patrolmen Thomas Gero, 35, who joined the force November 20, 1966, was also promoted to detective and assigned to the Intelligence Division under Sgt. Eugene Catalano.

The Detective Bureau was headed up by Captain Stanley J. Stankiewicz during the day and at night by Sgt. Edwin J. Blair. The Uniform Division was under Captain Dauro Baccoli, with two lieutenants and eight sergeants and fifty patrolmen. Captain Edgar D. Almstead was in charge of the Administrative Division and Captain Stanley Kobus in charge of the Traffic Division.

During the year three members of the department received training in special courses. Capt. Stanley Stankiewicz attended an emergency care course at Harvard, Sgt. Norman Bessette completed a course in firearms training and Officer William Mason attended a course in law enforcement photography.

Ten patrolmen attended the six weeks basic police school: Cosmo Spezzaferro, Gerald Lee, William Zoito, Gordon Saville, Robert Beals, Daniel Triceri, James Winn, Albert Hubbard, Gary Danford and Howard Fiske.

Late in 1970, the Identification Bureau was permanently staffed by Officer William Mason. Some of the duties of Officer Mason were the photographing and fingerprinting of everyone who is brought in for a crime, as required by law. As a public service, the department took fingerprints for pistol permits and job applications, naturalization papers and government security clearance. The duty of crime scene services was to search for and photo evidence for future uses. The evaluation of evidence and preservation of evidence was a major requirement for the ID officer. By the end of the year, the department had 4,000 fingerprints and 850 photographs in the criminal file and approximately 2,000 crime scene photographs.

The Traffic Division reported ten fatal accidents, for the year, one less than the previous year.

The department added an additional new ambulance to its fleet of vehicles, making 1,338 runs and 1,330 wagon runs. Total fleet mileage for the year was 378,905.

PART OF THE DEPARTMENTS FLEET OFFICERS
STRACUZZI   O'NEIL   SCIOLA   VINER

I KNOW EVERY COP IN PITTSFIELD

YOU DON'T KNOW ME!

Steve Salvini, who was a pharmacist at Samale's Pharmacy on the corner of Willis and Fenn Streets and a deputy sheriff for seventeen years, relates the following story:

> "Every morning before starting my shift at the pharmacy, I would stop in for breakfast at Court Square Lunch on the corner of Wendell Avenue and East Street just across the street from the Court House. After finishing I would walk down the street to the pharmacy. Chief John J. Killeen would also stop in for a coffee every morning before going to District Court for the morning arraignments. One morning a belligerent drunk was giving one of the waitresses a hard time. The waitress told the drunk to calm down and leave or she would call the police. The drunk got up from his counter stool and said "go ahead I know every cop in Pittsfield." Chief Killeen got up from his counter stool and said "You don't know me." The next thing I knew, the drunk was on the floor with the chief standing over him, on his walkie-talkie calling for the wagon. The wagon and two officers arrived, escorted the drunk to wagon and drove away to the station. The chief sat back down and finished his coffee. The waitress thanked the chief as he was paying for his coffee, leaving for court."

The next morning, Officer Thomas Harris was getting the prisoners ready to go to court. When he was giving the drunk back his property, the drunk asked him "Who was that red faced man who put me down on the floor?" Officer Harris told him it was the chief.

1971

During 1971, two members of the department retired: Officers Rosario Stracuzzi and Thomas Fitzgerald. Another one officer resigned.

Michael White was promoted from patrolman to sergeant and assigned to the Uniform Division. Seven patrolmen attended the six weeks basic police school which all new officers must attend within six months of their appointment. They were: Michael Bianco, David Boyer, Gary Crippa, Peter McGuire and Paul Therrien. These appointments left the ranks of the department only one short from a full complement.

The Identification Bureau, which was in effect since 1970, now had in its permanent records 4,500 fingerprints and 1,300 offenders' photographs. Approximately two hundred crime scene searches were conducted and approximately four hundred examinations for fingerprints were performed at these crime scene searches.

There was one motor vehicle fatality, compared to ten in 1970, and no murders during the year. There were 53,097 parking tickets issued by the two parking meter attendants and officers.

The Civil Defense Auxiliary Police worked a total of 3,620 man-hours. There were a total of twenty-five officers and men in this division.

The department and the Pittsfield Police Association sponsored a Junior Rifle Club in May of 1971. The club was an affiliated member of the National Rifle Association. The basic function of the club was to teach the basic fundamentals of firearms, and to bring out these qualities of sportsmanship, fair play, discipline, and co-operation so essential to success in life. The club had its own body of elected officers, plus adult leadership consisting of the department weapons officer Lt. Robert Jordan and Officer Thomas Harris. Upon joining the club each shooter received seven weeks of basic rifle instruction in the fundamentals of small bore shooting. On completion of the basic course the individual would receive a Certificate of Completion and any award they may have earned at that time, such as Pro-Marksman, Marksman, Sharpshooter and Expert. The club was very active as competitive shooters. Several matches were held at the Police Department Range with teams from Berkshire Community College, Holyoke, and other local groups of rifle buffs. The club also shot several matches out of town, one being the National Sectional Matches at the Lyman blue Trail range in Connecticut.

PITTSFIELD NATIONAL BANK HOLDUP THWARTED

OFFICER EDWARD DESCZ

It was a chilly spring morning in 1971. Officer Edward Descz was on his walking beat, Post 2, which ran from West Street to Fenn Street; Post 2 contained five banks. At a little after 9:00 a.m. Officer Descz received over his walkie-talkie a message to check out the walk up window at the Pittsfield Nation Bank, West Street. The bank's silent alarm had been tripped. The communication room at the station had about 40 different alarms that they monitored. All the bank alarms were located here and part of the communication officers duties, were to monitor them.

As Officer Descz ran down the hill he observed a young girl standing outside the walk-up window. Going up to the girl, the bank teller blurted out that this girl gave her a note demanding money. The note ordered the teller to fill up a bag with money and warned that the robber had a gun. The teller, herself only 19 years old, pushed the alarm button as she slowly filled a bag with money. Officer Descz placed the girl under arrest. She turned out to be only sixteen years old.

The FBI was called into the investigation because Pittsfield National Bank was a federal bank. She was charged with attempted bank robbery and turned over to Juvenile Probation.

STATE THEATRE PLAYS TRICK ON OFFICER DESCZ
AFTER HIS BANK ROBBERY ARREST

AUTO HITS PATROLMEN AT ACCIDENT SCENE

On Monday, June 28, 1971, Officers John Skumin, Raymond Shogry and John T. O'Neil were investigating a two car motor vehicle accident on Wahconah Street. Lights from two cruisers were flashing, as it was dark out. All of a sudden a car came down Wahconah Street at a high rate of speed striking O'Neil, throwing him on the roof of the on-coming car, breaking the window. O'Neil was knocked unconscious. The police ambulance was called and transported O'Neil to St. Luke's Hospital. The next thing he knew he was looking up at the nurses, nuns dressed all in white, with wide-brim, pure white hats, thinking he was in heaven. Back at the accident scene the driver refused to get out of his car. He was taken out through the driver's side window, placed under arrest, and transported to the station in the wagon to be booked.

POKER GAME RAID

On September, 28, 1971, Lt. William Dermody, Sgt. Eugene Catalano, two detectives and six patrolmen raided a poker game on Highland Avenue. Ten men were arrested and charged with gambling offenses. The owner of the house was charged with allowing his home to be used for gambling and the others were charged with being present where gambling was in progress. The card game was in progress in the kitchen with money and two decks of cards on the table when the officers entered the house. In District Court the next morning before Judge Frank W. Cimini, each of the 10 players were fined. Chief John J. Killeen said the search and seizure warrant was obtained because of complaints of gambling.

1972

In 1972, the Welfare Department moved from the Police Department Building to their new quarters. The new City Health Department Laboratory now occupied a portion of the upper northeast corner of the building. The police building was renovated and now occupied all the available space on the ground floor, the second floor occupied by the Detective Bureau and Administrative Offices.

During the year two Officers retired, William Potter and Ronald Dean. Officer Francis Savko was promoted to sergeant.

Seven officers graduated from a Crime Scene Search School: Capt. Stankiewicz, Detectives William Paris, Matthew Lennon, Richard Henault, Edward Sherman, Thomas Gero, and Officer William Mason.

Five new officers attended the eight weeks Basic Police School: Bernard Auge, Mark Danford, Leonard Pruyne, Benedetto Sciola, and Craig Strout.

The department made 1,274 ambulance calls and 1,435 wagon service runs. There was one murder and three fatal accidents during the year. The department ran on a budget of $1,246,731.00

MURDER OF WIFE WITH .22- CALIBER RIFLE

On Saturday, July 22, 1972, at 6:04 p.m., Charles V. Parise of Stearns Avenue found his neighbor, Dorothy Kurek Manship, 35, lying in the street in front of her house. On the lawn was a .22-caliber rifle. Mrs. Manship was declared dead on arrival at the Berkshire Medical Center's Pittsfield General Unit, where she was taken by police ambulance. Dr. Irvin I. Rubin, Medical Examiner, made a preliminary report. An autopsy was performed by Dr. George G. Katsas, state pathologist. Mrs. Manship was shot six times, one time in the left breast, one in the left arm, one each in the buttocks, one in the mid-back and one in the back of the head.

DETECTIVE RICHARD HENAULT
Picking up .22 Shell Casings

At about 6:30 p.m., Capt. Stanly Stankiewicz and State Police Detective Lt. Milo F. Brown Jr. arrested John Manship, Jr., 34, Dorothy's estranged husband, as he was walking up Fenn Street. Manship had called the station from a payphone at the corner of Appleton Avenue and East Street. According to members of her family, Mrs. Manship had feared for her safety and had, at various times, sought protection. On Monday morning Manship was appeared in District Court and pleaded "not guilty" on the charge of murder. Manship had been in court on three previous occasions to answer to show-cause complaints of non-support. Manship hired Attorneys Leonard H. Cohen and Harris N. Aaronson to defend him.

A bindover hearing was held before Judge Frank W. Cimini in District Court. Judge Cimini found probable cause to order Manship bound over to Superior Court on the charge of murder. Three witnesses testified, Medical Examiner Dr. Irving I. Rubin testified about the autopsy. Investigator William H. Mason testified he took photos of the body and of the interior of the house. An 11- year-old neighbor testified he was outside his house at 6:00 p.m. the day of the shooting and saw Mrs. Manship "come running out of her house." "He (Manship) was standing there with a gun, shot her once more and she fell on the ground."

In March of 1973 a jury trial was held in Superior Court before Judge Ken B. Smith. The jury consisted of 14 members.

Attorney Leonard H. Cohen filed several motions. One was to dismiss the indictment on grounds that the 1972 Grand Jury was improperly and unconstitutionally made up. A similar motion requesting dismissal on the grounds that the traverse jury, which will hear evidence in the case, was also improperly constituted. Judge Smith indicated that he considered the issues important and one that should be addressed by the legislature, denying the motions. Three days of the week were taken up in arguing the motions.

Assistant District Attorney William R. Flynn called several witnesses during the trail. The first one was Officer John Skumin, the first officer on the scene, who found Mrs. Manship lying face down in the street and the rifle on the lawn. Skumin stated he put a blanket under her head and discovered she was bleeding. He found a trail of blood from the cellar up the stairs and through the kitchen and back porch.

Investigator William H. Mason, who was the department's fingerprint identification officer, testified that he found John Manship's right ring finger print on the left side of the .22- caliber gun's pistol grip. This was the .22 rifle that was found on the front lawn of the Manship house.

Lead detectives in the case, Edward Sherman and Richard A. Henault, testified that at the Police Station. Manship said "I shot her, I just kept shooting. I just wanted to take my daughter out. She just wouldn't listen."

Dr. George Katsas, state pathologist, testified that the final shot, which hit her in the head, probably killed her.

In the fifth day of the trail, Manship pleaded guilty to second degree murder. When questioned by Judge Smith about the voluntariness of his guilty plea, Manship said that witnesses' description of the shooting was accurate. Judge Smith handed down the mandatory life sentence in prison.

Attorney Cohen, with the halt of the trial, said that the unanswered question of a pair of scissors found on the steps would never be answered. It was the contention of the defense counsel that Mrs. Manship had struck her husband with the scissors and thus provoked him to shoot her with the .22-caliber rifle.

1973

In April of 1973, the department started a Police Explorer Scout Troop 545. The troop had a membership of approximately twenty boys and girls. These members attended meetings two to four times a month and learned the various aspects of police work as well as the court system.

In 1973, Chapter 18, Section 1, of the City Code, authorized the department one chief, four captains, two lieutenants, twelve sergeants, seventy-eight patrolmen, seven of which assigned to the Detective Bureau, and on patrolman assigned to the Traffic Bureau as a Police Safety Officer, one policewoman, two Parking Meter Attendants, thirty-three School Crossing Guards, one Mechanic, three part-time Matrons, four Senior Clerks, and one Clerk- Stenographer. A total of two hundred and six School Patrol Officers helped out during the year.

As required by Massachusetts General Law, the department conducted in-service training for the force. Seven members received training in other special courses. Five officers graduated from the Crime Scene Search School; Captain Almstead, Captain Baccoli, Sergeant Polidoro, Sergeant Perrone, and Detective Lee. Captain Stankiewicz attended an Emergency Care School, and Sergeant Savko attended a Firearms School.

Three new members of the force attended the twelve weeks basic police school: Officers James Boland, Harry Giguere and Thomas Harris.

The department ran on a budget of $1,353,648, of which $9,734 was used to maintain the motor vehicle fleet, which traveled 361,741 miles. There were 1,234 ambulance runs and 1,057 wagon service runs. The number of fatal motor vehicle accident doubled from the previous year from three to six. There were no murders. The CD Auxiliary Police recorded a total of 6,074 man hours of work performed.

A total of $5,300 was turned over to the City Treasurer which was collected through the issuance of Hunting & Target permits and the sale of Licenses of Firearms, Shotguns, and Rifles, and Gunsmith permits. This was an increase of more than double from the year before and can be attributed to a changed in the law which provides that the Hunting & Target permits be issued for five years and increasing the fee to $10.00, instead of two years for a fee of $2.00. There was also a change in the law in the issuance of FID cards which made them valid until revoked or suspended.

The department expressed its gratitude to the Master Plumbers Association, for their generosity and kindness in furnishing a picnic in June for all School Patrol children. Their association had done this for the last several years.

1974

Sixteen new patrolmen were named to the department. This was the largest number of personnel to be added at one time and for the first time in years brought the force up to full strength. They were: Thomas Guinan, Robert Levesque, Robert D'Ascanio, Dermot Sporbert, Albert Hayford Jr., John Bartow III, Bruce Eaton, Raymond Griffin Jr., Michael Eastland, Allan Cook, Henry Ferris Jr., Richard LeClair, David Reilly, Kenneth Rivers, Joseph Ziemlak, and James Cota.

SIXTEEN NEW OFFICERS

Six officers retired during the year. They were: Howard Fiske, John Gogan, Edward Skowron, Lawrence Healy, Enrico Giardina and William Mickle. There were now 37 members of the force on the retirement roster, still living.

Five officers attended the twelve weeks basic police school, which all new officers must attend within nine months of their appointment: Robert D'Ascanio, Thomas Guinan, James Johnson, Robert Levesque and Dermot Sporbert.

A Rape Reporting unit was established by the department as required by law. This unit established a rape prevention and prosecution unit for the purpose of developing a method of reporting the crime of rape and the counseling of the victims of rape.

The Traffic Bureau investigated eight fatal accidents during the year and the Detective Bureau investigated two murders. The department's fleet put on 382,572 miles. There were 1,444 ambulance runs and 1187 wagon service runs. The Civil Defense Auxiliary Police recorded 6,811 hours for the year. Members of the Auxiliary Police were able to wear side arms when so directed by the chief of police. They had to first satisfactorily complete a 40 hour training course conducted by Lt. Robert Jordan.

FATAL ACCIDENT

BANK ROBBER NABBED 25 MINUTES AFTER ROBBERY

On January 14, 1974, a ski-masked armed robber entered the City Savings Bank branch office in the Bradley Plaza. The masked robber ordered the branch bank's manager, two tellers, and two teenage customers into a back room, took $3,500 in cash, and left. An elderly male customer in the bank strolled out the front door without being stopped by the robber while the holdup was in progress.

An employee at the CVS store next to the bank was able to provide a detailed description of the getaway car, a 1973 station wagon. A Berkshire Armored Car vehicle spotted the car on South Street, after hearing the description on a police radio. The owner of the armored car service Gerard S. Reder, who was out in another armored car, drove to the area. The station wagon pulled into the parking lot of the shopping center in Lenox on Route 7. Reder and his three guards, Thomas Kane, David Green and Peter Masoero, who were armed, confronted the robber, who surrendered to Reder and his men. They were joined momentarily by State Trooper Alan Chamberland, who held the robber until Pittsfield Police arrived.

The robber turned out to be Thomas H. Mario, 36, of Merriam Street, Pittsfield. The whole episode from robbery to capture took only 25 minutes. The gun turned out to be a toy pistol. Mario was also charged with the armed robbery of the Pacific Finance Co. office in the K-Mart shopping center on Merrill Road on January 7, when he got away with $1,022. In both cases the robber worked alone.

On May 29, 1974 in Superior Court, Mario was sentenced to 5 to 7 years in the state prison.

AUGUST 1974-SQUAD A

Squad B 4 P.M. to 12

AUGUST 1974
SQUAD B SHIFT, 4 PM TO 12

LEFT TO RIGHT, LT. ROBERT JORDAN, OFFICERS HARRY GIGUERE, LOUIS MARCEL, JAMES WINN, JOHN O'NEIL, JOSEPH COLLIAS, ROBERT BEALS, ANTHONY WONDOLOSKI, FRANCIS WIMPENNEY, COSMO SPEZZAFERRO, JON WHITE, ROBERT KARPECK, DAVID MACKEY, SGT. ROBERT ROZON AND SGT. FRANCIS SAVKO.

AUGUST 1974- SQUAD B

AUGUST 1974
SQUAD C SHIFT, 12 AM TO 8 AM

OFFICERS ROBERT BENOIT, THOMAS HARRIS, PAUL THERRIEN, GARY CRIPPA, GORDON SAVILLE, WILLIAM MICKLE, III, WILLIAM ZOITO, SGT. ANTHONY PIRES, OFFICERS BERNARD AUGE AND MARK DANFORD.

Squad C 12–8:00 A.M.

AUGUST 1974- SQUAD C

ARREST WITHIN EIGHT MINUTES OF BANK ROBBERY

On December 3, 1974, Isaiah Alexander Jr., 34, of Dewey Avenue, forced his in way into the City Savings Bank branch office at the Pittsfield Plaza shopping center on West Housatonic Street. This was just twenty minutes before the bank opened at 10:00 a.m. He grabbed the two tellers by their arms, demanding money. As this was happening, two other tellers who were reporting for work were at the front door of the bank. Quickly thinking, one of the tellers being held by Alexander, asked permission to tell the two tellers (customers) at the door that the bank was not opened yet, conveying a code that the bank was being held up. The tellers at the door walked next door and phoned the Police Station.

Alexander exited the bank with $9,600 and the keys to one of the teller's car. Detectives William J. Paris and Richard P. Reddy were investigating a burglary at Crescent Creamery at 85 South Onota Street, less than a mile from the bank. Standing in front of building, they heard the description of the stolen car being given out as it drove by them. Jumping into their unmarked cruiser they started to follow it. Within seconds the car pulled to the curb on South Onota Street and Alexander exited the car with the money in the paper bag. Arrested at gun point and transported to the station, Alexander admitted to the hold-up. Telling Paris, "I think the state owes it to me in a way, because of the 11 months I spent in jail before." Alexander had been charged with armed robbery of a package store and was held in jail. The case went through two mistrials and at the third trial he was acquitted.

During his trial in Superior Court, before Judge Raymond R. Cross, Alexander took the stand in his own defense. He said the detectives made up the statements attributed to him. The jury deliberated for less than an hour, finding him guilty. Assistant District Attorney Imelda C. LaMountain recommended to Judge Cross that he impose a sentence of 10-to-15 years for the robbery, and unauthorized use of the teller's car. Under this sentence, he would have to serve six and one half before he would be eligible for parole. Alexander pled guilty to three other indictments, forgery, passing a forged check and attempted larceny in his unsuccessful attempt to cash a forged check. Two charges of unarmed robbery and assault and battery were filed without a finding. These two charges were from a mugging of a man in early April. Alexander's lawyer was Assistant Public Defender Michael J. Ripps.

CHAPTER TWENTY-SIX

SCHOOL TEACHER CHARGED WITH DOUBLE MURDER

On December 23, 1974, Francis O. Hoben, an English teacher at Crosby Junior High School and part-time sports editor and reporter for the Eagle, beat to death his mother and sister at their home on Orchard Street.

According to Dr. Irving I. Rubin, Medical Examiner, Mrs. Christina V. Hoben, 79, and Elizabeth R. Hoben, 46, were severely beaten with a baseball bat.

Deaths were caused by multiple skull injuries and brain damage. Both victims were taken to Berkshire Medical Center, where Christina was pronounced dead and Mrs. Hoben died a short time later.

On December 24, 1974, Francis O. Hoben was arraigned before District Court Judge Frank J. Cimini who ordered that he be held without bail until his next court appearance and that he undergo a psychiatric examination by Dr. James Cattel, court psychiatrist. Hoben's attorney, Leonard H. Cohen stated that he would arrange for an additional private examination.

On January 3, 1975 a bind-over hearing was held before District Court Judge Frank W. Cimini. Hoben's statement to Detective William Paris was introduced as evidence. After reading the statement and listening to testimony of person who spoke with Hoben on the afternoon of December 23, Judge Cimini ordered that Hoben be bound over to the Grand Jury of the Superior Court on murder charges. The judge ordered that Hoben be held without bail. Hoben's statement, in which he described having been in "a very nervous state for the past three or four weeks," was put in as evidence at the initiative of defense attorney Leonard H. Cohen.

On December 20, Hoben had gone to Charles A. Bordeau, director of the school system's personnel service, to file a request for a leave of absence because of his feelings of nervousness. On the night before the deaths, Hoben told Detective Paris, he made up his mind to kill his mother, sister and both his aunts "because I decided to kill myself and I didn't want to leave them behind." He changed his mind about the aunts, who lived in the same house.

On the day of the murders Hoben went to his mother's house and told his mother he was very upset and wanted his sister home from work. Mrs.

Hoben called her daughter home. Following the beatings, Hoben went to the Berkshire Eagle where he had been a part-time employee for 10 years. There he spoke with assistant sports editor William E. Mahan, who tried unsuccessfully to reach an attorney that Hoben wanted.

Hoben was sent to Bridgewater State Hospital. Assistant District Attorney William R. Flynn received a psychiatrist's report from Bridgewater which stated that Hoben was mentally competent to stand trial. At his trial, on August 26, 1976, a psychiatrist testified that Hoben believed that he was being threatened with death by a "secret society" and planned suicide to avoid the killers and to kill his mother and sister to keep them from being murdered by the society." Hoben was found not guilty by reason of insanity and was sent to Bridgewater State Hospital. After five years of confinement in the state mental institution, Hoben was found sane and ordered released. Assistant District Attorney Francis X. Spina, at the August 21 hearing, filed an objection to Hoben's release plea, declaring that he still needed, "the care and support of the state facilities." The institution said he was in a state of "stable remission" and they recommended his release.

Hoben found housing in Northampton after his release. Less than two weeks after his released, Hoben committed suicide on Thursday, September 11, 1980.

1975

BEATING DEATH LEADS TO MURDER

On January 26, 1975, a Newton Avenue man was charged with murder in the beating death of a 4-year- old boy. The mother of the boy was also charged with, murder and accessory before the fact of murder.

Calvin T. Cadwell, 38, a General Electric Co. employee, was charged with the first degree murder after an investigation by the Detective Bureau, in the killing of Walter Gerwaski III. The mother of the 4 year old, Judith P. Gerwaski, was also charged.

Walter Gerwaski III was pronounced dead upon arrival at Berkshire Medical Center where he was transported by Police Ambulance from Newton Avenue.

Cadwell was originally arrested in the early afternoon on an assault and battery charge, and held on $1,000 bail. Cadwell had administered a severe spanking for disciplinary reasons.

Cadwell was charged with murder after a late-afternoon autopsy by Boston Pathologist Dr. Ambrose Keeley. The autopsy disclosed "multiple blunt force injuries" with the cause of death listed as "subdural hematoma," or bleeding under the scalp, which put fatal pressure on the boy's brain. This was caused by one or more blows to the head. There was evidence of head bruises in addition to bruises on the lower body.

Detectives reported that the boy was injured sometime after 9:00 a.m. by Cadwell who had disciplined him for not eating his breakfast. At 10:05 a.m. Walter's mother, Judith, had called for the police ambulance. Cadwell, a member of a ski-rescue team at a local ski area, attempted to administer oxygen from his rescue kit to the boy while the ambulance was in route. Officers manning the ambulance also made unsuccessful attempts to revive the boy.

The original assault and battery charge against Cadwell was dismissed by Judge Frank W. Cimini at the request of Assistant District Attorney William R. Flynn. Flynn said the murder indictment against Mrs. Gerwaski covered alleged action of the woman before the day of the boy's death, as well as on January 26. The accessory charge, which carries the same penalty as murder itself, life in prison, was based on the prosecution's belief that she may have urged Cadwell to discipline the boy that day and on previous occasions.

Assistant District Attorney William R. Flynn, who prosecuted the case in Superior Court, brought out evidence that Cadwell had repeatedly struck Walter with a paddle, forced him to sit on a hot furnace grating which burned him, made him sit in a toilet bowel, and stand bare foot on a pile of chains.

Cadwell was convicted of first-degree murder and sentenced to life in prison. Cadwell's case was appealed to the Supreme Judicial Court who in 1978 ordered the first-degree murder conviction reduced to second-degree murder. The court ruled that while evidence of Cadwell's guilt was indisputable, there was insufficient proof of either premeditation or "extreme cruelty and atrocity" necessary for a first–degree conviction. A person convicted of second-degree murder is eligible for parole in 15 years. Cadwell had to be brought back to Superior Court for a formal resentencing, in 1978.

Judith Gerwaski was found guilty on the charge of being an accessory before the fact of manslaughter and received a sentence of seven months to seven years. Judge Walter H. McLaughlin said he was influenced in his sentence by the fact she had agreed to testify against Cadwell, and in fact had been the major witness for the prosecution. Her lawyer, Attorney Leonard

H. Cohen, said her sentencing will not be her greatest punishment. That will come "when the gates open and she returns to this community." The punishment will be in the form of public ostracism for allowing her 4 year old son to be a victim of fatal child abuse, and will "take place for the rest of her natural life." Judge McLaughlin allowed her to serve her sentence at the Berkshire House of Correction.

Assistant District Attorney Flynn indicated Mrs. Gerwaski's indictment might never come about at all had authorities not felt she lied at a District Court hearing for Cadwell to protect him.

NEW COMMUNICATIONS CENTER

A new Communications Center at the station was dedicated during 1975. It was one the most modern, sophisticated communication systems in the country. It was the heart of the Police Department and one of the most effective tools to combat crime.

The integrated communications system cost $179,000 and was in the planning stage for more than two years. This center replaced a conglomeration of equipment in use for over 20 years and was literally on the verge of wearing out. Also put into service was a new phone number, 443-3511, with its capability of handling twice the number of calls as the old one. The new telephone system itself provided seven lines into the station instead of four under the old system. It also provided the capability of expanding up to 14 incoming lines for future years.

In December 1972, a six–member Pittsfield Police Communications Project Team was appointed by Mayor Donald G. Butler to design the new communications system. The team, headed by Civil Defense Director William H. Cooney, spent several months defining the communications requirements of the present-day department. A Waltham consulting firm was hired to help draw-up specifications for the maze of new communications components and design a system that could meet the city's needs for at least 10 years into the future.

The completely new and more powerful radio system included transmitters and receivers, portable units for the individual patrolmen and mobile radios for each cruiser. It was designed to provide instant communication virtually anywhere in the city. Several radio frequencies were added to expedite emergency calls and to tie into future county radio network.

A sophisticated console in a reconstructed communications room provided officers answering phone calls and dispatching officers vastly improved equipment. The console included a status board indicating the availability of each unit, radio monitoring of fire department activities, telephone tape recording apparatus, and an elaborate surveillance system for the police station security.

With the new system, ten radios were installed in the private cars of detective bureau personnel, enabling them to go directly to a crime scene when called in or to communicate with the station if they saw a crime in progress while off duty.

New radio codes and code cards were issued to each member of the department. There were fifteen codes and one of the most important was "10-33", meaning "officer needs assistance." When this code was heard, every officer dropped whatever he was doing and responded to assist a fellow officer. This code was very rarely used.

CHANGE IN RANKS

There were several changes in the ranks of the department due to the retirement of three sergeants and the resignation of a captain, and the sudden death of another captain. Sergeants Edwin Blair, Benjamin Kulesa and Eugene Catalano retired. Administrative Captain Edgar D. Almstead, Jr. resigned last year and Captain Stanley J. Kobus died in May of last year. Captain Stanley Stankiewicz took over as administrative as well as detective captain. Sergeant Michael White took over as night commander of the Detective Division. Sergeant John Perrone was moved to the Intelligence Unit from the uniform force and three new sergeants were moved to the uniform force. They were: Sergeants Cosmo Spezzaferro, 27, David Boyer, 27, and Gerald Lee, 35.

As required by Massachusetts General Laws, the department conducted in-service training for the force. Several members received training in other special courses: Officer Mason attended an advanced fingerprinting course as the State Police Academy in Framingham and Detective Lee graduated from the Crime Scene Search Training School. Captain Stankiewicz attended the FBI Academy in Quantico, Virginia, for three months; Lieutenant Jordan and Sergeant Bessette attended an Instructors' Firearm Training Course at Camp Curtis Guild. Seventy-three men received in-service firearm training. All members required by statute, attended First-Aid and Cardio-Pulmonary Resuscitation classes sponsored by Mass. Heart Association and the American Red Cross. Fifteen men were being trained as Emergency Medical Technicians because of ambulance requirements. At present, sixteen Emergency Medical Technicians are registered. Sergeant White attended the Rape Training Coordinator course at Brandeis University and gave in-service classes to all officers on the proper reporting of rape cases.

On October 7, 1975, the CD Auxiliary Police unit observed its 25 year birthday. Some 50 officer from Western Massachusetts Auxiliary Police Associations were on hand to celebrate. City Civil Defense director William H. Cooney reviewed the history of the local unit, beginning with its inception in 1950 under the direction of Police Chief Thomas E. Calnan. Chief John Killeen citied a recorded 8,650 man hours of duty donated to the city for the year. Auxiliary Commander Quentin N. Thompson presented to Police Lt. Robert L. Jordan a plaque: "In appreciation for the time and effort donated to the Auxiliary Police." Jordan was the CD training officer.

There were eight fatal motor vehicle accidents and one murder during the year. The ambulance answered 1,444 calls and the wagon made 1,187 service runs.

JUVENILE BUREAU CREATED

Due to the large number of juvenile cases, 458, which came to the attention of the department; a Juvenile Bureau was established on December 27, 1975. This bureau was recommended by the Herklots Commission report on the study of the police department. This bureau worked as a liaison with the Juvenile Probation authorities in all juvenile cases.

Sergeant Frank A. Polidoro, a 20 year veteran of the force was assigned to head the bureau. Sergeant Polidoro had a lot of experience with children, as he had ten children of his own and two grandchildren.

SERGEANT FRANK A. POLIDORO

DRINKING -SHOTGUN-MURDER

Ralph Delmolino and Peter J. Sondrini were both at Pittsfield's VFW Post on Linden Street drinking. The date was October 25, 1975. At their trial in Superior Court, in June of 1976, Delmolino's chief defense counsel, Leonard H. Cohen, said "they never saw one another "at the VFW and decided independently to go to Eric's Way bar in Canaan, New York just across the West Stockbridge town line, to continue drinking.

Stephen P. Warner, 21, and Delmolino were in Warner's car. Sondrini and two women companions were in his car. Both cars were driving on Route 41, when there was a bumper-to-bumper auto harassment incident. Both cars pulled to the side of the road and Sondrini leaped from his car, attacked Delmolino with a baseball bat. Delmolino fired a single, close range shotgun blast into Sondrini's left side, killing him.

Warner then drove Delmolino back to Pittsfield, abandoned his car and the shotgun in Coolidge Park, and reported the auto stolen to the Police Department. After an investigation, both Warner and Delmolino were charged with murder.

Through his chief council Attorney George Crane, Warner pleaded guilty to being an accessory after the fact of murder and was sentenced to 2 years in jail. The charge of murder was dismissed.

Delmolino, in explaining his actions to Judge Kent B. Smith, said Warner had wielded the shotgun when the cars stopped and that in the ensuing struggle he and Sondrini had wound up in possession of the gun. Sondrini was still beating him with the bat, when he got his hand on the trigger and the gun went off. Assistant District Attorney Flynn countered that "our evidence doesn't agree with what he says." Three witnesses, two women in Sondrini's car and Warner, were prepared to testify for the prosecution, saying Delmolino was the one who originally wielded the firearm.

Delmolino was given a sentence of from 12 to 20 years by Judge Smith after pleading guilty at the outset of his trail. The judge softened the sentence by recommending to the Department of Corrections that his sentence be served at the Berkshire County House of Correction rather than state prison.

1976

The city purchased two new ambulances which were the newest type and met all the specifications as set out in the rules and regulation of Emergency

Medical Service Department of Public Health State of Massachusetts and U. S. Department of Health, Education and Welfare.

One of these ambulances was obtained by a $12,000 grant from the state. The second ambulance was purchased because the city was able to participate in the state sponsored Collective Ambulance Purchase Program, thus enabling the city to purchase the second ambulance at a reduced price. The two new modular type ambulances were a windfall for the city since they represented a total of $52,000 worth of equipment and cost the City of Pittsfield a little less than $25,000.

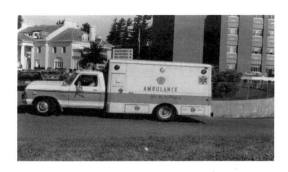

There were forty, Nationally Registered Emergency Medical Technicians-Ambulance in the department.

Twenty-five more officers had completed the course and were waiting to take their exam. The remainder of the department was waiting to be trained. Sixteen members had received their refresher training and will be recertified for a two year period as required by the National Registry of Emergency Medical Services. Officer Edward Fields was certified as an Instructor- Coordinator in EMT training after attending an Instructor's Course held in Springfield by the Chief of Training of the Office of Emergency Medical Services.

PROMOTIONS IN THE RANKS

Several promotions took place in the ranks of the department. On February 29, 1976, Sergeant Anthony J. Pires with a score of 83 and tops on the civil list was promoted to captain by Mayor Evan S. Dobelle. Chief John J. Killeen assigned the new captain to the Traffic Division.

Also on February 29, Lieutenant Robert L. Jordan was promoted to captain by Mayor Dobelle with a score of 80 and placed in charge of the Detective Bureau.

Patrolmen Gary Crippa was promoted to sergeant in the Uniform Division. Policewomen Thelma Thomas retired leaving this position open. There were now seven vacancies in the patrolmen ranks and a new position of dog officer within the department.

With the new communications system, incident cards were made out for every call. There was a huge increase in the total number of incidents recorded because all incidents were now recorded. In 1975, there were only 9,955 calls recorded and in 1976 there were 27,052.

The Pittsfield Police Association and the Pittsfield School Department sponsored the annual School Patrol picnic for the 250 members at Berkshire Community College.

There were six traffic deaths during the year and no murders. Wagon calls were reduced to 524, as some of the cruisers now had cages in them. There were 1,185 ambulance runs.

The Auxiliary Police recorded a total of 10,398 man hours for the year. The unit consisted of 30 members. Each officer was required to put in a minimum of 16 hours per month, but most of the personnel donated over 32 hours per month.

The Citizen Radio Division under, Commander Jack Shea, also assisted with their mobile equipment and manpower. They report in for all emergencies.

MANPOWER STUDY

A police manpower study sought by Chief Killeen since the fall of 1974 was about to happen. The Massachusetts Police Institute, a federally- aided arm of the Massachusetts Chief of Police Association, sent its executive director, Joseph Shannon, and four staff members to Pittsfield to meet with Chief Killeen, Mayor Evan S. Dobelle, and members of the City Council.

Chief Killeen speculated that a study would demonstrate a need for more policemen to supplement the 100 member force. His request for the study came at a time of increasing crime in Pittsfield and across the nation. Shannon said that this was the first request of this sort he had had from a chief in his visits to numerous Massachusetts police departments. He called it an "imaginative" approach and praised Chief Killeen for asking for it. Mayor Dobelle backed the study.

On September 16, 1976, the City Council unanimously approved a two-year labor contract with the police unions. The action followed a 30-minute executive session in which councilmen question why police officers were getting more vacation than other city employees. The councilors were told that the vacation time was not the result of union contracts, but a result of a 1970 Supreme Judicial Court decision interpreting state law as it applied to police in Holyoke, which defined a work week as seven days.

Starting in July of 1977, the base pay of a policeman would be $12,575, a sergeant would be $15,090 and a captain $17,605. The base salaries are increased by educational incentive pay and longevity pay.

CAPTAIN SUFFERED STROKE

Captain Robert L. Jordan, chief of detectives, suffered a serious stroke in August, 1976. Jordan was at a skeet-shooting match near Greenfield when stricken. He joined the force as a provisional officer August 18, 1957, and became a regular patrolman the following February. He was promoted to sergeant on May 1, 1966 and a lieutenant in July 1966, and to captain on February 29, 1976 after having been senior lieutenant. Jordan served for 20 years in the department. Jordan was a firearms enthusiast and in charge of firearms training for the department. He was granted a disability retirement in May, 1977.

All members of the department were required to take one week firearms training each year. Officers had to fire 50 rounds from the Thompson .45-caliber machine gun, along with other department firearms. The department was able to secure all the .45 ammunition they wanted from the military.

Jordan had established within the department a team of officers who traveled through New England in pistol competition with other departments. Each officer used his own .357 Smith and Wesson Revolver and had gunsmith Ralph Williams fine-tune it for the competition. Captain Jordan expertly reloaded all the ammunition for the team. Officer William Mason, a leather craftsman who made off duty holsters for officers, made leather bullet holders for each member of the team. Speed loaders were not allowed in competition. The holder was made so two bullets could be reloaded at a time. Everything was timed for speed and accuracy. Pittsfield's team won a great many trophies and medals in competition. Besides Jordan, team members were:

DETECTIVES EDWARD SHERMAN, RICHARD HENAULT, INVES-
TIGATOR WILLIAM MASON, OFFICERS JOSEPH COLLIAS, RALPH
PIVERO AND JOHN O'NEIL

AMERICAN REVOLUTION BICENTENNIAL
PITTSFIELD SPECIAL POLICE BADGE
1776-1976

There were several retirements and promotions during the year. Lieutenant William M. Dermody was promoted to captain on July 20, and took over the Traffic Division. Captain Anthony J. Pires moved from the Traffic Division to chief of the Detective Bureau. Captain Dauro J. Baccoli remained in charge of the Uniform Division. Sergeant Michael White was promoted to lieutenant and was assigned to the mid-shift in the Uniform Division. Detective Matthew Lennon was promoted to sergeant in the Uniform Division. Patrolman Daniel Grady was promoted to sergeant and headed the Records Bureau. Sergeants William Tuohy and Francis Savko retired from the Uniform Division. Retiring from the Traffic Bureau was Patrolmen Fred Strout and two detectives retired, Richard Reddy and William Paris.

RAYMOND SHOGRY

Richard Delphia, Safety Officer, transferred to the Detective Bureau and Officer Raymond Shogry became the department Safety Officer. Ronald Patti filled the vacant position of dog officer and two Federal Grant positions of dog officer were also filled by David Drake and Donald White.

Eight additional officers were added to the Uniform Division: Ronald Derby, Henry Dondi, Harold Finn, Judith Cormier, Owen Boyington, Michael Fitzgerald, William Ramsey, and Robert Smith.

All eighty-five members of the department were certified EMT-A's. Several members received training in other special courses; Captain Anthony Pires attended the F.B.I. Academy in Quantico, Virginia, for three months.

In the summer the city administration obtained funding through a Title VI CETA (Comprehensive Employment and Training Act) grant to finance a pilot program, one year in duration, for police aide and community service training. The new officers were called Community Service Officers and received training for answering non-enforcement calls. The conceptual thrust of the program as set up was that Community Service Officers are civilians serving within the structure of the Police Department and were intended to free the law enforcement officer from non-enforcement duties so that he or she may perform the greater effectiveness and to the detriment of crime in the community.

These officers received four weeks of classroom training and three of in-service on the job training. They were instructed in the policies and procedures of the Police Department and besides being addressed by each superior officer they had courses in report writing, criminal law, penal institutions, court clinic referrals and counseling. Joy Johnson was project assistant. Thirteen Officers were named: Raymond Bush, Joan Coughlin, Charles Cox, Paula Dupont, Theresa Eltoft, Sheryl Howard, Ann Johnson, Robert Liverseidge, Brian Marquis, Loraine Myers, Michael Penna, Rebecca Shea and Robert Wheeler.

The Auxiliary Police recorded 14,032 man hours. Civil Defense Director William Cooney retired after serving twenty six years.

The department during the year purchased two off-road motorcycles as an addition to its fleet of fifteen cruisers, one wagon, two ambulances, one dog van, two parking meter cars and two motorboats. A total of 503,491 miles were recorded during the year.

POLICE UNITS QUELL 3 DAY DISTURBANCE AT JAIL

On April 10, 1977, 59 law enforcement personnel quelled a three day disturbance at the Berkshire County House of Correction. The disturbance escalated into the setting of fires and smashing of equipment and windows. Heavy slate tiles were torn from the floors of cells and thrown at fluorescent light fixtures. Small fires were set with rolls of toilet paper and other flammables and thrown onto the outer windowsills. Toilets were smashed in cells.

CELL BLOCK DEBRIS
PHOTO BY MARC MITCHELL EAGLE STAFF

Sheriff John D. Courtney Jr., a former state trooper and Williamstown Police Chief, said the trouble started Thursday when inmates began fighting, banging on bars, chanting and igniting small fires, Courtney ordered all inmates confined to quarters except for the one-hour mandatory exercise period, and each cell was stripped of its contents, except for mattresses. Despite these actions, inmates continued their noisy campaign Friday night. Saturday, they started another small fire and began damaging floors, breaking windows and hurling debris into the corridor.

Sheriff Courtney called Chief John J. Killeen and State Police for their assistance on Saturday morning to put down the disturbance. Seventeen officers from the tactical unit, in riot equipment from Pittsfield, twenty state troopers from barracks in Western Massachusetts, and twenty-two deputy sheriffs and jail guards put down the disturbance. State Police were under the command of Capt. C. W. DeMyer of Williamston, Western Massachusetts troop commander. A cell-by-cell search of the main cellblock which housed 77 inmates was conducted.

CHIEF KILLEEN ON STEPS DIRECTING OFFICERS,
MILITANT POLICE CAPTAIN IN WWII
PHOTO BY MARC MITCHELL EAGLE STAFF

Thirteen prisoners, described by Sherriff Courtney as "real trouble makers," were transferred in a group out of the jail to four other correctional institutions. This lowered the jail population from 99 to 86, about the jail capacity, and brought about comparative peace to the jail. No one was injured in the disturbances.

1978

In Chief John J. Killeen's fourteenth and final Annual Report as chief, he noted the department was two sergeants and one patrolman short.

Chief Killeen retired on his 65th birthday, December 25, 1978. Four new officers were added to the force: Anthony Riello, Frank Hess, Gene Auge and Jacob Marby. Longtime mechanic Frank Hess retired.

The entire department had successfully completed classes in Hostage Situation, Rape Seminars, Stress Awardees, and Crisis Intervention. A total of eighty five officers were trained as Emergency Medical Technicians-Ambulance in the department.

Officer James Winn attended an advanced latent fingerprint and photography course in Framingham and another course in Rochester. In additional to his duties as a police officer on the second shift, he worked as a photographer in the Identification Bureau.

A total of 1,108 juvenile cases came to the attention of the Juvenile Bureau. There were eleven traffic deaths during the year and a total of 31,317 incidents recorded.

18th BIRTHDAY CELEBRATION LEADS TO MURDER

Leo's Bar at 534 Tyler St., near the intersection of Tyler and Brown Streets, was one of the hot spots for the late night crowd. Members of the Warlocks Motorcycle Club hung out there.

On May 19, 1978, Thursday, a crowd of about 30 were inside the bar drinking and playing pool. Eddie Dobson, 22, and several other young black males along with "birthday boy", Frank Number, a white male, joined the others in the bar late that night.

An altercation between a young black male and a member of the Warlocks Motorcycle Club took place. In another argument, Frank Number wanted to go outside to settle a dispute he had with one of the youths who came with Dobson. Number was carrying a hunting knife. He took if off and placed it on a table inside the bar. A member of the Warlocks was hit over the head with a pool cue. Soon everyone was outside fighting in the street. Leo Lepotakis, owner of Leo's, called the station requesting police.

Upon arriving, officers found 30 or so people fighting in the street. Upon hearing the sirens the crowd started to disperse. Lying on the sidewalk bleeding from his chest was a Warlocks member, William E. Limburg, 22. He had been stabbed in the left side of his chest. The police ambulance was called and transported Limburg to BMC, where he died, shortly after 2:00 a.m. Friday morning.

Two others were also taken to BMC. During the brawl, Frank Number was kicked in the head. He was admitted to BMC intermediate care unit. The other male was treated and released with facial cuts suffered when he was hit in the side of the face with a beer bottle.

Responding officers arrested five for disturbing the peace and confiscated four knives from different people. Another knife was found on the sidewalk.

All five knives were sent to the State Police laboratory in Boston to determine if any of them had Limburg's blood on them.

SWITCH BLADE KNIFE ON SIDEWALK

Detective Commander Captain Anthony J. Pires was called to the scene and had officers search the Morningside area near the bar. We used flashlights to search the rooftops of Tyler Street business buildings, looking for knives or any other evidence. In the morning officers found a trail of blood leading south on Brown Street to the railroad tracks. Officers believed this was from another brawler who left the scene. Detective Lt. Milo F. Brown Jr., head of the state police detectives assigned to the District Attorney's office joined Captain Pires and Pittsfield Detectives in the investigation. Captain Pires told the media that despite interviewing several defendants and others at the bar; exactly what went on was still unclear the next day.

An autopsy was performed by Dr. George Katsas, determining that Limburg died of massive hemorrhaging from a single stab wound in the left side of the abdomen, rupturing the aorta, the body's main blood artery.

A large group of motorcyclists and their female companions from the local Warlocks Club and other clubs from New England and New York State attended Limburg's funeral. After the service they rode their motorcycles in a procession behind the hearse to the Pittsfield Cemetery. Captain William Dermody was placed in charge of a contingent of officers for extra security during the funeral.

After an extensive investigation, Eddie Dobson, 21, was charged with the 2nd degree murder. Dobson was already in jail on the charge of disturbing the peace when he was arraigned.

Captain Anthony J. Pires said a hunting knife found "in the vicinity of Dobson's arrest", and a witness's statement saying he saw Dobson near Limburg with a knife, led to his arrest. The knife had human blood on it, type O, the same as Limburg's.

Assistant District Attorney Daniel A. Ford and Philip F. Heller represented the Commonwealth. Attorney George B. Crane was Eddie Dobson's lawyer.

In Attorney George Crane's closing summary he stated that Leo's was no Ritz, that the drinking that had been going on colored the evidence. All witnesses either had an ax to grind or had been drinking. He claimed that the state's witness could be color-blind, not knowing the color of the shirt that the person who stabbed Limburg was wearing. The blood found on Dobson's shirt, type O, was the same as 46% of the population. He told the jury that because Dobson did not testify should have no bearing on their decisions.

In his summary to the jury, Assistant District Attorney Ford cited testimony that a patron in Leo's said he saw Dobson give Limburg what appeared to be a big hug and back away with what "appeared" be a knife. He said the state must prove only the "essential facts" not every element of the case. He discussed and defined malice, the crucial element in finding a guilty verdict for second-degree murder.

A jury of seven men and five women deliberated for a total of 18 hours over a three day period. They were all housed at the Wendell Hotel for two nights, with deputy sheriffs to keep them company. They came back with two not guilty findings and two guilty findings

They found Dobson not guilty of second degree murder and carrying a dangerous weapon when arrested at Leo's. They found him guilty of armed assault with a knife and disturbing the peace. As it was Saturday morning, Judge Cross set sentencing for Monday, November 19, 1979.

Judge Cross released Dobson on a $5,000 personal surety bond for his appearance in court on Monday, as requested by Assistant District Attorney Ford. Ford said "that the jury was not convinced beyond reasonable doubt". Assistant District Attorney Heller said the jury believed Dobson was "in the rumpus" but that there was "not a good eyewitness to the actual stabbing".

On Monday morning, Judge Raymond R. Cross sentenced Dobson to 2 years suspended sentence on his assault conviction. On the disturbance of the peace charge he received one month but was given credit for the time he had served awaiting trial. There were also two conditions. One was that he continue to work with the Defenders Advocacy Program, and the other was that he undergo treatment for alcohol abuse.

CHAPTER TWENTY-SEVEN

GUN BATTLE WITH BANK ROBBERS

On the morning of July 20, 1978, the Dalton branch of the First Agricultural Bank was held up by two masked men at gunpoint. They got $7,400 in cash and were accompanied by a woman accomplice.

Officer Louis W. Marcel, a nine year veteran of the department, was on radar patrol when he heard his cruiser radio report the bank robbery. The getaway vehicle, a green Chevrolet, was headed West on Dalton Avenue. On a hunch, Marcel decided to cruise up First Street. As he was traveling North on First Street he noticed in his rearview mirror a green Chevrolet heading south. Making a U-turn, he activated his emergency lights for the car to pull over. He attempted to approach its male driver and two passengers, a male and female.

But as soon as he got out of his cruiser, the Chevrolet sped away. At Park Square, Patrick Rahilly, 24, one of the robbers, blew out the rear window of the Chevrolet with a shotgun blast from his sawed-off shotgun. Rahilly fired five or six shots with the shotgun and then began firing with his revolver.

The cruiser and Chevy tore down South Street. Sgt. Gary Crippa, working at construction traffic detail, had been listening on his radio when he saw the green Chevy coming at him. Sgt. Crippa jumped in his personal car and started to follow the two cars.

Officer Thomas M. Guinan, who was also working the same traffic detail as Sgt. Crippa, fired one shot at the Chevy when it was only a few feet from him. Guinan was almost hit by a bullet fired by Rahilly. Guinan's bullet hit Jerry J. Sarno, 24, the driver of the Chevy in the hand and shoulder, going first through the windshield.

As the chase proceeded at speeds of up to 80 miles an hour into the less settled South Mountain Road area, Officer Marcel returned fire, his right hand on the steering wheel and his left hand clinching his six-shot revolver.

Officer Marcel's cruiser's windshield and hood were peppered from blasts from Rahilly's shotgun. The radiator was steaming and spouting water. Now on Swamp Road, Rahilly flung his sawed-off shotgun and two revolvers into the roadside bushes. At this time, Marcel's cruiser's bumper was practically kissing the Chevy. Then the Chevy swerved back into the cruiser, tossing both vehicles off the road and into a guardrail. Sgt. Crippa pulled up and sandwiched the Chevy between the two officers' cars. Guns pointed at the trio they offered no resistance and surrendered meekly.

OFFICER MARCEL AND SGT. CRIPPA
PHOTO BY OFFICER WILLIAM MASON-PPD

The wounded driver, Jerry J. Sarno, 24, of South Boston was sentenced to eight to ten years. Patrick S. Rahilly, 24, of Dorchester who had participated in the robbery of the same bank only a few weeks earlier on July 6, was sentenced to 35 to 40 years in the state prison.

Linda J. Gouthro, 21, of Dorchester, the female in the car who had not participated in the actual robbery, pleaded guilty to being an accessory and was given a seven-year suspended sentence and two years' probation.

On May 13, 1981, three years after the robbers' capture and trail, Officers Marcel, Guinan and Sgt. Crippa were given the departments "Valor" award for their heroism in the arrest of bank robbers. This took place in a ceremony in front of the City Council. Police Chief Stanley Stankiewicz congratulated the three, saying they had "truly lived up to their professionalism".

SCHOOL CROSSING GUARDS AUGUST 20, 1978
PHOTO BY WILLIAM MASON PPD

AFTERNOON BANK ROBERRY WITH .30-30 RIFLE

At 3:15 p.m. a lone gunman with a .30-30 rifle entered the Union Federal Savings Bank branch office at the K-Mart Plaza, in the Coltsville section of the city. It was Monday, December 3, 1978. The young male didn't have a mask on to cover his face. The bank's surveillance cameras were able to capture the entire hold-up enabling detectives to make close range photos of the robber.

There were three tellers in the bank, but no customers. The gunman told the tellers he needed the money for an emergency and needed it more than the bank. The tellers emptied their cash drawers into two bags he brought with him. The cash from the third teller's drawer, $1,429, didn't go into his bag but dropped on the floor. He didn't bother to pick it up. After an audit the bank said there was $3,196 taken by the robber. After exiting the bank, he got into a Pontiac and drove away.

A sharp-eyed customer who was shopping in the store next to the bank observed a male with a rifle and two bags get in a greenish color, Pontiac and drive away. She was able to get the license plate number of the car and gave it to the detectives.

Detectives were able to trace the license plate number to Robert Santa. With the surveillance camera photo, detectives were able to make a quick arrest. Santa was indicted by the grand jury. At his Superior Court trail he was found not guilty by the reason of mental illness.

Acting Police Chief Anthony J. Pires

Upon the retirement of Chief John J. Killeen, the mayor appointed Captain Anthony J. Pires to Acting Police Chief. He served from January 2, 1979 to November 20, 1980.

Two new sergeants were approved: Walter Boyer and Anthony Wondoloski. Two officers retired: John Bartow and Albert Hubbard. This left one vacancy in the Uniform Division. Two new officers were added to the force: Michael Case and Mark White. Officer James Winn was moved to the Identification Division from the Uniform Division

A Crime Prevention Bureau was established to show the public the newest techniques to improve business and home security: identification programs for property, retail security, security lighting, electronic devices, locks, rape, armed robbery, and programs for elderly security. Billboards and road signs indicating that Pittsfield is a Crime Watch Community city were installed through donations of civic organizations. Talks were given to civic organizations concerning crime prevention and engraving machines were acquired by the department on a loan basis to the general public for marking property.

GAMBLING DEBT LEADS TO MURDER

On the morning of February 13, 1979, David T. Colvin, 32, of Hungerford Street was shot and killed. The shooter was Brian K. Matchett of Scituate, Massachusetts. Matchett was hired by Arthur W. "Lucky" Samson Jr., who paid Matchett $100.00 and expenses to drive him to Pittsfield and back to Boston. Samson needed to collect a $1,500 gambling debt from Colvin, whom Samson described as "a brawler."

Matchett was an ex-marine and a decorated Vietnam War veteran, who served in the early 1960 as a personal bodyguard to Presidents John F. Kennedy and Lyndon B. Johnson. A physical culture buff who weighed 198 pounds. He was just under 6 feet tall. Matchett could do a deep knee bend with a 500-pound barbell on his back.

The two men drove to Pittsfield in Matchett's 1972 Ford station wagon with Matchett's German shepherd. On the way the heater of the car broke; it was a cold, late night drive. The two men checked into the former Holiday Inn in Lenox, now the Best Western Inn, at about 1:45 a.m. As they were resting, Samson began efforts to locate Colvin. These efforts involved two phone calls to the Colvin's house, as well as a trip to Hungerford Street at about 3:30 a.m. Both men knocked on doors trying to find Colvin.

After the search proved to be unsuccessful, they returned to the hotel where they rested. At about 6 a.m. they went to Dalton and talked to Charles A. Coppola, who made arrangements for Samson to talk to Colvin on the phone about directions to his house.

When they arrived at Colvin's Hungerford Street house, Samson got out of the car and was met at the front door by Colvin, who shook his hand and ushered him inside. Because of the "freezing cold," Matchett got out of the car and began walking around. When he heard shouting from inside the house, he went in through the front door, which as ajar.

Matchett walked into the living room, where Samson and Colvin were seated opposite each other. Matchett sat down next to Samson. There were some words between Matchett and Colvin. Colvin lunged at Matchett with a lamp, threatening to break it over Matchett's head. Matchett said at his trial he was sunk deep in a chair and "I couldn't get out of it." Instinctively, Matchett said, his hand still in his pocket because of the cold, his fingers tightened around the .38-caliber handgun he was carrying. Matchett said he yelled, "Hold It," Colvin grabbed his right arm, pulling him out of the chair as the gun was inadvertently discharged twice in rapid succession.

Colvin was on the couch as they left. But before they could get out of the driveway they had to move a car. A neighbor, Brian Stack had parked his car in the driveway to block their car in. They moved it by bouncing and sliding it out of the way with their car.

Police were called and responded with the department's ambulance. Officer Ralph Pisani was one of the three officers manning the ambulance. At Matchett's trail, Officer Pisani testified that he dressed wounds in Colvin's shoulder and stomach and that Colvin was still conscious when they arrived at Hillcrest Hospital.

Trooper Joseph P. Orcechowski of the Massachusetts State Police was on patrol in the Chester- Becket area on Route 20. He received a radio bulletin, to be on the lookout for a 1972 Ford station wagon, with two men and a dog in it. About 11:30 a.m. he observed a car fitting the description heading east. He followed the car for six miles, noting that it was traveling in an erratic manner. He stopped the car in the parking lot of a bar called Cedars. Orcechowski called for back-up and Trooper William E. Godfrey arrived. They search Matchett and found a .38-caliber snub-nose, Smith & Wesson revolver, a pair of handcuffs and two leather ammunition pouches.

Also found in the car was another handgun and a sawed-off shot gun. After transporting both men to the state police barracks in Russell and making a more thorough search, they found a knife in a sheath strapped to Matchett's leg.

Both men were transported to the Pittsfield Police Station and held overnight for their appearance in District Court. Every morning prisoners would be transported from the station to District Court. On this morning Officer John O'Neil was court officer; he accompanied to both Matchett and Samson to court in the wagon. The prisoners talked, as like nothing had happened the night before, joking with O'Neil.

Prosecuting the case for the Commonwealth was Assistant District Attorney Francis X. Spina. At their trial in Superior court, a state ballistics expert testified that the bullet that killed Colvin was fired from the .38-caliber handgun found on Matchett. The Berkshire Superior Court jury deliberated for a total of 12 hours. Matchett was found guilty of second-degree murder and sentenced to life in prison. His co-defendant, Arthur Samson, known as "Lucky", was found not guilty.

Matchett's attorney appealed the conviction and in June of 1982, the appeals court ruled that Judge John F. Moriarty, who presided over the original trial, improperly instructed the jury before it began deliberating. In May of 1983, a new jury-waived trial which lasted seven days took place with Judge Lawrence B. Urbano of Williamstown, presiding over it. Matchett was found guilty of manslaughter and sentenced to 12 to 20 years at Walpole State Prison.

MILLONS IN PAINTINGS STOLEN IN HOUSE BREAK

On Memorial Day weekend in 1978, about nine months before he was murdered, David T. Colvin broke into a house in Stockbridge. The owners of the house, Michael Bakwin and his wife, collected priceless paintings, most of them post-Impressionist. These painting were worth millions of dollars. One of the paintings, a major still- life, "Bouilloire et Fruits" by Paul Cezanne sold for $29.3 million at an auction house in London. This burglary was one of the largest thefts in the history of Massachusetts from a private dwelling.

BOUILLOIRE ET FRUITS BY PAUL CEZANNE

Colvin brought all seven painting to his lawyer's office in Watertown, criminal defense lawyer Robert M. Mardirosian. Mardirosian at one time was also Bakwin's attorney.

Mardirosian kept these paintings hidden in his office until 1988, by building a false wall, hiding them behind it. At this time he moved them out of country, putting them in a Swiss Bank. Mardirosian was able to keep secret these paintings by creating a shell company to move them.

In April 2005, Mardirosian wanted to sell these paintings in London. But a London company, who has a database listing all stolen art work, notified the auction house that paintings were stolen. After an extended investigation in 2007 federal authorities were able to retrieve the paintings. In US Federal Court, in 2008, Mardirosian was charged with possessing the stolen paintings. It only took the jury three hours to convict Mardirosian. He was sentenced to seven years in prison.

The US attorney's office returned the stolen paintings to Michael Bakwin who had not seen the paintings for more than 30 years.

FIFTH BANK ROBBERY IN ONE YEAR

LARGEST BANK ROBBERY IN THE
HISTORY OF BERKSHIRE COUNTY

On June 25, 1979, at 11:15 a.m., four men pulled off the biggest bank robbery in Berkshire County's history. Three of the armed and masked robbers entered the Allendale branch office of Berkshire Bank & Trust. They held more than a half-dozen employees and customers at bay with their automatic pistols. The trio that went into the bank was described as white, wearing blue jeans, windbreakers and felt hats with brims, all wore brown ski masks.

One of the trio vaulted the tellers' counter. There were no glass or metal barriers to prevent anyone from doing so. In yester years, tellers were in sort of a cage so this couldn't happen. He began to scoop money from the tellers' drawers. The second robber came around the counter to help. The third bandit, with gun in one hand, grabbed the teller nearest him by the arm and forced her to accompany him into the branch's office, where the safe was located. He kicked open the door and took money from the safe. They now had a quarter-million dollars.

The trio then ran outside and got into a tan Plymouth Volare station wagon, driven by a fourth man. They drove north in the parking lot, beside Cheshire Road and then turned west around the back of the shopping center. In the back of the shopping center next to the Sears & Roebuck Store, they dumped the Plymouth and each man jumped into his own car: a 1978 red Oldsmobile, a 1976 Dodge, 1975 blue and white Chevrolet, and a green Pontiac. These four cars had been parked there previously.

The abandoned tan Plymouth station wagon was stolen 10 days before from the Albany Airport parking lot. The ignition was "popped" and new Massachusetts plates were put on it. The plates were stolen from a tan Plymouth station wagon the night before the robbery, from a car parked near the Union Square Theater on Union Street. In their haste to get in the four other cars, they left a brown duffel bag with some $11,000, in the still running tan wagon.

With the help of several witnesses, detectives were able to identify one of the robbers as Michael R. Donahue, 33, of Quincy. Donahue, two other men, and one woman, rented two motel rooms, and one cottage in Lanesboro, just prior to the robbery. Quincy Police arrested Donahue for the Pittsfield Police for armed robbery while masked. Warrants were also issued for two other well-known Boston underworld characters, Ralph Petroziello and Kenneth Wightman. Wightman, who escaped from Walpole State Prison on April 17, was serving time for attempted murder of a Boston Police Officer while attempting to hold-up a Boston bank.

A trial was held in Superior Court on September, 1980, before Judge Kent B. Smith which lasted six days. First District Attorney Daniel A. Ford prosecuted the case for the Commonwealth and Attorney David P. Connor, court-appointed counsel, represented Michael Donahue.

One of the commonwealth's witnesses, Francis Mazza, who First Assistant District Attorney Ford had talked to while preparing his case, suffered a "memory lapse" when it came to his turn to tell about a conversation that he had in Donahue's cell in the Berkshire County House of Correction. Mazza had been brought into the courtroom with the jury out. Mazza repeatedly said to the court that he couldn't remember the statements he had made earlier to Ford. Because of his refusal to testify, Ford decided not to put Mazza on the stand in front of the jury.

One of the Commonwealth's witness stated that he had dropped his mother-in-law off at the bank. He and his 9-year-old son were sitting in their car in front of the bank waiting for her. Then his son called out look "dad there are three men coming out of the bank with guns in their hands and bags with money". The men stared at the father and son sitting in their car. The father jotted down the license plate number of the tan Plymouth getaway car. He then ran into the bank and grabbed the phone away from one of the tellers, who was talking to the police and gave them his information.

In Ford's closing argument, he stressed that while no one's testimony described Donahue as being in the bank at the time of the June 25 holdup, there was evidence showing that Donahue had been part of the trio that held up the bank and kept employees at bay with their guns. Ford also had one witness testify as to a conversation at the Berkshire House of Correction in which Donahue told about the bank robbery. Another witness a Lanesboro man placed Donahue behind the wheel of the getaway car. Donahue's attorney tried to discredit all of the Commonwealth witnesses.

Plainclothes officers were assigned to assist courthouse guards in the courtroom. For the first time Superior Court's new weapon's detector was used to check persons, entering the courtroom.

The jury was out for less than two hours before finding Donahue guilty of armed robbery while masked. Judge Kent B. Smith sentenced Donahue to life in prison.

SECOND ROBBER ARRESTED

Ralph Petroziello, 33, was arrested later on a warrant for the bank hold-up. In April, 1984, a trial was held in Superior Court before Judge William W. Simons. First Assistant District Attorney Daniel A. Ford prosecuted the case for the Commonwealth. Attorney Earle C. Cooley of the Boston law firm of Hale & Dorr was the defense counsel for Petroziello.

The defense brought in a surprise defense witness, Patrick J. O'Shea, an inmate at Walpole State Prison who was serving a life term plus 85 years for murdering one police officer and shooting another. O'Shea testified that he had been one of the men who robbed the bank. O'Shea was able to relate many details of the crime. Assistant District Attorney Ford said that he didn't believe O'Shea as he had "nothing to lose" by confessing to the crime. The same witnesses who testified in the Donahue trial in 1980 also testified in Petroziello's trail.

Several plain clothes state detectives and Pittsfield Detectives, along with six uniformed state troopers and deputy sheriffs, took their posts in the courtroom. Petroziello was led into the court room with his ankles shackled and his hands cuffed to a chain around his waist.

The jury who deliberated for four hours consisted of four women and eight men.

Clerk of Courts Deborah S. Capeless read the verdict after Judge Simons had looked at it. When she read the words "Not guilty", defense lawyer Earle C. Cooley, a large, gruff-voiced red head, threw his arms around his handcuffed client. Petroziello's brother, Joseph, shouted an approving "All right!" with Judge Simons banging his gavel saying "That's enough."

No handcuffs or ankle shackles were removed from Petroziello, as he still had to stand trial for an $110,000 bank robbery charge for robbing the Brockton Savings Bank. Petroziello had been indicted but not arraigned in the 1974 shooting murder of Boston Policeman Donald A. Brown, who was killed as he attempted to stop a holdup in Boston's Roslindale shopping center.

Defense attorney Cooley attributed his victory to police blunders. Smudged fingerprints were discarded after an investigator said they were "worthless." Evidence was lost after it was seized including the duffel bag in which the money was carried, some clothing and a pair of glasses. There was also conflicting testimony about how evidence, especially fingerprints, was gathered inside the bank.

First Assistant District Attorney Daniel A. Ford said he was "extremely disappointed and very surprised" at the verdict. He couldn't believe the jury would acquit someone accused of bank robbery just because the Police Department made a couple of mistakes. Nor did he understand how the testimony of four good, decent, law-abiding citizens could be ignored. All the officers who took part in the investigation were also surprised and disappointed, as they had put many hours into investigating the well planned bank robbery.

1980

Chief Stanley Stankiewicz

On November 20, 1980, Mayor Charles Smith appointed Captain Stanley Stankiewicz, Chief of Police. He served as chief until he retired on January 17, 1986. Captain Anthony Pires returned as commander of the Detective Division.

The department now had five vacancies: one Lieutenant, Michael White resigned and Sgt. Robert Rozon and three patrolmen retired.

In-service training classes were carried on during the year, thirty hours of training was required for every officer, each year. Included were: Firearms Training, Report Writing, and Sensitivity Training with various minority groups and Hostage Situations taught by the FBI.

An Internal Affairs Bureau was established, replacing the Intelligence Unit. Detectives Thomas Gero and Richard Henault, along with Officer

William Sturgeon were assigned to this bureau. Sergeant John Perrone returned to the Uniform Division. Sergeant Walter Boyer was assigned as the Department Court Prosecutor. There was one pedestrian traffic death.

CHIEF STANKIEWICZ AND OFFICERS
ON STEPS OF CITY HALL

1981

January 1, 1981 to June 30, 1981

Under Chapter 18, Section 7, of the City of Pittsfield Code, the reporting period changed, from a Calendar Year to a Fiscal Year. This Annual Report covered the last six months of 1981.

There were several changes in the structure of the department. Two new sergeants were appointed, LeRoy Fowler and David Reilly; one sergeant, John Perrone, retired. There were eleven vacancies: one captain, one lieutenant and nine patrolmen.

On January 1, 1981, under new requirements by the National Registry of Emergency Medical Technicians, all EMT-A's were required to meet the following qualifications: successful completion of the National Standard Refresher Course, twenty one hours; Annual Certification in CPR, twelve hours; completion of forty eight hours of additional continuing education. All officers were required to be certified.

There were three hundred School Patrol members, who performed their duties in all kinds of weather to safely assist their fellow students to and from school.

There were three fatal motor vehicle accidents and 1 murder during the first six months of the year. $1,103,183 was appropriated to run the department.

BANK ROBBERY ON EAST STREET

On January 28, 1981, Richard J. Sarkis, 41, unemployed, held up the East Street branch of the Berkshire Bank & Trust Co.

Sarkis, wearing a snowmobile suit, stepped up to a teller at 2:37 p.m., handed her a note demanding money, and held out a bag while the teller filled it. The teller put $1,835 into the bag. Sarkis held his hand inside the snowmobile suit, telling the teller he had a gun. Bank employees watched the robber disappear through a cluster of houses on Cove Street, at the rear of the bank.

At about 3:30 p.m., Sarkis took a taxi to the Holiday Inn in Lenox, where he rented a room. Sometime between 4 and 7 p.m. he hitchhiked backed to Pittsfield. Sarkis told detectives that he wedged a .357 magnum revolver between the back seat cushions of the car he rode in. Capt. William Dermody requested the motorists who picked up a man in a snowmobile suit from the area of the Holiday Inn in Lenox to contact the department. Family members said Sarkis was going to the Police Station to turn himself in. He was arrested on East Street at about 8:15 p.m. after detectives learned he was going to the GE Company to pick up a brother who worked there. Four cruisers converged on East Street and blocked off Silver Lake Boulevard, where he was arrested by Captain William Dermody, Detective Peter McGuire, Officers Thomas Guinan and Robert Levesque.

The department monitored all bank and some business alarms inside the station's communication room. There were around 30 alarms in the room, mounted on the wall next to the portable radio chargers. They were gray boxes about three inches by three inches with the bank's name or other business's names glued to them. Each box had a small, about the size of an eraser head on a pencil, red and green light and a reset button on it. When an alarm went off, a buzzing noise would alert the communication officer, the green light would go out and the red light would come on. At 2:37 p.m., the East Street alarm of Berkshire Bank & Trust Company went off inside the communication room. The communication officer sent a cruiser officer to the bank. Upon arriving at the bank, the officer found out it was a real bank robbery. Detectives were sent to start their investigation. The department's

Page 218

fingerprint expert, William Mason, lifted prints at the scene.

A Grand Jury indicted Sarkis of armed robbery. Sarkis was arraigned in Superior Court before Judge William W. Simons on February 5, 1981. Sarkis was not at his arraignment as he was undergoing psychiatric examinations. On July 29, 1982, Judge William W. Simons sentenced Richard Sarkis to five to seven years at Walpole State Prison. He was given 546 days credit for time spent in confinement awaiting disposition of his case.

NEARLY $20,000 STOLEN IN OLD COLONY BANK HOLD-UP

At the same time that Sarkis was being arraigned in Superior Court, another nearby bank was being held-up. February 5, 1981, was a cold winter day in Pittsfield, the temperature was in the single digits. Two men and a third one in a getaway car parked on West Street were holding up the Old Colony Bank on the corner of North and West Streets. The three made off with $19,866. Captain Anthony J. Pires, head of the Detective Bureau, stated that "Old Colony Bank job was the work of professionals, well-executed, perfectly timed and expertly cased beforehand". The entire operation was carried out in less than five minutes and was executed so flawlessly that customers and other employees in the bank did not find out about it until after the robbers had left.

Two men entered the bank from the West Street entrance at about 10:45 a.m., while a third man sat in the getaway car, which was parked illegally on West Street. The men made their way up the flight of stairs leading to the main banking area. They knew the exact location of the head teller's station next to the stairs, and went directly to it. One man brandished a handgun, while the second jumped over the counter into the station where bags of currency were awaiting shipment by armored car to the bank's branch offices. The pair grabbed the bags, ran down the stairs and sped off in the awaiting getaway car.

Vice-president and cashier Joseph Duffy, standing near an open window facing West Street, saw the two men get into the getaway car. He shouted out a series of numbers, which was the plate number on the car. He also phoned the Police Station with the plate number.

The getaway car was reported stolen at 7:30 a.m. from Commonwealth Avenue. It was later recovered on South Church Street. The plates on the car were stolen from a car parked at Riverview West. A resident of South Church Street told detectives she watched three men transferring canvas bags from the getaway car to a dark brown car. She made several attempts to call the Police Station, but couldn't get through.

Detective Edward Sherman, one of the detectives working on the robbery, said that both men were believed to be in their 30s, had treated their hair with a streaking or graying hair spray, and were wearing false gray mustaches. One of the mustaches was found in the getaway car. No arrests were ever made in the case.

CHAPTER TWENTY-EIGHT

AUCTIONEER SHOT IN HEAD

On February 18, 1981, shortly before 10:00 p.m., John L. Fontaine, 53, of Gamwell Avenue was shot in the head at close range. Fontaine was an auctioneer, antiques dealer and restaurateur. Fontaine was sitting in his late model Cadillac Biarritz parked outside El Italia Sub Shop at 416 Tyler Street. He was shot with a handgun; several empty cartridge casings were on the pavement near the car, indicating that the weapon was an automatic and not a revolver.

EMPTY CARTRIDGES
FOUND ON GROUND

Customers who were inside the sub shop when the shooting occurred said several shots rang out immediately after Fontaine's car had parked. Moments later, a car roared out of the parking lot on the west side of sub shop and drove across Tyler Street and up Glenwood Avenue. Customers rushing outside were able to give a description of the assailant and his car, a maroon Chevrolet Camaro.

A woman appeared near Fontaine's car and began screaming. She had come out of a house next to the sub shop, wearing a dress but not coat. She fainted and sank to the ground. Later identified as Mrs. Arthur R. Martin, she was inside the house negotiating a lease for a shop to house her antiques business. Fontaine was parked in his car waiting for Mrs. Martin.

Chief Stanley Stankiewicz was at the scene with Detective Captain Anthony J. Pires and night shift commander, Capt. William Dermody. From Mrs. Martin, it was determined they were looking for Arthur R. Martin, 55, her ex-husband. A 13-state bulletin was immediately filed for Martin.

Subsequent investigation determined that Martin had left Pittsfield about a year ago and was living in the Albany, New York area. A combined task force from the New York State Police, Albany Municipal Police and Bethlehem Police Department spotted Martin's car outside a bar where he had been living. Martin was inside the bar and surrendered without a struggle.

District Attorney Anthony J. Ruberto Jr. and First Assistant District Attorney Daniel A. Ford prosecuted the case for the Commonwealth. Martin was found guilty of 2nd degree murder. He was sentenced to the mandatory sentence of life in prison by Judge Lawrence A. Urbano in his eight day trial in Superior Court.

Martin's attorney George B. Crane made an appeal to the sentence, which was automatic. Crane did not deny any of the state's allegations about the how, when and where of the murder. Instead he entered a defense calling for a finding of not guilty by reason of insanity. Martin's conviction was overturned by the Appeals court in 1984 because of testimony given by a psychiatrist that Martin had been aware of the wrongfulness of his act. The Appeals Court said the evidence violated Martin's right to confidentiality in his statements during mental examination. Testimony about the defendant's mental state is admissible, but testimony in which the defendant admits guilt to an examining doctor is not admissible.

Martin's appeal was won after his case was taken up by former Western New England College law professor, John Thompson. Work on the case was done through the college's Prisoner Legal Assistance Clinic, made up of 10 to 15 students taking a semester-long course. The students did research, wrote briefs and drafted motion in the case. Thompson argued the appeals.

In October of 1985, Martin pleaded guilty to the reduced charge of manslaughter before Judge John F. Murphy and was sentenced to 14 to 20 years at Cedar Junction State Prison in Walpole. Martin was also given a sentence of 3-to-5 years to run concurrently, for carrying a gun without a firearm identification card.

1982

FISCAL YEAR
July 1, 1981 to June 30, 1982

Chief Stanley Stankiewicz, in his second Annual Fiscal Year Report, stated that four new officers were added to the department: John Grady, Terrance Donnelly, Ronald Kitterman and Ronald Dean. Veteran Officer Edward Descz retired and one officer resigned, leaving vacancies in the following ranks: one captain, one lieutenant, eleven patrolmen.

There were three fatal accidents during the year, a decrease of two accidents from the previous year. There were three murders. A $5,000.00 grant was received from the Governor's Highway Safety Bureau and an Operation Aware Program was implemented, allowing extra cruisers to patrol the streets during the peak hours on the weekend and when fatalities usually occur.

THE NEW POLICE EMBLEM

Representatives from both the Pittsfield Police Association and Police Union went to Chief Stanley Stankiewicz wanting to change the department's uniform patch. The triangular patch, worn on the left shoulder of uniform shirts, was an embroidered figure of an Indian beneath the words "Pittsfield Police." The triangle shape was once popular, but most departments in the state had changed to some version of the shield shape. The representatives wanted a design that better represented Pittsfield.

OLD EMBLEM

Chief Stankiewicz assigned Officers John T. O'Neil and Robert Benoit to work out a design. The officers did research at the Berkshire Athenaeum to help pick a new symbol that represented Pittsfield. Park Square was chosen because it was a historical and prominent part of the city. The patch featured a 19th-century view of Park Square, with the Civil War Memorial in the center. The dates when Pittsfield was established as a town and then as a city were placed on the sides. Theresa Chamberland, an artist from Richmond and close friend of O'Neil's wife, drew the sketch that was submitted to the uniform company. This design would also replace the blue-and-white seal that marked the sides of the cruisers.

The first patches were a light gold, both border and lettering. After a year, the patches were changed to a silver border and silver lettering for patrolmen and a dark gold border and lettering for superior officers.

DOUBLE MURDER AND SUICIDE

On March 9, 1982, the bodies of Melinda Daniels, 33 , and her two children, Lisa 5, and Dale 9, were found shot to death in a car in the Pittsfield Cemetery just off of Wahconah Street. Detectives who investigated the deaths reported that Melinda used a .22-caliber pistol she bought from a gun shop. After driving to the cemetery, she put cotton in the kids' ears, blindfolds over their eyes, shot both of them in the chest, and then took her own life. Mrs. Daniels, a former mental patient, had received from the Pittsfield Police, on March 3, a permit to purchase a pistol and firearm identification (FID) card, but never obtained a permit to carry the weapon. The permit allowed her to buy a gun and have it delivered to her home address within 10 days. But Melinda didn't want to wait that long. The following day, she drove to a gun shop where she had known the owners since she was a young girl, and somehow managed to walk out with the .22- caliber revolver in her hand.

40th BIRTHDAY PARTY LEADS TO MURDER

On Wednesday, April 7, 1982, a fight broke out between James Gerwaski, 24, and James E. McGovern, 19, while they were celebrating the 40th birthday of Rena Howard at her Christopher Arms apartment. The day had been one of drinking at several local bars, pot smoking, and continuing rounds of fights, particularly between Gerwaski's two girlfriends, Rena Howard and Linda Graham.

A joint investigation was conducted by Pittsfield Detectives and detectives assigned to the District Attorney's office. Gerwaski gave two written, signed statements and three oral statements, admitting that he stabbed McGovern; all statements different.

First Assistant District Attorney Daniel A. Ford prosecuted the case for the Commonwealth in Superior Court before Judge F. Moriarty, in a jury-waived trial. Robert E. Santaniello of Springfield was the court-appointed lawyer representing Gerwaski. This was the second time Gerwaski was found guilty of the fatal stabbing. Judge Charles L. Albert had accepted a guilty plea early in September, after Attorney George B. Crane had negotiated the charge from murder to manslaughter with the District Attorney's office.

Judge Alberti had delayed imposing sentence, pending a pre-sentencing report from Berkshire Superior Court Probation Department. Gerwaski told the probation officer that he had pled guilty to something he didn't do. The judge ordered the plea withdrawn and a trial held. At his trial he said he "confessed" to the stabbing because "I was trying to tell them what they wanted to hear so they would get off my back." He told the judge that he signed the statement, produced by Assistant District Attorney Ford, "because I had been drinking beer and smoking pot all day and I was mellowing out and was tired." Gerwaski said he had only pretended to read the statement because he signed it and that it was "all a blur."

Assistant District Attorney Ford accused James of lying "all over the place" in his cross-examination, recommending that Judge Moriarty return a verdict of second-degree murder, pointing out that it was "a very violent crime". Dr. John Valigorsky Medical Examiner said it was a single stab wound in the upper abdomen that caused the death. He described the wound as being 5 to 6 inches deep, severing the main artery or aorta. He also said that the knife that penetrated the victim's abdomen was stopped by the victim's spinal column, and indicated that the fatal wound was delivered with "some force."

Judge Moriarty noted that Gerwaski had a previous record of violent crimes, saying, "I am satisfied that the defendant did, in fact, stab the victim. I think he stabbed him intentionally, but I don't think he intended to kill him." Ruling it was a case of "sudden combat", he found Gerwaski guilty of manslaughter and sentenced him to 10 to 15 years in Walpole State Prison.

1983

FISCAL YEAR
July 1, 1982 to June 30, 1983

In his Annual Report, Chief Stanley J. Stankiewicz stated, that under new regulations all officers must be trained as Emergency Medical Technicians-Ambulance. Under the new requirements by the National Registry of Emergency Medical Technicians, all EMT-A's must successfully complete the National Standard Refresher Course of 21hours; annual certification in CPR, 12 hours and additional continuing education classes. The department made over 1,000 ambulance runs during the year. One officer from the communication room would drive the ambulance and picked up two officers walking their beat on North Street, usually post 3 and 4. The city collected over $109,000 in ambulance fees.

Chief Stankiewicz noted that the Civilian Defense Auxiliary Police, which were established in 1941, during World War II, donated 9,811 manhours during the year. They assisted the regular force in vandalism patrols and directed traffic at the accident scenes. There were 1,185 accidents, with 3 fatal accidents during the year.

CHAPTER TWENTY-NINE

1984

FISCAL YEAR
July 1, 1983 to June 30, 1984

STABBED AND BEATEN TO DEATH

On December 15, 1983, Karen A. Gromacki, 23, was found dead by her sister on the kitchen floor in their family house. Death was caused by three or four hammer blows to the head. She had also been stabbed 15 times in the right chest with steak and butcher knives.

Miss Gromacki and Timothy A. Spaniol, 27, had dated for four years and had lived together briefly in Florida, returning to Massachusetts in October, 1982. They lived for a while with her mother and sisters on Plinn Street and then for three weeks at his Center Street home.

On December 11, Miss Gromacki did not show up for work. On December 12 she moved back home with one side of her face bruised black and blue. On this day she also petitioned for and received in Pittsfield District Court a restraining order preventing Timothy Spaniol for contacting her. On December 13, Spaniol went to the Plinn Street home attempting reconciliation and on December 15, he returned to the Plinn Street house. They had an argument in the kitchen where Spaniol killed her with a claw hammer with blows to the head. She was also stabbed 15 times in the right chest with steak and butcher knives.

Police received an anonymous phone call that Spaniol was still in the neighborhood, where he once lived. They had been searching the Keeler Street area all night long. At about 8:00 a.m., Officer Michael Case spotted Spaniol on a hill in back of St. Joseph's Cemetery. Spaniol was near a tree with a rope dangling from one of the branches.

Captain William Dermody, Detectives Edward Sherman and Joseph Collias, along with Officer Case, began the chase for Spaniol, which lasted for about 10 minutes before Spaniol surrendered himself in the woods near Orlando Avenue. Captain Dermody said several warning shots were fired during the chase. Spaniol owned several firearms, but was unarmed when arrested.

Five and one-half hours after his 8:00 a.m. capture at gunpoint, Spaniol pleaded not guilty to killing his former girlfriend. Judge Bernard Lenhoff appointed attorney Francis X. Spina to be Spaniol's counsel. Defense attorneys for indigent accused murderers are chosen from a list of judge-approved lawyers, who are generally more experienced in capital-offense cases. Besides Spina, only two other attorneys were on the county's list, Attorney George B. Crane and Leonard H. Cohen, both of whom had recently tried murder cases. The Public Defender's Committee, which normally represents indigent defendants, is prohibited by law from representing murder defendants.

A grand jury secretly indicted Spaniol on murder charges. On his arraignment in Superior Court, Judge William W. Simmons appointed attorney Francis K. Spina to represent Spaniol. First Assistant District Attorney Daniel A. Ford handed the arraignment and requested a bail of $100,000, which Judge Simmons set.

On May 4, 1984, the facts of the case were presented to Judge Charles R. Alberti in Superior Court. Judge Alberti questioned Spaniol having him explain what had happened. After hearing Spaniol's explanation, Judge Alberti asked Spaniol, "You are freely and willingly accepting the fact that you murdered her?" Spaniol said "Yes". Judge Alberti then accepting, Spaniol pleaded guilty to second-degree murder. Judge Alberti sentenced Spaniol to life in Walpole State Prison.

EMERGENCY 911 CALL NUMBER

On June 9, 1984, Pittsfield's new 911 emergency telephone number was hooked up and ready to receive emergency calls. At a press conference in the communications room of the department, Mayor Charles L. Smith, Chief Stanley Stankiewicz, and Civil Defense Director Thomas Grizey explained that any emergency call, including fire, police and ambulance, may be made by dialing the universal number, 911. Chief Stankiewicz said the 911 system should reduce the number of false accident and fire calls by making it possible to trace calls, even when the caller hangs up first. Decals depicting a black phone dial, with a red center and the number 911, were affixed to police cars to help publicize the system.

The fire alarm dispatchers, who were housed in the Fire Alarm building on Tyler Street next to the old fire station, were moved into the Police Department Communication Room. They now became part of the department's dispatchers unit.

1985

FISCAL YEAR
July 1, 1984 TO June 30, 1985

TWO MASKED BANK ROBBERS

On January 20, 1985, two masked and armed males held up the branch office of City Savings Bank on Williams Street. The pair, described by Captain William Dermody as "knowing what they were doing", struck at 11:26 a.m. Both dressed in "army-type" olive green one piece suits, and green knit masks, wearing glove. One was armed with a sawed-off double-barreled shotgun the other with an unknown type pistol.

The four female employees were forced at gun point to lie on the floor in the small back office. A lone male customer was forced to sit in the middle of the lobby floor. The robber with the sawed-off shotgun kept watch on the employees and the male customer. The robber with the pistol went behind the counter and filled two duffel bags with $18,500, from the safe and tellers' drawers. One of the tellers was on the phone with the main office talking to a bank officer. She dropped the phone when the robbers came into the bank and started ordering them around. The bank officer heard the yelling and called the department reporting the hold-up.

They escaped by getting into a 1977 Pontiac Trans Am sports car, stolen from the Albany, New York Airport. Its ignition had been popped so it could be started without a key. This car was found on Dillon Street about a half-mile from the bank, with the engine still running. It had on it a stolen plate that was taken from a similar make Pontiac parked on Union Street. Officer Robert Karpeck was dispatched to the bank, arriving within two minutes after the robbers sped off in the Pontiac Trans Am.

Acting Police Chief Anthony J. Pires arrived at the bank with a team of detectives. Talking to a witness, who was in her parked car waiting to go into the bank. They were able to get a description of the male with the sawed-off shot gun. He was about 5 feet, 10 inches tall, in his mid-20s, with brownish-red hair just below his ears, and a long Fu-Manchu-style mustache. The male with the pistol was about 5 feet, 8 inches tall. No one saw his face or could describe any special characteristics he had.

Within hours a Ford station wagon that the robbers had parked on Dillon Street was found still running in a Coltsville parking lot, with one of the duffel bags behind the front seat. There were a few bills still in the bag. No witnesses could be found by detectives as to what kind of car they escaped in. Investigator James D. Winn of the department's ID bureau dusted both cars for prints but none were found. No arrests have ever been made in this robbery.

TWO STABBED-ONE FATALLY

On April 21, 1985, John Scaduto, 63, of Woodlawn Avenue, stabbed Evan B. Smith, 28, of Lincoln Street multiple times. Evan B. "Herbie" Smith was pronounced dead on his arrival at Berkshire Medical Center. His brother Cary Smith, 30, of Grant Street, Springfield was also stabbed multiple times. Cary underwent lengthy surgery for stab wounds to the chest and abdomen and was in critical condition.

Dr. Jeffrey S. Ross, Berkshire County Medical Examiner, who performed an autopsy on Smith, said that his throat had been cut and that there were five stab wounds in his chest. Dr. Ross determined the cause of death as homicide.

The Police Department received a call at 2:33 a.m., reporting that two victims of a knifing were lying at the corner of Lincoln and Cherry Streets, outside the apartment of Scaduto's daughter.

The event that led up to the stabbings was an argument between Scaduto and the Smith brothers. The two brothers had been drinking with Scaduto's daughter at Danny's Bar on Fourth Street all evening. Scaduto had been babysitting for his grandson all evening. Scaduto was angry because his daughter remained at the bar and because Evan Smith had reportedly beaten her up that night. The argument started at Danny's Bar and continued up to the corner of Lincoln and Cherry Streets, where the stabbings occurred.

Witnesses at the scene said that police arrived almost immediately, while the suspect's car was still there, but were unable to pursue Scaduto, because the bodies were in the road. Officers blocked off traffic at the Fourth and Lincoln and at Cherry and Lincoln and conducted an on-site investigation while Scaduto's car was being sought. Scaduto was stopped about 45 minutes later on Route 8 in Cheshire by State Troopers Erin Thompson and

Frank Hart, who were assigned to the Cheshire barracks. The troopers acted on the description given police by witnesses who said they saw the alleged assailant flee the scene in a silver gray older model Chevrolet Impala. Captain William M. Dermody and Lt. Walter M. Boyer went to the scene and arrested Scaduto for murder after being notified of his capture.

At his trial in Superior Court before Judge John F. Murphy, Scaduto's defense counsel, Francis X. Spina, presented six witnesses to testify for Scaduto. Their defense was that Scaduto acted in self-defense. Scaduto said Evan Smith pulled a knife on him, which he took away and used to stab both men. Hospital tests showed the two Smiths to have blood-alcohol levels far above the level considered to indicate intoxication.

First Assistant District Attorney Daniel A. Ford told Judge Murphy that people could understand and sympathize with Scaduto's motives, but not his actions. He called the slaying an act of extreme violence and cruelty.

Scaduto pleaded guilty to the reduced charges of manslaughter and attempted manslaughter and was sentenced to 8 to 12 years at Cedar Junction State Prison in Walpole. He also pleaded guilty to a charge of assault and battery with a dangerous weapon.

1986

FISCAL YEAR
July 1, 1985 TO June 30, 1986

Chief William M. Dermody

Promotions, appointments, retirements, and resignations highlighted Chief William Dermody's first six months Annual Report. Chief Stanley J. Stankiewicz went out on disability on January 17, 1986, and Captain William M. Dermody was appointed chief on January 21, 1986 by the Mayor

Charles Smith, serving until his retirement on October 1, 1988. Patrolman Robert Karpeck was appointed sergeant on July 1, 1985, and resigned from the department on March 29, 1986. John Grady and Benedetto Sciola were appointed sergeants on June 29, 1986. Two patrolmen, Robert Smith and Samuel Dean, resigned. Seven new patrolmen were appointed: John Mc-Grath, James Hunt, Thomas Bowler, David Herforth, Matthew Pictrowski, Michael Ortega and Walter Powell. Five patrolmen retired during the year: James Danford, Ralph Pivero, Thomas Guinan, Bernard Auge and Ralph Pisani.

The Detective Bureau was now actively involved in putting on seminars on child abuse, child kidnapping and other related crimes where children are victims. These seminars were being presented to parents' groups. The bureau has established its own investigator for suspicious fires and worked in liaison with the fire department in the investigation of these cases.

There were a total of six fatal accidents and no murders during the year. The Auxiliary Police donated in excess of 10,000 man hours during the year.

ELM STREET BANK ROBBERY

On Monday, September 16, 1985, three men one, armed with military.45-caliber automatic pistol, robbed the Elm Street branch of the First Agricultural Bank of $42,000. The three men arrived at the bank at 9:38 a.m., the designated time for Berkshire Armored Car to make a pickup at the bank. This was the third bank robbery that had taken place just before an armored car pick up. Two men, both described as white males in their mid-30s to early 40s wearing sunglasses, entered the bank. The male with the .45- caliber automatic told the customers waiting in line "Nobody move." The other kicked open the door to the tellers' area and grabbed two bank bags. One bag had $42,000 in cash the other held only canceled checks, food stamps and paperwork. They were in and out within 30 seconds. They escaped in a white four-door Chevrolet Chevette. They obtained the two moneybags and fled just before the armored car arrived.

The car was found some 10 minutes later by Officers Thomas Harris and Craig Strout in the parking lot of the A&P Supermarket just up the street from the bank. The car was stolen Sunday in East Greenbush, New York, and Massachusetts tags were placed on it by the robbers.

Detective Bureau Captain William (Bill) M. Dermody said the robbers didn't leave many clues. They were professionals who didn't panic and weren't nervous. Captain Dermody assigned Detectives Joseph D. Collias and Gary W. Danford to the case along with the FBI from the Springfield Office. The FBI was called in because the money was guaranteed by the Federal Deposit Insurance Corp.

The white four-door Chevrolet Chevette that was found in the A&P parking lot was towed to the department's garage. FBI agents dusted the car for prints and also dusted the teller's door at the bank. No prints were found because all three of the robbers wore gloves. The bank's observation cameras did not effectively identify the robbers because it was too dark in the bank.

Investigators brought in an artist to do a composite drawing of the two that were in the bank. Wanted posters were made up and distributed. The composite drawings were published in the Berkshire Eagle and other papers, posted in post offices and other public places. No arrests were ever made in this robbery and the case is still open.

COMPOSITE DRAWINGS OF
TWO WHO HELD UP BANK

1987

FISCAL YEAR
July 1, 1986 TO June 30, 1987

ONE SHOT TO HEAD

On Monday, September 8, 1986, Edward L. Poole, 23, shot Richard Lusignan, 34, of Lincoln Street. Lusignan was shot with a stolen .25-caliber handgun with one shot behind the right ear. The shooting occurred during an argument between the two men. Lusignan was taken to BMC shortly after police found him at his home at 1:30 a.m. Monday morning after being called to his apartment. Poole was originally charged with assault and battery with a dangerous weapon and attempted murder. These charges were dismissed when the murder charge was brought, after Lusignan died at Berkshire Medical Center. The murder stemmed from "bad blood" between Poole and Lusignan over the woman Lusignan lived with, according to facts presented in court by First District Attorney Daniel A. Ford. The two men shared "some degree of affection" with Alice Lee, 23, of Lincoln Street, though she was living with Lusignan.

MURDER BY .25-CALIBER HAND GUN

On the night of the shooting, Lee returned from a bar, saw Lusignan on the couch, and assumed he was asleep. After taking the last cigarette from a pack next to Lusignan, she left to get more cigarettes. She met Poole outside her door and walked with him to a store on Tyler Street. On the way back from the store Poole asked her, "What would you say if I told you I shot him?" When Poole convinced her he was serious, Lee ran back home and found a gunshot wound on Lusignan's head. Alice Lee called the Police.

Poole made a confession to Lt. Gerald M. Lee, after being arrested. A search warrant was obtained by Detective Peter T. McGuire, based on this confession. The warrant was so that a gunpowder test could be made of Poole's hands to determine if he had fired a gun recently. A search warrant was needed because this test is technically a search.

In his confession, Poole said he said had stolen the gun from a former landlord earlier that summer. He broke into Lusignan and Lee's apartment by reaching through a broken window on a side door. After an argument with Lusignan, he shot him. Poole met up with Lee when he returned to the apartment to see if Lusignan needed any help. Poole stated he had been drinking prior to the shooting at a bar on Tyler Street.

The charges against Poole were reduced to second-degree murder. The mandatory sentence for second-degree murder is life in prison with parole eligibility after 15 years. Assistant District Attorney Ford said the charge could be reduced to second-degree murder because some people who saw Poole earlier on the night of the shooting and said he was intoxicated. Premeditation is required for first-degree murder. Ford said intoxication is considered a valid argument against premeditation. Judge Lawrence Urbano agreed that a sufficient amount of alcohol can eliminate premeditation.

In addition to the life sentence, Urbano imposed sentences of 10 to 15 years and three to five years in Walpole for burglary with an assault on an occupant, carrying a firearm without authority, and assault in a dwelling. All sentences were served at the same time as the life sentence and did not change the parole eligibility date.

JULY 4, 1986-CHIEF WILLIAM DERMODY

SIX NEW OFFICERS

On October 19, 1986, six new officers were appointed to the force. They were: Charles Bassett, Thomas Harrington, John Mullin, Russell Quetti, Mark Lenihan and Karen Smith

On March 15, 1987, Officer John T. O'Neil was appointed to sergeant by Mayor Charles Smith and Chief William M. Dermody assigned him to Administrative Sergeant in the Records Bureau.

On November 18, 1987, six more officers were appointed to bring the force up to full strength. They were: James Stimpson, Thomas Barber, Robert Conklin, Christopher Kennedy, John Kubica and James McIntyre.

1988

FISCAL YEAR
July 1, 1987 TO June 30, 1988

Chief William M. Dermody submitted the department's Annual Report to the mayor and city councilors. In it he described the functions of each of the divisions of the department. He noted that the Identification Bureau had now been in existence for seventeen years, Investigator William Mason worked the day shift and Investigator James Winn work the second shift. These two officers did all the crime scene work in conjunction with the detective bureau.

The Traffic Bureau under Sgt. David Boyer and five officers investigated 5 fatal accidents during the year. They supervised 35 School Crossing Guards and 300 schoolboy patrol members.

Safety Officer Raymond Shogry taught children safety programs in all the schools. His talks were on the dangerous consequences of alcohol, drugs and driving while under the influence of alcohol. He also talked to other businesses, such as the telephone company, banks, bus terminals and insurance companies. The Chief also noted that there were 42 retired officers still alive.

1989

FISCAL YEAR
July 1, 1988 TO June 30, 1989

SHOOTOUT ON UPPER NORTH STREEET

For the first time, the department's Tactical Operations Unit was called into service at 6:00 a.m. on Friday, July 22, 1988. The unit had been training for some time without any call outs. On that morning, the department received a call from Mrs. Maryann M. Peck, saying that her son David L. Peck, 53 had barricaded himself inside his bedroom and threatened to blow up the house and kill anyone who tried to stop him. Mrs. Peck was worried because her son had not taken his medication.

The house was on upper North Street, Route 7 morning traffic from Giovanni's Restaurant to the Lanesboro town line was shut down. At about 7:40 a.m., David Peck climbed out of his bedroom window onto roof firing a .22-caliber rifle at an officer who was in the bedroom of the next door neighbor's house. Peck had been throwing furniture, clothing, golf clubs and numerous items out of his window. Among them were two realistic-looking homemade explosive devices; these were turned over to the State Police Bomb Squad who determined that there were no explosives in them. Peck had stuffed cardboard tubes with a substance and used nylon rope to make the devices look like bombs. Peck also started a small fire in his bed-room. Before climbing onto the roof, he shot through the wall into the hall-way where two officers were stationed trying to talk him into surrendering.

Just as Peck took aim to fire another round at the officer in the next door neighbor's house, a member of the Tactical Unit fired one round striking Peck in the right arm with fragments of the bullet lodging in his chest. He was taken by ambulance to BMC where he underwent surgery.

Peck was arraigned in his hospital bed on the following Monday, charged with 5 counts of assault with intent to murder, four counts on a police of-ficers and one on a civilian. Six days later, Peck appeared in District Court before Judge Clement A. Ferris who ordered him to undergo a 20-day psy-chiatric examination at Northampton State Hospital. In Berkshire Superior Court David Peck was found incompetent to stand trial and was remanded to a State Hospital.

STABBED 21 TIMES - STRANGLED - SEVERE BEATING - BROKEN BACK LEADS TO MURDER

On August 30, 1988, Nancy M. Fallon, 32, of Dalton, stopped by Dan-ny's Bar on Fourth Street for a few cocktails. Nancy left the bar just before midnight by herself, heading home. She lived with her boyfriend, Richard C. Grace, and her 5 year old daughter, Jocelyn. On September 2, Grace reported Nancy missing. The Berkshire Eagle ran a story about her disap-pearance.

An investigation was started, and on September 3 Nancy's car was found abandoned on a street in Marlboro with blood stains inside and out. Blood stains, a tire iron, car floor mats and a blood-stained jacket belonging to Nancy were found at the rest area, in Hancock on Route 20. A state police tracking dog found Nancy's body partially buried under tree limbs, dirt and leaves in the woods along Route 20 in Hancock. A palm print was found on the outside window of Nancy's hatchback. Checking the fingerprint data base, a match was found. The print belonged to David Talbot. After his arrest, blood matching Nancy's type was found in the seam of Talbot's cow-boy boots.

Detectives learned that while at the bar she had a conversation with Patrick Michael Burke, 24, of Fitchburg. Burke had been out of jail on parole for less than two months. He had served almost 5 years of a 6-10 year sentence for aggravated rape in 1983. Seated next to Burke was David Talbot, 25, of Pittsfield, who was just out of prison, on parole for four days. Talbot severed almost 8 years of a 15-year sentence for an armed robbery conviction in 1981 of a Cumberland Farms Store with two older men. Burke and Talbot met each other while serving time in Concord State Prison.

PATRICK MICHAEL BURKE   DAVID TALBOT

While in prison Talbot became "President" of the Northern Gentlemen's Club. The club was a small group of inmates who communicate in secret code and anyone who dishonored the trust of the group would be killed.

Trooper Patricia A. Driscoll became the lead investigator into the murder case, as the body was found in Hancock and not in Pittsfield.

After an intensive investigation by State Police Detectives and Pittsfield Detectives, both Patrick Burke and David Talbot were arrested and appeared in District Court, eight days after the murder. Before their arraignment attorneys George Crane and Francis X. Spina were appointed to represent them. Assistant District Attorney Lee D. Flournoy was prosecutor for the Commonwealth, assisted by Assistant District Attorney Robert J. Carnes. Carnes stated that the murder was an "extreme atrocity involving strangling, stabbing, facial fractures, a broken back and a serve beating. The official cause of death was multiple stab wounds. Talbot had made some incriminating statements the day after the murder. Burke had visible blood stains on his clothing the day after the murder and had a deep cut on his hand. He also confessed to a 15-year-old girl that he himself "killed a woman and threw the knife in the woods." This was Nancy's pocket knife.

In his three day trial in Superior Court before a deliberating jury of eight women and four men, Burke was found guilty of first-degree murder on May 26, 1989. Assistant District Attorney Lee D. Flournoy was prosecutor for the Commonwealth. In her closing statement Flournoy said Fallon had been so brutally stabbed and beaten that "she was killed three times

The jury was only out for less than three hours before returning their finding. Judge George F. Keady, Jr., sentenced Burke to mandatory life term in the state prison at Cedar Junction in Walpole without the possibility of parole.

The trial of David A. Talbot charged with first-degree murder began one month after Patrick Burke's did in June. Assistant District Attorney Lee D. Flournoy was also the prosecutor in this case. She put the premise before the jury that Talbot and Burke followed Nancy out of Danny's bar. Burke was in the driver seat, Nancy in the passenger seat and Talbot in the back. Burke made advances to Nancy, but she said no and pulled out her pocket knife. Burke grabbed the pocket knife and began stabbing her. Talbot in the back seat grabbed Nancy, holding her while Burke repeatedly stabbed her. Blood splattered all over the windshield.

The pants worn by Burke and Talbot had human bloodstains on them and both men and Nancy had similar soil stains on their clothing. After burying Nancy in the woods on West Mountain, they drove to Marlboro, drank heavily with friends, and forgot where they left Nancy's car.

Attorney William J. Fennell of Springfield put his client, Talbot, on the stand. Talbot blamed Burke for the murder. Burke didn't testify at his trail. The jury was only out for four and one-half hours before bring a verdict of second-degree murder and larceny of Nancy's car.

Superior Court Judge William W. Simons sentenced Talbot to life in prison. That sentence would begin after he finished any sentence he was now serving. Talbot also received a 3 to 5 year sentence for the larceny of Nancy's car, to be served concurrently with the life sentence. By statue a person serving a life sentence can be eligible for parole in 15 years.

CHAPTER THIRTY

DIED IN THE LINE OF DUTY
OFFICER TIMOTHY M. SHEPARD

On September 19, 1988, four members of the department started their 14 week basic training class at the Massachusetts Criminal Justice Training Academy, Agawam. They were officers: Timothy M. Shepard, Jeffrey J. Kemp, Dwane Fosiy and Glenn S. Civello. There were 50 trainees from 18 different police departments in Western Massachusetts.

It was Monday and all cadets were on the track jogging. Cadet Shepard and Civello were keeping up well. Civello said "we went around a corner, when Timothy kept going straight ahead. Then he fell down." Civello said classmates had no idea when he collapsed that he was seriously ill. "We figured it was heat exhaustion or something. That first day was a tough day."

Shepard, 25, was taken to Baystate Medical Center in Springfield in critical condition and place in the intensive care unit and placed on life support systems because of serious kidney damage. He was unconscious.

Two more cadets became ill Tuesday and two more Wednesday, all with one or more of a group of symptoms that included muscular pain, fever, nausea, abdominal pain and dark urine. A total of 21 cadets were stricken seven hospitalized the other 14 were treated and released. None of the academy staff members were affected. The cadets suffered from kidney problems brought on by exhaustion and dehydration.

After learning of Shepard's condition, Mayor Anne Everest Wojkowski had the remaining three Pittsfield cadets interviewed and sent to Berkshire Medical Center for examination and tests. As a result, Cadet Jeffrey J. Kemp was admitted to BMC intensive unit and put on intravenous therapy.

All cadets were called at their homes and told to get blood and urine tests at their local emergency rooms.

Gary F. Eagan, director of the Massachusetts Criminal Justice Training Council, said that although cadets had been told to drink only bottled water, some had taken drinks from taps in the bathroom sinks at the academy. The academy is at the end of the town water line and staff members avoided drinking tap water because it is discolored.

Timothy emerged from the coma he was in after about four weeks. He had a liver transplant on September 27 at Presbyterian University Hospital in Pittsburgh and was able to recognize his mother and pregnant wife, Holly. He was able to respond to questions by shaking his head. Doctors had been able to remove his respirator for brief periods of time. He was even able to write his wife, "I made it," although he was too weak to breathe or speak on his own.

Then on October 31, he fell unconscious again and was rushed into emergency surgery to remove a blood clot on his brain. He never regained consciousness and was pronounced dead at 11:00 p.m. on Wednesday, 44 days after collapsing. An autopsy revealed that Shepard died from complications which were attributed to inadequate water and excessive exercise during the training session.

Shepard's death was the subject of an inquest to determine whether criminal charges should be brought against the state troopers in charge of the training. The two state troopers in charge of cadet training requested and received a transfer from the academy. The head of the state's police training program resigned.

Five days before Shepard's death, Attorney General James Shannon released the results of a month-long investigation into the illnesses. The investigation found a "massive failure" of the system that led to abusive training.

Officer Timothy M. Shepard's funeral was held on Tuesday, November 8, 1988, at St. Joseph's Church with the Most Rev. Joseph F. Maguire, bishop of the Roman Catholic Diocese of Springfield, celebrating the Liturgy of Christian Burial. Also on the alter with the bishop were twenty white-robed priests

The funeral was one of the largest in recent memory in Pittsfield. It was marked by precision and pomp of 500 police officers, sixty cruisers, motorcycles and four horses all while keeping step to a solemn drummed cadence up North Street from the Berkshire Hilton Inn to St. Joseph's Church for Mass and then to the cemetery for the burial.

At first Shepard's family requested that the state police cancel their plans to participate in the cadet's funeral. Then Mayor Anne Everest Wojtkowski, who had acted as press liaison for the family said the request that the state police not participate in the funeral was "made impulsively by a grief-stricken family. That the family reconsidered and agreed that there are many fine and compassionate state policemen and they should be made welcome." The state police did scale back on their plans, and about 10 troopers from Western Massachusetts did attend.

At least 50 cities and towns from as far as Nantucket and Albany were represented. Boston's Metropolitan District Commission sent 50 officers, four mounted on horses. Most of the 86 officers from Pittsfield had white gloves and black shrouds on their badges marched with Acting Chief Cosmo Spezzaferro at the helm. The 46 cadets still in training at Agawam and 40 officers from Springfield also marched.

Flying in from Boston by helicopter to attend the funeral were Lt. Gov. Evelyn Murphy, state Public Safety Secretary Charles Barry, Public Safety Commissioner William McCabe, and Peter Agnes, who abolished stress training for cadets as his first duty as the interim head of the Massachusetts Criminal Justice Training Council. U.S. Rep. Silvio O. Conte was among the mourners, as were Mayors Anne Everest Wojtkowski of Pittsfield and John Barrett III of North Adams.

In the front row St. Joseph's Church was Shepard's family: his wife Holly, her mother Joy Mendel, her father Bruce Mendel, a former Pittsfield Police Officer himself. Timothy's parents, Thomas and Ellen, his brothers, Thomas and Christopher, and his sisters, Teresa and Sarah.

All the flags in the city flew at half-mast. Each year for Memorial Day a Police Flag his placed on Timothy's grave, as well as on the graves of the entire department's deceased members.

CHANGING OF CHIEF'S

In early September, 1988, Chief William M. Dermody informed Mayor Ann Everest Wojtkowski that he was going to retire as of October 1, 1988. Saying "I have several other interests I wish to pursue after retirement." Chief Dermody was an avid outdoorsman and wanted to spend more time hunting and fishing.

ACTING CHIEF CAPTAIN IN CHARGE
COSMO SPEZZAFERRO

Mayor Wojtkowski appointed Captain Cosmo Spezzaferro as acting chief while Chief Dermody used up his vacation time. As of October 1, the official date of Chief Dermody's retirement, Spezzaferro officially became acting chief. As the chief's position was not Civil Service, Spezzaferro had to take a leave of absence from his Civil Service position as captain.

On February 16, 1989, Chief Spezzaferro informed Mayor Wojkowski that he wanted to step down from the position of acting chief and resume his position as Civil Service Captain. This was done to preserve his civil service seniority. If he had stayed in the chief's position for more than six months, on a leave of absence, it would have affected his seniority. Mayor Wojkowski then appointed him as Captain-in-charge. This had a descending effect. Administrative Capt. Gerald Lee returned to lieutenant; Lieutenant David Boyer returned to the rank of sergeant, and Sergeant Anthony Riello, returned to the rank of patrolman.

CHILD-CUSTODY DISPUTE LEADS TO DEATH

Patricia A. Furlani, 34, and her husband David D. Furlani, 32, were in a child-custody dispute. In September, 1987, Patricia filed a motion asking that her husband be ordered to leave the house. The motion had not yet been decided. Earlier in the dispute David Furlani filed a motion asking that his wife be ordered to leave the house, which was denied. In October 1987, Patricia filed for divorce in Probate Court. In the complaint she sought custody of their two young sons. The divorce and custody case was scheduled for trial in Berkshire Probate Court on December 8 and 9, 1988.

David Furlani was an electrical engineer and a GE employee. On November 10, Furlani wrote a letter of resignation to GE; because his job had involved high security clearance, he promised never to divulge any sensitive information or to travel to a communist country. He already had obtained Social Security numbers and passports for his children, and he also had withdrawn money from various GE savings accounts.

In a statement to police, Furlani said that the family woke up early on Sunday, November 13, 1988, and Patricia was preparing to meet her parents for church. While she was getting ready for church, he went to pack the children's clothing and an argument broke out between them over the children's schooling.

Furlani said he went into the basement to collect some laundry and that his wife followed him. Then she went back upstairs returning with a small paring knife, accused him of wanting to take the children away, and threatened him with the knife. A struggle followed and they both fell to the floor. She began to cry out for the children, who were upstairs in the house. When she did not stop screaming, he put his hands on her neck and strangled her.

Mr. and Mrs. Robadue, Patricia's mother and father, had become concerned when their daughter did not meet them for church. They drove to her house at Longfellow Avenue and saw David leaving with his sons in the car. They became suspicious, and finally entered the house, finding their daughter dead in the basement.

An all-points bulletin was issued for the arrest of David Furlani. At 12:35 p.m. New York State Police stopped David Furlani on Interstate 90 in the town of Guilderland, just outside of Albany. The children were in the car with him. He was arrested and arraigned in the town on Sunday afternoon. In searching Furlani's car, state police seized $18,000 in cash, maps of Canada and passports for Furlani and the children.

District Attorney Robert J. Carnes prosecuted the case for the Commonwealth in Superior Court. He said an autopsy revealed that Patricia Furlani had been killed by asphyxiation caused by three to four minutes of pressure on her neck.

Furlani pleaded guilty to voluntary manslaughter before Superior Court Judge Elizabeth Porada, who imposed the maximum sentence of 18 to 20 years in state prison. Conviction of voluntary manslaughter means that the murder was committed "in the heat of passion" with adequate or reasonable provocation that might cause a person to lose self-control and act impulsively, without reflection.

1990

FISCAL YEAR
July 1, 1989 TO June 30, 1990

TWO STATE MURDER INVESTIGATION
BY FIVE POLICE DEPARTMENTS

On April 14, 1990, Marilyn Roy Bigelow, 29, was last seen. Bigelow, who was divorced, had two sons, ages 9 and 11. She was reported missing after she failed to show up for work at McCarthy's Variety Store on Tyler Street. Later that day she did not attend a friend's wedding.

The night before, she had worked until 11:00 p.m. and then called her two sons to tell them she would be home soon. She had money in her pocket from a recently cashed income-tax refund check, she went to several local bars and left one unnoticed by her friends. She was last seen outside the Riverside Bar on Columbus Avenue with Robert Beverly, 35, of Lenox Avenue. They were in his green 1976 Ford, a vehicle that was unregistered and uninsured. It was suspected that the two were using drugs together.

At 2:34 a.m. Lee Police stopped Beverly for speeding as he was traveling south in the Ford on Route 7, through Lee. The woman with Beverly fit Marilyn's description. But for an unknown reason, the Lee Police did not report the incident to Pittsfield officials until two months later in the investigation. Beverly told the Lee officer who stopped him that the woman was his wife, who was ill, and that he was taking her to Fairview Hospital in Great Barrington. He was not ticketed or charged.

Beverly was also seen in Canaan, Connecticut, at 3:30 that morning. This report was a factor in directing the investigation toward Southern Berkshire County.

When Bigelow did not return home to her two children, her family became concerned. Police described her disappearance as suspicious and expressed fears that she might be dead, the victim of either murder or a drug overdose.

Within 24 hours of her disappearance, the department had linked Bigelow to Beverly and questioned him twice. Beverly turned his car over to police voluntarily on April 15, and they obtained a search warrant to search it for clues. Detectives working on the case would make an arrest if they could only find Bigelow's body. Without a body, the case was legally only one of a missing person. With no evidence of a crime, there were no grounds for criminal charges even though detectives believed they knew who was responsible for her disappearance.

The investigation into Bigelow's disappearance got new movement on June 12, when Lee Police contacted Pittsfield and reported stopping Beverly's car. After that, searches zeroed in on areas near Sheffield and Ashley Falls without any luck.

Then, police received one of many anonymous tips, this one pointing them to the Pfizer quarry off Daisy Hill Road in Canaan, not far from Route 7. Police were cautious, as they had many such tips that had come in over the months, even some urging them to search quarries in Southern Berkshire. This man's information seemed specific and credible, as he told them he had taken a trip to Canaan with Beverly on April 15. Detectives took the man to Canaan, "where he showed a specific location." This man had been out of town and on returning recently, had learned that Beverly was being investigated. Checking the location, they found a belt later identified as Bigelow's.

On the next day detectives had arranged for help from Connecticut State Police, who brought in search dogs. Bigelow's body was found at 10:41 a.m., 41 minutes after the search began, her skull fractured.

A surveillance team was then dispatched to keep track of Beverly during the day, in anticipation of an arrest warrant from Connecticut.

Through the rest of the day and well into the night, detectives and state police followed Beverly around Pittsfield and back and forth to Lee. He finally caught a cab to Springfield from Lee.

Finally at 1:20 a.m. an arrest warrant was completed by a Connecticut judge. A squad of Massachusetts State Police troopers, some with tracking dogs, stopped the taxi at Exit 4 and arrested Beverly on a fugitive-from-justice warrant. Beverly was held overnight in Springfield on $250,000 bond, but at his arraignment in Hampden Court, he was ordered held without bail. Beverly agreed to go voluntarily to Canaan, Connecticut. He appeared in Litchfield County court on murder charges. It was believed the murder took place in Connecticut.

Connecticut authorities would not confirm that the body found in Canaan was Bigelow's until after official identification had been made through dental records. A Pittsfield detective who was at the quarry immediately recognized Bigelow's body because it was clad in the clothing she was wearing when she disappeared April 14. Even her rings were still on her fingers.

In May of 1991 after a month long jury trial in Litchfield Superior Court,

Beverly was found guilty of murder.

The experienced defense attorney for Beverly commented that he had never seen an investigation and prosecution that involved two states and five police departments conducted so smoothly without even a hint of "turf war" among the agencies.

ROBERT BEVERLY
PHOTO BY CRAIG F. WALKER EAGLE STAFF

Massachusetts and Connecticut State Police and those of Pittsfield, Lee and Sheffield had been involved in the case. Each of the 12 officers assigned to the detective bureau in the department had been involved in the case. Detective Gary Danford was the case officer for the Pittsfield Detective Bureau.

1991

FISCAL YEAR
July 1, 1990 TO June 30, 1991

23-YEAR-OLD CHARGED WITH FATAL KNIFING

On Sunday, July 1, 1990, around 11:00 p.m., an argument broke out in the kitchen of a second-floor apartment on Danforth Avenue. The argument was between Edward D. Messer, 23, and Raymond G. Sour III, 25. The argument led to an altercation in which Messer stabbed Sour. Messer lived in an adjacent residence on Danforth Avenue and Sour lived on Second Street.

Several witnesses were in the apartment. A quick investigation by Sgt. Benedetto Sciola and Detective Jack McGrath developed a suspect, Messer.

All city units were alerted. Messer was arrested about 10 minutes later by Officers James Stimpson and Walter Powell in the vicinity of Columbus and Circular Avenues, roughly one-half mile from the scene of the incident. Messer was held overnight on $500,000 bail, pending his arraignment in District Court.

EDWARD D. MESSER
PHOTO BY JOEL LIBRIZZI EAGLE STAFF

During the District Court hearing Assistant District Attorney Robert Carnes noted Messer's prior record and violation of probation in requesting that he be held without bail. Messer's defense attorney Leonard H. Cohen requested that the case be continued to give him time to determine the family's financial resources. Judge Bernard Lenhoff subsequently ordered Messer held without bail until the case was heard again.

Dr. Loren Mednick, Associate Medical Examiner for the Commonwealth, determined the cause of death to be a stab wound. The initial charge against Messer was assault and battery with a dangerous weapon, a knife, which was recovered at the scene. The charges were later changed to murder.

In February, 1991, a trail was held in Superior Court, with Judge William W. Simons presiding. District Attorney Gerard D. Downing presented his case to the jury of 10 men and two women. Downing wanted a conviction for 1st degree murder.

Attorney Cohen admitted that Messer stabbed Sour and Sour died as a result of that wound. The only issue, Cohen said, was whether Messer was guilty of first-degree murder, second-degree murder or manslaughter. Cohen believed that the case was never first-degree murder, that it was second-degree or some possibility of manslaughter.

The jury deliberated for just over four hours and found Messer guilty of second-degree murder.

Judge William W. Simons imposed the mandatory sentence of life at Massachusetts Correctional Institution at Cedar Junction. Messer, 24, would be eligible for parole when he was 39 years old.

STRANGLED TO DEATH
WITH AN ALARM-CLOCK CORD

On September 28, 1990, the body of Louise M. Wright, 75, of Dickinson Avenue was found in her up stairs hallway, between a bathroom and guest bedroom. She was lying face down on the floor, bound hand and foot. Around her neck was the cord of an alarm clock, and attached to that was a device made from a coat hanger, which was used to tighten the cord around her neck so as to strangle her.

Mrs. Wright's body was found by her life-long friend Ethel Lasher, 75, and her nephew Charles Wright, 42, shortly after 4:00 p.m. Upon finding the body, they turned around and left the house as fast as they could to call the Police Department.

Ethel Lasher had dropped Louise off on September 26, from their weekly Bible class. Mrs. Wright's Berkshire Eagle was in still in the mailbox at the front door, two days' worth of mail spilled out of the mailbox. Upon arriving at the scene police found a white bucket that was usually on the front step filled with sand tipped over underneath side living-room window.

Crime Scene Investigator James Winn, dusting the house for fingerprints, found fingerprints on the outside of a window pane, where the white bucket was. Back at the station, Winn was able to match the prints to a Mark Banister, 20.

PRINT LEFT BY MARK BANISTER

Police detectives and uniform officers were at the house for several hours. Also at the scene were, District Attorney Robert J. Carnes, District Attorney-elect Gerard Downing, members of the District Attorney's officers and several neighbors.

After an autopsy in Springfield, the state medical examiner's office determined the cause of death was strangulation.

Detectives arrested Banister on Saturday afternoon on outstanding warrants charging him with breaking and entering in the nighttime, larceny of a motor vehicle, and other offenses. Banister confessed to murder and robbery after his arrest and interviews with detectives.

Upon being booked police found two rings and a check on his person, all belonging to Louise Wright.

In December, 1988, Banister was sentenced to serve a year in jail for earlier charges involving checks taken Mrs. Wright. Banister and Gerald S. Scott, her step-grandson, stole checks from her house. Scott was successful in cashing one of the checks, which had been made out to him for $200.50.

Banister's attempt to cash the second check for $1,000 but was unsuccessful when a bank teller told him there were insufficient funds in the account. Both were arrested.

Attorney George B. Crane represented Banister in District Court before Judge James Scullary, who held him without bail.

In May of 1991, a Superior Court Trial was held which lasted almost two weeks. Superior Court Judge Daniel A. Ford presided over the trail. District Attorney Gerard D. Downing and Assistant District Attorney David F. Capeless prosecuted the case for the Commonwealth. Attorney George Crane represented Banister.

Downing put several prosecution witnesses on the stand, including a detective who read aloud the sworn confession. A forensic expert linked fingerprints and footprints at Wright's house to Banister. Downing also linked Wright's blood to stains on clothes of Banister's.

The jury heard final arguments and deliberated for only four hours before finding Banister guilty of first- degree murder.

Judge Daniel A. Ford sentenced Banister to life in prison with no prospect of parole. In addition to the mandatory life sentence carried by a first-degree murder conviction, Ford gave Banister concurrent sentences of 45 to 60 years on assault charges, 15 to 20 years on a burglary charge and 3 to 5 years on other charges, all to be served at Massachusetts Correctional Institution at Cedar Junction.

After the trail District Attorney Downey commended Pittsfield detectives, especially Peter T. McGuire and Gary Danford and members of the uniformed branch for their investigation.

MARK BANISTER

FAREWELL FUNERAL TO CONGRESSMAN

CONGRESSMAN SILVIO O. CONTE

On February 13, 1991, friends and political figures from around the United States attended the funeral of long-time Congressman Silvio O. Conte. The funeral drew the largest assembly of national, state, and county public figures ever gathered in Pittsfield. Congressman Conte served in Washington, D.C. for 32 years. Conte was a native of Pittsfield and graduated from Pittsfield Vocational high School in 1940. He served with the Seabees in the South Pacific in World War ll.

Vice President Dan Quayle arrived at the Pittsfield Airport aboard Air Force 2. Speaker of the House of Representatives, Thomas S. Foley, former speaker of the House Thomas "Tip" O'Neill, Senator Edward M. Kennedy, Governor William F. Weld, former Governor Edward J. King and Pittsfield Mayor Anne Everest Wojtkowski were among the political figures in Pittsfield to attend the funeral.

Needless to say, the department was out in full strength for an event with unusual logistical and security considerations. All off-duty officers were ordered to work. Also on hand were Secret Security Agents, Massachusetts State Police and Auxiliary Police to help with traffic, crowd control, and security.

Thousands filed through All Souls' Church to pay their respects the night before the funeral. It took two hours to reach the altar where Conte rested. The funeral was held at St. Joseph Church with a military honor guard.

CHAPTER THIRTY-ONE

GUNMEN ROB ARMORED CAR OF $1.23 MILLION

On April 9, 1991, three masked men robbed the Berkshire Armored Car Services of $1,233,000. This was the largest robbery in the history of Berkshire County. The robbery took place at the Armored Car headquarters in the old Berkshire Woolen Mills complex at 343 Pecks Road after 3:30 a.m. as two armored car guards were loading their armored car with money from main vault for delivery to out of town banks.

ARMORED CAR HEADQUARTERS
PHOTO BY JOEL LIBRIZZI-EAGLE

Three masked men, one with a shotgun, surprised the two guards. One guard was in the back of the armored car loading the money, and was ordered out by the shotgun bandit. Both guards were handcuffed and hogtied. One of the guards was struck in the back of his head. The masked gunmen also stole the guards' guns, one a 9-mm semiautomatic pistol, the other a .357 revolver.

One of the guards managed to get free after about 10 minutes to get to a phone to call police even though he was handcuffed. Duct tape was not put over his mouth thus enabling him to talk.

This robbery now became the largest robbery in the history of Berkshire County. On April 2, 1989 four men stole $434,900 from an armored car in Williamston. They were arrested within minutes by North Adams Police and were all convicted in Berkshire Superior Court of the robbery.

The armored car company was engaged in interstate commerce, with some of the money connected to federal banks. According to Gerard S. Reder, owner of the armored car company, the building contains both alarms and surveillance equipment at a variety of spots. The company was in business for 36 years.

Detectives, with the assistance of the FBI from the Springfield office, started their investigation. Plaster cast tire tracks were taken in the dirt parking lot from the getaway car. The joint investigation was continued by detectives from Pittsfield, the FBI, Internal Revenue Service and Massachusetts State Police assigned to the district attorney's office. It was almost two years before any arrests were made in June of 1993.

Chief Gerald M. Lee said police had an idea early on who might be responsible for the robbery. "It wasn't long after it occurred that the detectives started picking up rumors and getting information." The case stayed on the front burner for the whole two years and two months, and all the detectives from the day shift worked on the case at one time or another.

On June 17, 1992 investigators executed search warrants for robbery proceeds, including cash, checks, guns, bank records, real estate purchase records, furniture and jewelry. Also sought in the search were articles used in the robbery, including ski masks, duct tape, Firestone tires, a car, and a shotgun.

The first warrant was for the house and business of Francis J. Procopio Jr., 48, of South Onota Street, who helped to plan the robbery, provided the getaway car, and disposed of it later. Procopio was arrested on an outstanding warrant for larceny by check. As a result of the search, Procopio was charged with 10 counts of gun possession and possession of a car that had been reported stolen in Hampden County. Procopio had collected $250,000 for his share of the robbery.

The second warrant was for the apartment and 27-foot cabin cruiser moored at the Pontoosuc Lake property of Bernard J. Kiley, 56, of Brockton, formerly of Taubert Avenue in Pittsfield, the "mastermind," of the robbery. Kiley was sentenced to prison in 1959 for the beating death of 71-year-old Michael Koza, but the conviction was reversed on a technicality and he served only 10 years. In 1976 Kiley was convicted in a $7 million securities scam and sent to prison. In 1981 he was jailed on drug charges, police describing him as the head of a major drug-trafficking operation in Western Massachusetts. While searching the Brockton apartment used by the men, agents found a collection of firearms, five handguns, two Glock 9 mm pistols, a Smith and Wesson 38-caliber revolver, a Colt .45 pistol, and a SKS semiautomatic assault rifle. A listing of Berkshire County radio frequencies, a police scanner, state police uniforms, ski masks, a mold to make police badges, state police badges, beards and a wig were found. An informant told agents that they were planning to rob another armored car in Western Massachusetts posing as state troopers.

The third warrant was the house of Charles R. Gattuso Jr., 31, of Crane Avenue, who worked as a guard/driver at Berkshire Armored Car for two months in early 1991. He was fired from the job for excessive lateness. Gattuso was recruited by Kiley and provided information about the routes, scheduling and security. In exchange for this information, he received $55,000. He used this money to remodel a restaurant, "The Breakfast Club," which was located across the street from Procopio's garage. He also purchased several vehicles and treated his family to a California vacation. Gattuso was cooperating with the FBI and was put in the federal witness protection program.

The fourth warrant was the house of Vincent A. Lattanzio, 37, of Hyde Park Avenue, Boston. Vincent was one of the actual robbers. Kiley and Lattanzio met each other while serving time in a Massachusetts prison. Lattanzio was convicted of two prior armed robberies.

The fifth warrant was the house of Donald J. Abbott, 25, of Colwell Road, Burrillville, Rhode Island, who was the third robber who held the two guards at gun point. Abbott cooperated with the FBI and was freed on $250,000 bail when he was executed by shotgun blasts to the back of the head in August of 1993, while driving down a rural road near his home. Rhode Island State Police said that his murder was a professional hit. Abbott met Kiley while they were both serving time at a federal penitentiary in Danbury, Connecticut.

On June 20, three days later, agents searched the Brooks Avenue home Kiley's brother, Donald, looking for records of financial transactions.

After a trial in federal court the jury who deliberated for about 91 hours over a two day period found Kiley, Procopio and Lattanzio guilty on all 16 counts of armed robbery and conspiracy. Both Kiley and Procopio were also convicted of money laundering.

In a separate verdict, the jury found that the government could seize $30,000 in an investment account in the name of Kiley's brother, who invested some of the money from the robbery for his brother Bernard. Agents were able to determine that at least $330,000 was spent in an eight month spending spree on cars, boats real estate and travel. This was done by using a ledger found inside a teddy bear at Kiley's home. $348,000 in cash still remained unaccounted for.

Senior U.S. District Federal Judge Frank H. Freedman determined Kiley was a career criminal and sentenced him to 49 years in prison. Under federal sentencing guidelines, a person must serve at least 85 percent of his sentence. Kiley wouldn't be eligible for parole until he was 96 years old. Kiley had only been out of prison two months when he robbed the armored car company.

Francis Procopio was sentenced to eight years in prison for his role. Judge Frank H. Freedman, who presided over the trial, said he was not convinced that Procopio's role was "as severe" as that of the other participants. Judge Freedman could have given him 10 years.

Charles R. Gattuso Jr., received two years in prison in exchange for his cooperation with investigators and was placed in the federal witness protection program.

Lattanzio received a sentence of 29 years in jail for his part in the robbery.

STABBED TO DEATH

On Wednesday, April 24, 1991, officers discovered the body of Earl "Cornbread" Lewis, 52, in his Melville Street apartment after a welfare check at 3:00 p.m. Lewis lived alone in his second-floor apartment across from the Pittsfield Boys' and Girls' Club and adjacent to the former Coaches Corner bar, where he often drank.

Lewis was known as "Cornbread Junior" to many of his friends from his days as a CB operator. He was born with polio, which affected the entire left side of his body, leaving his left arm crooked and clenched. He walked with a cane.

EARL (CORNBREAD) LEWIS

District Attorney Gerard D. Downing said it was a "brutal and savage" murder. Lewis being stabbed in excess of 15 times in the chest, back, neck and head.

Detective Sergeant Benedetto Sciola and Elizabeth A. Keegan of the district attorney's office escorted Joan Lewis to the scene to identify the body of her former husband. They were divorced from each other six years previously, but remained on good terms, often visiting one another. Only two days before his death he had stopped over her house. She often sent him leftovers for his meals.

Detectives had linked Annette Leitzsey, 41 of Linden Street, to the crime "by statement in the nature of admissions she had made to other individuals." An arrest warrant for first-degree murder was issued for her arrest. Officers were stationed on the rear porch of her second-floor apartment, between 8 p.m. and 10:30 a.m. waiting for her return. Leitzsey was arrested Thursday morning at 10:23a.m. on Robbins Avenue. She was also known as Annette Stewart, Annette Coker, Annette Cummings, Annette Ward and Ann Johnson. In the department computer she was flagged as armed and dangerous, use caution when dealing with her. She was known to carry and use dangerous weapons.

ANNETTE LEITZSEY
PHOTO BY CRAIG F. WALKER EAGLE STAFF

A search warrant was executed at her apartment to gather physical evidence that linked her to the murder. Detectives found Leitzsey's white blouse bearing a blood- spray pattern consistent with a stabbing. The murder weapon, the knife was found in her bleach bottle. Lewis's wallet was also found in her dresser.

In her arraignment in district court, District Attorney Gerard D. Downing requested that bail be set at $500,000, claiming that Leitzsey showed an "extreme risk" of flight. He pointed to her history of using aliases and her use of different Social Security numbers. Two weeks prior to the murder she was charged with assault with a dangerous weapon, a meat cleaver.

Attorney Francis X. Spina was appointed by the court to represent Leitzsey. In statements given detectives, Leitzsey accused 33 year-old Herman "John"

Kempson, who had lived with her for roughly a month before the murder. Leitzsey claimed that Kempson stabbed Lewis when he wouldn't tell him where to find cocaine he allegedly had stashed in his Melville St. apartment. Detectives found no cocaine when they searched Lewis's apartment and the Linden Street apartment that she and Kempson shared.

At Leitzsey and Kempson's trail, First Assistant District Attorney David F. Capeless based the Commonwealth case on the theories of deliberate premeditation and extreme atrocity and cruelty.

Leitzsey was found guilty on both murder theories of first-degree murder. She was sentenced to the mandatory sentence of life in prison without the possibility of parole.

Kempson, who was represented at his trial by Attorney George Crane, was found not guilty of being an accessory after the fact of murder.

District Attorney Gerard D. Downing commended the department for its work in solving the murder, commending Detective Sergeant Benedetto Sciola, Detective Owen Boyington and Detective Terrance Donnelly. For their work on the case, the department awarded each officer the "Honorable Service Medal."

1992

FISCAL YEAR
July 1, 1991 TO June 30, 1992

JULY 4, 1991- CAPTAIN IN CHARGE COSMO SPEZZAFERRO

Acting Chief Walter M. Boyer

On August 4, 1991, acting Chief Walter M. Boyer announced a series of "realignments of responsibilities" designed to "move the department forward" in the absence of a permanent chief.

The list of changes included elevating Lt. Gerald M. Lee from day shift commander to head of the Detective Bureau. Changes in administrative areas were made, Sgt. John T. O'Neil shifted from administrative sergeant to a supervisor of the uniform division on the 4 to 12 shift. Many administrative duties had been handled by Sgt. O'Neil when Captain Cosmo Spezzaferro served in the dual role of acting chief and administrative captain. Boyer said there was no longer a need for both a sergeant and a captain in administration. Boyer said looking around there was a lacking of uniform supervisors for the evening shift.

Officer Robert Benoit who had handled the processing of District Court complaints will now assist Capt. Spezzaferro. District court responsibilities now fell to the detective bureau. One detective on the day shift was assigned to that duty. Five detectives were sent to a one-week "prosecutor's school."

Lt. John Grady was designated as the liaison officer between the department and the civil defense auxiliary police. Grady was assigned as training officer for the volunteers, who served under the direction of CD director Thomas G. Grizey.

The final change involved the assignment of outside overtime details for construction and road-repair sites. The responsibility for assigning officers to fill these jobs was shifted from the uniform division to the head of the traffic bureau, Sgt. David R. Boyer.

COUSINS SMASHED THROUGH
WALL TO ADMINISTER FATAL BEATING

Tuesday evening, December 10, 1991, cousins Chester Brazee and Joseph Brazee administered a fatal beating to 40-year- old Donald J. Haber.

The encounter took place at the apartment house at the corner of Columbus and Daniels Avenue. Although Chester Brazee and Haber's addresses are on different streets, their apartments were actually in the same building, which stands on the corner. The Brazee apartment is entered from Columbus Avenue by way of a walk that leads to its entrance in the rear. The Haber apartment is entered by an outdoor stairway rising from the Daniels Avenue sidewalk around the corner. There was a package store built into the front of the building on Columbus Avenue. There were five apartments in the building. Chester Brazee lived at 236 Columbus Avenue and Donald J. Haber lived at 2 Daniels Avenue. Also living at 2 Daniels Avenue with Haber was, Burt F. Rockwood, 54. Both Haber and Rockwood drank heavily at times. Haber, known variously as John, Don and J.J., was a disabled veteran of the Vietnam War who received a government allotment. Less was known about Rockwood who had lived in Bennington, Vermont, for some years but had drifted down to Pittsfield. The apartments were connected by a door over which a panel had been nailed.

The encounter took place when Haber and Rockwood made a great deal of noise that disturbed Chester Brazee's child and his girlfriend, who was eight month's pregnant. Chester Brazee, followed by his cousin, Joseph, opened a locked door separating the two apartments and then broke through a panel that covered the doorway on Haber and Rockwood's side. Once inside Haber's apartment, the Brazee's administered a brutal beating with a blunt instrument to Haber and Rockwood. The club like instrument was used to beat Haber in the head. Though the attack occurred on the evening of the 10th, Haber did not seek medical or police assistance and continued to drink heavily even though he had severe head injuries.

Police were called to 2 Daniels Ave on December 11 to give medical assistance and found Haber bleeding from the nose and mouth, as well as bleeding heavily from lacerations. Rockwood suffered fractured ribs and injuries to his face and spine. Both Haber and Rockwood were taken to Berkshire Medical Center.

Lt. Gerald M. Lee and Sgt. Benedetto Sciola were in charge of the investigation for the department. Both Brazees were arrested on warrants following the Detective Bureau investigation.

They appeared before Judge Alfred A. Barbalunga in District Court, each charged with two counts of assault and battery by means of a dangerous weapon and one count each of burglary and armed assault on an occupant of a dwelling.

Following the death of Haber, District Attorney Gerard D. Downing charged the Brazees with murder. The autopsy report showed that Haber bled to death as a result of "blunt force trauma to his face." The autopsy results also gave as a secondary cause failure of the blood to coagulate and the effects of a severe alcoholic condition.

At their trial in Superior Court before Judge Daniel A. Ford, Chester K. Brazee, 29, pled guilty to one count of manslaughter, and two counts of burglary, and armed assault on an occupant. He was sentenced to 15 to 20 years on the manslaughter charge and to concurrent 12 to 15 years on the other charges.

Joseph H. Brazee, 33, who was also charged with murder, pleaded guilty to one count of burglary, armed assault on an occupant, and was sentenced to 12 to 15 years at Cedar Junction.

CHESTER K. BRAZEE & JOSEPH H. BRAZEE
PHOTO BY JOEL LIBRIZZI EAGLE STAFF

1993

FISCAL YEAR
July 1, 1992 TO June 30, 1993

TV SHOW "PRIME SUSPECT" LEADS TO ARREST

On Monday, March 1, 1993, the department's dispatch center received an anonymous call. The caller stated they were watching the TV show "Prime Suspect" and saw that their neighbor was wanted by the Atascosa County Sheriff's Department in Jourdanton, Texas. In talking to the Sheriff's Department, it was found out John Paul, 47, was wanted for fleeing their jurisdiction prior to being sentenced on a narcotics charge. John Paul's prints and photo were faxed to the department. A stake-out was set-up on his apartment by Officers Mark Lenihan, James Hunt, and Detectives Terence Donnelly, Thomas Bowler, and Sgt. Benedetto Sciola. At 10:15 p.m. Paul was arrested and charged with being a fugitive from justice. Upon questing, it was found out that Paul lived in the area for about five years. He led a quiet life in Pittsfield, not coming in contact with the department. Paul looked just like his five-years- old mug-shot. He was placed on $200,000 cash bail or $2 million surety, waiting for the Texas authorizes to return him to Texas.

CHAPTER THIRTY-TWO

RETIRED SCHOOL TEACHER MURDER NEVER SOLVED

On July 1, 1992, the body of Byron E. Filkins, 60, a retired Taconic High School teacher, was discovered at this home on Lebanon Avenue. The discovery was made by his fiancée, attorney Dorothy M. Crane, when she returned home at about 6 p.m. Mrs. Crane called 911, a fire engine and police cruiser responded.

BYRON E. FILKINS

Filkins taught machine technology in the vocational department at Taconic High from the late 60s until he retired in 1988. He was married in 1950 and was divorced in 1976. The couple had seven children.

An autopsy was done by Worcester County medical examiner, Dr. Joanne Richmond, who determined death was caused by multiple blows to his head with a blunt object. The unofficial report was that the murder weapon was a hammer, a crowbar or similar instrument, which was never found.

There was no evidence of forced entry into the home, nothing of value appeared to be missing, and the dwelling was not ransacked. Filkins' wallet was found on him, which contents including cash, appeared undisturbed.

Witnesses reported that they saw him drive away from his home about 1 p.m. toward the West Housatonic Street. Not one neighbor noticed what time he arrived back home. Detectives made appeals for any possible witnesses to come forward. Detective questioned many of Filkins' family members and acquaintances, without any luck. To this day, the case remains open.

RED MAZDA B2000 PICKUP MURDER WEAPON

On Saturday, night September 5, 1992 at The Gathering Bar at 236 Tyler Street, a fight broke out and spilled out into the parking lot behind the bar. The time was about 11:30 p.m. The fight was between Jayson Moore, 22 and two brothers, Martin VanBramer, 21and his older brother, Mathew VanBramer, 27.

Although The Gathering fronts on Tyler Street, its parking lot is entered from Burbank Street, across from Morningside Community School. The Gathering is in a two-story building, and a sidewalk and a narrow grassy strip are between the parking lot and the street.

SKID MARKS IN PARKING LOT
PHOTO BY JOEL LIBRIZZI EAGLE STAFF

Inside the bar observers said Martin VanBramer apparently became engaged in a dispute with Moore and three or four of his friends. Drinks were thrown. Martin VanBramer, Moore and his friends went outside to the parking lot. VanBramer came back inside, noticeably upset. He called his brother Mathew and another brother.

It was after one or more of the VanBramer brothers arrived that Moore went outside and got into his pickup truck and drove out of the parking lot. Martin VanBramer and his brother Mathew were in the street. Moore drove into them. When the truck struck Martin his head hit the windshield, shattering it; he then landed in the eastbound lane of Burbank Street. Mathew VanBramer who landed on the truck, slid into the bed of the truck.

Officer Thomas Barber saw Moore's truck as it came out of Tyler Street turning left through a stop sign into North Street. There was a man in the truck's bed yelling "Stop the truck." Officer Barber then turned on his cruiser's blue lights and pulled behind the truck. Moore pulled over immediately. There three people got out of the truck and started yelling at one another.

Officer Bruce Hugabone on his way to the accident scene on Burbank Street passed Officer Barber and the red pickup truck. At the accident scene Officer Hugabone learned that a red pickup truck had hit the two VanBramer brothers. Returning to where Officer Barber had the red pickup stopped Officer Hugabone, placed Moore under arrest. Both brothers were taken to Berkshire Medical Center, where Martin died the following day. Mathew VanBramer was treated and released from the hospital.

Medical Examiner Loren J. Mednick of Springfield said the cause of death was multiple injuries, the most severe of which was a massive skull fracture consistent with "motor vehicle impact-type injuries." There were also lacerations and scrapes on the chest, legs, arms and hands. VanBramer's blood-alcohol level of .259 as determined at BMC. Any reading over .10 was defined as intoxication in drunken driving cases.

Two days after Martin's death, 65 family members and friends marched quietly around The Gathering. Billed as a peaceful protest, the march was nonetheless tainted by violence after an apparently angry woman tried to disrupt the otherwise orderly event. Carlene Coral, 25, was arrested and charged with disturbing the peace and two counts of assault and battery on a police officer. Coral was led yelling from the lines of marchers by Sgt. John O'Neil and Officer Thomas Barber. As the woman was driven away by Sgt. O'Neil, the marchers stopped momentarily to applaud the efforts of the police. They then resumed their path around the block carrying lit candles and placards.

SGT. O'NEIL AND OFFICER BARBER WITH PRISONER
PHOTO BY CRAIG F. WALKER-EAGLE STAFF

In May, 1993, a trial was held in Superior Court before a jury of six men and six women. Judge Daniel Ford was the presiding judge. District Attorney Gerard Downing presented the case for the Commonwealth. Downing called more than a dozen witnesses, many of whom were at the bar that night, to give their recollections of what had happened that night. Defense attorney Robert J. Carnes had built a defense that portrayed Moore as a victim of Martin VanBramer's drunken misidentifications. He said that Moore was not trying to run down the brothers, but was trying to escape from them after they had accosted him.

The jury deliberated for about six hours on Thursday and Friday before returning its verdict of manslaughter. Judge Daniel Ford ordered Jayson Moore to serve a 16 to 20 year term at Cedar Junction on the manslaughter charge. Moore was also given a concurrent 7 to 10 year term on one count of assault by means of a dangerous weapon (motor vehicle).

JAYSON MOORE
EAGLE PHOTO

District Attorney Gerard Downing had praise for the investigators. "Members of the uniform branch and traffic division of Pittsfield Police Department, specifically officers James Boland, Bruce Hugabone, Thomas Barber, and Sgt. John O'Neil, did outstanding work. Detective Jack McGrath for his coordination of the investigative effort, especially the defendant's statement, was crucial to our success."

Downing thanked the jurors for their efforts, "This was a difficult case and the jurors did an excellent job. They neither overlooked nor ignored any of the evidence presented to them."

LT. GERALD LEE NAMED CHIEF OF POLICE

Chief Gerald M. Lee

On November 25, 1992, Lt. Gerald Lee took the helm of the department after four years of controversy. The question was: "Should the Chief of Police be a Civil Service Chief or not?" According to the voters of Pittsfield, it should be.

Under the Acts of 1981, Chapter 204 the position of chief was taken out of Civil Service. Chief John J. Killeen was the last Civil Service Chief retiring in 1978 on his birthday, December 25. Mayoral appointments were then made and served at the discretion of the Mayor. There were five in total. First was Acting Chief Anthony J. Pires, second was Chief Stanley J. Stankiewicz, and the last full time Chief was William M. Dermody who retired in 1988. Then Acting Chief Cosmo Spezzaferro ran the department for three years. Taking over when Spezzaferro stepped down was Acting Chief Walter M. Boyer, who ran the department until Chief Lee was appointed.

In 1988 the Public Safety and Health Committee said that the chief's job should be put back under Civil Service, but no action was taken.

In 1990, Lt. Lee was one of six applicants in a nationwide search for chief. He was ranked number one during the assessment part of the search for a chief. Each candidate was asked a series of hypothetical questions. This was done by an independent consulting company with no ties to Pittsfield. The company ranked Caption Larry Jetmore of the Hartford Police Dept. as best overall. The captain had 20 years' experience in the 500 officer department. Capt. Jetmore had commanded all of the different units in the Hartford Department.

Mayor Anne Everest Wojikowski said Lt. Lee did not have the command experience and put Jetmore's name before the City Council for appointment as Police Chief of Pittsfield. Capt. Jetmore was first outsider in the department's history to be considered as chief.

On the night the council was to confirm Capt. Jetmore as chief. Capt. Jetmore withdrew his name. He informed Mayor Wojikowski that he was retiring from the Hartford Dept. and taking another police-like job. Mayor Wojikowski was very disappointed, but still would not appoint Lt. Lee as Chief. There was a question if the Mayor had enough votes in the City Council to confirm Capt. Jetmore.

The department's superior officers and patrolmen's unions started a petition drive to get a referendum. The question was "Should the job of Police Chief of Pittsfield be Civil Service?" At the polls the voters overwhelmingly wanted the job to be Civil Service by over 2,000 votes.

A Civil Service written exam in addition to an oral exam was held with Lt. Lee scoring the highest. Mayor Edward M. Reilly appointed Lt. Gerald Lee as Chief of Police and the City Council confirmed his appointment effected November 25, 1992. Chief Lee served as chief until his retirement on January 3, 1997.

1994

FISCAL YEAR
July 1, 1993 TO June 30, 1994

DRUG RAID AT MAJOR CRACK HOUSE LEADS TO DEATH

On October 20, 1993, eight members of the department, Lt. David R. Boyer, Sgt. John T. O'Neil, Detectives Owen Boyington, Jack McGrath, David R. Granger, and Officers Glen F. Decker, Dwane J. Foisy and James Hunt attended a search warrant briefing at the Massachusetts State Police CPAC office on West Street. The State Police Narcotic Unit had a NO KNOCK search warrant for 111 Linden St. The department is a member of the County Drug task force along with other departments. North Adams was represented by Detective E. John Morroco. The warrant was for controlled substance, crack cocaine. The briefing on the warrant was done by Trooper Joseph McDyer. Present from the State Police were Lt. Robert Scott and Trooper Chris Meiklejohn. Trooper McDyer said there were two guns in the house, a sawed-off shotgun and a handgun. This house was doing a massive business in selling crack cocaine. The best approach to the house was planned and each officer's was given their assignment for serving the search warrant.

Detective Granger and Officer Decker were assigned to be the first in on the entry team. Det. Granger was assigned to use the battering ram to gain entry as the search warrant authorized entry without announcement because of the firearms. The other officers on the entry team were Lt. Smith, Lt. Boyer, Troopers McDyer, Meiklejohn, and Brian Foley, Detectives Boyington and Morroco.

Officer James Hunt was assigned to cover the back door with another battering ram. Also at the rear door which was on the East side of the house and towards the rear were Detective John McGrath, Officer Dwane Foisy and Sgt. John O'Neil.

The task force arrived at 111 Linden Street at about 12:55 a.m., hooking up with the stake out officers, and took up their positions, one team to the front door and the other to the rear door.

Detective Granger and Officer Decker upon approaching the front door, saw a male looking out of the front door window then disappear. Hitting the front door with the battering ram, the door swung inward then back toward them. Both officers pushed the door back forcing the door inwards towards the living room along with the male holding it.

Officers shouted in loud voices, several times, "Police Officers, Search Warrant, get down on the floor." Several males began to run into the kitchen, failing to comply with the officers' commands to get on the floor. Three males ran into the bath room followed by Det. Granger. One male shut the door, but Det. Granger was able to force it open. They were trying to flush the toilet. One male had his hand in the water with the water running out of the toilet bowl. Det. Granger was able to push them out of the bathroom into the hands of officers from the raiding teams.

The back door team could hear the front entry team shouting "Police" and persons running inside the apartment. Someone was trying to open the kitchen door that leads on the porch. Officer Foisy opened the outer door and officers saw 5 or 6 males trying to exit the kitchen coming right at us. They were trying to run by each other, running right into the rear arrest team. There was a pantry in the corner of the kitchen. One male ran into the pantry not realizing that there was no door to escape by.

Two of the males attempting to make their exit by the kitchen door turned around and when back into the kitchen. The third one was cornered on the porch and handcuffed by Det. McGrath and Sgt. O'Neil.

Detective John Morocco was chasing a young male who was trying to escape through the kitchen door onto the unlit porch. A struggle ensued on the back porch; Det. Morocco and the male landed on Officer Foisy's right foot. Det. Morocco's Glock .9-mm handgun accidently discharged, when the young male jerked his head up and he hit the weapon. Det. Morocco almost lost control of the gun when it went off. A bullet struck the male in the head.

Det. Morocco applied pressure over the wound in an attempt to control the bleeding. Sgt. O'Neil radioed the station for an ambulance as did Officer Foisy. Sgt. O'Neil used his flashlight and spotted a .9-mm handgun on the floor of the unlit porch; picking it up with two fingers to secure it. It was not known who it belonged to at the time or whose fingerprints were on the weapon.

The ambulance arrived and the crew began treatment, transporting the subject to Berkshire Medical Center, where he was pronounced dead.

The name of the 19-year- old who was accidently shot was Eric Jermaine Hunt, whose last known address was Bronx, New York. He had several aliases, Shawn Hunt, Henry Davis, and Shaun Davis among them. In checking his record, it was found out that he had been arrested in Albany and the Bronx, on possession of cocaine, auto theft, grand larceny, loitering for the purpose of using or selling controlled substance, possession of a weapon, using a false name and receiving stolen property.

There were a total of thirteen in the apartment at the time of the raid. Twelve were arrested and charged with possession of cocaine with the intent to distribute. One was charged with one count of possession of shotgun ammunition and some were charged with possession of cocaine or marijuana.

During the search of the arrested and apartment, 250 rocks of crack cocaine were recovered with a street value of about $5,000. A sawed-off shotgun and ammunition for it were also recovered along with $4,000 in cash.

The next morning at their arraignments before Judge Alfred A. Barbalunga in District Court, all pleaded not guilty. Assistant District Attorney David F. Capeless requested bail on all twelve. It was brought out that investigators were not sure of their true names until they were confirmed by fingerprints from the FBI. Judge Barbalunga placed bail on them ranging from $500 to $40,000, on the ones that their identity was in question, they were held without bail.

Detectives learned from fingerprints that one male who said he was a juvenile was actually an adult and was an escapee from a jail work-release program in New York City. He was charged with being a fugitive from justice and held without bail.

District Attorney Gerard D. Downing asked Attorney General Scott Harshbarger to investigate the shooting. Each officer who was at 111 Linden Street was interview by the attorney general staff. None of the people at the apartment would talk to the investigators.

After two months of investigation the Attorney General rendered his report, that the shooting was an "ACCIDENT." Which everyone on the raiding team knew

CHAPTER THIRTY-THREE

SERIAL KILLER BROUGHT TO JUSTICE BY TWELVE YEAR OLD-HAD MASTER PLAN FOR ABDUCTING CHILDREN

Friday, January 7, 1994, was a cold, snowy winter morning in Pittsfield. Notre Dame Middle School student Rebecca Savarese, age 12, was walking up West Street on her way to her school on Melville Street. Rebecca lived with her mother Christine Paoli in their apartment at the Riverview West Housing Complex. Her apartment was about one-quarter of a mile back down West Street near the Western Mass Electric Company building.

Rebecca was almost to North Street when she noticed a man next to her saying something, but she could not hear what he was saying as she had a set of headphones on, listing to her favorite music. As she removed the headphones, she could see he had a gun. He grabbed her by the arm saying "Everything will be OK just do everything I say." He had a truck parked on the corner of North and West Street and he was trying to get her to his truck. Rebecca had taken DARE classes at her school, put on by the department and taught by Officer Kim Bertelli.

KIM BERTELLI

Rebecca faked an asthma attack and tried to sit on the curb, enabling her to break free from this man's grasp. He still had a hold of her purple knapsack, but she was able to slide out from it which she had on her shoulders. Rebecca ran to a man clearing snow from the side walk, blurting out what had just taken place.

Stopped at the red light at North and West Streets was Russell Davis, a nurse's aide at Berkshire Medical Center. Russell had just finished working the 11 to 7 shift. This was not his regular shift; he usually worked days but was filling in to cover the 11 to 7 shift.

His attention was called to a man struggling with a young dark- haired girl. At first he thought it was a father and daughter argument. The man saw Russell looking at him. Russell didn't see the gun in the man's hand. Rebecca had broken away from this man. The man started running to a black, 1975 GMC pick-up truck which he was parked by the curb.

Continuing down South Street, Russell saw in his mirror, the front license plate on the pickup truck and made a mental note of some of the numbers. The black pickup went through two red lights on South Street and turned left on to East Housatonic Street, where it disappeared.

At the Mobil gas station on South Street, Russell saw a police cruiser parked. Russell stopped and reported to the officer what he had just witnessed, giving a description of the truck, plate number and what the man looked like.

In the meantime, Rebecca was telling the officers at the station what had taken place. A radio transmission was given out about the incident and the cruiser officer at the Mobil station radioed in the information that Russell had given him.

Rebecca, Russell, and the detectives sat down with a Indent-a-kit and made a composite of the man who tried to abduct Rebecca. Copies were made and distributed to officers.

DETECTIVE OWEN BOYINGTON

With a copy of the composite, Detective Owen Boyington began a search for the black pickup truck and driver. Driving into Lanesboro, he saw a truck looking like the one involved in the incident parked in a drive way on Summer Street. As this was out of his jurisdiction, he went to the Lanesboro Police Department. With Officer Timothy Sorrell, Det. Boyington returned to the Summer Street house where the truck was parked. The owner of the truck was Phillip Shallies, who lived there with his mother. Shallies explained to the officers that he and his mother were legally blind and he didn't drive the truck. He said he had friends drive him around in it to do his errands. Shallies didn't resemble the composite sketch. Inside the house having lunch was Lewis S. Lent, Jr., 42, years old, who resembled the composite sketch. Lent told Officer Sorrell that he had driven the truck that morning, but not in Pittsfield. Lent was given his Miranda rights.

LEWIS S. LENT JR

Lent said he heard about the attempted abduction on the radio and a friend of Shallies had called, joking with Shallies about his black truck. Also parked in the yard were a 1983 Delta 88 Oldsmobile and a 1983 light blue Ford Econoline van.

Det. Boyington told Lent that he looked just like the person in the composite sketch that he had and asking Lent to come down to the Police Station so they could straighten things out. Lent was more than willing to go with Det. Boyington to the Pittsfield Police Station. Lent wanted the up-stairs tenant, Chester Forfa, who owned the 1983 Oldsmobile, to come with him to the station.

At the station, Lent was brought upstairs to the Detective Bureau which is on the second floor. There Det. Boyington again gave Lent his Miranda rights, which Lent also read and signed. Chief Gerald M. Lee and Detective Peter T. McGuire were also present. The time was about 2:30 p.m.. Det. Boyington told Lent he was not under arrest and didn't have to talk to him. Lent was asked if it was OK to take his picture. Lent agreed without hesitation. Detective Thomas N. Bowler was put in charge of setting up a 10 man photo array and seven-man lineup. Officers went out into the street and brought back to the station 6 men who resembled Lent. These six men, along with Lent, were put in the line-up. From the photo array, both Rebecca and Russell picked out photo number 6, who was Lent. They also picked Lent out of the seven man line-up. Each member of the line-up had to repeat "Everything will be OK" when their number was called to step forward. These were the words Lent said to Rebecca on West Street. Detectives videotaped the line-up. This videotape was later shown in Superior Court where Lent's defense team tried to get Rebecca and Russell's identification of Lent thrown out, saying it was flawed.

By 3:00 p.m. detectives were aware that Lent had worked as a janitor at the Pittsfield Cinema Center on West Housatonic Street. This is where 12 year old Jimmy Bernardo was abducted from on October 22, 1990. Jimmy's body was found a month later, in the woods in Newfield, New York, about 220 miles from Pittsfield. This was the first break investigators had gotten in three years of their investigation.

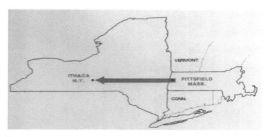

220 MILES FROM PITTSFIELD TO ITHACA, NEW YORK

Detective Peter McGuire was the department's liaison with the Bernardo family. Det. McGuire talked daily sometimes twice a day, to New York investigators, sharing any information on any likely suspects. Within the hour, Det. McGuire was talking to his fellow detectives in New York; giving them the information about Lent. Lent's mother lived within 10 miles of where the hunters hand found Jimmy's body.

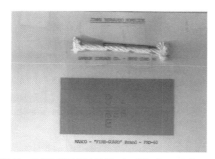

GREY, VINYL, DUCT TAPE & SPOT CORD # 8 ROPE

At about 6:30 p.m., investigators from New York were at the station. Detectives from the department were questioning Lent about the kidnapping. He still claimed he didn't do it. Lt. David Boyer asked the New York State investigators to stand-by until Pittsfield could finish their questioning of Lent.

Lent wanted to talk to the New York investigators. He didn't want to go back to his cell and go to sleep. He told them he would talk all night. Pittsfield detectives interrupted the interview a couple of times. One was to bring Lent downstairs to the booking room. Officer Glenn Decker and Det. David Granger brought Lent from the Detective Bureau to the booking room, where they search him. Searching him they found $60 in cash, a wallet with personal papers, a driver's license, and a wrench. Unfolding one of the papers, Det. Granger found a receipt from Dave's Sporting Goods Store for the purchase of a 9 shot, 22- caliber revolver.

Joint Homicide Task Force
39 Allen Street   Pittsfield, MA 01201

Sergeant John T. O'Neil, PPD

Telephone: 800-296-4115   FAX: 800-296-4117

Sergeant John T. O'Neil was the booking officer for the night. He read Lent his Miranda rights and asked him all the standard booking questions. It was the standard procedure to videotape and voice record the booking procedure. The time was 10:07 p.m.. The tape number was 39. The charges were kidnapping, armed robbery and assault by means of a dangerous weapon. Lent gave a verbal response to all the questions. He was returned to the Detective Bureau by Granger and Decker to finish his questioning by the New York investigators, which lasted until 3:00 a.m.. Lent wanted to keep talking. At 3:00 a.m. he was returned to his cell.

DETECTIVE PETER MCGUIRE

On Saturday morning, January 8, upon arriving for work, the desk sergeant told Det. McGuire that Lent wanted to use the phone and talk to him. In the Detective Bureau, Lent told Det. McGuire he remembered driving in Lanesboro with the black, 1975 GMC pick-up truck, but not into Pittsfield.

Investigators from New York State questioned Lent again. Finally, Lent admitted to them his taking part in the failed attempt to kidnapped Rebecca. Lent told New York State Police senior investigators James G. Ayling and John F. Murray where he had hidden Rebecca's L.L. Bean purple backpack and his gun. He signed New York's consent forms which allowed them to search his van and North Adams apartment.

Pittsfield detectives were told of Lent's confession. Detective Gary W. Danford took a written statement from Lent. Lent signed the statement and the department's consent forms. He again told the detectives where the backpack and gun were. Lent's lawyers tried to get the confession disallowed in a Superior Court hearing. Detective Danford testified that Lent was very alert to what was going on. In fact, Lent told Danford he had a couple of words misspelled and corrected his grammar. He told Danford he hoped he didn't scare Rebecca too much.

On Sunday, January 9, Lent wanted to talk to the New York State investigators. Lent told Ayling and Murray that he had been interviewed in the Jimmy Bernardo murder and he didn't own a car at that time. Ayling found out that this was not true and suspected that Lent had something to do with the case. While talking, Lent volunteered to talk about the Bernardo case. He admitted that he abducted Jimmy and described the abduction in detail. Lent was working at the Pittsfield Cinema Center on West Housatonic Street. Jimmy was outside of theatre waiting to meet up with some of his friends who hung around there. It was about 5:30 p.m. Lent came out and saw Jimmy, went over to him and offered him $5.00 to help move some chairs. From his van he got his abduction kit. Once inside, Lent pulled out a knife and put it to his throat. He then took some duct tape, and taped Jimmy's hands and feet. Jimmy started yelling, so he taped his month. Jimmy kept trying to get loose. Lent said that the duct tape was real strong as it was a commercial strength, fire retardant, that he used to fix any ripped seat in the theatre. As Lent was bringing some trash bags outside when he saw Jimmy's Mongoose bike up against the building. He placed it in the back of his van and later threw it into Silver Lake. Officers recovered the bike right where he said it would be.

JIMMY BERNARDO

Lent waited until all businesses were closed and the parking lot was empty of cars before he brought Jimmy out of the theatre and put him in his van. He brought him to his second floor apartment that he rented at 304 Tyler Street. There Lent sexually assaulted Jimmy. On October 23, the next day, Lent drove Jimmy in his van to Newfield, New York. There he forced Jimmy into the woods, where he strangled him with a rope. He tied it to Jimmy and pulled his body up so he was off the ground. A month later, three deer hunters found the body of Jimmy lying on the ground with a rope around his neck.

After Jimmy was found, a task force was set up at the station. Detectives went to the Pittsfield Cinema Center, where Jimmy was last seen. There they talked to the manager Richard Baumann and got a list of employees that worked there. This list didn't have Lent's name on it, because Baumann considered Lent a transitional employee, not a full time employee. Lent fell through the cracks at this time. After a month with no leads, members of the task force were reassigned to other cases and returned to their departments. Detective McGuire and Senior Investigator David McElligott of the Ithaca State Police barracks in New York State stayed in touch, looking for any new developments and prepared for when a break would come. Pictures of Jimmy in his baseball uniform were posted everywhere.

On Sunday, January 9, Lent, in a five-page statement which he signed, told how he raped and killed Sara Ann Wood, 12. Driving around New York State in his van, he saw Sara pushing her bike up a hill carrying some books. He stopped the van; with a knife in his hand, he jumped out and came at her. She started running but he caught her by tripping her. He threatened her with his knife. He got her into the van and taped her hands up with duct tape, taken from his abduction bag, which he always had with him. He then drove to a remote area, where he raped her. He then made her walk some distance into the woods. He then picked up a large stick and with both hands on it, hit her in the head, killing her. He then went back to the van and got a pick and shovel and dug a grave where he buried her.

On his way home, Lent stopped at a shopping plaza and tossed Sara's clothes in a trash bin. The next day, Lent broke the pick and shovel in small pieces and got rid of them.

MASTER PLAN FOR ABDUCTING CHILDREN

Lent told officers that he had a *MASTER PLAN FOR ABDUCTING CHILDREN*. He was building in his North Adams apartment a secret room with drawers so he could keep the kids he kidnapped in them, and then later kill them. He would take them out when he needed sex. These girls would be between the ages of 12 and 17. Lent wanted strong walls so no one could hear the kids if they screamed. Lent had mapped several places out, where he planned to take kidnapped kids and have sex with them.

On Monday morning, January 10, Lent was taken to District Court for his arraignment on the kidnapping of Rebecca Savarese. He was wearing a bulletproof vest under his jacket. Pittsfield Officers Glen Civello and Thomas Harrington were on each side of him. Lent was afraid someone was going to do something to him.

Head public defender Richard D. LeBlanc asked Judge Rita S. Koenigs to excuse Lent from being present in the court room during his arraignment. LeBlanc had filed a motion challenging how Lent was identified. Lent was kept in a holding cell just outside of the court room.

District Attorney Gerard D. Downing presented the Commonwealth case. He requested that bail be set at $200,000 cash or $2 million in surety. In the meantime New York filled a fugitive from justice warrant for the murder of Jimmy Bernardo, which has no bail.

TASK FORCE

On Tuesday, January 11, 1994, Chief Gerald M. Lee, Capt. Frank Page, Lt. Robert Smith and F.B.I. Agent Robert Confort, agent in charge of the Boston office, announced a multi- agency task force was beginning formed.

The purpose was the continue investigation of crimes Lent was charge with: murders of James Bernardo, Sara Ann Wood, and the attempted kidnapping of Rebecca Savarese; to connect Lent with open abduction/homicide case unsolved in the Northeast and other locations where he lived; to work-up a timeline of his life, where he lived and what cars he ever owned. The task force consisted of 25 detectives from New York State, 24 from Massachusetts State Police, 2 from Pittsfield Police and the 5 from the FBI. The squad room in the basement of the department was taken over by the task force. Roll call had to be held in the locker room. The pistol range was converted into a break and lunch room. A room next to the janitor's office was taken over as the command post.

When the case broke, Chief Lee had only been chief for a little more than a year. Between running the department and his involvement in the Lent case he was putting in between 10 and 12 hours a day. He had attended every news conference and meeting of the task force. The news media would not let up, 10 to 15 TV and 10 or more reporters with cameras were camped outside the station and court room in the bitter cold. America's Most Wanted and 48 Hours wanted to do one-on- one interviews. With four different agencies on the task force and four different media policies there had to be one individual who released information, so everyone received the same information. Special Agent William J. McMullin of the FBI became the taskforce spokesman. In his 24 years with the F.B.I. He has served as the liaison officer for the FBI with the media.

FBI agent Clint Van Zandt of the Behavioral Science Unit, who specialized in the pathology of child killers, joined the task force. He came from the FBI's headquarters in Quantico, Virginia. He was brought in to develop a profile of Lent from the information the task force had gathered so far. The Behavioral Science Unit that Van Zandt worked for was the subject of the movie and novel "The silence of the Lambs."

After reviewing the evidence, the Behavioral Science Unit believed that Lent would own up to certain things, but that he didn't want anyone to know where to find any bodies. This was because if you found a body in a timely fashion it could be determined what he had done to the body. There could also be other bodies in the area. The FBI now uses the Bernardo case as a model for similar task force cases involving missing children.

Chief Lee told the media that there was tremendous support from the community. Some business loaned desks and chairs to the task force. Pittsfield High School's Culinary Art program made lunches for the members of the task force, so they wouldn't have to leave the building and cut into valuable investigation time. Other restaurants also donated lunches, coffee and pastry for breaks. AT&T donated two 800 numbers for tips; these numbers were answered from 9 a.m. to 12 mid- night seven days a week by officers. On off-hours a answering took the calls. Nynex installed 13 free phone lines. Martin Marrietta Corp opened an account for office supplies.

INVESTIGATOR JAMES WINN

The black, 1975 GMC pick-up truck and Lent's Ford van were towed from Summer Street in Lanesboro to the department's garage after his arrest. Crime Scene Investigator James Winn searched the van and found Rebecca's L.L. Bean back pack and a gun, just where Lent said they would be.

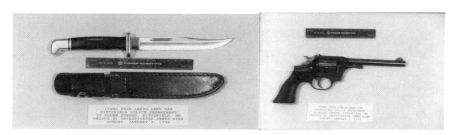

PHOTOS BY INVESTIGATOR JAMES WINN

On Monday, January 10, investigators impound a 1983 Delta 88 Oldsmobile belonging to Chester Forfa who lived with the Shallies on Summer Street. Forfa told investigator that Lent frequently used the car. He told them on one occasion Lent showed unusual concern about the cleanliness of the interior of the Olds. He thought this strange because he didn't keep his own van clean.

The Grand Jury brought indictments against Lent in the Savarese case, adding one addition charge of A&B. A special session of the Grand Jury was called on February 12, 1994, and indicted Lent for the kidnapping and murder of 12- year- old James Bernardo. In Tompkins County, New York,

Lent was also charge with the murder of Jimmy and being a fugitive from justice.

Under the Savarese indictments, Lent didn't have to appear in Superior Court before Judge Francis X. Spina. His lawyer, Richard LeBlanc of the public defender's office, stood in for him. Under the murder charge of Jimmy Bernardo, Lent had to appear in person and the charge read out loud, according to Massachusetts court rules. Lent was brought from the Berkshire House of Correction to Superior Court within an hour after the indictments were handed down. There was only one reporter in the court room when he was arraigned. Judge Francis X. Spina order District Attorney Gerard D. Downing and public defender Richard LeBlanc not to talk about the case to the media.

Lent's lawyers, Richard LeBlanc and Alan M. Rubin of Northampton, tried to suppress evidence that could link Lent to the murder of James Bernardo, and the kidnapping of Rebecca Savarese. A hearing was held on November 3, 1994, before Superior Court Judge Richard F. Connon. In question were two seats that were taken from Lent's North Adams attic that were in Lent's van at the time of Bernardo's death. The search warrant was for his apartment only, not the basement or attic where the seats were found.

Officers found a gun, duct tape, and rope in the North Adams apartment. Pieces of the rope and duct tape were cut into lengths. Lent's lawyers wanted to prove the officers had no right to go into the attic or basement because they were not named in the search warrant issued by Superior Court Judge Daniel A. Ford.

First District Attorney David F. Capeless argued that the attic and basement were shared with other tenants. The keys to both were given to the officers by another tenant. There was no expectation of privacy of an area to which others have access. Lent was given keys to both of these areas when he moved in.

Lent's lawyers also questioned the search of Lent's blue van where a gun was found inside a canvas bag, along with Rebecca Savarese's purple knapsack. Lent's lawyers said Pittsfield's Investigator James Winn went beyond the scope of the search warrant when he opened the canvas bag. First District Attorney Capeless told Judge Connon that the officer had a full search warrant for the entire van and its contents.

Attorney LeBlanc also questioned the finding of the receipt that Detective David Granger found in Lent's wallet during the booking procedure. This showed Lent purchased a gun at Dave's Sporting Goods Store. LeBlanc stated Granger didn't have to unfold the receipt. The inventory of his wallet was used as a pretext for an investigative search. Det. Granger said he was following standard procedure to check for items that could be used to inflict harm, such as razor blades. Second Assistant District Attorney Anne M. Kendal argued that Granger followed procedures very explicitly.

TASK FORCE DOWNSIZED END OF APRIL 1994

After four months of intention investigation and over 40,000 hours put in by over 60 officers, the task force was downsized to five officers. There was one from MSP, Trooper Gene Baker two from NYSP, Senior Investigators James G. Ayling and John F. Murphy, Special Agent T.J. Roberts from the FBI, and Detective Richard LeClair from Pittsfield. These five officers still worked full time on Lent with back up officers as needed.

The task force members searched 20 or so different dwellings, businesses and vehicles. They established a time line on Lent's life and the 70 some vehicles he owned or had use of. Collected close to 2,000 pieces of evidence and cataloged it. They also interviewed close to 2,000 persons and followed up on over a 1,000 leads. They talked and disseminated Lent's profile to 39 departments who had similar unsolved abduction/homicide cases.

In January, 1994, members of the task force and volunteers, numbering 150, searched in 15 to 20 degrees below-zero weather in the Adirondack Mountain for the body of Sara Woods. This was the area Lent told investigators they would find her body. Officers were using earth-moving equipment and ground-penetrating radar equipment on loan from the FBI. Members searched over 2,600 acres which took 55 days. They also had a specially trained dog from the Rhode Island State Police. The search turned out to be fruitless.

In July, 1994, task force members, under the command of Det. Lt. Robert G. Scott, search of a wooded area off of Notch Road, Adams, near Mount Greylock. They also used the specially- trained dog from the Rhode Island State Police. The National Guard set up three tents next to the search area, where searchers spent the night. Officers received information that Lent spent a lot of time in this area.

TRIAL

In October, 1994, Judge Ford ruled that the trial would be held in Berkshire Superior Court. The jurors would be composed of Hampden County residents.

One of Lent's attorneys, Imelda LaMountain, requested that the trial be held outside of Berkshire County, stating that Lent would not be able to get a fair trial because of the publicity it had received from the media.

One other motion by Lent's attorneys was also disallowed. It was to bar the identification of Lent in both the lineup and photo array at the Pittsfield Police Station, saying the two were unnecessarily suggestive. Rebecca Savarese and Russell Davis both picked out photo number six which was Lent. Judge Ford also allowed Savarese and Davis to make a personal identification of Lent during the trail. The judge also refused to have another judge hear the case. Lent's attorneys claimed Ford should not hear the case because he issued the search warrants for Lent's van and his North Adams apartment.

In January, 1995, the trail of Lewis Lent Jr., for the kidnapping, armed robbery, larceny from a person, assault with a dangerous weapon and assault and battery on 12- year- old Rebecca Savarese began in Berkshire Superior Court. Judge Daniel A. Ford was the presiding Judge. The trial lasted four days.

District Attorney Gerard D. Downing prosecuted the case for the Commonwealth. Defense attorneys for Lent were public defenders Richard LeBlanc and Alan M. Rubin.

District Attorney Downing called fourteen witnesses during the trial. The defense didn't put anyone on the stand. They tried to convince the jury that the officers intimidated and coerced Lent into giving statements about crimes he did not commit. They tried to show that the officers deprived him of sleep and food, and that they interrogated him, for three days without giving him his rights.

District Attorney Downing showed that Lent was very talkative and would talk willingly all night. That he gave a five page statement, which he signed. He related how he tried to abduct Rebecca. He told how he kidnapped Jimmy Bernardo and Sara Ann Wood. He told about his *MASTER PLAN FOR ABDUCTING CHILDREN*. He admitted how he was in the process of building his secret room where he was going to keep other victims he kidnapped.

After closing arguments, the case went to the jury which consisted of six men and six women from Hampden County. At 8:45 p.m., the jury returned with their verdict of guilty. Superior Court Clerk Deborah S. Capeless read out loud the jury verdicts. They were out for less than five hours before finding Lent guilty of kidnapping, larceny from a person, assault with a dangerous weapon, and assault and battery. The charge of armed robbery was dismissed by Judge Ford. Lent was taken back to the Berkshire County House of Correction for the night to await sentencing.

On Friday morning, January 14, 1995, Judge Daniel A. Ford sentenced Lent to 17 to 20 years in Cedar Junction State Prison. This was the maximum sentence he could give. Lent received 9 to 10 years for kidnapping and 4 to 5 years on each of the charges of larceny and assault with a dangerous weapon, which would add up to 17 to 20 years. Judge Ford was not happy with the sentence. He called it "insufficient punishment" for a convicted kidnapper. Lent would be eligible for parole in about 11 years. He was taken out of court in handcuffs and was in his cell at Cedar Junction by noon.

Judge Ford impounded the jury list so the media could not badger them on how each of them felt about the case.

There was a disagreement on where Lent should be tried for the murders, as he had been indicted in both Massachusetts and New York State.

Sara Anne Wood's father, the Rev. Robert D. Wood, and Herkimer County District Attorney Michael E. Daley, wanted Lent to stand trial in New York. They had hoped Lent would reveal where he buried Sara. Rev. Wood met with US Attorney General Janet Reno in Washington to see if she could help to get Lent tried in New York State.

LENT PLEADS GUILTY

On Monday, June 3, 1996, Lent admitted killing James Bernardo. This was only one day before his trial was to start in Springfield. Judge Daniel A. Ford decided to move the trail to Springfield because of heavy media publicity. Lent also waived his right to fight extradition to New York.

In May, a competency hearing was held to see if Lent was fit to stand trial for murder. Judge Ford found that he was able to stand trial and set the trial day for June 4, 1996 in Springfield Superior Court. Lent and his attorneys talk to District Attorney Gerard Downing right after the hearing, trying to make a deal so that Lent would serve his time in a federal prison. The inmates at Walpole did not like pedophiles and beat Lent regularly. Lent thought he would be safer in a federal prison. Lent would have to tell where the body of Sara Ann e Wood was.

The District Attorney's office was going to have 54 witnesses testify in court at the trial. Each officer who testified in the Savarese case in January of 1995 was given a transcript of his testimony so they could review it in preparation for the trial.

Judge Daniel A. Ford sentenced Lent to the mandatory sentence for first-degree murder, life in prison without parole.

In June, 1996, Lent was turned over to NY State authorities; he was to stand trial in January. Lent pled guilty to killing Sara Anne Wood. Judge Patrick Kirk levied in his Herkimer courtroom the maximum penalty for second-degree murder, 25 years to life. Judge Kirk thanked Lent for answering a question in his mind. Could he impose the state's new death penalty on anyone? This was a new law in New York, which Lent was not eligible for. He told Lent that he could with no question. Judge Kirk also stated "I'm sure God has a place for you in hell."

Lent was returned to Massachusetts where he is serving life without parole sentence.

Sara Anne Woods body has never been found, along with other of Lent's victims.

STILL UNSOLVED MURDERS

1. Gordon Eyerly, 13, of Lake County, Florida. In 1977, Eyerly was found hanging by a white rope. Lent lived 50 yards away in a trailer.

2. Robert Gutkaiss, 15, of Stephentown, New York. His body was found in July 1983, in a wooded area. He was last seen picking strawberries. Lent traveled through Stephentown on his searches for victims.

3. Holly Piirainen, 10, of Grafton. Massachusetts. Abducted on Aug. 5, 1990, her body was found on October 23. Holly looked a lot older than 10 years old. This was another town where Lent traveled.

4. James Lusher, 16, of Westfield, Massachusetts. He disappeared on November 6, 1992, and has never been found. His bike was found in a pond, just like James Bernardo's.

5. Lynn Burdick, 18, of Florida, Massachusetts. She was kidnapped out of a store she worked in, on April 17, 1982. She was 18 years old, but looked younger. She had a slight build, and weight only 80 to 90 pounds. Lent prowled this area for victims.

(All the above were dark-haired, white youths in their early teens.)

1995

FISCAL YEAR
July 1, 1994 TO June 30, 1995

On July 3, 1994, Sgt. John T. O'Neil was appointed lieutenant by Mayor Gerald Doyle. Chief Gerald M. Lee assigned him as Commander of Squad B. On September, 23, 1994, Chief Lee assigned him to represent the department on the City of Pittsfield Traffic Commission.

SIX YEARS TO ARREST BANK ROBBER

It was August 3, 1994, when a single male with scarf covering his face entered the City Savings Bank branch office on Williams Street. He was average height about, 5'-8" to 5'-10", and weighted between 160 to 175 pounds. He wore a black, baggy, hooded, short-sleeve sweatshirt with black and gray stripes over his dark shirt; pants were dark in color with bright white sneakers. He yelled to the three tellers, one manager, and one customer that it was a hold-up; he said he had a bomb in the duffle bag he was carrying, and demanded money.

Tellers handed over a total of $2,109 to the robber. Exiting the bank the robber got on his getaway vehicle, a ten speed mountain bike. The bank customer, a 75 year old male, went out the door right after him. The 75 year old tried to block the bike from getting out of the parking lot with his car, tapping him once. In doing so, the scarf and hood became loose and revealed the robber's face. He then followed the bike and rider up Doreen Street into the sand pits, where he lost him.

One teller ran to the front door and locked it, while another pulled the hold-up alarm, sounding in the police station at 11:15 a.m. Captains Anthony J. Pires and Anthony J. Riello, along with crime scene services and detectives, responded to the bank. The bank was closed for the rest of the day.

Going to the sand pits, officers found the mountain bike in a river. They also found part of the stolen money hidden in some bushes. Only two to three hundred dollars was missing. A composite sketch showing the robber wearing a mustache was able to be made with the 75 year old's detailed description.

Detectives worked on the bank robbery for six years, with no results. Then, in January 2001, Lanesboro Police Officer Timothy Sorrell received some information that a John J. Chipechase, of Madison Avenue, had committed the bank robbery. Officer Sorrell contacted Detective Peter T. McGuire with his information.

After a little digging, Det. McGuire found out that Chipechase was on probation. Calling Chipechase's probation officer, John A. Torchio, McGuire asked if he would bring Chipechase to the station for an interview. Torchio told Det. McGuire that he couldn't transport anyone in his personal vehicle, as it was against his department's rules.

Detective McGuire made arrangements for a cruiser to pick up Chipechase the next morning. Torchio met both Chipechase and Det. McGuire in the Detective Bureau along with Det. Glenn Civello. At this time Chipechase was not under arrest, but McGuire gave him his Miranda rights. Torchio told Chipechase to be truthful with McGuire.

Chipechase was on parole for a conviction of possession of burglar's tools. He also had failed a recent drug test. Det. McGuire told Chipechase he wanted to talk about a bank robbery that happened back in 1994. Chipechase looked down at the floor and said, "I'm not saying I did or didn't do it. I just don't want to go to jail tonight." McGuire told him that he would summons him to court. Chipechase then gave a written statement to Det.

McGuire and Civello on how he held-up the bank. He had waited in the parking lot for almost an hour until it was empty of customers' cars before he went into the bank for the hold-up.

Torchio called over to court and talked to his supervisor, who told him to arrest Chipechase on the parole violation. As he was already under arrest, Det. McGuire told him he was charging him with armed robbery while masked, assault and battery, and four counts of assault with a dangerous weapon, a bomb.

In Superior Court before Judge Daniel A. Ford, Chipechase's attorney, Nathaniel Green, filed a motion to have the statement Chipechase gave to Det. McGuire and Civello kept out of evidence at his trial. Green said that the statement was involuntary and that he was under the influence of marijuana when he gave it. Assistant District Attorney Joan McMenemy put three witnesses on the stand to testify that they didn't think Chipechase was under the influence, that he was alert and coherent when he gave the statement. Judge Ford took all the evidence under advisement and said he would give a decision before the case went to trial, placing $5,000 bail on Chipechase. Judge Ford ruled that a person under Chipechase's circumstances could believe he was in custody and not free to leave and that Det. McGuire acted properly in giving Chipechase his rights.

On March 13, 2002, in Superior Court, before, Judge Thomas J. Curley Jr., almost 8 years after the robbery, Chipechase pleaded guilty to the charges and was sentenced to five to six years in the state prison.

BADLY BEATEN FEMALE, RUN OVER, LEFT TO DIE

In the early morning hours of November 15, 1994, two bow hunters found the badly beaten body of Kristal Hopkins, 16. The two hunters were camping out on the mountain and at about 4:00 a.m., heard a car take off from the area where they found the body.

Kristal was dying from multiple blunt trauma and hypothermia, as she lay in a fetal position on Berry Pond Circuit Road in Pittsfield State Forest. It was a frigid morning. Kristal was rushed to Hillcrest Hospital by Pittsfield Police Ambulance. She was pronounced dead at the hospital.

Lead investigator was Sgt. Richard Smith of the Massachusetts State Police attached to District Attorney Gerald Downing's office, with the assistance of Pittsfield detectives.

A state police crime scene unit was brought in. Three K-9 units and their dogs were also brought in to search the area. Divers searched Berry Pond a short distance downhill from the summit. Berry Pond is the highest natural body of water in the state. From the summit you had a view of Lebanon Valley, New York.

BERRY POND

STONE WITH TAR

Kristal was found on the edge of the road. The road was a smooth, hard surface, made from small pieces of stone mixed with tar. Blood was found in three spots: spatters at the top, then more about 10 feet away. The last stain, an irregularly shaped spot about 6 inches wide, was about 35 feet from the first spot.

After an investigation, Adam Rosier, 23, was arrested for her murder.

The Rosier case became a long grind for District Attorney Gerard Downing's staff. Assistant District Attorney David Capeless had won favorable decisions in crucial pretrial hearings in the fall that allowed testimony about blood spatters on Rosier's car and a DNA comparison of blood.

This was believed to be one of the first times that one aspect of DNA tests, the Short Tandem Repeat technique of polymerase chain reaction analysis, was introduced at trail in the Commonwealth. Dr. Charlotte Word, a senior scientist with Cellmark Diagnostics of Maryland, testified at the trail that the STR technique added three genetic markers to the suite of six identified by other polymerase chain reaction methods. With the STR factored in, Word estimated the chances of the spatters found on the underside of Rosier's 1985 Mercury Capri, that he drove the night of the murder being someone other than Hopkins' was 1 in 770,000. If STR was excluded and only six markers analyzed, the odds dropped to a much lower 1 in 5,500.

At a preliminary hearing in late November and early December, Rosier's defense attorney, Robert Carnes, argued without success that the STR data and Cellmark's statistical analysis of it should not come in front of the jury.

At the trail, Dale Burke, a prosecution witness, said Rosier appeared at his bedside the day after his Capri was impounded to ask Burke if he and Barry Secord, who both said they saw Rosier speeding away from the forest about the time Hopkins was killed, would provide him with an alibi.

Burke said he was stunned to hear Rosier tell him that he beat Hopkins during an argument after they had sex in Rosier's car at the lookout point over Berry Pond. Burke testified that Rosier told him that he threw Hopkins, who was naked from the waist down, out into the night. He got out of the car, punched Hopkins in the face several times, stomped on her with his foot when she finally fell, backed over her with the car, and then drove over her again as he sped away, watching in his rearview mirror as she writhed on the pavement.

ADAM ROSIER

Carnes, who declined to put Rosier on the stand, told the jurors that inconsistencies in the prosecution's theory of the crime should provide the seeds of the reasonable doubt they needed to acquit his client. There was no physical evidence, like blood, skin or semen, conclusively linking Rosier to the crime. Carnes also attacked the testimony of Burke and Secord, both of whom, he noted, had charges pending at the time of the trail and stood to gain from their cooperation with the district attorney's office.

The Berkshire Superior Court jury deliberated less than two hours before finding Adam Rosier guilty of first-degree murder, on January 22, 1996.

Judge Daniel A. Ford imposed the mandatory sentence of life in prison without the possibility of parole.

CHIEF LEE AND COMMAND STAFF - MARCH 23, 1995

1996

FISCAL YEAR
July 1, 1995 TO June 30, 1996

ARRESTED UNDER NEW LAW-RESISTING ARREST

On March 2, 1996, Officer Jeffrey Bradford responded to a complaint of a disturbance at a residence on John Street at 5:50 p.m. Upon arriving, Paul B. came at Officer Bradford with his fists clenched. Bradford pepper-sprayed Paul B. and with the help of Officer Thomas Barber was able to handcuff and ground-stabilized him. While doing this, Paul B. managed to kick Bradford several times.

Aside from assault and battery on a police officer and disorderly conduct, Paul B. was charged with the new law of resisting arrest. The law only took effect on February 22, which provided for a maximum term of 2 years in the House of Correction and/or a maximum fine of $500 for those convicted. Massachusetts had been one of only a few states that did not have such a statue on the books. This was the first arrest under the new law.

MAN ARRESTED AFTER HIDING IN HOT CHIMNEY

On April 1, 1996, police were called to a disturbance on Hawthorne Avenue. It was Friday night at about 7:15. Upon arriving, Florence G. was arrested for disturbing the peace. Detective Owen Boyington heard a noise in the attic above them. Florence G. informed the officers that Jackie T. was hiding in the attic, and officers went upstairs to investigate. Jackie T. locked the attic door behind him, forcing Officers Dwane Foisy and Thomas Barber to remove the door.

When they did, Jackie T. was nowhere to be found in the attic. But officers heard Jackie T.'s footsteps on the roof. Officer Foisy looked out a window and saw Jackie T.'s head disappear down a chimney located on the adjacent roof.

The Pittsfield Fire Department was called to furnish its ladder truck to extricate Jackie T. The furnace was on! But just as the ladder truck arrived Officer Foisy and Detective Thomas Bowler managed to talk him out of the chimney unharmed, although his clothes and hands were a little sooty.

Jackie T. was arrested on an outstanding warrant for being an idle and disorderly person. He was released on $100 bail for his arraignment in District Court and told to clean up before he appeared. Florence G. was released on her own recognizance and ordered to appear in District Court the next morning.

1997

FISCAL YEAR
July 1, 1996 to June 30, 1997

The department received a $4,000 trunk-mounted audio-video recorder with a double camera, low-light capability and portable microphone. This unit was a gift from the local chapter of Mothers Against Drunk Driving. One camera was mounted on the windshield of the cruiser and could be activated manually, in conjunction with the cruiser's lights, or by voice command by a portable microphone that communicates with the VCR by radio waves. The second camera was inside the cruiser. The video feed is switched to the inside camera when an arrestee is placed in the back of the cruiser. The recorder and playback unit were safely stored in a locked, weather-proof, shock-resistant steel box in the trunk of the cruiser. Tapes are kept for 90 days and cannot be stopped, rewound or erased after the camera is started. This cruiser was assigned to the Traffic Division.

During the year the department investigated 1,353 accidents, 7 fatalities, 274 with personal injury, 1,072 accidents with property damage, and 366 hit and run accidents.

FREE-WHEELING ON NORTH STREET

During the month of August on Sundays the department shut down the northbound lanes on North Street between Melville Street and Maplewood Avenue.

This was done so roller bladers, skateboarders, and bikers would have a place to perfect their skills. Ramps were set up in the middle of the street. Hundreds of kids and their families turned out to watch. This was done as the department was receiving complaints about skateboarders and bikers on the sidewalks knocking down shoppers. The department received a grant for a mobile skateboard ramp that could be transported to different parks and community events.

GOVERNOR WILLIAM F. WELD AND SECRTARY OF PUBLIC SAFETY. KATHLEEN M. O'TOOLE- HER GRANDFATHER WAS A PITTSFIELD POLICE OFFICER

CHANGING OF CHIEFS

Chief Anthony J. Riello

On January 3, 1997, Chief Gerald M. Lee retired. Chief Lee became chief on November 25, 1992, and served as chief for a little more than 4 years.

On January 4, 1997, Chief Anthony J. Riello started his tenure as chief for the next ten years, retiring on December 1, 2007.

1998

FISCAL YEAR
July 1, 1997 to June 30, 1998

JULY 4, 1997-CHIEF ANTHONY RIELLO

SGT. LOSES FIGHT WITH CANCER

On September 11, 1997, Sergeant Terrence P. Donnelly, 41, died of cancer at Brigham & Women's Hospital in Boston. Sergeant Donnelly was a sixteen- year member of the force. He had been undergoing treatment for leukemia for several months.

Before being promoted to sergeant, Terry worked in the narcotics unit. His partner in the unit, Patrick Barry, now Captain Barry, a close friend, said Donnelly brought kindness and a sense of humor to a tough job. "He was the very best we had in narcotics, and we are going to miss him."

During Donnelly's months in Boston, officers made regular trips to visit him, to boost his spirits and check on his progress. Detective Thomas Bowler, a close friend of Terry's, spoke of Terry's love for his three minor children, Kayla, Sean and Terrence Jr.

A morning funeral procession drew merchants and downtown residents to their doorways and sidewalks along North Street and Columbus Avenue, where they watched the passing of the hearse containing Sgt. Donnelly's body.

Marching behind the hearse were Pittsfield officers, state police and other officers from surrounding cities and towns. Bringing up the rear were Berkshire County District Attorney Gerard Downing and members of his staff, court officers, probation officers and others. Outside the fire station on Columbus Avenue, the funeral procession passed under a flag- draped arch formed by joining two fire truck ladders across the street.

SGT. TERRENCE P. DONNELLY FUNERAL PROCESSION
PHOTO BY CRAIG F. WALKER-EAGLE STAFF

At St. Mark's Church, the church bells rang as the pews inside filled with friends and colleagues. The Rev. Henry Dorsch imparted comforting words and prayers.

The casket was taken out of the church, through two orderly columns of saluting police officers with their badges covered with black shrouds.

Three school buses brought officers and friends to St. Joseph's Cemetery. At the grave site, Donnelly's purple Mongoose police mountain bike was parked. Father Dorsch said the final words and prayers. A volley of shots was fired, taps were played, a police siren wailed in the background. A bagpiper played the familiar sound of "Amazing Grace."

REVERSE STING

On Friday, January 30, 1998, Sgt. Patrick Barry and members of the drug unit set up a reverse sting. Two undercover officers posed as drug dealers on Francis Avenue. It didn't take long before a city man tried to buy crack cocaine from them. He wanted to broker a deal with them. He offered them sexual favors from a woman friend of his, in exchange for the drugs.

The man left and returned with his female friend. The undercover officers negotiated a deal and turned over some drugs to them. After they received the drugs, the officers identified themselves and placed the pair under arrest. They were charged with soliciting sex and possessing crack cocaine. In District Court, the male denied a charge of enticing a person for prostitution and possession of cocaine. An additional charge of assault and battery on a police officer was also brought. During the booking procedure the male attacked Officer Jeffrey Bradford. The female pleaded not guilty to a charge of prostitution and possession of cocaine.

Moving their reverse sting operation to the corner of North and Melville Streets; within two hours they had another male under arrest.

This reverse sting was one of 18 that the drug unit had done since the last half of 1995. Forty-one persons were arrested in less than three years for trying to buy drugs. These stings caused street sales to almost come to a halt in the city, driving the dealers inside. Buyers were fearful that they could be buying from an undercover police officer.

OPERATION CRACKDOWN PHASE II

On Friday and Saturday, February 6 and 7, 1998, members of the department's drug unit and members of the Berkshire County Drug Unit executed seven search warrants, making 26 arrests. They confiscated 80 grams of cocaine with a street value of about $16,000.

On phase one of Operation Crackdown, which took place on January 22, 16 were arrested in a predawn raid on 103 Bradford Street in which 10 apartments were searched and $1,400 of crack was recovered. 103 Bradford had become a haven for drug dealers and drug users. In this raid only dealers were targeted.

Operation Crackdown was a five-month undercover operation. A total of 41 people were arrested. Eleven firearms were taken off the street. $8,000 in cash and $17,400 in crack cocaine was retrieved in the raids.

On Monday morning, twenty-five suspects were in Central Berkshire District Court, which caused somewhat of back log in their arraignment before Judge Anthony J. Ruberto. One of the defendants failed to show up and a non-bailable warrant was issued for her arrest. Each suspect scrambled to get a lawyer. Fifteen were released after their arraignments on their personal recognizance. Six were held on $100,000 bail and the other four on lesser amounts.

All the suspects were brought before the Grand Jury and indictments were handed down; their cases were dismissed in District Court and heard in Superior Court.

The department's drug unit, which consisted of Sgt. Patrick Barry, Officer Thomas Harrington, and Officer Glen Decker, were assisted in the raids by members of the Detective Bureau and uniform officers.

Sgt. Patrick Barry notified all the landlords that they were expected to evict the suspects who were arrested and charged in the two raids or face criminal charges themselves.

NEW FOUR LEGGED MEMBER OF DEPARTMENT

In April of 1998 the department, under a $3,000 dollar federal grant, purchased a new German shepherd, named Jack. Officer Marc Strout became the city's newest K-9 officer.

Up until now the department for the last seven years had only one K-9, Iyox, with its handler Officer Dwane Foisy.

Officer Strout had to learn to give his new partner commands in Czech because this was the language he was trained in. German shepherds are often used in police work because of their intelligence and obedience.

1999

FISCAL YEAR
July 1, 1998 TO June 30, 1999

JULY 4, 1998-OFFICER JEFFREY COCO ON RUNNING BOARD
CARRYING .45 THOMPSON MACHINE GUN

CHAPTER THIRTY-FOUR

FIRST LADY HILLARY CLINTON VISITS PITTSFIELD

On Tuesday, July 15, 1998, First Lady Hillary Rodham Clinton visited Pittsfield and its Historical Colonial Theatre at 113 South Street. The first lady's motor caravan had three buses in it. The caravan was escorted down West Housatonic Street to South Street by four police motorcycles. An estimated crowd of 20,000 citizens awaited her. It was a beautiful, hot, sunny summer day; the temperature in the upper 80s. The caravan was almost two hours late, due to one of the buses breaking down on the Garden State Parkway.

The First Lady was on the White House Millennium Council's tour to "Save American's Treasures". She was to visit two locations in Berkshire County, the Colonial Theatre in Pittsfield and The Mount, home of Edith Wharton, in Lenox.

Members of the crowd started to gather at 1:30 p.m., at this time the blocked off area opened. For admittance to the area, one of three different passes was required. A white pass that would admit 2, to the general area, a red pass for special guest, and a blue one for honored guest. No signs or lawn chairs were permitted.

Mrs. Clinton was introduced, following remarks by Mayor Gerald S. Doyle Jr., U.S. Rep. John W. Olver, and National Endowment for the Arts Chairman William J. Ivery, and Friends of the Colonial Theater Restoration President Robert Boland. Mrs. Clinton gave her speech to a flag-waving crowd. After her speech, she stepped down from the platform and shook hands with many members of the crowd.

BEHIND THE SCENE WORK

The protection of the first lady was the job of the U. S. Secret service. The Pittsfield Police Department's job, with the help of the Sheriff's Department and State Police, was crowd and traffic control. A meeting with the Secret Service was held at the Hilton Hotel on July 10, 1998. Present were members of the Secret Service, Chief David W. Berkel of the Lenox Police Dept., Pittsfield Fire Chief Raymond Risley, three members of the Mass. State Police, two lieutenants and one Bomb Squad Technician. From the Pittsfield Police Department were Chief Anthony J. Riello, Uniform Captain Cosmo Spezzaferro, and Lt. John T. O'Neil. Lt. O'Neil coordinated this event for the department between the many agencies involved. Information packets for internal police use were passed out by the U.S. Secret Service.

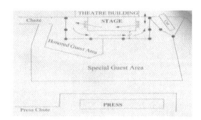

MAP DEPICTING AREA OF STAGE

The department had 32 officers on the detail throughout the afternoon as well as 12 deputy sheriffs and five auxiliary police officers. Six officers from the department special reaction team patrolled rooftops. One sharp-shooter was placed in the South Congregational Church steeple. Extra dispatchers were also brought in. Over 365 hours were put in for security. Security was extremely visible for the event. There were also a number of plain- clothes officers from Pittsfield and the State Police, mingling among the crowd.

South Street between Park Square and the intersection of South Streets and East and West Housatonic Streets was closed to traffic from 6:00 p.m. the night before until 8:00 p.m. the night of the visit. The department's mobile command vehicle was set up on South Street. The Pittsfield Fire Department had four squads of EMT's strolling through the crowd. Six people were overcome by the heat, four were treated on the scene and two were transported to the hospital.

The event ended without any arrests or incidents. Everyone waved as the caravan headed out of Pittsfield, toward the Mount in Lenox, breathing a sigh of relief.

OFFICER GETS SPRAYED BUT NOT WITH MACE

August 4, 1998, was a warm summer night. Officers Leonard H. Pruyne and Jeanne M. Veltri were dispatched to Leroi Drive where a baby skunk had become entangled in a rolled-up volleyball net. Upon approaching the unmoving baby skunk the officers thought it was dead. Officer Pruyne borrowed a pair of hedge clippers from the home owner, cutting away the net to free the baby black and white. As soon as it was free, it thanked Officer Pruyne, by blasting him in his arm with his powerful smelly spray. Officer Pruyne picked up the skunk and carried it to a nearby field, where he released it. The home owners thanked the officers, but from a distance.

LEONARD H. PRUYNE

Thinking that he could be a risk of contracting rabies, Officer Pruyne went to the ER at Berkshire Medical Center. There he was advised to begin a series of rabies shots as a precaution. After his shot, the ER staff told Officer Pruyne he could leave and they would take care of the paper work later.

Back at the station no one wanted to spend much time talking to Officer Pruyne. One of the officers found a bottle of perfume, sprayed it into the air, trying to get rid of the skunk smell. Lt. John O'Neil excused Officer Pruyne from the rest of his shift as no one wanted to get near him.

ARMED MAN ROBS BANK

It was Saturday, November 14, 1998, when a heavy-set male in his late twenties entered the City Savings Bank branch office at the Big N Plaza on West Housatonic Street. Displaying a handgun, he ordered the tellers to place money into a beige plastic supermarket-type bag. He then fled out the front door at 9:20 a.m., going around the building heading up the embankment toward the railroad tracks.

Uniform officers and a K-9 unit searched the area with any luck. The bank's surveillance cameras took several photos during the robbery. One of these photos was published in the Berkshire Eagle. That morning the phone in the detective bureau rang off the hook from callers who saw the photo in the paper. Andrew Constantinos, 29, was the name they put to the photo.

Det. Sgt. Patrick Barry was in charge of the investigation. Members of the Detective Bureau and uniform officers arrested Andrew Constantinos at his house. They had a warrant charging him with larceny by check in addition to the armed robbery charge. Bail was set at $50,000 for the night. He was arranged in District Court the next morning.

ANDREW CONSTANTINOS

Several months later in Superior Court, Constantinos pleaded guilty and was sentenced to 10 to 12 years in state prison.

NEW CAPTAIN, LEUTENANT AND SERGEANT

On December 6, 1998, Mayor Gerald S. Doyle Jr. and Chief Anthony J. Riello announced the promotion of three veteran officers with a total of 70 years' service between them. The three would be in an acting position until confirmed by the City Council at its next meeting.

Lt. John T. O'Neil filled the position of Administrative Captain. An opening occurred when Captain David R. Boyer retired.

Katherine M. O'Brien was promoted to lieutenant, the first female lieutenant in the history of the department. She was also the first female sergeant in the department. She filled the lieutenant slot vacated by Lt. O'Neil. Lt. O'Brien became the commander of the third shift or mid-night to 8 a.m.

Craig A. Strout filled the vacant sergeant position created by the promotion of Lt. O'Brien. Craig's father, Freddie, was a member of the department, retiring as senior traffic investigator. Craig's son, Marc, is also a member of the department, working the midnight shift.

$100,000 WORTH OF STOLEN GOODS SEIZED

On May 8, 1999, a department task force executed several search warrants and seized stolen property worth close to $100,000. There were ten arrests made in connection with the investigation.

The task force was formed after 308 tires on 81 vehicles were slashed at Johnson Ford at 694 East Street on April 12 for a value of $30,000. The task force arrested the persons responsible for the vandalism of the tires, a twenty-one year old male and a sixteen year juvenile. Detective Glen F. Decker obtained information about the Johnson vandalism while he was conducting an unrelated investigation.

While looking into the vandalism at Johnson Ford, the task force came across several individual property crimes. The task force zeroed in on thefts from places under contract to Sentry Security Service. Sentry was a family-owned security service where two brothers, James J. Tarjick, 27, and Aaron Tarjick, 23, worked.

The task force of eight consisted of five uniformed patrolmen, Michael Maddalena, Michael Ortega, James Parise, Michael Winston and Michael Wynn. Two detectives, Richard LeClair, and Peter McGuire. Detective Sgt. Patrick F. Barry was in charge of the task force.

Detective Sergeant Patrick F. Barry said not all of the arrests were related to the theft ring. They all came as a result of the task force's investigation into a series of property crimes in the city.

Property seized on search warrants included six all-terrain vehicles; four Chevrolet Corvette tires; two snow blowers; two large-screen television, including a 52- inch RCA color TV; generators; police scanners; motor vehicle parts or engines with defaced, altered or obliterated serial numbers; all-terrain vehicle helmets, tires and rims; property from Hancock Shaker Village, a bicycle and other items. The department had to rent a U-Haul truck to move all the items that were recovered by the search warrants.

MOVING STOLEN ITEMS FROM U-HALL VAN

The 52-inch RCA color TV was believed to have been taken from the General electric Athletic Association on Crane Avenue which Sentry Security Services was under contract to watch.

After a concentrated investigation on the Tarjick brothers, arrests and search warrants were issued. The Tarjick brothers ran an operation that relied on electronic equipment. It was sophisticated in the sense that James and Aaron had portable radios, had lookouts, and wore headsets. They would radio to one of their associates on the headset to where they would be doing the crime. The gang also was able to commit crimes by monitoring police activities. Many of the incidents happened when shift changes were in progress at mid-night, or when units were tied up with something else, like at an accident scene or large disturbance, where officers were called off their beats to help out. The Tarjick's were able to monitor police movements by scanning the main radio frequency and the detective bureau's private radio channel. The detective bureau's radio channel was found in scanners during the search of their house.

Aaron was arrested when the department executed a search warrant at his home on Pontoosuc Avenue on May 7. Almost a month later on June 4, his brother James turned himself in.

At their trials in Superior Court in February, 2000, before Judge Daniel A. Ford, both brothers pled guilty to a multitude of charges. Assistant District Attorney Paul Caccaviello prosecuted the cases for the Commonwealth. Lawyers for the defendants were Elizabeth Quigley and Brigid Hennessey. Both sides were able to come to a sentence agreement which was presented to Judge Ford.

There were a total of 33 charges brought against them. Among them were disturbing the peace, carrying a dangerous weapon, receiving a stolen motor vehicle, altering or removing a vehicle I. D. number, uttering a false document, a bill of sale, five counts of breaking and entering in the nighttime with the intent to commit a felony, two counts of armed robbery while masked and one counts of conspiracy to commit armed robbery, eight counts of receiving stolen property, five counts of obliteration of I.D. numbers on a machine, larceny in a building, and possession of marijuana. The time frame of their crimes was between December 1997 and April 1999.

Judge Ford sentenced James to concurrent, five to seven years at Cedar Junction and his brother Aaron to four to six years. They were also given probation for three years on the charges of conspiracy to commit armed robbery while masked and armed robbery while masked for the Pampered Pets armed robbery in December, 1997.

Both brothers could have received a sentence of five years to life in the state prison for the armed robbery charges. When they get out of prison, if they violate any parts of the probation, they could face the above sentence.

2000

FISCAL YEAR
July 1, 1999 to June 30, 2000

MAYOR DOYLE BECOMES JUNIOR POLICE OFFICER

On Friday, May 5, 2000, Chief Anthony J. Riello, Captain Patrick F. Barry, and Captain John T. O'Neil went to City Hall and swore Mayor Gerald S. Doyle in as a junior police officer. Chief Riello presented the mayor with a Pittsfield Police Officer's junior badge to make it official.

On Tuesday night, Mayor Doyle helped officers arrest a couple who stole a pocketbook from a woman who was shopping at the Price Chopper Store on Hubbard Avenue. Mayor Doyle and his son were watching a softball game at the Berkshire County Softball Complex on East Street. Sitting in his car with his son, they were watching the game and listening to the Red Sox game on the radio. The Mayor heard over his police scanner the license plate number of the truck that the duo took off in.

Within minutes, the truck drove into the Softball Complex. The duo got out of truck and hid some items under a car. Mayor Doyle got on his cellphone, calling the station. The truck left the complex and headed West on East Street. Mayor Doyle followed it until he saw Officer Thomas Barber who was dispatched to the complex. Officer Barber stopped the truck on the East Street Bridge. Officer Dale Easton was also dispatched to the complex where he found the women's pocket book underneath a car. Officer Barber placed the couple under arrest for larceny over $250 and larceny from a person.

Chief Riello said "we felt the Mayor's quick action deserved some recognition. Showing how police can make arrests when citizens assist them."

ARRESTED FOR ATTEMPTED MURDER IN TENNESSEE

In the last week of February, 2000, Captain Trent Harris of the Johnson City, Tennessee, Police Department called the department. Captain Harris reported that they had received information that a Michael T. Harper, 21, was living in Pittsfield. His street name was "C-Murder." Harper was wanted in Tennessee for one count of attempted first- degree murder. He was also under investigation for two other counts of attempted murder, one in another nightclub and one at a school dance. Johnson City Police had obtained a warrant for his arrest.

Captain Harris stated that Harper was accused of shooting a Melvin Kirkland, 27, in a Johnson City nightclub on May 29, 1999. He was seriously wounded but the wound was not fatal. Johnson Police worked on the case for four months before they obtained an arrest warrant. Captain Harris said it took them another five months to track him down. Harris received information that Harper, left Johnson City shortly after the shooting and was now living in Pittsfield. Capt. Harris said if Harper was convicted, he could receive a sentence of between 15 to 25 years in a Tennessee State Prison.

Johnson Police considered him to be "ARMED AND A DANGEROUS FELON." They sent his photo and prints to the department.

Michael Kirkland, the victim in the shooting, was later murdered in another nightclub a few months later. Johnson City Police arrested and charged a John Harrington for the murder. A shootout between Kirkland and Harrington took place in the bathroom of a nightclub. Harrington was shot once in the back of the heard and died.

In Pittsfield, detectives and members of the department's drug unit were given the information on Harper. Investigator Glen Decker, the lead investigator, developed information that Harper was living in a second floor apartment building on Linden Street.

A team of detectives, drug officers and uniform officers, along with Det. Capt. O'Neil and Det. Sgt. Mark Bushey, made a raid on the apartment. All officers had their bullet vests on as Johnson Police said he was always armed. Four officers went up the front stairs and four the back stairs. Upon entering the apartment and making a searching, the team found no Harper.

A stake out of the apartment was set up. At 2:00 p.m. on Friday, March

3, Harper was spotted walking up Linden Street heading for his apartment. He was arrested at gun point. He told Detective Thomas Bowler his name was Travis Campbell, but the picture detectives had showed he was Harper.

Bail was set at one million dollars for his appearance in district court on Monday. Harper's attorney on Monday was Veronica J. Fenton of Lenox; Assistant District Attorney Richard M. Locke represented the Commonwealth. Harper signed a waiver of rendition to return to Tennessee. Johnson City Police returned Harper to Tennessee. The charge of giving a false name to a police officer was dropped.

DEATHS CAUSED BY EXTRA-PURE HEROIN

Heroin users were warned on June 3, 2000, to use extreme caution if they purchased any heroin in Holyoke. Two deaths had been traced back to an unusually potent strain of heroin coming from that city. Detectives were investigating the death of a male in his late twenties who died from this heroin in his house off of East Street. Only a few days before this death, another male in his early twenties died from the same batch of heroin. Detectives were able to trace this heroin back to two different dealers in Holyoke.

LARGE-SCALE MARIJUNANA OPERATION

On June 16, 2000, sixteen officers under the command of Lt. Katherine O'Brien, with a search warrant in hand, raided a house at 18 Atwood Avenue. Pittsfield's special response team was used, because it was known that guns were at the house.

Six were arrested and charged with a variety of drug charges, with included distribution of marijuana, possession of marijuana with intent to distribute, and distribution of the drug ecstasy. Undercover officers had made hand-to-hand buys at the house for this designer drug.

Also seized were a .30caliber rifle, a Marlin.44-.40-caliber rifle, a Mauser rifle, and a quantity .22 caliber ammo. Plastic bags, a cigarette rolling machine, hand-held scales, two large pit bull dogs, and more than two pounds of marijuana with a street value of around $12,500 was seized.

Detective Glen Decker was the lead investigator on this case. The house had been under surveillance for over a month.

2001

FISCAL YEAR
July 1, 2000 to June 30, 2001

The department embraced the community policing philosophy by decentralizing police services and staffing five neighborhood police offices with civilian volunteers and beat officers. Each section of the city had a neighborhood police office. There locations were:

Coltsville	954 Crane Ave
Morningside	636 Tyler St
Wilson Park	76 Memorial Drive
West Side	314 Columbus Ave
Madison Ave.	15 Francis Plaza

The Wilson Park and Madison Avenue offices were located in Pittsfield Housing Authority Neighborhoods where they were shared by police and tenants.

Each office was unique in that it reflected the diverse needs of neighborhood residents. The department was able to operate these offices and other projects from the $305,450 grant money it received from the Executive Office of Public Safety.

Some of the other projects this money paid for were:
      Neighborhood Crime Watch
      Neighborhood Police Officers
      National Night Out
      Cops in Shops
      Downtown Ambassador Program
      Night Light
      World Wide Web Access to Pittsfield Police
      Public Access Television Show

BEHIND THE BADGE

"Behind the Badge" was the name of the show the department produced for public television which was an informative program that showed the viewers all aspects of the department and police work. The show was produced at the Pittsfield Community Television Studio. It aired each Thursday at 7:00 p.m. with different guests and aspects of police work each night.

"Cops and Kids" was another program that was funded with grant money. This program was an after-school, community-based collaboration comprised of the police, public and parochial school system, and youth service agencies. It provided a wide range of coordinated prevention, intervention, treatment, and adventure-based programs for 50 city students between the ages of 12 and 14 who were projected to drop out of school or would benefit from such a program.

In 2001, the total strength of the department was 87 sworn officers, with 43 civilian personnel. Among the civilian personnel were 13 dispatchers and 18 school crossing guards. Captain Cosmo Spezzaferro was in charge of the Uniform Division, Captain John T. O'Neil in charge of the Detective Bureau and Captain Patrick Barry, the Administrative Division. There were three lieutenants in charge of the three shifts. There were eleven sergeants, nine in patrol, one in dispatch and one in the drug unit. Eight detectives, two investigators, one narcotics investigator, one DARE officer, four school resource officers, three traffic officers, two K-9 officers, and forty-eight patrol officers.

The detective bureau completed a total of 1,352 investigations. The ID branch of the detective bureau issued 538 Firearm Identification Cards and Licenses to Carry.

The Narcotics Unit confiscated drugs worth $170,290, made 122 arrests, executed 9 search warrants, and arrested 162 persons for possessory offenses.

The total calls for services for the year were 30,856: the midnight shift handed13, 598, the evening shift, 10,491, and the day shift 6,767. The detective bureau reported there were no murders during the year and no fatal accidents were investigated by the traffic bureau.

There was a 7.2% reduction in violent crimes during the year.

CHAPTER THIRTY-FIVE

BOMB IN RED BOX=BANK ROBERY

On Thursday, August 31, 2000, a white male in his mid-30s, about 5'-9" to 5'-10" tall, walked into the Berkshire Bank's branch office at 75 Cheshire Road. He came in by the rear entrance of the bank. Once inside he yelled to the employees that he had a bomb in a reddish shoe box he was carrying. He ordered tellers to put their drawer money into a bag he brought with him. There were no customers in the bank. Then he ordered all ten employees into a back room, telling them he was leaving the shoe box with the bomb in it on the counter. He left by the back door. The robber wore a wig with dark dreadlocks, a bandana, a green T-shirt under a plaid vest, and dirty blue dungarees. His right arm was wrapped in a bandage. He had a tattoo similar to a cross or swastika on his forehead, just above his sunglasses. The bank's security camera captured the whole event while it was taking place.

ASSISTANCE OF THE PUBLIC IN HELPING TO IDENTIFY THE
PERPETRATOR OF THE BERKSHIRE BANK ROBBERY ON 08-31-00
THE FOLLOWING IS A COMPOSITE SKETCH OF THE ROBBER

Witnesses in the parking lot saw the robber leaving the bank, heading to a gray older-model van which had windows all around it. They noticed this van because it was next to the bank facing a northerly direction, taking up four parking spaces.

The Pittsfield Fire Department responded as a bomb was thought to be in the building. After a search of the bank no reddish shoebox could be found.

Officer Dwane Foisy and his K-9 dog Iyox were called to the bank. This was done to see if the dog could pick up a track of the robber and follow it to the van.

Captain John T. O'Neil, commander of the Detective Bureau and Drug Unit, assigned Detectives Peter McGuire and Glenn Civello as lead investigators with FBI agent T.J. Roberts of the Springfield Office. The FBI was called in because the bank's money was insured by the Federal Deposit Insurance Corp. Detectives took statements from all the tellers and did several line ups, with no luck.

ONE OF SEVERAL LINE UPS

BREAK IN BANK ROBBERY

A break in the instigation came on June 6, 2001, almost a year later, when a Troy, New York, branch bank was robbed. It was about 11:00 a.m. when a man wearing a wig, fake mustache, fake goatee and a homemade tattoo on his forehead with some kind of a bandage on his arm entered the bank. He handed a teller a note saying he had a bomb. He fled the bank without any money when an armed armored-car guard entered the bank.

An observant teller snuck into a back room and called the Troy Police. Officers were waiting outside when he fled the bank. A short-lived chase ensued but the robber was arrested. He had a loaded .22- caliber handgun in his waistband. The robber was identified as Robert L. Krug who was indicted by a New York Grand Jury of attempted first-degree robbery and second-degree criminal possession of a weapon. He posted bail and was released from custody.

Recognizing the similarities between the two cases, the threat of a bomb, and the homemade tattoo on forehead and bandage on arm, Pittsfield investigators began working with Troy Police. In November a case was presented to the Berkshire Grand Jury by the District Attorney Office, which returned a true bill.

On December 6, 2001, Robert L. Krug, 52, of New Baltimore, New York, pleaded not guilty to one count of armed robbery while masked. Judge Thomas J. Curley Jr., in Berkshire Superior Court, set bail of $1,000 cash or $10,000 surety. Krug posted bail and was released for his trail. Krug was found guilty in New York State and sentenced to prison. Massachusetts lodged an arrest warrant with the New York authorities, to be served when he is released from prison. As of August 20, 2011, Krug was still severing his time in New York.

DEPARTMENT'S SECOND HAUNTED HOUSE

On October 27 and 28, 2000 the department staged its second annual haunted house at 70 North Street. The first haunted house was in the basement of the station, which was found to be too small. With the help of two dedicated volunteers, Jack and Betsy Roy, who started working on props just after Christmas, the haunted house took shape.

About 40 students from Taconic High School played the parts of ghosts, goblins and other creatures in the graveyard. Officers took kids' fingerprints and passed out candy.

Over 3,000 people went through the haunted house. Numerous people and businesses donate supplies to make the event possible. Captain John T. O'Neil was chairman of the haunted house committee.

80 YEARS OF TRADITION ENDS

The retirement on Friday, November 3, 2000, of Sergeant Gary Danford, ended the long tradition of having a Danford on the police force. Back in the 1920's Gary's grandfather, Stanley C. Danford was a patrolman. Then came his father, Malcolm J. Danford, better known as "Pinky." Malcolm was 6 foot plus and weighted a good 200 pounds. You didn't want to get in a tousle with him.

Before Gary joined the force, he was in the army and he fought in Vietnam. He was a recipient of a Purple Heart. Gary joined the force in November, 1969. Soon after his brother, Mark J., became an officer. Now there were four members from the Danford family on the force. His father's brother, James Danford was also on the force. Gary's father, Malcolm, passed away while still on the job in the 1980's

Gary made detective in 1984 and worked on several murder cases. In 1997 he made sergeant and was transferred to the uniform division. After his father died, his uncle Jimmy retired and his brother, Mark, left the department after fifteen years, and became a parole officer in the state of Florida.

Gary had the longest service of the Danford family, serving 31 years.

STANLEY   MALCOM   JAMES   GARY   MARK

DA GERALD DOWNING SAYING GOOD LUCK
PHOTO BY INV. STIMPSON

OFFICERS GIVING HAND SALUTE

THREE PIT BULLS VS THREE OFFICERS

It was Wednesday, December 27. 2000, and cruiser Officer James Stimpson was on regular patrol. It was about 3:30 p.m. with only a half hour left on his shift. He was on Robbins Avenue when he saw people running out of a house screaming. They were yelling that pit bulls were attacking them.

Not knowing what he had, Jim called for backup. Sgt. Delmont Keyes and Officer Michael Wynn arrived. Going up to the second floor, they could hear dogs fighting. There they found Rita, baby-sitting for a friend. The friend had two pit bulls that were fighting with a third pit bull. The third pit bull belonged to Rita, who had locked her pit bull in a bed room, from which he somehow escaped. Rita tried to break the fighting dogs up, but to no avail. Other friends in the apartment, in fear of getting bit, ran down the front stairs and out into the street yelling.

The three officers tried to break the dogs up by spraying them with Mace, emptying four or five cans on them with no luck. Officer Wynn retrieved a 12-gauge shotgun from his cruiser. The shotgun was loaded with bean-bag shells. Officer Wynn fired five rounds off in attempt to stun and break up the fighting pit bulls. All five rounds were direct hits, but had no effect on them. They just kept on fighting. The rounds didn't do any physical damage to the dogs because they didn't open upon contact. Finally the officers were able to distract the most hostile dog long enough to lock him in the back

Page 316

stairway. Once he was out of the picture the other two stopped fighting.

Pittsfield Animal Control Officer Joseph Chague was dispatched to the scene and removed two of Rita's friend's pit bulls from the apartment. Rita's pit bull was taken to her veterinarian to be patched up. Luckily, no one was injured

200 GRAMS OF CRACK COCAINE COMING FROM NEW YORK

Members of the department's drug unit and Berkshire County Drug Task Force received information from a confidential informant, that on Monday January 15, 2001, a large shipment of crack cocaine was coming into Pittsfield from New York City.

The informant gave a description of the suspects, the car, and its registration number, and the route and the time they would be coming into the city. Members of the task force set up surveillance on Route 295 in Richmond to Route 41 going into Pittsfield.

The suspect's car, a 2001 Ford Focus, was spotted on 295 followed by a Pontiac Grand Am. Occupants of both cars stopped at a convenience store on 295 and had a conversation. Getting back into their cars, they continued toward Pittsfield.

On Route 41 on the Pittsfield and Richmond line, both cars were stopped by police. In the trunk of the Focus officers found 263 grams of crack cocaine, with a street value of more than $26,000. The drugs were discovered by Officer Marc Strout and his canine partner, Nick.

Both occupants in the Focus were charged with trafficking a class B substance and conspiracy to violate the controlled substance act. All three in the Pontiac were also charged with trafficking a class B substance and conspiracy to violate the controlled substance act. Because there was more than 200 grams of crack cocaine, conviction for trafficking would carry the minimum mandatory 15-year state prison sentence. It was a good night's work for the drug task force.

2002

FISCAL YEAR
July 1, 2001 to June 30, 2002

July 4th 2001
Steps-Berkshire County Superior Court House-East Street
Chief of Police Anthony J. Riello

L-R Sgt. Delmont Keyes-Off. Marc Strout-Sgt's Michael Fitzgerald- Mark Bushey-Capt. John T. O'Neil-Chief Anthony J. Riello
Act. Capt. Henry Dondi-Lt. Katherine O'Brien-Sgt's David Granger- Michael Winston-Off. John Murphy
2nd Row Off. Marc Maddelena-Gary Traversa-Det. Richard LeClair-Off. Charles Bassette-Off's Shaun Osborn-Dale Eason-Patrick Duffy
-James Parise-Gary Herland
3rd Row Off's Kim Supranowicz-unkown-Matthew Ortega-David Hallas-James Stimpson-Walter Powell-David Kirchner-Curtis Jasey
4rd Row Off's Russell Quetti, Christopher Kennedy-James McIntrye-Michael Ortega-Raymond Bush-Miles Barber-Gary Herland

JULY 4, 2001

THREATS BY HANDGUN LEADS TO DEATH

It was Tuesday, August 8, 2001, a hot and humid night in Pittsfield. At 5:46 p.m. the dispatch center in the department received a 911 call that a man with a gun was in his apartment attic and was threatening to commit suicide. Two beat officers were first on the scene at 152 Wahconah Street, radioing back to the station that they had a male in his attic with a handgun. Shift Command Lt. David Reilly, a 28- year veteran of the department, who had talked numerous suicidal individuals down, responded to the scene. Also responding was Officer Jeffrey Bradford, an 8- year veteran of the department. Officer Bradford was also a member of the department's tactical team and a medic.

Dispatch alerted members of the department's tactical team to respond to 152 Wahconah Street. Cruiser officers began to block off Wahconah Street and keep back curious spectators who had started to gather. They also evacuated the other residents of the building complex.

Sgt. David Granger, Detective Glenn Decker, and Officer Matthew Ortega joined Lt. Reilly and Officer Bradford in the apartment. They learned that the man in the attic with the handgun was 54 year old John C. Boyd.

Page 318

Boyd told the officers that he had a gun and he would shoot anyone who came near him. The officers could not see him in the attic.

John C. Boyd was despondent; his wife had been put in a nursing home a few months earlier, and she was waiting to have a liver transplant. John would take her out for a drive every Sunday, ending at their apartment. They had also made several trips to Springfield checking about the liver transplant.

Two body bunkers were brought in for Lt. Reilly and Officer Bradford. (A body bunker is a hand- held portable bullet resistant shield with a bullet proof clear window. This window enables the officer to see in front of him without having to expose his head. The bunkers are about two feet wide and three feet tall.)

Lt. Reilly and Officer Bradford tried to convince Boyd to surrender his gun and come down from the attic. While talking to him a single shot rang out. There was dead silence. Both Reilly and Bradford started up the narrow stairs, holding the body bunkers in front of them. Finally Boyd answered the officers back. Then another shot rang out; this time Boyd didn't answer. Thinking he had committed suicide, both officers climbed to the top of the stairs. There in front of them was Boyd with his handgun, cocked and ready to fire. The officers ordered Boyd to drop the handgun, but Boyd started advancing toward them. Fearing for their lives both officers shot. A total of three rounds rang out, striking Boyd.

Officer Bradford rendered first aid, calling for the ambulance crew to come in. Boyd was transported to Berkshire Medical Center where he was pronounced dead.

Crime Scene Service Investigator James Stimpson found one of Boyd's rounds on the roof of 148 Wahconah Street, the house next door. The round went through Boyd's attic wall into his neighbor's attic and through that wall, landing outside on the roof of 148.

As in all police officer shootings, District Attorney Gerald D. Downing had Lt. Richard Smith of Massachusetts State Police Detective Division, start an investigation. Chief Anthony J. Riello placed all five officers on paid administrative leave, which is standard police practice.

After a two month investigation, Berkshire County District Attorney Downing announced that Lt. Reilly and Officer Bradford acted legally when they shot and killed John Boyd.

CHAPTER THIRTY-SIX

$500,000 MISSING FROM WAL-MART

On September 21, 2001, Detective Captain John T. O'Neil, received a call from the Wal-Mart Store in the Berkshire Crossing shopping plaza off Hubbard Avenue. The store reported that on September 14, a cash office associate noticed that only three of the four deposit bags placed in the safe the previous night were in the safe. The discovery led to an audit, which found that between August 3 and September 14, 21 deposit bags had not been deposited in the bank. The 21 bags contained $304,003 in cash and $189,803 in checks made out to Wal-Mart. Captain O'Neil assigned Detective Peter T. McGuire to head up the investigation. The FBI was called and Special Agent T.J. Roberts, of the Springfield office, who worked with Pittsfield on many occasions, was assigned the case.

The joint investigation led to Lucas R. Smith, 20, of Dalton, who was an assistant manager. He worked for Wal-Mart from August 2000, until he resigned to take a job with a local financial service on August 25, 2001. While working for Wal-Mart, Smith had an annual salary of $29,500. He had access to the cash office, where store revenues were kept in a safe. His duties included reconciling bank records with internal deposit records and verifying that the daily deposit slips for each deposit accurately reflected the amount of cash and checks in the deposit bag. Smith had keys to the office and the combination to the safe.

Following Smith's August 25 resignation, it was learned that he was seen in the store at various times after the 11:00 p.m. closing time, with a set of keys and a laptop computer briefcase.

A search warrant was issued for Smith's Dalton residence. FBI Agent T.J. Roberts, Detectives Peter McGuire, Richard LeClair, and Joseph Collias executed the search warrant. A 2001 Cadillac Escalade was seized and towed to the Pittsfield Police Department garage. Smith bought the vehicle in Albany, New York, on September 22, paying $42,000 in cash and financing $5,000 for it. Smith also bought a BMW in Latham, New York, and paid $61,233 in cash for it.

Found in Smith's apartment under the search warrant was $84,000 in cash and $190,000 worth of checks made out to Wal-Mart. Several thousand dollars' worth of purchased merchandise was also seized, including roughly $4,000 worth of computer equipment. There was $13,000 in cash in the Cadillac when it was searched in the police department garage.

Following the search, a federal warrant was issued for Smith's arrest. At 1:30 the next morning, Officer Gary Herland spotted Smith driving a Cadillac in the area of East and Elm Streets. Herland stopped Smith and placed him under arrest. At the time Smith was wearing a $3,500 Rolex watch.

Smith was charged with transporting stolen money in interstate commerce for purchasing the vehicles in another state, a federal charge, rather than a state charge of larceny.

Smith was transported to Springfield for his arraignment in U.S. District Court. He pled guilty to Interstate Transportation of stolen property. He received a sentence of 28 months in Federal Prison. A forfeiture verdict was granted and the money was turned over to the Wall-Mart Store.

ANTI-TERRORISM UNIT ESTABLISHED

The department created an anti-terrorism unit on October 16, 2001 that would research, plan and train for the possibility of terrorist attacks. The unit was formed when the department was overwhelmed with more than 30 calls about suspicious mail and packages, including one delivered to the police station. The package sent to the department contained a book about negotiations and a picture of Osama bin Laden. Inside the envelope was a handwritten note saying "everything is negotiable." After an investigation it was traced back to the sender who thought he was helping by sending the book on negotiations.

Captain Cosmo Spezzaferro, the commander of the uniform division with 32 years on the department and commander of the Berkshire County Special Response Team, was placed in charge of the unit. This meant he would have to be reassigned to the detective bureau where the other two members of united worked, Sgt. Mark Bushey and Officer Michael Grady. Grady helped develop the school critical incident response project.

CAPTAIN COSMO SPEZZAFERRO

Captain John T. O'Neil, commander of the Detective Bureau, would transfer to the Uniform Division for a year. Capt. O'Neil remained as the department's public information officer. He returned to the Detective Bureau and Drug Unit on October 27, 2002.

The unit worked along with the FBI to investigate all threats and to bring charges against anyone issuing a threat, even if it was a prank.

Later, Officer John Gray was assigned full time to the task force and worked out of the Springfield Officer of the FBI for over a year. Then Detective Richard LeClair was assigned to the task force and remained there until he retired in December of 2007.

FALSE ANTHRAX CALL

On Sunday, November 4, 2001, the phone rang at the Dakota Restaurant on South Street. The caller, John D. Jones, 26, of Chapel Hill, North Carolina wanted to speak to the manger. Jones had worked as a bartender at the Dakota for a couple of months, but got fired for being rude to customers. Once on the phone Jones said, "Did you have any salad tonight?" The manager told him yes. Then Jones said "Well I took care of you and your guests, and if I were you, I'd start taking "Cipro." Cipro is an antibiotic used to treat anthrax.

The manager called the Pittsfield Police Department to report the phone call. Detectives, along with the Fire Department and the Berkshire County

Hazmat team, responded to the restaurant. No anthrax was found. Detectives traced the call to Jones in North Carolina; within an hour, they talked to Jones who admitted it was a hoax.

The case was turned over to the FBI because it was a federal crime. Jones was arrested ten days later and appeared in U.S. District Court in Durham, North Carolina. He was held by U.S. marshals and transferred back to Springfield, Massachusetts to U. S. District Court. Jones was incarcerated in a Federal Prison awaiting trial. This was the fourth anthrax case to be prosecuted in Massachusetts. Jones was placed on three years' probation after being found guilty in Federal Court.

OFF THE STREET FOR 7 TO 9 YEARS

On January 24, 2002, Superior Court Judge Daniel A. Ford sentenced Craig A. Hill to the state prison for 7 to 9 years. Hill pleaded guilty to two counts of distribution of cocaine, one count of possession of cocaine with intent to distribute, and one count of possession of marijuana with intent to distribute, all second offenses. He also pleaded guilty to two counts of assault and battery by means of a dangerous weapon and assault and battery on a police officer.

Assistant District Attorney Paul Caccaviello prosecuted the case for the Commonwealth. The defense attorney was Imelda LaMountain.

On May 7, 2001, Officer James Stimpson tried to stop a car driven by Hill. Stimpson knew Hill didn't have a driver's license. Hill jumped from his car on Prospect Street and tried to make it into a house. Stimpson was able to grab Hill and a struggle took place. Hill threw a bag of crack cocaine to his girlfriend who was in the doorway, but she dropped it. The bag contained 38 grams of crack with a street value of about $7,600. Backup officers arrived and subdued Hill. Found in Hill's car was a small amount of marijuana and $1,715 in cash.

Hill was out on $1,000 bail and under indictment for other drug charges. Hill had sold crack to an undercover officer on January 11 and 19. After the last transaction officers went to arrest him. But he drove his car straight at a cruiser, slid into it. He had 7 grams of crack on him with a street value $1,400 and three bags of marijuana when placed in handcuffs.

MAKE OVER OF CRUISERS

On February 1, 2002, the department showed off the new design of the department's cruisers. The old red and white design consisted of multiple stripes covering most of the car doors and about 25 percent of the entire car. The stripes became ripped or torn when a cruiser door was bumped or from normal wear and tear. It was expensive to continually keep the cruisers looking professional.

The new design was a simple silver stripe, with a police patch near the front of each side and Pittsfield Police in letters on both sides.

Chief Anthony J. Riello said that Officer Marc Maddalena wanted to know if the department could look into a new design for the cruisers. A poll was taken among the officers and the navy blue cruiser with the silver trim won out. The new design was a simple silver stripe, with a police patch near the front of each side, and Pittsfield Police in letters on both sides. It cost $5,000 to paint five of the cruisers with the new design. Two new cruisers came with the new design. Now the department had seven professional looking cruisers for patrol.

LT. O'BRIEN VOLUNTEER OF THE YEAR

On February 27, 2002 Lt. Katherine O'Brien, commander of the midnight shift was voted Volunteer of the Year at Pittsfield Girls, Inc. On February 13, Lieutenant O'Brien celebrated 19 years on the department. Lt. O'Brien belongs to the Berkshire Professional Women's Association, the Girl Scouts, and the National Center for Women in Police Work and the Women's Law Enforcement Association. The Lieutenant is also a member of the Pittsfield Mobile Home Park Rent Control Commission, and a volunteer at the Berkshire Museum.

"CAPTAIN" ANNA BENHAM RETIRES

After 38 years on the job in the Traffic Bureau, Anna Benham retired on Friday. March 1, 2002. But only just for the weekend. She returned part time, on Monday, March 4, 2002, for a few hours a week Anna started to work in the Traffic Bureau after passing a Civil Service test. Her first day of work was April 27, 1964. Anna worked under six police chiefs, starting with Chief Thomas H. Calnan. At the time, there were the only two females in the department.

With no female officers to search a female prisoner, Anna was asked to do the searching. Anna also had to accompany male detectives to homes of females who had to be questioned or arrested.

When she started to work, all tickets were either typed or hand written. Each day she would have to go to the Registry of Motor Vehicles, which was located on Bank Row. There she would get the information on newly registered motor vehicles, to keep the departments records up to date.

In 1982, she became one of the department's hearings officer for parking and animal control tickets. She also did the scheduling for the department's 22 school crossing guards, calling in substitute if someone called in sick.

At a surprise party in the squad room, Anna was presented with a 35-year service pin by Chief Anthony J. Riello, saying members of the department referred to her as "Captain Benham" because she ran the traffic bureau when there was no captain there.

CHIEF RIELLO AND ANNA BENHAM

Also present at the party were retired Chiefs William M. Dermody and Gerald M. Lee. Chief Lee said in his joking manner that he only came to make sure she was leaving. She had outlasted 6 chiefs. Chief Dermody said he worked with her for 10 years and that she straightened him out a few times.

OREGON ESCAPEE ARRESTED

On March 12, 2002, a Tuesday, the department received a call from a North Street homeless shelter. They reported that a man and woman with a sick toddler were at their shelter seeking assistance. The toddler had no shoes or winter clothing and appeared to be sick. Officers responding to the call found that the couple and toddler were not there, telling the shelter manager to call back if they came back.

Within an hour the shelter called back, stating the couple was back. Officers responding spoke to a man. He told them his name was Anthony Day, he was 29 years old, and he came to Pittsfield looking for a relative of his. Officers were able to locate Day's relative. Upon speaking to the relative to see if they could help out the couple and child, officers were told she didn't know who Anthony Day was. But she had a relative, named Francis Potter, 38, of Oregon, who had a small child. He was wanted in Oregon for escaping from jail. She showed the officers a picture of Potter who turned out to be the man in the shelter, going by the name of Day.

Contacting Oregon authorities, it was learned that Potter was serving 13 months at Mill Creek Correctional Facility in Salem, Oregon. This was a minimum security state prison with no fences. On February 23, 2002, Potter was in the recreation yard when he walked away. He was picked up by an unknown person who was waiting for him a short distance down the road.

Returning to the shelter, officers arrested Potter for being a fugitive from justice. In district court the next morning, Potter waived extradition and voluntarily returned to Oregon.

2003

FISCAL YEAR
July 1, 2002 TO June 30, 2003

WARRANT ROUNDUP

On November 25, 2002, 34 police officers, deputy sheriffs and probation department personnel took part in an operation to arrest anyone who had an outstanding warrant. Captain John T. O'Neil stated to the news media that there were about 1,800 outstanding warrants just from Central Berkshire District and Berkshire Superior Courts. There were about 6,000 people who were subjects of warrants issued in Berkshire County. This operation had been planned for months. The operation was limited in length so if a person could not make bail there would be room in the cell block to keep him, until he could be brought to the House of Correction for court the next day.

Five teams of four officers were given warrants to serve, arresting an average of five defendants per hour, for a total of 28. Sheriff Department vans were used to transport prisoners to the station, where they were finger-printed and photos taken.

Eighteen defendants were released on bail. Ten were brought to the House of Correction for the night. The roundup started at 8:00 a.m. and lasted until 2:00 p.m.

PAWN SHOP ROBBED AT GUNPOINT

Thursday, December 19, 2002, was a regular day at the department. There was snow on the ground and the temperature was in the 20s. Early in the afternoon dispatch received a 911 emergency call that a holdup had taken place at Luisa's Precious Metals and shots had been fired. The pawn shop was located at 93 First Street at the corner of Eagle Street.

Detective Sergeant Mark Bushey and Detective Peter McGuire were at the corner of Eagle and North Streets. They responded to the Pawn Shop with uniform officers. Upon entering the store they could smell fresh gun smoke in the air.

Talking to the owner, Luisa Economou, who is confined to a wheelchair, and her 72 year-old father, Manuel DoCarmo, detectives, learned that two men entered the store. One man, Hosea Jackson of Wallkill, New York, carried in a duffel bag and put it on the glass counter. Pulling out a black .357-magnum, handgun from the bag, he announced it was a holdup.

Manuel grabbed the barrel of the .357 and a struggle took place with two shots ringing out, one smashing a glass showcase. Manuel and Jackson were rolling around on the floor. Jackson yelled to his partner, Andre Jaheem Decker of Albany, New York to get the gold and platinum chains in the showcase. Decker had to make his way around Luisa who was in her wheelchair blocking the way. Managing to get by Luisa, Decker started to fill his pockets with the chains. Jackson and Luisa's father Manuel were rolling on the floor. Decker came around the counter after taking an envelope from Luisa with $200 dollars in cash. Decker then helped Jackson get up from the floor. Manuel was struggling with a man more than half his age.

Both men bolted from the pawn shop to a waiting minivan, driven by Antonio Castro of Schenectady, New York. The trio drove back to Albany.

Meanwhile, Crime Scene Services Investigator Bruce Eaton dusted for prints and retrieved the bullet fragments. Investigator Eaton found that one of bullets had lodged in the counter, being stopped by a sheet rock screw, hitting it dead center. If the bullet had not hit the screw, it would have hit Luisa in her chest, possibly killing her while she was sitting in her wheelchair. After getting a description of the jewelry, detectives put out an all-points bulletin on the stolen goods. The total value of the chains was $5,000. Pawn shops have a network between themselves where they pass information back and forth. In addition to the department putting out the information about the robbery, so did Luisa to her fellow pawn shop owners.

Decker and the getaway driver Castro were arrested in an Albany pawn shop. They were trying to sell some of the chains. The shop owner said he would give them $600 dollars for the chains, stalling them until Albany Police arrived to make the arrest. Detective Sgt. Bushey and Detective Michael Maddalena, lead investigator on the case, drove to the Albany Police Department that night to confer on the investigation. Jackson was arrested shortly after.

The Albany Police Department charged the trio with receiving stolen property and they were found guilty and sentenced to prison in New York State.

Almost eight years after the robbery the trio had their day in court in Massachusetts. New York State wanted them to serve all their time in New York before releasing them to Massachusetts. First Assistant District Attorney Paul J. Caccaviello prosecuted the case for the Commonwealth.

In 2009, Andre J Decker, who was in his early twenties at the time of the robbery and was on parole, pled guilty to three counts, armed robbery, armed assault with intent to rob a victim older than 60 and using a firearm during the commission of a felony. He was sentenced to nine years in the state prison.

In 2010, Antonio Castro, the getaway driver, pled guilty to one count of being an accessory to armed robbery in Superior Court. Judge John J. Agostini sentenced him to 2 to 2 1/2 years in prison at Cedar Junction, as he was already serving time in prison; Judge Agostini ordered that this sentence run concurrently with his other time. All other charges were dropped, including armed robbery, carrying an unlicensed firearm, armed assault with intent to rob a victim older than 60, and using a firearm during the commission of a felony

DAY BEFORE CHRISTMAS BANK ROBBERY

It was Tuesday, December 24, 2002. The Pittsfield Cooperative Bank at 110 Dalton Avenue had just opened for the day's business at 9:00 a.m.

Michael S. Baggett, 41, of Barton's Crossings, walked into the bank and handed a teller a note saying he wanted money and he had a gun. The teller handed him a packet which contained $2,831 with four marked bills inside it. Exiting the bank, Baggett got into an awaiting Kia, with Nancy E. Leone, 29, of Adams. Witnesses were able to get the license plate number of the car. The department ran the plate number and found it was reported stolen out of Springfield.

All units were given the description of Baggett and the Kia. Television and radio stations picked up the information from police scanners and broadcasted it to the public. Both Baggett and Leone worked at Old Country Buffet. At the time of the robbery Baggett was wearing his Old Country Buffet shirt. Within three hours the station was flooded with calls saying that Baggett could be a suspect in the bank robbery. Officers spotted Baggett riding as a passenger in a green van on First Street. Both Baggett and the driver were placed under arrest. The driver was charged with operating a motor vehicle without a license. When officers searched Baggett, they found the $2,831 on his person with the four marked bills. He still had on his Old Country Buffet shirt.

The Kia was spotted parked on Orchard Street. A stake out was placed on the car and within a few hours Leone was arrested. A line up was held at the station and five tellers from the bank identified Baggett as the bank robber.

At their arraignment in District Court, before Judge Michael Ryan, Assistant District Attorney Robert W. Kinzer, presented the Commonwealth's case.

Baggett had 63 separate convictions. In 1990 he was convicted of armed robbery and was sentenced to five to seven years in the state prison. He had twenty-five default warrants on his record and used a host of aliases. He was processed in nine different states for his crimes.

Leone had ten previous convictions on her record. Besides armed robbery, she was also charged with trying to cash a $1,200 stolen check

On November 22, the couple tried to open a bank account at a Legacy Bank branch by cashing a stolen $1,200 check. They stole a checkbook and a driver's license from a Pittsfield woman who was in a restaurant on January 2002, watching the Super Bowl with some friends. Baggett was also charged with one count of uttering a false check, attempting to cash a false check, and receiving stolen property under $250.

Both pleaded not guilty to all charges. Assistant District Attorney Kinzer asked for $100,000 cash bail which was set for Baggett and $5,000 for Leone. They were both incarcerated at the House of Correction, waiting their arraignment in Superior Court. On Friday, January 31, 2003, both defendants were arraigned in Berkshire Superior Court before Judge Daniel A. Ford.

Michael S. Baggett, also known as Miguel Baggetta, was charged with one count of armed robbery, one count of receiving a stolen motor vehicle, one count of receiving stolen property under $250, one count of larceny under $250 and one count of attaching plates to a motor vehicle in connection with the bank robbery. He pleaded not guilty to all the charges.

The District Attorney's Office dropped the bank robbery charges against Leone because Baggett later gave signed statement saying he drove the car to the bank and Leone didn't know he was going to rob the bank. But she was charged with one count of uttering, one court of forgery and one count of attempt to commit a crime: larceny over $250. She pleaded not guilty to all the charges. Judge Ford ordered Baggett held on $100,000 cash or surety bond and Leone on $10,000 cash or surety bond.

In Superior Court on May 2, 2003 before Judge John Curley, Leone retracted her not guilty plea and pled guilty to uttering a false check, forgery of a check, and attempt to commit a crime. Assistant District Attorney Joan M. McMenemy represented the Commonwealth and Attorney Nathaniel K. Green of the public defender's office was counsel for Nancy Leone. Leone received eighteen months in the Berkshire County House of Correction, six months to be served with credit of 130 days the balance suspended. She was also placed on two years' probation and had to participate in a drug program. In July of 2004 she was found in violation of probation and sentenced to one year in the House of Correction.

Michael S. Baggett was remanded to the Franklin County House of Correction. Robert J. Bray, of the law firm of O'Sullivan & Bray of Greenfield,

Massachusetts, was counsel for Baggett and Assistant District Attorney Joan McMenemy represented the Commonwealth. In June, 2003, Baggett's lawyers filed a motion that the charges against him be dismissed. Judge Daniel A. Ford denied this motion.

On November 14, 2003, Baggett was sent to Bridgewater State Hospital for observation. On December 29, 2003, a little more than a year after the bank robbery, he withdrew his not guilty to armed robbery and pleaded guilty to unarmed robbery. Judge Daniel A. Ford sentenced Baggett to 6 to 9 years at Cedar Junction Prison and credited him with 219 days served. The other four charges were placed on file.

CHAPTER THIRTY-SEVEN

MURDER BY STRANGULATION

Danielle DiOrio was only 23 years old when she met her death by strangulation. Danielle and three others shared an apartment at 68 John Street. Two of the three roommates were away for the weekend. The third, 29 year old Daniel L. Lowry, was under arrest and in a cell at the police station. It was Saturday, January 18, 2003, a cold, wintery night in Pittsfield.

Lowry was arrested when he went next door to 66 John Street to see the landlord, who was not there. Two other renters, Karen and James, were there. An argument took place and Lowry picked up a frying pan and assaulted the couple. The department was called at about 8:30 p.m. and Lowry was placed under arrest for assault and battery by the means of a dangerous weapon. Officers had no reason to check out anything next door at 68.

On Sunday morning at about 9:00 a.m., a friend of Danielle's, Jane, went to 68 John Street to visit her. Jane found Danielle lying on her bed, unresponsive. Jane called 911, and the department dispatched an ambulance to the apartment. The ambulance crew found that Danielle was dead, calling the station for officers to respond. Officer James Stimpson and David Kirchner responded, determining that this was not an ordinary death. Chief Anthony J. Riello, Det. Captain John T. O'Neil, and Det. Sgt. Mark Bushey were notified. Senior Detective Peter McGuire was lead detective in the case.

District Attorney Gerard D. Downing was notified along with the state police crime scene service. Danielle was taken to Holyoke where an autopsy was performed by Associate State Medical Examiner Loren Mednick. Dr. Mednick determined Danielle's death was asphyxiation by manual strangulation, occurring some time Saturday. Her death was ruled as a homicide.

Detectives learned that Danielle had moved into 68 John Street in November. Before that she lived with relatives across the street from her new apartment. She moved because she had a disagreement with her foster-brother and wanted to be on her own. She graduated from Pittsfield High School and had a job at Stop & Shop. Danielle and her sister were adopted by the DiOrio family, when they were 5 and 3 years old.

Danielle's roommate, Daniel L. Lowry, became a suspect in the murder. Lowry lived in Edison, New Jersey, until November 2002, when he moved to Pittsfield. He moved into 66 John Street with two other former residents of New Jersey. He moved into 68 John Street with Danielle and two others in December. Lowry wanted to become a member of the Hells Angels motorcycle club. Danielle's family was not happy with the living arrangements. They believed that the others were taking advantage of Danielle and having her pay all the bills. The only heat in the apartment was from the stove.

Daniel gave a statement to Detective McGuire saying that he and Danielle were on the bed wrestling. He had been drinking a great deal and became violent. That the last thing he remembers, he had his hands around Danielle's neck.

Lowry was arrested and charged with murder on Monday afternoon, after he was interviewed and gave his statement to the detectives. He was held on $1 million bail for his arraignment in Central Berkshire District Court on Tuesday morning. At his arraignment in District Court, Lowry had long black hair down to his shoulders. In Superior Court, Lowry had all his hair shaved off.

In January 2004, Lowry pleaded guilty to voluntary manslaughter for the murder of Danielle DiOrio. He also pleaded guilty to two counts of assault and battery by means of a dangerous weapon, and two counts of intimidation of a witness. These were the charges that were brought for the incident with the frying pan, on his next door neighbors.

First Assistant District Attorney David F. Capeless told the court that Lowry was allowed to plead guilty to manslaughter because Danielle's death was not premeditated. Danielle's death was considered to have occurred during the "heat of passion as a result of argument." Daniel told detectives he did not intend to kill her. Attorney Nathaniel Green was Lowry's lawyer.

The judge ordered Lowry to serve18 to 20 years on the manslaughter charge, and 7 to 10 years on the assault and battery by means of a dangerous weapon and intimidation of a witness charges.

Lowry had to serve his sentences one after another, not concurrently. The total time he would have to serve is 25 to 30 years. He would be eligible for parole after serving 25 years.

SECOND BANK ROBBERY IN THIRTY DAYS

On Friday, January 24, 2003, a lone male about 6-feet- tall, medium build, with a moustache, and a birth mark on the left side of his face, walked into the Banknorth branch office on Dan Fox Drive. He was wearing a barn jacket and a baseball hat with a Michael Jordan sportswear logo on the front and sun glasses.

It was 10:10 a.m. when robber handed a teller a note demanding money. The teller handed over $1,700. The lone male turned and headed out of the bank as the teller pushed the silent holdup alarm. There were no other customers in the bank at this time. The tellers could see him walk toward Stop & Shop Supermarket then lost sight of him.

Chief Anthony J. Riello, Captain John T. O'Neil, Investigator James Stimpson and an undercover detective, along with Banknorth President Donna Beck, watched a replay of the robbery from the bank's surveillance camera.

The picture was crystal clear. A still copy of the robber was made and given to several television stations that aired it. The branch office closed for the day, so Investigator Stimpson could dust for prints.

Officer Dwane Foisy and his K-9 German shepherd, Iyox, were called in to see if they could pick up a track as to which way the robber went, after the tellers lost sight of him.

After the robber's picture was seen on TV, the detective bureau was flooded with calls. Callers identified Daniel T. McArdle, 39, of Thompson Lane, Brainard, New York, as the robber. McArdle worked at Berkshire Services for Youth in Canaan, New York. He was well known in the area. After looking at his picture, one of the second shift officers said "I know him. He played on my softball team."

A fugitive from justice warrant was issued for his arrest. Information was also received he had a .22-caliber pistol, which was never found.

Detectives learned McArdle had a girlfriend who lived in Ghent, New York. New York State Police, with Pittsfield Detectives Thomas Harrington and Michael Maddalena, arrested McArdle without incident at 9:20 p.m. at his girlfriend's house.

McArdle was held without bail and appeared before a County Court Judge where he voluntarily returned to Pittsfield. Detective Sergeant Mark Bushey and Detective Peter T. McGuire escorted McArdle back to Pittsfield for his appearance in District Court where he was charged with unarmed robbery.

GUN TO FIST FIGHT EQUALS MURDER

At 10:34 p.m., April 15, 2003, the department received a phone call from Berkshire Medical Center's Emergency Room, reporting that a 20 year old male, David J. Killbary, had just been dropped off by two female friends. Killbary was suffering from a small caliber gunshot wound to his chest.

Officers were dispatched to the ER to talk to the two female friends that had brought Killbary to the hospital. Officer Cynthia Brown was able to get a detailed description of two males who had shot Killbary. One was a dark skinned, heavy set black male wearing a dark blue baseball cap approximately 6' tall. The second one was a heavy set white male with reddish hair, approximately 6' tall. He wore a gray sweat suit.

Dispatch notified the Detective Bureau where Detectives Owen Boyington, Jack McGrath and Thomas Harrington were on duty. Detectives Boyington and McGrath left the station to go to the crime scene, the A-Mart Store on North Street. Detective Thomas Harrington called Detective Captain Patrick Barry and briefed him on what was going on. Captain Barry was an experienced murder investigator who had worked on ten murder investigations at this time in his career. Captain Barry designated Det. Thomas Harrington, a seasoned detective who had worked on numbers murder cases, as lead investigator in the case.

Captain Barry and Det. Harrington responded to the ER. Captain Barry instructed Officer Walter Powell to stand by with Killbary. Officer Powell went with Killbary and the staff to the operating room. A team of physicians tried to save Killbary's life, with no luck, and he was pronounced dead at 12:45 a.m.. Killbary's clothing and his possessions were taken by Officer Powell and turned over to Investigator James Stimpson, the department's crime scene and evidence officer. The shooter's description was broadcast to all units.

In the meantime, Milton J. Gasson, Jr., one of the participants in the shooting, called a friend who lived on Lenox Avenue, asking him to meet them outside of his apartment. Still at the A-Mart Store, Quasim Hastings, another participant, went in the store and told the driver of the green car, who was purchasing some beer, to hurry up they needed to get out of the area. The driver drove them up to Lenox Avenue and they got out of the car. Hastings started to demonstrate to the two males they met, how he shot Killbary. A loud dispute took place about the shooting.

Fourteen minutes after the shooting, at 10:48 p.m., a neighbor from Lenox Avenue called the station, stating that she was watching TV with her windows opened, and that four males were arguing about a shooting. Officers were dispatched to Lenox Avenue. Detectives Owen Boyington and Jack McGrath responded to the call with uniform officers John Soules, Rick

Saldo, Thomas Barber and Raymond Bush.

Upon seeing the cruisers' headlights approaching, the group broke up and started to walk away. The two other males ducked back into their apartment.

Upon approaching Lenox Avenue, Officers Barber and Soules saw only two males walking south away from the house where the argument took place. Officers didn't know until later that two of the males ducked into their apartment. The two males matched the description that was given out about the shooters. One later identified as Quasim L. Hastings, took off running up a driveway on Weller Avenue.

Officer Soules went up the driveway where he encountered Hastings, who he brought back to his cruiser and pat frisked him for weapons, finding none. Upon arriving Officer Bush, was shown by Officer Soules where he encountered Hastings. With his flashlight, Bush began searching the driveway area, where he found a silver .25- caliber automatic pistol, with wooden grips.

Detective Boyington went to where the gun was found and took several pictures of the gun lying on the ground next to the house's deck and fence.

Detectives Boyington and McGrath talked to the other male, whose name was Milton J. Gasson Jr.. Gasson was asked if he wanted to talk about the shooting that just happened on North Street Gasson told the detectives he did not know anything about any shooting.

With the .25- caliber pistol in hand and the description matching the one broadcasted over the air, both suspects were placed under arrest for armed assault with intent to murder. This charge was brought as Killbary was still alive at this time. Both suspects were eighteen years old.

While the units were at Lenox Avenue, Captain Barry interviewed one of the female friends who had brought Killbary to the hospital. Det. Harrington interviewed the other friend. Both gave the same description of the shooters and what took place at the store. Later that evening they signed written statements.

They explained how Killbary and one of his female friends, Jan, picked the other friend, Roane, up from work and drove to the North Street store to buy a pack of cigarettes. They drove into the parking lot of the store. As they drove in the two shooters were leaning up against a green car. The shooters looked at them as they drove by and parked the car. Roane went into the store to buy some cigarettes.

Killbary and Jan stayed in the car. Milton Gasson and Quasim Hastings walked up to car. Hastings asked Killbary "What the f---- you looking at?" Gasson told Killbary to get out of the car. More words were exchanged. Jan kept telling Killbary to stay in the car. She knew that he recently just got out of jail. Then the three, Killbary, Hastings, and Gasson, walked behind the store, where a physical altercation took place. Hastings pulled out a .25- cal--iber pistol from his waistband and shot Killbary in the chest. Both Hastings and Gasson walked away, laughing, toward North Street. Killbary started walking toward his friend's car, saying that he'd been shot. A red spot on his shirt started to get grow larger. Killbary got into the back of the car and passed out. His friends drove out of the parking lot afraid that they might get shot at, driving as fast as they could to the ER about four blocks North.

After Killbary died, District Attorney Gerard D. Downing was notified about the murder. Both suspects, Hastings and Gasson, were charged with murder, under the joint venture theory. This means a defendant and co-defendant are assumed to be acting together when they commit a crime.

Back at the crime scene, Officer Jeff Coco located a spent .25-caliber Smith and Wesson casing on the ground, where witnesses said the shooting took place. He knew that it had to come from an automatic pistol, because an automatic kicks the casing out of the gun. A revolver keeps the casings in the revolving cylinder until ejected.

After being booked by Sgt. Michael Winn, while walking up to the Detective Bureau with Det. Boyington, Hastings said he wanted to take full responsibility for the shooting. He told Det. Boyington that Gasson had nothing to do with the shooting. Det. Boyington did not ask Hastings any questions, while given Hastings his rights before taken his statement. Hastings told Det. Boyington he changed his mind and didn't want to give a statement. Hastings was returned to his cell.

Gasson had been asked if he wanted to give a written statement, telling the detectives he didn't want to. He wanted to see a lawyer. Around 6:00 a.m. Captain Barry heard banging coming from the cell Gasson was in. Upon entering the cell area Gasson said he wanted to give his side of the story. Captain Barry reminded him he wanted to talk to a lawyer first. Gasson told Captain Barry that he had changed his mind.

Detective Harrington took a three page statement from Gasson after he was given his rights and signed the proper forms. Gasson told about what they did during the day and how they ended up at the A-Mart Store on North Street looking for someone old enough to buy them some beer. While Hastings and Gasson were leaning up against someone's car, an older car pulled into the parking lot and a girl got out and went into the store. Hastings said did you see that dude icing us. They then walked over to the car where Killbary was sitting in the back seat, asking Killbary if he had a problem? Words were exchanged between the three. Hastings told Killbary to get out of the car and come out in back of the store. The girl in the car kept telling Killbary not to go. The three went in back of the store. Gasson thought that they were going to square up when he heard a shot. He saw Killbary grab his chest and start running to the front of the store. Gasson said he asked Hastings, what just happened? Hastings said that he just popped that boy. Gasson said he called his friend John and told him to meet them outside of his apartment. They got a ride to Lenox Avenue. They met up with John Crossin and Peter Morgan and Hastings told them how he just popped someone. They got a bit loud and someone yelled the cops are coming. John and Peter went into their apartment as they saw the cruiser's lights coming up the street. Gasson and Hastings started to walk south, and then Hastings ran up a driveway. An officer asked why Hastings took off running; Gasson told him he didn't know. They were then placed under arrest and taken to the station.

Early that morning Officer John Gray took a written statement from John Crossin about the phone call Gasson made to him, recording what Hastings told him about the shooting in front of his apartment on Lenox Avenue. John's cell-phone was examined to see what time Gasson had called him.

The next morning, both defendants were arraigned on murder charges before Judge Alfred A. Barbalunga in District Court. They were held without the right to bail. Their cases were continued until May 21 for a pretrial hearing. Judge Barbalunga ordered that no media could take pictures of the defendants in his court room or on the courthouse grounds. Gasson's attorney, Nathaniel Green, requested this. He told Judge Barbalunga that he believed their identification could be a significant factor at their trail in Superior Court. Both defendants were indicted by a Berkshire County Grand Jury on the murder charges.

The next morning, Det. Sgt. Mark Bushey took at statement from Peter Morgan, the other male who met with Hastings and Gasson on Lenox Avenue. Peter told Sgt. Bushey that Gasson had called their apartment and wanted to see them. When Hastings and Gasson arrived, Hastings said that he just shot someone. He again repeated he just shot someone and told what happened at the North Street store. Peter said he and John didn't know how to deal with this and didn't want them around. They went into their apartment when the cruisers arrived. Later they went to Clapp Park and had a few beers with some other friends and stayed a couple of hours. When they got home, John's mother told them the police wanted to see them about a shooting. They both were brought to the station by a police cruiser and gave their statements.

Detectives took statements from John and Peter's friends who were at Clapp Park. There were a told of six statements taken. There was a difference of opinion as to what caused the shooting. Some heard that it was over a girl that Killbary and Gasson had both dated. Others thought it was over a look that Killbary gave to Hastings or Gasson. Officer John Gray went to Clapp Park and found evidence that there had been a beer party on top of the hill. Officer Gray retrieved several 40 oz. bottles, which he traced back to the North Street store.

An autopsy was performed on David Killbary the next day in Holyoke at the State Medical Examiner's office. This confirmed he was shot in the left chest and died from the gunshot wound.

Detectives were later able to trace the .25-caliber pistol back to an individual who gave a statement stating he sold the gun to Gasson a few months earlier for $120. During questioning, Gasson admitted he purchase the .25-caliber handgun that was used in the murder. Later it was found out the gun was bought with a quarter of an ounce of marijuana, which was worth $120 on the street.

Ten days after the murder, a witness came forward and gave Det. Boyington a written statement. In the statement he told how he was in the North Street parking lot, in his truck listening to the radio and smoking a cigarette. He stated that he knew Hastings and Gasson and watched them with a third male walk down to the end of the lot. He thought it look like they were going to fight. He rolled down his window and turned down his radio. He watched Gasson back up and then Hastings pulled a gun out of his waistband and shot the white male. He heard the shot and saw the male stumble backwards. Hastings yelled something to the effect "That what you get." Both Gasson and Hastings ran off. He was shocked at what he had seen, but didn't want to get involved. He drove out of the parking of as fast as he could. He didn't tell anyone of what he had just witnessed. Next day he saw on TV that it was David Killbary who was murdered. It took him a few days, and then he told one of his friends what he saw and said he was going to the police and tell them.

Captain Barry took a statement from another witness who stated he was walking through the parking lot going to the store to buy some cigarettes. He walked by David Killbary, who he knew. The other two, Gasson and Hastings, he didn't know until he heard their names the next day. He heard Gasson call Killbary a punk. Then Hastings told Gasson to beat him up. A few punches were exchanged. Then Hastings pulled a gun from his waistband and shot Killbary. The witness stopped to watch the fight, a few feet away. The shot wasn't that loud. Then Killbary walked right past the witness holding his right hand to his left chest. The witnesses went into the store and purchased his cigarettes and walked home. When get got home he told a couple of people in his house about the shooting. A couple days passed, while talking to a couple at a baseball game, he mentioned the shooting. They told him he had to go to the police and tell them.

Detectives continued with their investigation and in August the Commonwealth dropped the murder charge against Gasson. District Attorney David F. Capeless told the court that the Commonwealth had not found any additional evidence linking Gasson directly to the murder. Gasson was there when the murder took place, but the shooting was "strictly the act" of Hastings.

The Grand Jury on July 23, indicted Gasson for being an accessory after the fact of murder and possession of a firearm without a FID card.

The grand jury indictment read "WELL KNOWN QUASIM L. HASTINGS TO HAVE COMMITTED MURDER DID HARBOR, CONCEAL, MAINTAIN OR ASSIST QUASIM L. HASTINGS WITH THE INTENT THAT SAID PERSON SHOULD AVOID OR ESCAPE DETECTION, ARREST, TRIAL OR PUNISHMENT."

Judge Daniel A. Ford set bail for Gasson at $20,000 cash or $200,000 surety. District Attorney Capeless told the court that Gasson was on probation for an assault charge as a juvenile. Just two days before the murder he was arraigned in district court on another assault charge.

On March 12, 2004, Hastings, in Superior Court, pleaded guilty to second-degree murder and was sentenced to life in the state prison by Judge Daniel A. Ford.

QUASM L. HASTINGS WITH OFFICERS
DAVID KIRCHNER AND MICHAEL McHUGH
PHOTOS BY C&B VIDEO

In November 2004, Milton J. Gasson Jr. pleaded guilty to the two reduced charges and was sentenced by Superior Court Judge Daniel A. Ford to Cedar Junction State Prison for three to five years on the accessory charge and two years' probation for the firearms charge. He was credited with 480 days he spent in jail awaiting his trail.

MILTON J. GASSON WITH OFFICERS
DAVID KIRCHNER AND MICHAEL McHUGH
PHOTOS BY C&B VIDEO

As in all major investigation, members of the detective and drug unit worked together as a team to solve the crime.

ANNUAL REPORT FOR FISCAL YEAR 2003
July 1, 2002 to June 30, 2003

Chief Anthony J. Riello stated in the Annual Report for the fiscal year 2003, that the department was a progressive agency that had embraced the community policing philosophy to improve the level of service. The department answered 32,272 calls for service.

State and Federal Grants awarded to the department helped run many programs that reduced the fear of crime and improve the quality of life for the residents and visitors of the city.

The following grants were active during the year:

Community Policing $325,450
Berkshire Regional SRT $299,340
COPS in Schools $250,000
Universal Hiring $225,000
Domestic Violence Aftercare Program $125,356
Homeland Security Overtime Protection $49,318
Local Law Enforcement Public Safety Equipment $44,500
COPS MORE $26,720
Local Law Enforcement Block Grant $22,333
Identix $11,000,
Traffic Safety Enforcement $10,000
Click It or Ticket $9,600
Juvenile Accountability Incentive Block Grand $6,951
Cops in Shops $5,000
Car Seat Safety $2,000

KNIFE ATTACK ON OFFICERS LEADS TO DEATH

There is no such thing like an ordinary domestic call; every call is different. On Tuesday, July 15, 2003, Officers Diane Caccamo, David Kirchner, and Michael McHugh were dispatched to a husband and wife domestic call. A neighbor called the department at 3:30 p.m., when she saw a domestic disturbance going on in the front yard of 84 Lyman Street. Forty year old James P. Xavier and his wife, Amy, lived in an apartment at 84 Lyman Street. The department's records show that officers had been to 84 Lyman Street several times before. When the officers arrived, the couple was back in their apartment.

Before entering the building, Officers Caccamo and Kirchner stopped at the entrance to listen. Officer McHugh started around the building to the rear entrance, when he heard Officer Kirchner call out that Xavier had a knife. McHugh came running back to join the other officers. Entrance to Xavier's apartment was gained from a hallway. As Kirchner and Caccamo entered the hallway, James Xavier came out of his apartment's door, greeting the officers with a 10 inch knife. He waved the knife in the air daring them to come and get him. James's wife, Amy, could be heard screaming despondently in the apartment. Amy tried to get past James and leave apartment, but he grabbed her and threatened her with the knife. Officers kept on ordering James to drop the knife and let his wife go. Officers Kirchner, McHugh and Caccamo had their guns now pointing at James and again ordered him to let go of his wife and drop the knife. He finally let his wife go and Officer Kirchner grabbed her and handed her off to Officer Caccamo. All of a sudden James charged the officers, yelling. Officer Kirchner, in self-defense, fired three rounds, hitting James in the chest and hand. Securing the knife, they began to administer first aid. An engine company from the fire department and ambulance arrived and transported James to Berkshire Medical Center where he was pronounced dead.

In all police shootings, an investigation is conducted by the District Attorney Office. District Attorney Gerard Downing had Lt. Richard Smith and Lt. Patricia Driscoll of the State Police Detective Division carry out the investigation. Chief Anthony J. Riello, as standard police procedure, placed the three officers on paid leave until the investigation was completed.

Detectives found out that Xavier had a criminal record. In 2000 he was charged with assaulting a female and stealing her pocket book and he received a 30 day sentence to the Berkshire County House of Correction. He also had a pending case in Superior Court for trying to deliver a drug, "OxyContin" to a female friend of his who was an inmate at the Berkshire County House of Correction.

Lt. Smith and Lt. Driscoll found that the officers acted legally in the shooting of James Xavier. Case Closed!

PROMOTIONS and RETIREMENTS

*During the fiscal year 2003 there were
several personnel changes as shown below:*

[PROMOTIONS]

NAME	POSITION	DATE
David Reilly	Acting Patrol Captain	10/28/02
Henry Dondi	Acting Lieutenant	11/17/02

Michael Winston	Acting Lieutenant	11/10/02
Marc Strout	Acting Sergeant	11/17/02
Gary Belknap	Acting Sergeant	6/22/03
Michael Nykorchuck	Drug Investigator	7/04/02

NAME	POSITION	DATE
James Stimpson	Crime Scene Investigator	2/07/03
Gary Traversa	Dare Officer	10/01/02
Jack Tobin	Dispatch Supervisor	5/28/06
Thomas Barnaby	Dispatch Asst. Supervisor	5/28/03

[RETIREMENTS]

NAME	DATE
Officer Leonard Pruyne	07/10/02
Officer John Kubica	8/11/02
Captain Cosmo Spezzaferro	10/21/02

DA DOWNING SAYING GOODBYE

GOOD LUCK ON YOUR
RETIREMENT MAYOR
SARA HALFAWAY

Upon the retirement of Captain Cosmo Spezzaferro of the Special Operations Bureau, Chief Anthony J. Riello assigned Captain Patrick Barry to head this position. Captain David Reilly was assigned to head the Patrol Division with Lt. Henry Dondi as shift commander from 8:00 a.m. to 4:00 p.m. shift. Captain John T. O'Neil resumed his duties from Uniform Captain & Administrative Captain to Administrative Captain and Public Information Officer.

CHAPTER THIRTY-EIGHT

MURDERED FOR KENO WINNINGS

At 9:30 a.m. on Saturday, August 17, 2002, the body of 62- year- old Robert L. Vincent was found in his apartment at 236 Tyler Street. Vincent was the manager of Tyler Home Supply at 711 Tyler Street. He had worked at the store for over 45 years and was the manager for the last 40 years. He opened the store every morning. When he failed to report to work, two other employees went to his apartment to check on him. When Vincent failed to answer the door, they called the police department. Vincent lived alone in his second-floor apartment above two small businesses. Vincent was lying on the floor in a pool of blood. He had suffered visible trauma to the body.

Vincent was well-known in the Tyler Street neighborhood. He left his apartment every morning and went downstairs to Soup-N-Such or across the street to Bev's Pittsfield Diner for breakfast, then walked to work. Every afternoon after work, he went to the Tyler Café on Tyler Street and the corner of Woodlawn Avenue, formerly known as Charlie's Bar. He drank a few beers, played Keno, and then returned home before dark. He was a regular customer for over 40 years.

Vincent never married nor had any children. His two sisters live in Florida and a brother lived in Pittsfield. Vincent was an easygoing man who liked to laugh and helped anyone in need. He often loaned money to acquaintances and never demanded to be paid back. He was known by friends and patrons of the Café as "Vinnie, Prince Vince and Rack of Legs", because he was so thin.

On Friday night, he won two games of Keno on one ticket; he hit four out of the five numbers by playing the numbers of his birthday: 9-4-19-39 and 62 his age. He would have turned 63 on September 4. He then matched all five numbers on computer-generated ticket, winning $460. With some of his winnings, he brought a round of drinks for his friends at the bar. Vincent then bought 3 more Keno tickets, said good-by to his friends, left the café, and headed home to his apartment. The three tickets were all winners and just had to be cashed.

District Attorney Gerard D. Downing said that evidence found at the scene led police to believe Vincent was most likely murdered. Downing said the initial review of the evidence at the scene, including the condition of the body and the apparent injuries, led them to draw that conclusion.

Chief of Police Anthony J. Riello assigned Captains Patrick F. Barry and John T. O'Neil to oversee the department's murder investigation. The entire Detective Bureau and Drug Unit were assigned to different tasks in the case. The department was assisted by detectives assigned to the district attorney's office and members of the state police's Crime Scene Services Unit.

Detectives interviewed all the patrons of the Tyler Café, and took written statements from each one.

In one interview, detectives learned that a patron, Frank P. LeBeau Jr., 34, who had no permanent address but recently stayed in an apartment on Maplewood Avenue, had shown up at Vincent's apartment. Vincent stated that he thought it was strange that LeBeau knew where he lived and had shown up unexpectedly at his apartment.

In another interview, it was learned that LeBeau had come into the restaurant and acted very friendly, as if he knew everyone. He played a few games of Keno and always said "thank you" when handed the ticket.

LeBeau learned that Vincent had won the Keno money when he showed up at the Café later that night and stayed until closing time. A number of things had raised suspicion of LeBeau, including the fact that he immediately left town after the murder

The department's Special Response Team was called out to search the two block area between Vincent's apartment and where LeBeau was staying on Maplewood Avenue. Retracing possible paths between the, two locations, for the murder weapon.

Tips from the community led detectives to a residence in Agawam, where detectives used a caller identification to track LeBeau to Brimfield. Four days after the murder, LeBeau was arrested. LeBeau gave two statements during a nine-hour interview with Detectives Glen F. Decker and Thomas Bowler. In the first, LeBeau said he had no knowledge or involvement in the homicide.

LeBeau gave the second interview after police recovered the stolen Keno tickets, which matched receipts found in Vincent's apartment, from LeBeau's wallet.

District Attorney Gerard D. Downing said LeBeau gave a statement that included "admissions," but he would not characterize the statement as a confession.

1980 ELKS RING   1.25 CARAT
                   DIAMOND RING

Two rings were also taken from Vincent's fingers; one a was a Fraternity of the Elks ring that showed a 1980s year on it and the second was a man's gold ring with a 1.25 carat diamond in the center. A regional broadcast was sent out about the rings and detectives were sent to cities where LeBeau formerly lived to talk to departments who had dealings with LeBeau for any information they could give. The broadcast asked police departments to check their pawn shops.

At 2:00 p.m., on August 23, 2002, Frank P. LeBeau Jr. was arraigned before District Court Judge Alfred A. Barbalunga on a charge of murder. Attorney George B. Crane was assigned to represent LeBeau. Crane asked that bail to be set without prejudice, so that he could argue the issue at a later date when he had more information on the allegations.

District Attorney Downing stated that LeBeau had lived in Great Barrington for a short time, lost his job there, and moved to Pittsfield where he had a few ties. Downing asked for no bail. Judge Barbalunga ordered that LeBeau be held without bail and continued the case to September 19 for a pretrial conference.

In Superior Court, in October, 2004, one of LeBeau's attorneys, Joseph A. Franco, said his client was intoxicated during the attack and argued that there was a mitigating circumstance and he should not be found guilty of first- degree murder.

In Superior Court, Trooper Carol Zullo of the state police crime services, testified that 70 prints were taken from Vincent's apartment. One of the prints was that of LeBeau.

Associate State Medical Examiner Dr. Joann Richmond, who did the autopsy, stated that Vincent died from being hit in the head with a blunt object numerous times.

First Assistant District Attorney David F. Capeless asked the jury to find LeBeau guilty of first- degree murder.

The trial lasted for two weeks and the jury of seven women and five men after only four hours of deliberation, found LeBeau guilty of first degree murder, larceny under $250, and three counts of larceny over $250. The jury found that the crime possessed both the premeditation and the "extreme atrocity of cruelty" to necessitate a first-degree murder case.

Superior Court Judge John J. Agostini issued the mandatory life sentence without the possibility of parole on the murder conviction.

Capeless singled out lead investigator, Detective Owen Boyington and State Police Detective Lt. Richard Smith Jr., for their work on the case. Chief Anthony J. Riello commended all the officers of his department that worked on the case.

Outside the courthouse, family members and friends of Vincent said the verdict on the case gave them a sense of closure.

2004

**FISCAL YEAR
July 1, 2003 to June 30, 2004**

.38 COLT THREE SHOTS = MURDER

Shortly after 9:00 p.m., on July 1, 2003, a hot summer night in Pittsfield, the department received reports of gun shots from the area of 65-67 Cherry Street. Upon responding, officers found 27 year old Anthony Raubeson of 67 Cherry Street lying on the ground bleeding from three gunshot wounds. One shot from a .38 Colt entered the chest, penetrating the heart. Sergeant Jeffrey Bradford, one of the responding officers to the call, notified dispatch of situation. Sgt. Bradford began a search for the murder weapon, without any luck.

The department's Drug Unit was familiar with the area and the players as they executed several successful drug raids in the area. Sergeant David Granger of the Drug Unit was notified, along with Detective Captain Patrick Barry and Chief Riello. Detectives Glen Decker and Thomas Bowler were designed as lead investigator for the department. The detectives and drug investigators began to round up witnesses to the now- murder investigation and to take written statements from them.

Several witnesses gave the name of the shooter as Tyhien McQueen (street name "Primo"), age 23. He lived in the upstairs apartment, which was number 65 Cherry Street. Anthony Raubeson lived downstairs at number 67 Cherry Street with his mother.

An arrest warrant was obtained for Tyhien McQueen for murder and possession of a firearm during the commission of a felony. Detectives learned that McQueen hid out in the area for about a week. He then went to his mother's house in Brooklyn, New York where he was arrested two weeks after the murder. While awaiting extradition back to Pittsfield, McQueen was held in a New York City Jail.

After almost two years, in May of 2005, Tyhien McQueen was put on trial in Berkshire Superior Court for the murder of Anthony Raubeson. Judge John A. Agostini was presiding Justice. District Attorney David F. Capeless prosecuted the case for the Commonwealth and defense attorneys were Harry Miles and Cornelius Moriarty.

A jury of six women and ten men were picked for the jury. All sixteen would hear the case. When it came time to deliberate, four would be excused. District Attorney Capeless had contemplated that the trail would last two weeks.

District Attorney Capeless with his first witnesses and defense witnesses brought out the facts that there was tension between Anthony Raubeson, who lived in the downstairs apartment, 67 Cherry Street, and the upstairs tenants 65 Cherry Street, who were selling cocaine out of their apartment. At times drug business was done in the street in front of Raubeson's downstairs apartment. Joseph "Brick" Wiggins, 28, rented number 65. Wiggins had only lived in the upstairs apartment for five months.

On the morning of the shooting, the sons of Wiggins were given permission to take bike parts from the basement of the building by the landlord. These parts belong to Raubeson's brother. Raubeson was gone all day, but upon returning home he saw one of boys riding the pieced together bike. He yanked the boy off and pushed him to the ground. Raubeson went into his house and got his pit-bull dog and started to chase the boys.

Raubeson left the area for a few minutes, then returned with five or six of his friends armed with a bat that had screws sticking out of it and swastikas on it. One of the defense attorneys showed the bat to the jury. Other weapons were sticks and crow bars. They got into a fight with two of the residents of 65, the upstairs apartment. A verbal argument was going on when a cruiser officer who was driving by stopped because he saw the weapons. No one wanted any charges, so the officer scattered the group.

Wiggins, the upstairs tenant, arrived home shortly after 9:00 p.m.; he had been fishing the whole day. Learning of the happenings while he was gone, he wanted to confront Raubeson. They had differences before and were able to work them out.

Raubeson returned home at about 9:30 p.m.. Wiggins confronted him in the parking lot next to their building. Also arriving at this time was Tyhien McQueen, of Brooklyn, New York who was a drug runner and stayed in the upstairs apartment. A fist fight ensued with Raubeson on top of Wiggins. McQueen, who was standing next to them, pulled out from his waist band a .38 Colt, revolver. McQueen fired two shots, Raubeson fell to his knees. McQueen moved closer and fired one more round. Raubeson was hit in the chest, piercing his heart. McQueen and all the witnesses took off running. Raubeson was rushed to Berkshire Medical Center where he was pronounced dead on arrival.

Investigators learned that McQueen and a 15 year old, who was a drug runner for Joseph "Brick" Wiggins, renter of 65 Cherry Street, ran about two blocks after the shooting. At the corner of Spring and Curtis Streets, they hid the murder weapon, the .38 Colt, in the bushes. This information was developed six days after the shooting. Detective Sergeant Mark Bushey and Crime Scene Investigator James Stimpson recovered the weapon with three spent shots in the cylinder, two live rounds and one empty chamber. The .38 Colt was sent to the Massachusetts State Police Crime Laboratory. DNA that was recovered from the revolver came primarily from McQueen. Ballistics from the Colt showed that it was the weapon that killed Anthony Raubeson.

In a statement given to detectives, McQueen admitted that the .38 Colt was his. He got it from a friend because he was being harassed by his girlfriend's ex-boyfriend and he needed it to frighten him. He stated that he gave it to the 15 year old, who ran drugs for Wiggins and lived with them at 65. McQueen said he took the gun back from the 15 year old before he shot Raubeson. Both fled the area of the shooting, hiding the gun in the bushes two blocks away. They hid out for a week before going to McQueen's mother's house in Brooklyn, New York, where he was arrested.

District Attorney Capeless put on witnesses, some of McQueen's fellow drug dealers, who stated they saw McQueen shoot Raubeson. McQueen's defense team maintained that the 15 year old was the one who murdered Raubeson.

The 15 year old boy refused to give a statement to the detectives until he was arrested for failure to appear in court to testify in the case. He was held on $100,000 bail. On the stand and before the sixteen jurors, he stated that he saw McQueen shoot Raubeson, also stating that Joseph "Brick" Wiggins saw the shooting.

On the fifth day of the trial with the Commonwealth still only putting on half of its witnesses, the defendant, Tyhien McQueen, pled guilty to a reduced charge of manslaughter, admitting he had shot and killed Raubeson.

Judge John A. Agostini thanked the jury for serving. On the joint recommendation of District Attorney David Capeless and the defense team of Harry Miles and Cornelius Moriarty, Judge Agostini sentenced McQueen to 12 to 15 years in prison. McQueen was credited with 602 days for the time he was awaiting trial. The charge of possession of a firearm during the commission of a felony was dismissed.

Joseph "Brick" Wiggins, one of Commonwealth's witnesses, pleaded guilty in Superior Court to distribution of cocaine. He was sentenced to 2 years of a 2 1/2 year jail term. Due to the fact he spent two years in jail, waiting for the trail, he was given 2 years' credit, placed on probation and released.

Detective Captain Patrick Barry commended the officers who worked on the case, particularly Det. Sergeant David Granger and lead Detectives Glen Decker and Thomas Bowler.

District Attorney David Capeless praised the department and the detectives for putting together an investigation that led to McQueen's successful conviction.

WELCOMING THE SENATOR
PITTSFIELD AIRPORT-JUNE 18, 2004-DET. GLENN CIVELLO
CAPT. O'NEIL-SENATOR TED KENNEDY- DET. THOMAS BOWLER

FIFTH ANNUAL HAUNTED HOUSE

Mayor Sara Hathaway took time out of her busy schedule to support the department's fifth annual haunted house. Dressed in her favorite Halloween outfit, she greeted many small goblins at the door giving out treats to each one.

TICKET TO HAUNTED HOUSE

The haunted house was held at the Arena, 10 Lyman Street, on the weekend of October 24, 2003. Over two hundred volunteers took part in setting it up, working evenings and weekends for a month. It brought members of the community together.

This year's haunted house was dedicated to Betsy Roy, who with her husband, Jack, had helped out each year to make the event possible. Betsy, who was battling cancer, was unable to take part this year.

Volunteers dressed in Halloween costumes took groups through the maze of spooky rooms, stopping to allow volunteers to act out their terrifying skits. The hallways were lined with spider webs and plastic spiders.

Many Wal-Mart employees were involved under the coordination of Beth Barbarotta, who has helped out for the last four years. Beth dressed as a witch and had her own room, called the "witch's room."

Carr Hardware and Supply Co. manager John Magner set up his "Mad Scientist" display. A skeleton inside a metal cage shot bolts of sparks from the skeleton to the metal cage, lighting up the skeleton and cage.

FOUR BANK ROBBERIES IN A YEAR

On January 26, 2004, at 9:30 a.m., Harley D. Traverse, 18, of 341 West Street walked into the Greylock Federal Credit Union on the corner of West and Center Streets. Traverse was carrying a blue lunch bag which he placed on the counter in front of a teller He handed a teller a note saying the bag contained a bomb. He told the horrified teller that he would kill her if she didn't give him money.

Traverse had on sunglasses, headphones, a baseball cap, and the hood of his sweatshirt concealed his face. Traverse fled the bank with $30,000 leaving the lunch bag on the counter in front of the teller.

Uniform officers and detectives responded to the credit union. Seventy-five employees and customers were evacuated from the building. The State Police bomb squad was called in. The bag was removed from the bank and placed outside. The area was blocked off because a large audience had gathered. The bomb squad blew up the blue lunch bag. The bag contained a device that was made out to look like a pipe bomb.

After the smoke had died down and it was considered safe to approach the bag, it was found that the pipe bomb was made out of an aluminum bat, duct tape, and sockets.

Traverse didn't get to spend much of the $30,000. He was arrested the next day, after a little more than twenty-four hours had elapsed. The department received a tip the next morning from a citizen who stated he recognized Traverse's picture from surveillance-camera photographs. These photographs had been published in the Berkshire Eagle the next morning. They were also broadcast over the local television stations. The credit union has a highly sophisticated security system, which takes crystal- clear pictures.

Traverse gave a signed statement to the detectives. He admitted writing the demand note, robbing the credit union of $30,000 in cash, and creating a hoax device inside the blue lunch bag.

In searching Traverse's apartment, detectives were able to recover most the money taken from the credit union.

HARLEY D. TRAVERSE
PHOTO BY BEN GARVER-EAGLE

The next morning in District Court, bail was set at $200,000 cash or $2 million surety bond. A public defender was appointed to represent Traverse on all charges. The public defender's office had a cloth placed over his head to cover up his identity. The thought behind this was that he had sunglasses, a baseball hat and a hood on when he robbed the credit union, his identity was obscured. However the person who gave the tip to the department that led to his arrest, had no problem in identifying him after they saw his picture in the Berkshire Eagle.

While at the Berkshire County House of Correction, Traverse sent a threatening letter to the man who turned him in to police. He was arraigned in District Court on a charge of intimidation of a witness. Later the charge was taken up in Superior Court.

In Superior Court before Judge John A. Agostini, Traverse pleaded guilty to armed robbery while masked, possession of a hoax device, threatening to commit murder, intimidation of a witness, and false reporting of a bomb. Traverse was sentenced to six to ten years in the state prison,

ROBBERY NUMBER TWO

OFFICER FOISY AND HIS PARTNER IYOX
PHOTO BY BEN GARVER EAGLE STAFF

On November 3, 2004, Derrick D. Ranzoni, 21, of Crane Avenue, using a .22- caliber Ruger rifle, robbed the branch bank of Banknorth at the Stop & Shop shopping center on Merrill Road.

Ranzoni, masked, went into the bank with the .22 rifle at 9:35 a.m. and held up the bank. Ranzoni dropped much of the money, fifty and one-hundred dollar bills, in the parking lot and behind the shopping center as he ran through them trying to escape into a wooded area. $2,500 dollars was strewn across the parking lot. Shoppers began to help officers retrieve the money; no question some ended up in some shopper's pockets, but most was recovered. The total taken from the bank was around $15,000.

Investigators received leads from members of the public, responding to scanner reports and a reverse-911 message that was sent out to area businesses to be on the lookout for the bank robber. Within minutes, officers received a tip that a man fitting the physical description of the robber was walking by a swamp area next to the Pittsfield School Department's bus garage on Merrill Road. Hearing sirens, Ranzoni jumped into the high grass as the officers arrived on the scene.

When K-9 Officer Dwane Foisy and his partner Iyox arrived on the scene, officers yelled to Ranzoni to surrender. He refused to come out of the grass or show his hands. Officer Foisy unleashed Iyox who ran right to Ranzoni, clamped down on his thigh, and held him in place. Foisy and Officer Michael McHugh made their way into the swamp where Iyox held the fugitive. Foisy and McHugh were concerned that Ranzoni still was armed with the .22. When they saw the suspect had no weapon, Foisy ordered Iyox to release his hold on him so he could be handcuffed and placed under arrest. Two deputy sheriffs who were working road details joined in to help bring Ranzoni out of the swamp. Both Ranzoni and McHugh, who twisted his knee in the marshy area, were treated for minor injuries and released from Berkshire Medical Center.

A specially trained weapons detection dog from the state police recovered the .22 Ruger later in the afternoon.

Many of the officers arrived at the scene in their dress uniforms as they had just come from the funeral of longtime Fire and Police Dispatcher Richard F. Benham, better known to the officers as "Mr. B."

DERRICK D. RANZONI ARRESTED
PHOTO BY BEN GARVER-EAGLE

Ranzoni was charged with robbery with a firearm while masked and possession of a firearm during the commission of a felony. Ranzoni plead guilty in Superior Court and was sentenced to seven years to be served at the Berkshire County House of Correction.

BANK ROBBERY- THREE- BY SENIOR CITIZEN

On November 23, 2004, Tuesday, shortly after 10 a.m., Joel M. Boyce, 66, of 155 Francis Avenue, with a dark-colored winter hat pulled over his face, entered the Berkshire Bank building at 66 West Street, told a teller that he had a gun, and demanded money. Bank employees handed over under $2,000 in cash to Boyce. Boyce headed directly to the package store in the Big Y supermarket building on West Street, about 2,000 feet from the bank.

Employees of West Street Wine & Sprints said Boyce purchased a 750-milliliter bottle of Absolut vodka and a pack of cigarettes.

On the way back from the package store, Boyce was stopped by Officer Ronald Kitterman and released after Kitterman took down his personal information. This initial interaction between Boyce and Kitterman was captured on film by Eagle photographer Ben Garver and a local TV news cameraman.

OFFICER RONALD KITTERMAN TAKING DOWN INFORMATION
PHOTO BY BEN GARVER

Photographer Garver, back in his dark room, was able to enhance the photo of Boyce. Once this was done it was compared with the bank's security photos, making a perfect match.

BEN GARVER

Page 358

Cruiser Officer Kitterman's stop was one of several threshold inquiries made by officers with men matching an early description of the robber. Boyce was wearing a pair of khaki pants similar to those worn by the robber.

With the new evidence of the two matching photos, Officer Kitterman and Detective Dale Eason went to Boyce's Francis Avenue apartment. There they found him and his bottle of Absolut vodka. He only got one drink from the bottle. He had already changed his clothes. Officers observed a large sum of money sticking out of the hood of a jacket hanging on a nail. Boyce was placed under arrest for armed robbery while masked, and transported to the station for booking.

Taken to the Detective Bureau, Boyce gave a two-page signed confession to Detective Dale Eason. Boyce said he had thoughts about robbing the banks for about three weeks. In his statement Boyce said, "I am broke and I have no money."

Boyce received Supplemental Security Income and his rent was subsidized by the Red Cross. He decided to go through with the robbery after coming back from breakfast at the Salvation Army on West Street. Boyce used his green knit cap that had the top cut off to cover his face. He went into the bank and over to a teller and said "This is a robbery I want all your money." The teller didn't believe him a first thinking it was a joke because everyone knew Boyce in the Bank. Then Boyce told the teller he had a gun, putting his hand in his jacket. Boyce regularly cashed his Social Security check at this bank every month. The horrified teller gave him the money and he left the bank. He then threw his green knit cap in a trash barrel outside the bank, and walked to the package store to buy his vodka.

In Berkshire Superior Court, Boyce was charged with armed robbery while being masked. Assistant District Attorney Richard M. Lock prosecuted the case for the Commonwealth. Assistant District Attorney Lock brought out that Boyce had a criminal record going back over 30 years. Boyce's attorney was Thomas Donahue. Boyce rejected Lock's statement that he was masked during the robbery. Boyce pled guilty to armed robbery after the Commonwealth dropped the charge of being masked. Attorney Donahue wanted a sentence of five or six years, saying that anything more would be a life sentence, due to Boyce's age. Superior Court Judge John A. Agostini sentenced Boyce to six to ten years in the state prison.

CHAPTER 39

FOURTH BANK ROBBERY OF THE YEAR

Just three days before Christmas, a cool Berkshire day, Wednesday, December 22, 2004, two masked men with handguns, wearing baggy clothing, entered the Credit Union of the Berkshires at 744 Williams Street, just before 3:30 p.m.

One the masked men walked right up to one of the terrified tellers pointing a Sig 22/45 caliber semiautomatic pistol in her face, saying "give me the money or I will shoot you dead." Customers and staff were made lie down on the floor.

After all the cash drawers were emptied, he forced one of the tellers at gun point into the vault. He made her hold a plastic bag while he scooped money into it from the main safe drawer, with one hand. In his other hand he was holding his pistol.

A regular patron of the Credit Union was sitting in his truck outside in the parking lot, when he saw two men pulling masks over their faces and entering the Credit Union. He drove around to the drive-up window and peered inside. Seeing the two masked men holding guns on the tellers and scooping money from the tellers' drawers into plastic bags, he called 911 and reported what he just saw.

The gunmen then ran out of the credit union and into a wooded area behind the shopping center, toward Alfred Drive, with $100,000 in cash. A good citizen of Alfred Drive saw the two men get into a Pontiac Sunfire driven by a third man. The resident had seen the Pontiac circling around in the neighborhood telling officers that it hadn't been acting right, so he took down the car's license plate number. This was the big break the department needed. The description of the car and plate number was given out to all units.

The Pontiac was found within fifteen minutes by Officers Raymond Bush and Cynthia Brown, parked in front of the Dalton Apartments complex on April Lane. Crime Scene Investigator Mark Trapani was able to left footprints from the parking lot in back of the Credit Union.

Trapani went to April Lane and was able to match footprints from the robbery scene to prints leaving the car and going to the apartment at 107 April Lane. A stakeout was conducted.

The person living at 107 April Lane turned out to be a girlfriend of Marco

Sostre, one of the robbers. Consent was given to search the apartment; therefore no search warrant was needed, saving time. Found in the apartment were three loaded handguns, $11,000 and clothing thought to be worn in the robbery. Also found was a police scanner to monitor police activity. One of the guns, a loaded Sig 22/45 caliber semiautomatic pistol with a defaced serial number, was identified as one of the weapons used in the stickup.

A short time after the car was discovered, Angel Lamboy, 27, of Plunkett Street was spotted walking to the vehicle. Lamboy denied that he had any involvement in the robbery. Questioned by officers as what he was doing in the complex, he stated that he was delivering crack cocaine to somebody in the complex. Questioned about the white Pontiac Sunfire, Lamboy said the car belonged to his girlfriend. After further questioning Lamboy was arrested on probable cause, transported to headquarters and booked. Later that night Lamboy gave a statement in which he admitted to being the getaway driver.

Officers also stopped and questioned two men coming from behind 107 April Lane, but at the time not having enough probable cause to make an arrest, they were let go. One was Marco Sostre, 30, of Onota Street and the other was Robinson Figueroa, 18, of Robbins Avenue. Sostre was initially identified as Marco Rivera, but also went by the names of Rubin Muriel and Mark Rivera. Figueroa also went by the alias of Robinson Figuerosa-DeJesus.

After taking statements from the Credit Union employees and from several other witnesses to the robbery, detectives had enough evidence to arrest Sostre and Figueroa. Upon arresting Sostre and booking him, they made an inventory of his property, finding twenty-six thousand dollars in three large wads of cash in his pockets.

In questioning Sostre, detectives learned that he was with Figueroa all day. Figueroa told detectives he was with his aunt all day. Figueroa "lawyered up " during questioning, so detectives had to stop their interview and returned him to his cell.

In further investigation it was found that both Lamboy and Sostre recently moved to Pittsfield from the Springfield area. Sostre had armed robbery charges against him in Springfield.

The next morning in District Court, Lamboy, Sostre and Figueroa covered their heads with their jackets while in the prisoners' docket.

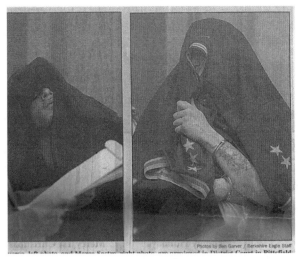

FIGUEROA & SOSTRE
PHOTO BY BEN GARVER-EAGLE

First District Attorney Paul J. Caccaviello represented the Commonwealth. Attorney Thomas M. Sherman, Jr. was the defense lawyer for Figueroa, Anthony Andrews for Sostre, and Edward O'Brien for Lamboy. All three lawyers said their clients knew nothing about the robbery or fit the description of the robbers. Judge Barbalunga placed bail on the trio.

All three were charged with armed robbery with a firearm while masked, larceny over $250, possession of a firearm in the commission of a felony, possession of firearm without an identification card, possession of ammunition without a FID card, and possession of a firearm with a defaced serial number.

At his trial in Berkshire Superior Court before Judge Daniel A. Ford, Angel D. Lamboy, in February 2006, pleaded guilty to being the wheel man in the robbery. First Assistant District Attorney Paul J. Caccaviello and Lamboy's attorney, Thomas J. Donohue Jr., came to a plea agreement. Judge Daniel A. Ford sentenced Lamboy to six to eight years at Cedar Junction on the armed robbery charge. Lamboy was also given concurrent sentences of five to six years on the firearm charge, and four to five years on the assault and firearm possession charges and a concurrent sentence of two years on the larceny and ammunition possession charges.

NO MARIJUANA LEADS TO 50 TO 60 YEARS IN PRISION

On Thursday May 5, 2005, Lance R. Norris, 26, drove up to a group of four standing in the parking lot at Dower Square housing project. Lance asked the group if they had any marijuana he could buy. Telling him no, Lance pulled out a pistol and started firing at the group. Bullets from his gun struck two males and one female; the second female escaped without a scratch. Other bullets struck nearby cars. All three victims were treated at Berkshire Medical Center. Their wounds were not life-threading. Detectives were called to BMC to interview the victims and start their investigation. Norris fled to New York City to get lost in the crowd.

Detectives learned that Norris had lived in different apartments in Pittsfield and Bronx, New York. Norris was wanted by Bronx, New York, detectives for a stabbing that took place in November, 2005. In December 2005, Norris was arrested in a Bronx apartment by detectives.

Pittsfield Detectives had put together their case against Norris and presented it to the Grand Jury, who indicted him on December 16, 2005. The charges were four counts of armed assault with intent to murder, assault and battery with a dangerous weapon, use of a dangerous weapon, and use of a firearm during the commission of a felony, four counts of assault with a dangerous weapon, and possession of a hand gun without a firearms identification card. Detectives lodged their warrants with New York authorities.

Norris was returned to Pittsfield. On October 30, 2009, four years after the shooting, Norris was arraigned in Berkshire Superior Court. Norris pleaded not guilty to all counts.

On March 31, 2010, a three day trail started in Berkshire Superior Court. First Assistant District Attorney Paul J. Caccaviello prosecuted the case for the Commonwealth. Norris's defense attorney was Raymond J. Jacoub, of Great Barrington.

The jury deliberated for only two hours before bringing in a guilty finding. Three of the charges were dismissed at the request of the District Attorney's office, armed assault with intent to murder, use of a gun during the commission of a felony and assault by means of a dangerous weapon.

Superior Court Judge John A. Agostini sentenced Norris to serve a total of 50 to 60 years at Cedar Junction State Prison. Before the sentence started, Norris had to finish serving a prison sentence in Attica State Prison, New York.

Berkshire Museum
June 3, 2005
Officers Miles Barber, Davids Hallas, Lt. Michael Winston U.S. Sen. John F. Kerry,
Capt. John T. O'Neil, and Sgt. Jeffrey Bradford

VISITING PITTSFIELD-JUNE 3, 2005
U.S. SENATOR JOHN KERRY

TWO BANK BANDITS ON TRIAL

On May 23, 2006, Marcos A. Sostre and Robinson Figueroa went on trial in Berkshire Superior Court. Judge Daniel A. Ford presided over the jury trial.

First Assistant District Attorney Paul J. Caccaviello was prosecutor for the Commonwealth at the five day trial. Sostre's attorney was Timothy M. Farris of Springfield and Figueroa's attorney was Edmund St. John of Adams.

One of the main witnesses at the trial was Richard Petricca Jr., who was sitting in his pick-up truck in the parking lot just outside of the credit union. Petricca saw Sostre and Figueroa put on their masks and enter the Credit Union. He drove his truck to the drive-up window and witnessed the robbery taking place and called 911. Several others testified including the terrified teller who Sostre put his gun in her face. A cellmate of Sostre's for two months at the Berkshire County House of Correction stated that Sostre boasted of how he and Figueroa robbed the Credit Union.

The jury was made up of eight women and four men who deliberated for six hours before finding both guilty as charged.

They were charged with armed robbery while masked, use of a firearm during the commission of a felony, possession of a firearm without a license to carry, possession of ammunition without an firearm identification card, possession of a firearm with a mutilated serial number while in the commission of a felony, and three counts of assault by means of a dangerous weapon.

Upon finding both defendants guilty, Judge Daniel A. Ford sentenced Sostre to serve 20 to 30 years, and Figueroa to 12 to 18 years on the armed robbery charge. On the remaining charges they received concurrent sentences to be served in the state prison.

After the verdict was in, First Assistant District Attorney Paul J. Caccaviello and Chief Anthony J. Riello congratulated Captain Patrick Barry, Investigator Mark Trapani, and lead investigator Detective James Casey, Credit Union employees, officers who worked on the case, and the alert citizens who helped solve the case. Without the help of the alert citizens, the case might have never been solved.

Detective Casey later resigned from the department to became an officer in the Houston Texas Police Department.

PIPE BOMB EXPLODES AT TACONIC HIGH SCHOOL

It was Wednesday, June 9, 2004, at 7:10 a.m. when a pipe bomb filled with .22-caliber nail-gun cartridges exploded just as students were arriving for the classes at Taconic High School. Luckily there were no injuries.

The bomb was placed a blue rubbish barrel near the rear entrance of the school. When the bomb went off, it smashed windows in the rear entrance, and scorched the area. The barrel contained most of the explosion. When the Fire Department arrived they pulled the fire alarm box after finding it was a bomb. Their original call was for a dumpster fire. Students evacuated the building by the front and side doors. Classes were cancelled for the day.

The 2004 senior class had had their prom at the school the night before, so the seniors had the day off. If the seniors had school, there could have been injuries because they usually park their cars in the rear of the school and enter through the rear entrance.

The Berkshire County Tactical Response Team was called in for the manpower to conduct a room- to- room and locker-by-locker search. The search of the school didn't recover any other bombs. The state police bomb squad and agents from the Bureau of Alcohol, Tobacco, Firearms and Explosives were also called into examine the bomb.

Detective Sgt. Mark Bushey and the Detective Bureau were put in charge of the investigation. Sgt. Bushey had been a school resource officer at Taconic High School for a number of years.

An 18-year-old senior became a "person of interest." He was described by detectives as a disgruntled student who was barred from attending graduation and the senior prom. A search warrant was issued to search his house, but no evidence turned up.

After questioning at the station and taking a lie-detector test, given by the ATF. The 18-year-old was no longer a "person of interest" because he passed the lie-detector test.

One witness reported he seen a man wearing a red hooded sweatshirt and blue jeans running from the blue rubbish barrels and jumping over the concrete barrier just before the bomb blast.

Detectives went to several local hardware stores to see if any store sold any materials used in making bombs or bought a quantity of .22-caliber nail-gun charges, with no luck.

A week later, a reward up to $5,000 was offered for information leading to the arrest and conviction of the person or persons responsible for the pipe bomb. The reward was from the Insurance Agencies of Massachusetts through its Arson Watch Reward Program.

After spending hundreds of hours investigating this case, no arrests were ever made and no one collected the reward. The case is still open.

45 YEARS IN STATE PRISON FOR SHOOTING SPREE

On June 22, 2004, a jury of three women and nine men found David K. Baxter, 25 years old, street name "D-Boy", guilty of one count of armed assault with intent to murder, two counts of assault with intent to kill, possession of a large capacity weapon during the commission of a felony, possession of a firearm with a defaced serial number, possession of a firearm without a permit, possession of a large capacity firearm without a permit, attempting to procure perjury, and two counts of intimidation of a witness. The jury deliberated for just under eight hours before finding Baxter guilty. The trial lasted almost two weeks.

District Attorney David F. Capeless and his staff prosecuted the case for the Commonwealth. Defense lawyers for Baxter were Juliane Balliro of Boston and Pittsfield Attorney Leonard H. Cohen.

On December 14, 2002, on North Street between the Advance Auto Parts and Family Dollar Store, Baxter, with a 9 mm pistol in one hand and a .357

revolver in the other hand, fired into a crowd. The crowd was there to watch a fight between Baxter and another party, but Baxter backed down from a fight.

The party that Baxter was going to fight missed being hit, but another party in the crowd, Isaac Pizarro, was wounded. He was taken to Berkshire Medical Center where doctors removed a 9 mm slug. Ballistics tests showed that the 9 mm bullet taken from Pizarro matched the 9 mm that Baxter shot into the crowd.

While recovering from his wound at Berkshire Medical Center, Captain Patrick Barry had Pizarro register under another name for his safety. Pizarro would not cooperate with detectives about the shooting.

A good citizen, whose apartment was next to Advance Auto Parts on Madison Avenue, heard the gunshots. As he was looking out of his window, he saw a black male with a knit watch cap bury something in a snow bank. Investigator Bruce Eaton of the department's crime scene services recovered the 9 mm pistol and the .357 revolver in the snow bank. The revolver had one spent casing in the chamber. Found in the parking lot were a dozen or so spent 9 mm casings fired from the semiautomatic pistol.

9 MM PISTOL   357 REVOLVER

Several weeks later, on January 24, 2003, Pizarro's cousin, Ernest Phaire, Jr., was shot by Baxter in a driveby shooting. Phaire was in a parked car outside of Pizarro's Wahconah Street apartment.

Pizarro still would not cooperate with detectives. He told them he didn't know who the shooter was and didn't see Baxter in the area. Then Pizarro was arrested in Albany, New York, on drug charges. Pizarro was on probation in Massachusetts; this brought about a violation of probation hearing. After the hearing, Pizarro began to cooperate. He gave a written statement and testified in Superior Court that Baxter was the shooter in both incidents.

Also testifying for the Commonwealth about the shooting was Baxter's cell- mate whom he admitted that he was the shooter in both incidents. Baxter's ex-girlfriend also told the jury about the shootings.

Officers Dwane Foisy and Miles Barber, who were among the first officers on the scene of the North Street shooting, told the jury what they found upon arriving.

The perjury charge was brought after investigators received a letter from a girl who Baxter wrote to asking her to lie for him in court. The two intimidation charges were brought as results of Baxter trying to hire a lawyer for a witness, so he could not testify in court against him. The other one was the result of Baxter having a man threaten a witness, who was in jail, so he would not testify in court against him.

After the jury returned the guilty findings, Judge Daniel A. Ford sentenced Baxter to 35 to 45 years in prison.

District Attorney David F. Capeless told the media "These convictions and sentences are important ones for the people of Berkshire County. They signal the end of one major criminal career and reaffirm the dominant position of law enforcement in the battle against crime."

He also commended the lead investigators in the case, Investigator Michael Nykorchuck of the department's Drug Unit and State Police Sgt. Brian Foley, who was assigned to the District Attorney's office.

ARRESTED FOR TENNESSEE MURDER

Two men who moved to Pittsfield in August, 2002, were arrested on fugitive-from-justice warrants; one was accused of murdering a 76-year old woman in Harriman, Tennessee. A Chevrolet S-10 pickup truck stolen from the murdered woman was driven from Tennessee to Pittsfield and sold to a man in Dalton. Both men were charged with the theft of property valued between $1,000 and $10,000.

In the later part of January, 2004, Investigator James Stimpson of the department's Crime Scene Unit received a call from Investigator Bruce Nelson of the Tennessee Bureau of Investigation. They were working with the Harriman Police Dept. to solve the murder of a 76 year old resident of Harriman. The Tennessee Bureau of Investigation had obtained an arrest warrant for a David William Cosgriff, a 61 year old male, accused of the murdering Kathleen Taylor. They also obtained a warrant for 36 year old Christopher J. Zamisz, Mrs. Taylor's, grandson. Both her grandson and Cosgriff were indicated by a Grand Jury for larceny of her truck. At the time of her death, all three lived together in her house. First-degree murder in Tennessee carries the death sentence.

Investigator Nelson explained that Mrs. Taylor's daughter, who lived in Texas, reported her missing in July, 2002, after not hearing from her. Officers from the Harriman Department questioned both Cosgriff and Zamisz. Officers were told that she was in Florida having a knee operation. Soon after being questioned, the duo left Harriman, Tennessee, in Mrs. Taylor's Chevrolet S-10 pickup truck, heading to Pittsfield.

Investigators in Harriman learned that over $20,000 was missing from Mrs. Taylor's bank account. On February 25, 2002 she was in her bank placing a stop payment order on one of her checks. This was the last time anyone saw her.

On December 27, 2003, hunters in Harriman found a severely decomposed body in a shallow grave. After an investigation, the body turned out to be the missing Kathleen Taylor. The grave was only about four miles from her house.

After further investigation, it was learned that Cosgriff formerly lived in Pittsfield. Tennessee was putting out feelers to departments where Cosgriff had formerly lived.

Investigator Stimpson left a report for Det. Captain John T. O'Neil and Det. Sgt. Mark Bushey about his conversation with Investigator Nelson of Tennessee.

Tennessee sent pictures of both parties and their descriptions to the department. A description of the truck and its vehicle identification number was also sent. Detectives and members of the drug unit were now on the lookout to see if the pair was in the Pittsfield or Berkshire County area.

In querying the truck's VIN, it was found out that it was now registered to a resident of Dalton. In talking to the new owner, it was learned that he had purchased the truck from Cosgriff and Zamisz. They gave him the title, so the truck could be registered in Massachusetts. Investigators learned that the duo lived someplace on Bartlett Avenue.

In talking to staff members of the Pittsfield Library, it was found out that the duo spent a lot of time in the library. One staff member told Capt. O'Neil that the duo gave her the willies.

A stake out of the area was conducted and their apartment building was located. Not knowing if they possessed any weapons or how dangerous they were, it was decided to use the SRT unit to enter the apartment. Investigator Nelson from the Tennessee Bureau of Investigation came to Pittsfield for the arrests.

On June 26, 2004, Bartlett Avenue was blocked off at East Street for-safety reasons, while the entry was made into their apartment. Zamisz was found in the apartment and placed under arrest without an incident. While searching the apartment, officers found two marijuana plants in Zamisz's room. He was charged in District Court for possession of the plants. While inquiring about Cosgriff, it was found out that he was working at a North Street store as an assistant manager.

Upon receiving this information, Investigator James Stimpson and Detective Thomas Bowler went to the store. Inquiring at the store, they found Cosgriff was in the back warehouse, stocking supplies. Cosgriff was placed under arrest. This was nearly 2 years after the murder.

Arraigned in District Court before Judge Alfred A. Barbalunga the next day, they were held without bail.

Their cases were transferred to Superior Court for extradition hearings before Judge Daniel A. Ford. The Commonwealth was represented by Assistant District Attorney Joseph A. Pieropan. Cosgriff was represented by Attorney John M. Bernardo and Zamisz by Attorney Dennis Buckley. In separate hearings, both agreed to sign extradition papers to return to Tennessee.

Investigator James Stimpson and Detective Thomas Bowler received a summons from Tennessee to appear in Roane County, Tennessee Superior Court for the trail of Cosgriff. Before the trail began they were notified that Cosgriff pled out and their testimony was not needed.

2005
FISCAL YEAR
July 1, 2004 to June 30, 2005

The following promotions occurred during the year:

Name	Position	Date
Michael Wynn	Acting Lieutenant	02/06/05
Michael Wynn	Lieutenant	03/08/05
Matthew Hill	Acting Sergeant	02/13/05
Jeffrey Bradford	Acting Sergeant	02/13/05
Jeffrey Bradford	Sergeant	03/08/05
Gary Belknap	Acting Sergeant	02/13/05

The following retirement occurred during the year:

Name	Position	Date
Bruce Hugabone	Lieutenant	08/10/04

ARSON AT McDONALD's

On July 4, 2004, the next door neighbor to McDonald's at 445 West Housatonic Street, reported that the east side of the building was fully engulfed in fire. The east side of the building is where the drive-up window is located. The clapboard siding was charred black. A tarp had to be placed over the drive-up window and roof as there was a huge hole in the roof, exposing the inside of the store.

Thirty employees were put out of work. The store was closed for a couple of weeks while repairs were made. The owner tried to relocate some of the employees in the two other stores he owned.

The fire originated underneath the drive up window. Captain-in-charge Patrick Barry was asked if the Taconic Pipe Bomb incident on June 9 was related to the McDonald's fire. He said that the McDonald's fire appeared to have involved an accelerant, not an explosion like the one Taconic High School.

Det. Sgt. Mark Bushey was put in charge of the investigation for the department. A small task force was put together, which included Sgt. Bushey, Chief Stephen Duffy of the fire dept. a member of the State Fire Marshall's office, an ATF agent, and a FBI agent from the Springfield Office.

Detectives interviewed all thirty of the employees of the store. All evidence from the fire was sent to the state police crime lab.

A $5,000 dollar reward for information leading to the arrest and conviction of those responsible was offered.

On July 10, the FBI offered and additional reward for information, but to this day no one has collected any of the rewards or been arrested for the arson.

CHAPTER FORTY

PLUMBER FOUND DEAD IN VAN

On January 19, 2005, Wednesday, the department received several calls that a man was slumped over inside his van. The temperature in Pittsfield plunged to minus10 between 7:00 p.m. Tuesday and when the body was found just before 7:00 a.m. on Wednesday. The van was on Circular Avenue near the road's intersection with Division Street.

The fire department was called to gain access to the van. Firefighters broke the van's rear window in order to gain entry. The red van had the name of Adornetto Plumbing & Heating written on the side. Inside was the body of 45- year- old Gerald Adornetto. Adornetto, who had long been a Pittsfield resident, was now living in Cheshire. Neighbors said they had spotted the van in the area several times in the last few weeks. The van had been parked in the same place since at least Tuesday, according to witnesses.

ADORNETTOS VAN

The van was towed to the Police Station garage at Police Headquarters. A forensics team from the department and state police crime lab combed it for evidence.

Detectives John Gray and Michael Maddalena were assigned as lead investigators.

The death was classified as apparent homicide. According to the state Board of Plumbers and Gas Fitters., Adornetto's plumber's license, which is required to work in Massachusetts, expired in May and had not been renewed.

On September 2, 1997, Adornetto had been sentenced to serve three to four years in state prison and placed on five years of probation after he admitted in Berkshire Superior Court to a vicious domestic assault on his then wife. Adornetto had thrown his wife down the basement stairs of their home on Gamwell Avenue, smashed her head into the floor, and then used a broom handle to choke her. He pleaded guilty to armed assault with the intent to murder, assault and battery by means of a dangerous weapon, and assault and battery.

Adornetto was also arrested in the summer for burglarizing a Sunset Avenue house in Lenox, where he had previously done work. Among other items, he stole a 300-pound safe. When arrested, police found the stolen items in his possession, He pled guilty in Southern Berkshire District Court to breaking and entering in the nighttime to commit a felony, wanton destruction of property over $250, and two counts of larceny over $250.

Adornetto, whose arrest triggered a Superior Court probation violation, served several months in jail and was placed on two years of post-release supervision in connection with the theft charges.

District Attorney David F. Capeless, after receiving the autopsy results, reclassified the death of Adornetto as "suspicious" from the original belief that he was a victim of a homicide. It was initially thought that he was murdered because of "several injuries to the body," knife wounds. The exact cause of death was not determined until the results of the toxicological testing were returned.

The autopsy was performed by Associate Medical Examiner Dr. Loren Mednick at the Officer of the State Medical Examiner in Holyoke. Dr. Mednick determined that Adornetto died of a heart attack due to acute cocaine ingestion.

A statement given to detectives on January 19, unsealed in August, seven months after the body was discovered, revealed that Anthony Carnute, 23, had received a call from Adornetto from a pay phone on January 17, and they made plans to take a ride together.

Carnute's cell phone was found in Adornetto's van. Detective John Gray was granted a search warrant on February 2, to search the cell phone.

Also found in the van were two pieces of crack cocaine, with an estimated street value of $140. Detectives were not able to definitively link the drugs to either Carnute or Adornetto. Carnute had known Adornetto for about a year and admitted to selling drugs to him in the past.

Carnute met up with Adornetto on Circular Avenue and an altercation took place with Carnute stabbing Adornetto. A silver knife was used in the stabbing, which was never found. Detectives believe that someone, after learning of altercation, removed and disposed of the knife. Carnute suffered some injuries of his own during the altercation and was taken by ambulance to Berkshire Medical Center, a short time after fleeing the van. The stabbing came to the attention of the detectives. Carnute, however, was uncooperative with authorities and offered no information on how he was hurt until two days later.

District Attorney David Capeless said, "Carnute did not break any laws by failing to alert police to any possible injuries to Adornetto. Under these circumstances, there was nothing criminal that he had done, if there was, we would have charged." The official finding was that Adornetto died of a heart attack.

Chief Anthony J. Riello said "The detectives, the drug investigators and our patrol officers did a superb job in investigation that incident, from the moment that we made the discovery to the follow-up investigation when we took several statements."

FEBRUARY 2, 2002-BOYS CLUB- RED SOX TROPHY

CHAPTER FORTY-ONE

MURDERED FOR $150 DEBT

On February 6, 2005, Brandon LaBonte, 21 years old was lured away from his Pittsfield apartment. LaBonte owed Damien Lamb 25, a debt of $150. LaBonte was told that he could work off the debit. LaBonte was taken by Damien Lamb, 25, Steven J. Fish, 21, and David A. Davies III, 21, to a wooded area in Washington. They handcuffed LaBonte, asking him if he want a beating or a finger cut off. LaBonte told them he would take a beating. The trio then beat LaBonte. Lamb was a judo and kickboxing expert.

Ten days later, on February 16, 2005, LaBonte was enticed to go with Fish and Lamb to Lamb's father's house in Becket. Lamb told LaBonte that he could work off a $1,200 debt he owed to another friend. LaBonte was never seen again.

LaBonte was reported missing and an investigation was started by Pittsfield Detectives. The questioning of Damien Lamb solved the mystery of LaBonte's disappearance and eventually led to Lamb's arrest.

State Police Detectives assigned to District Attorney David F. Capeless's office were called in to take over the investigation as it was out of Pittsfield's jurisdiction. Trooper Stephen R. Jones was lead investigator for the State Police Detectives.

A seventeen day trial in Superior Court before Judge John A. Agostini took place. First Assistant District Attorney Paul J. Caccaviello was lead prosecutor. This was his first murder case. Assisting counsel for the District Attorney's office was Richard M. Lock. Court appointed attorney for Lamb was William A. Rota; assisting Rota was attorney Anthony Gianacopoulos.

Steven Fish became one of the Commonwealth's lead witnesses. Fish told the court that he accompanied Lamb and LaBonte to Lamb's father's house in Becket. Fish testified under oath that Lamb told him to wait in the car while he and LaBonte went inside Lamb's father's house. A while later Lamb told Fish that he wanted to show him something. Getting out of the car and walking to the front of a parked truck, he saw LaBonte's body on the ground. A shovel was covering his face, with a rope around his neck. They placed put him on a tarp and put him in the trunk of the car. The following day, Lamb, Kendra Keith and Fish dove to Lamb's mother house in Peru. They dragged the body to a beaver hut in a swampy area and hid it there.

An extensive search was made for LaBonte's body by officers and cadaver dogs. The body was never found or any trace of it on the 83 acre tract of land.

BEAVER HUT

The Commonwealth put forth the theory that his mother may have brought the body to an incinerator where it was disposed of. His mother worked for the state Division of Fisheries and Wildlife in Pittsfield. Part of her job was disposing of dead animal carcasses in an incinerator. Under Massachusetts General Laws, Chapter 274, Section 4, parents, brothers, sisters, grandparents, grandchildren and spouses cannot be charged as accessories after the fact in felony cases, because of their intimate relationships with a defendant.

Kendra Keith, 19, who met Lamb at the Martial Arts Academy in Pittsfield, testified in court that they were romantically involved. Lamb wanted the relationship kept hidden as he was living with the mother, with whom he had a daughter.

Lamb came to Keith's apartment at 3:00 a.m. that morning showing her LaBonte's body in the trunk of the car. He wanted her to help dispose of the body. Keith was terrified of Lamb. She stated that she, Fish, and Lamb drove to Peru and hid LaBonte body inside a beaver hut.

A jury of seven women and five men deliberated for two days before finding Lamb guilty of second-degree murder. He was also found guilty of assault and battery, assault and battery by means of a dangerous weapon, and assault and battery to collect a loan.

Superior Court Judge John A. Agostini sentenced Lamb to life in prison at Cedar Junction. He also received a 3 to 4 year sentence for the other assault and battery to be served if he made parole in 15 years.

Both Steven J. Fish and David A. Davies III pled guilty to assault and battery, assault and battery with a dangerous weapon, and assault and battery for the purpose of collecting a loan. Fish also pled guilty to accessory to murder after the fact. Both men were sentenced to time already served and were placed on probation. This was the agreement worked out with the District Attorney and their attorneys for testifying at the trail.

Kendra Keith pleaded guilty to accessory after the fact of murder and was placed on probation for five years. Two of the conditions of her probation were that she continue counseling and have no contact with Lamb. Timothy J. Shugrue was her attorney.

KNIFE TO MAJOR ARTERY LEADS TO DEATH

TYSON BENOIT
PHOTO BY BEN GARVER EAGLE STAFF

On May 30, 2005, Tyson Benoit and a 13 year old boy had been sitting with friends outside of 299 Francis Ave. in the early morning hours, when 18 year old Anthony Hopkins passed by. Benoit told his young friend about an incident, where Hopkins made racial remarks to Benoit and his friends resulting in a brawl that left one of Benoit's friends with severe facial injuries. Benoit told his friends "Let's go mess with him."

They followed Hopkins to his parents' house on Robbins Avenue and started throwing rocks at him as he banged on his front door. Hopkins then turned and charged at Benoit, who had armed himself with a knife, and a fight ensued. Benoit stabbed Hopkins in the torso and neck area, which cut a major artery. Hopkins later died from blood loss at Berkshire Medical Center.

Benoit was arrested after an investigation by the detective bureau and state police assigned to the District Attorney Office. Benoit spent 475 days at the Berkshire County House of Correction awaiting his trail.

The trail was held in Berkshire County Superior Court in January 2007 before Judge Daniel A. Ford. First Assistant District Attorney Paul J. Caccaviello and Assistant District Attorney Richard M. Locke sought the first-degree murder charge against Benoit, alleging that he intended to kill Hopkins to settle the bad blood between them. Caccaviello cited the incident of racial remarks and the brawl that left one of Benoit's friends with severe facial injuries.

Public defender Nathaniel K. Green had argued that his client hadn't intended to kill Hopkins and he should only be found guilty of manslaughter.

The jury of six men and six women, including three women alternates, deliberated for close to 2 hours before returning a verdict of second-degree murder.

Judge Daniel A. Ford sentenced Benoit to serve life imprisonment, as required by a second-degree murder conviction, at Massachusetts Correctional Institution at Cedar Junction. He was credited with the time he awaited trial toward his 15 years before he would be eligible for parole.

2006

FISCAL YEAR
July 1, 2005 to June 30, 2006

The mission of the department was to work in partnership with the community, to protect life and property, and enhance the quality of life in our city. This was done with a total 89 officers. The department was broken down in three divisions each headed by a captain all working together to make a progressive agency. Each division reported to Chief Anthony J. Riello. *The three divisions were:*

Administrative	Captain John T. O'Neil
Special Operations	Captain Patrick Barry
Patrol	Captain David Granger

There were thirty-seven officers in patrol with one officer on military leave, Officer Gary Garand, and ten openings. Fifteen officers served in the Special Operations Bureau. There were four officers in the schools, one DARE officer and three in the Traffic Division. There were 26 support personnel one full- time animal control officer, Joseph Chague, and part-time officer, Terrence Moran.

The Special Operations Bureau, under the command of Captain Patrick Barry was comprised of the Narcotics Unit, with one sergeant and five drug investigators. During the year they took part in "Operation New Year" which resulted in the arrest of over 30 people for heroin distribution and related charges. This was the largest heroin round up in the history of Berkshire County. Heroin, cocaine, and marijuana are the predominant drugs of choice in the community. This unit also assists the detective bureau with the investigation of major cases.

The Detective Bureau had six detectives and was responsible for the complex investigation of all major crimes, such as homicides, robberies, and rapes. They investigated six shootings and one murder case, among other crimes, during the year.

The Crime Scene Services Unit had two crime scene investigators and is responsible for processing crime scenes and solving crimes based on evidence obtained.

The Anti-Terrorism Unit had one detective, Richard LeClair, who serves as the department's liaison to the FBI Joint Terrorism Task Force and investigates any terrorism related activity in Berkshire County.

The Patrol Division commander was Captain David Granger. This division was the back bone of the department. Under Captain Granger were three lieutenants each in charge of a shift with three sergeants on each shift. Lt. Michael Wynn was in charge of the day shift, 8 a.m. to 4 p.m., Squad A; Lt. Michael Winston was in charge the 2nd shift, from 4 p.m. to midnight, or Squad B; and Senior Lt. Katherine O'Brien was in charge of the midnight to 8 a.m. shift or Squad C. Total calls for the year were 42,473.

Traffic enforcement, accident investigation, taxi cab and wrecker inspections, hit and run follow-up investigations are the main function of the Traffic Bureau. The unit consisted of Sgt. Michael Fitzgerald, Charles Bassett, Marc Maddalena and James McIntrye. The department issued 7,408 citations during the year and investigated 1,994 motor vehicle collisions. Of these accidents, 268 had injuries and three were fatalities.

Part of the Administrative Captain's duties was to interview all persons applying for a license to carry a firearm. Captain John T. O'Neil was the issuing authority for the department. The total number of licenses issued during the year was 486. The total fees collected was $37,700, out of this the city received $9,500 and the state $28,200. Sue Wheeler, the FID/LTC clerk, processed all persons by taking their fingerprints and photographs. One of the new provisions of the Gun Control Act was that a person applying for any firearms permit who was not licensed as of 06/01/98 must submit a basic firearms safety certificate with his application. Another provision was that the disqualifying categories for FIDs and LTCs were significantly broadened.

During the year Information specialist Alan Zawistowski, with the help of capital funds and grant funds, was able to acquire the following technology: Five new MDTs (mobile data terminals) that were placed in the field: three were placed in new patrol cars: one was placed in the sergeant's vehicle and one was placed in the new lieutenant's vehicle. Also added were two new digital cameras to the Patrol Division. A digital system supplied by the District Attorney's office with some funding from the department was set up in the station. This unit records audio and video during interviews and statement. This video captures the suspect's, victim's, and witness's true emotions, records both audio and visual actions from suspects, victims, and witnesses, and is more reliable reporting to help increase convictions.

Qwest E911 Language translator services lets an interpreter be merged into a 911 call within 23 seconds. The interpreter/translator can immediately start translating what the calling party is saying and then interpret what the dispatcher is saying to the calling party. There are over 140 languages that are supported by this service.

The department increased building security and building accessibility by adding a phone intercom system both at the main window and the handicap access ramp/door. The phone and intercom system tie directly to the Dispatch Center, which is staffed 24/7.

On May 9, 2006, the department launched the program "A Child Is Missing." This program notifies local residents that a child, Alzheimer patient, or disabled adults has wandered off or has been abducted. This is done by sending out phone calls to the neighborhood from where the person is missing. Over 1,000 calls per minute can be sent out asking the neighbors to check their area for any signs of the person. This program is available to police departments at no cost through the national nonprofit agency.

To activate the system the department would call A Child Is Missing with the name, description, and last known location and time the person was seen. A ACIN technician would pull a satellite image of the area, and with the help of the department would determine if there are any likely places where the person could be, such as parks, ponds or shopping centers. Then the technician would send out a tape-recorded message to that area with the information. The first few hours are critical in finding a missing person. Only 2 percent of people receiving a ACIN message will hang the phone up and not listen to the message and help. The ACIN database only can call listed phone numbers, but citizens can contact ACIN and have their unlisted phone number put in the database.

PROMOTIONS–RETIREMENTS–RESIGNATIONS

On September 13, 2005, Sgt. David Granger was promoted to Captain.

Retirements	Date
Henry Dondi	03/04/06
Ronald Kitterman	07/01/06

Resignations	Date
Thomas Barnaby	11/26/05
Adam Cruz	01/24/06
Felix Aquirre	01/31/06
Cynthia Brown	04/30/06
Brian Sayers to Trooper NY State Police	05/07/06

ARREST OF BEVERLY'S MOST WANTED FELON
TWO DAY STAKEOUT ON NORTH STREET BUILDING

On January 12, 2006, the department received a call from the Beverly Police Department. Detective Thomas Nolan stated that they held a warrant for a Louis Gonzaelez, 28, of Lynn, Massachusetts. The warrant was for armed car-jacking and carrying a firearm without a Firearms Identification Card. Back on September, 27, 2005, Gonzaelez stole a car at gunpoint in Beverly. The driver was not injured. The car was recovered a short time later with Gonzaelez's fingerprints on the driver's wheel.

Gonzaelez had eight other warrants outstanding in the Commonwealth. He went by five different names. Most of the warrants were under his aliases. Beverly Police made him their "Most Wanted Felon."

Beverly detectives received information that Gonzaelez was in Pittsfield, staying with a friend in his North Street apartment. They didn't know the friend's name except that the live in apartment building on North Street given a description of the building. They sent the department his picture and prints.

A two day stake-out of the building was conducted by detectives. Finally, on Saturday, January 14 2006, a male fitting Gonzaelez's description left the building. As he left the doorway he pulled his hood up to block his face. As he was getting into a parked car, Detectives Dale Eason and James Roccabruna approached him. Gonzaelez gave one of his aliases, but the picture they had of him matched perfectly. He was placed under arrest and was arraigned in District Court on Monday. Beverly Police transported him back to their city.

In talking to Beverly's Detectives it was learned that Gonzaelez had taken off from a halfway house where he was paroled to. He was serving a five year sentence at the state prison.

58 STABB WOUNDS
THREE WEEK
MANHUNT FOR MURDER

Family and friends reported to Pittsfield Police that Michelle Townsend, 27, mother of four children, ages 22 months to 7 years, went missing over the weekend of March 4, and 5, 2006. They expressed concern over her whereabouts because of a volatile history between her and her husband.

A friend, Michele Matthews, said Michelle Townsend left a desperate phone message from her husband's, Seymour Townsend, Lincoln Street apartment early Friday, March 3, 2006. Friends called police after Michelle Townsend failed to show up for breakfast with a friend on Friday and did not respond to their calls. Her mother filed a missing person's report on Saturday.

Based on these concerns, police made several attempts to reach her on Saturday and Sunday.

On Monday morning, Sergeant Matthew Hill, with the assistance of firefighters, kicked down Seymour Townsend's apartment door shortly after 9:30 a.m. after receiving another request from the state Department of Social Services and Michelle Townsend's family.

Inside the apartment was the body of Michelle lying on the living-room floor covered with a white sheet. The kitchen floor, which adjoins the living room, was covered with blood.

OFFICER JAMES McINTYRE GUARDING CRIME SCENE
PHOHO BY BEN GARVER EAGLE STAFF

Pittsfield and state police crime scene investigators were called in. Found in the living room was a bloody fingerprint which investigators matched to Seymour Townsend's fingerprint. Investigator James Stimpson videotaped the entire crime scene.

Detective Dale Eason was able to get an arrest warrant from District Court for Seymour Townsend for the murder of Michelle Townsend, based on the bloody fingerprint that was discovered at the crime scene and the desperate phone call Michelle made to her friend from her husband's apartment. Townsend went by several aliases "Rohan Davies, Sidney Downing and S. T."

Detectives also searched for Michelle's vehicle, a green, 1998 Dodge Grand Caravan with Massachusetts plate number 30WF28. Seymour frequently drove this vehicle.

Michelle had encountered her husband's violent behavior in the past. On August 24, 2005, he was arraigned in court on charges of assault and battery and destruction of property over $250. Officer Kipp D. Steinman investigated the incident and stated that Seymour had punched his wife with a closed fist and "went from room to room destroying things." She had endured physical abuse from him in the past and lived in fear of him. On September 28, 2005, she dropped the charges against him.

District Attorney David F. Capeless and the Pittsfield Police appealed for the public's help in finding Seymour Townsend, an unemployed Jamaica, New York, native.

After a three week search, on March 23, 2006, Pittsfield Detectives Thomas Harrington and Thomas Bowler, along with New York City Police and federal agents, caught Townsend staying at a friend's apartment in Jamaica, Queens, New York.

Detective Harrington stood in the rear of the apartment making sure no one fled out the back. Detective Bowler went to the apartment front door with the others members of the arrest team.

Detective Harrington stated in court that "I saw a person's head look out the apartment window, look toward the street and then look toward the yard" "I didn't know if he was going to flee, so I moved closer." It turned out to be Townsend, who asked the detective who police were searching for. Harrington said, "You'll see-go and answer the door."

SEYMOUR TOWNSEND

During an interview with police at the 113th Precinct the next day, Townsend admitted to killing his wife and then driving her green Dodge Caravan to the city by day-break. He had parked the van across the street from a Bronx Hospital, had thrown away the license plates and keys, and had gone to another hospital to get treated for a cut on his right pinkie finger that he received from the attack on his wife. He then walked around for hours before arriving at his friend's place in Jamaica.

During the five day trial, District Attorney David Capeless and his First Assistant, Paul J. Caccaviello, argued that Townsend was guilty of first-degree murder based on both theories of premeditation and extreme atrocity or cruelty. A first-degree murder conviction requires a finding of only one of the theories.

Defense attorney John M. Kaufman argued that Townsend "snapped" when he killed his wife and instead should be found guilty of the lesser charges of second-degree murder or of voluntary manslaughter.

Dr. Loren J. Mednick, of the state medical examiner's office, described the 58 stab wounds that Townsend had inflicted on his wife, Michelle Padgett Townsend. She said that she was likely near death from blood loss before she suffered the last dozen stab wounds in her upper back.

Brian Cunningham, a DNA expert, said Michelle's blood was found on her husband's clothing, on the kitchen knife he used to kill her, and throughout the apartment where the body was found.

On Thursday, May 17, 2007, a jury of 10 women and two men returned the verdict of first-degree murder after 4 hours of deliberations over a two day period.

Superior Court Judge Judd J. Carhart sentenced Townsend to the mandatory sentence of life in prison.

Berkshire County District Attorney David F. Capeless thanked the family, friends and witnesses who testified during the trail, and the members of the Pittsfield Police and Massachusetts State Police Crime Scene Services and Crime Laboratory who assisted in the investigation.

MEMORIAL DAY – MAY 19, 2006

2007

FISCAL YEAR
July 1, 2006 to June 30, 2007

The strength of the department throughout the fiscal year 2007 was stable. Two long time officers retired: Officer Thomas Harris on December 23, 2006, and John McGrath on January 24, 2006. Jonathan Garson resigned on June 3, 2007. Five officers were added to the uniform force on Tuesday, December 12, 2006: Tyrone Price, James Lowsaw, Brett Wallace, Christopher Whitney and Gnacio Matos.

With the help of Community Policing Grant money, the department was able to expand the K-9 unit from one officer to three. One team was assigned to work each shift, giving the city around the clock coverage. The K-9 Unit had existed since 1991. The unit was started with grant funds to purchase and train one dog and handler.

JAMES PERISE & NERO

JENNIFER JAYKO & CERO

The new K-9s were Nero, a German shepherd from Czech Republic and his handler James Parise, and Cero, another German shepherd also from the Czech Republic and his handler, Officer Jennifer Jayko.

There are several benefits of the K-9 unit, because of a superior sense of smell and hearing and potential for controlling aggression. The trained law enforcement K-9 is a valuable supplement to the police officer power.

The K-9 dogs are trained as patrol and narcotics detection dogs. The dogs perform a variety of police duties, including tracking, narcotics searches, and perimeter containment.

MEMORIAL CEREMONY FOR K-9 IYOX

On January 23, 2007 a reflection service was held at the Elks Club on Union Street as a tribute to K-9 Iyox. Iyox died on January 9, a veteran of

10 years with the department. His partner was Officer Dwane Foisy. Iyox was cross-trained in patrol and narcotics detection. About 50 officers from departments throughout the Berkshires and officers who trained with Iyox from Albany, East Greenbush, and Columbia County in New York attended.

Chief Anthony J. Riello presented Iyox with a posthumous commendation for his many years of service and for his capture of the Bank North Bank robber in November of 2004.

CRIME REPORTING

The department submits all "part one crime" to the FBI according to its national reporting criteria of the Uniform Crime Reporting Program. The following were reported; homicide 0, rape 107, robbery 47, assault 973, burglary 437, larceny 499 and auto theft 87.

The department, by the way of the Communication Center, answered 48,915 calls for service. They also received 8,415 calls for the ambulance and Fire Department, 15,000, 911 calls and approximately 30,000 non-emergency calls. The center is comprised of one supervisor, Jack Tobin, one assistant supervisor, Scott Connors, nine full time emergency telecommunications operators, and two part time operators. Their duties include answering 911 emergency calls and dispatching the proper police, fire and or ambulance response and answering non-emergency phone calls. They speak with citizens, who walk in to the lobby with a question, problem, or concern, and they monitor public building alarms for fire or burglar.

Among the duties of the Administrative Captain were the Auxiliary Police. The unit consisted of 9 active members who worked 1,352 man hours. Sixty eight of these hours were for the 4th of July parade. During the year, they were called in six times for emergency purposes, three for fires and three weather related emergencies. When officers were available on Tuesday, Thursday and Friday evening they did their usual patrols of public buildings. The Auxiliary Unit augments the department in a vital non-law enforcement role.

On September 29, 2006, Chief Anthony J. Riello appointed Administrative Captain John T. O'Neil, Captain in charge of the Traffic Bureau and Special Events.

The Traffic Bureau officers, Officer Charles Bassett, Marc Maddalena, and James McIntyre, handled 469 motor vehicle accidents including three fatalities. They issued 2,431 motor vehicle citations, made 72 arrests for motor vehicle violations, and served 73 arrests warrants.

Under information specialist, Alan Zawistowski, the cross-agency networking took place. This technology uses the state CJIS network to connect all full- time Berkshire County Police Departments IMC (Independent Media Center) records databases together. This allows any full- time officer to query reports, photos and calls from any other full- time police department. This feature is available in the station as well as in the cruisers. The ability to see what police involvement someone has throughout the county is a huge officer safety and crime- solving tool.

The department's new state-of-the-art radio system, called "The MASTR III P25", is an industry leader in interoperability, performance, and reliability. This system provides secure digital communications for mission critical applications. In addition to the base station, two MASTR III repeaters were also purchased. The repeaters improve the signal strength of the police frequency throughout the city. Additional incident command channels were also added, which allow an event to have a dedicated radio channel. All the new equipment was placed in the new dispatch center with acoustic walls and ceilings, ergonomic furniture made from recycled materials, state of the art E911 system upgrades and 3 position TDM-150 radio consoles.

The department has six officer candidates in the Lowell Police Academy who will graduate in November. Once they complete the department's field-training program, they will be ready for unaccompanied patrol in the spring.

4th OF JULY PARADE

CAPTAIN JOHN T. O'NEIL'S LAST PARADE AFTER
40 YEARS OF SERVICE

MARINE PATROL BACK ON
LAKES AFTER EIGHT YEARS ABSENTS

Due too many complaints from the boating public on Onota and Pontoosuc Lakes, and with a $10,000 grant from the state's community policing funds, the department's boat was taken out of moth balls. It had been taken out of service due to a lack of funds and volunteer patrolmen to operate the boat. Funds were needed for more pressing enforcement priorities.

The boat sat idle in storage for nearly eight years and required a major tune-up. Local boat dealers donated parts and labor to restore it to tip top shape, along with a new paint job.

Twelve officers, who own personal boats or knew how to operate a boat, signed up for the detail. Sgt. Mark Bushey and Sgt. John Murphy were the first officers to operate the boat on its shake-down patrol, on August 17, 2007. The marine patrol works closely with the Environmental Police, who have jurisdiction over all state water ways, but are spread thin, due to their budget.

SERGEANTS' BUSHEY & MURPHY

Word spreads quickly among boaters and Jet Ski operators when the department's boat is on the lake. The marine patrol checks to make sure all watercraft obey the 45 mph speed, limit carry a fire extinguisher and proper life preservers. If driving at night or dusk, navigational lights are required.

PROMOTIONS–RETIREMENTS

NAME	RANK	DATE
Lt. Michael Wynn	Acting - Captain	08/18/2007
Sgt. John Mullin	Acting Lt.	08/18/2007
Det. Glenn Decker	Acting Sgt.	08/18/2007
Inv. Michael Grady	Acting Sgt.	08/18/2007
Act. Det. Timothy Koenig	Detective	08/18/2007
Off. John Soules	Drug Investigator	08/18/2007
Off. David Kirchner	Drug Investigator	08/18/2007

ASTRONAUT STEPHANIE WILSON SEPTEMBER 12, 2006

CAPTAIN-IN-CHARGE

Michael J. WYNN

On November 28, 2007, the Mayor of the City of Pittsfield appointed Acting Captain Michael Wynn to the position of Captain-in-charge of the department. This was due to the fact that Chief Anthony J. Riello retired from the department and accepted the position of Chief of Police in Falmouth, Massachusetts, effective December 1, 2007. Wynn was only an acting captain as there were no openings in the captain's rank. The position of full time captains was filled by Captains Patrick Barry, David Granger and John T. O'Neil. Senior Captain O'Neil was out on leave preparing to retire, thus creating an acting position.

CHAPTER FORTY-TWO

LAST ROLL CALL

On December 27, 2007 Captain John T. O'Neil and Detective Richard LeClair attended their last roll call. (The officers had total of 73 years of combined service to the City of Pittsfield). Captain O'Neil had 40 years of service and Detective LeClair had 33 years of service. Also present were members of Squads A and B the Detective and Drug Unit and some off duty officers. Captain-in-charge Michael Wynn, on behalf of the department, presented each officer with a plaque stating their years of service and a gold retirement badge. Upon the official retirement of Captain O'Neil, Captain Wynn was made a permanent captain.

JOHN O'NEIL, MICHAEL WYNN AND RICHARD LECLAIR

ON TO RETIREMENT...

LIST OF SOURCES

The History of Pittsfield (Berkshire County) Massachusetts:
From the year 1734 to year 1800
By J.E.A. Smith
Published by Lee & Shepard
149 Washington St.
Boston, Mass.
1869

The History of Pittsfield (Berkshire County) Massachusetts:
From the year 1800 to year 1876
By J.E.A. Smith
Published by C .W. Bryan & Co.
Springfield, Mass.
1876

The History of Pittsfield -Towns Government
From the year 1876 to 1891
By Edward Boltwood
Published by Eagle Printing & Binding Co.
Pittsfield, Mass.
1916

The History of Pittsfield Massachusetts:
From the year 1876 to year 1916
By Edward Boltwood
Published by City of Pittsfield
1916

The History of Pittsfield Massachusetts:
From the year 1916 to year 1955
By George F. Wilson
Published by City of Pittsfield
1957

Annual Report of the selectmen of the Town of Pittsfield
For the year ending April 1, 1852
Steam, Press of Axtell & Marsh
1852

Inventory of the Town and City Archives of Massachusetts
No. 2 Berkshire County
Vo. XXII. Pittsfield
The Historical Records Survey
Service Division
Work Projects Administration
1942
War Duty, July 1942
Federal Bureau of Investigation
J. Edgar Hoover, Director
1942

Encyclopedia Wikipedia - Queen Withelmina
Wikipedia i, English. Started in 2001

Annual Chief's Reports from 1876 to 2008

CHIEF JOHN M. HATCH	1876-1881	April 1876 to June 1881
CHIEF JAMES McKENNA	1881-1886	June 1881 to Nov. 13, 1886
CHIEF JOHN NICHOLSON	1886-1905	Nov.13,1886 to April 1, 1905
CHIEF WILLIAM G. WHITE	1905-1913	Apr.1, 1905 to Jan. 6, 1913
CHIEF DANIEL P. FLYNN	1913-1915	Mar.10,1913 to May 8, 1915 * Died
CHIEF JOHN L. SULLIVAN	1915-1947	Sept. 13,1915 to Feb,18, 1947
CHIEF THOMAS H. CALNAN	1947-1964	Feb. 26,1947 to June 10, 1964
ACT-CHIEF CAMILLE L. MARECL	1964-1964	June 9, 1964 to Nov. 29, 1964
CHIEF JOHN J. KILLEEN	1964-1978	Nov. 30,1964 to Dec. 25, 1978
ACT. CHIEF ANTHONY J. PIRES	1979-1980	Jan. 2 1979 to Nov. 20,1980
CHIEF STANLEY J. STANKIEWICZ	1980-1986	Nov. 20,1980 to Jan.17,1986
CHIEF WILLIAM M. DERMODY	1986-1988	Jan. 21,1986 to Oct. 1, 1988
ACT. CHIEF COSMO SPEZZAFERRO CAPT-IN-CHARGE	1988-1989	Oct. 1, 1988 to Feb. 16,1989
COSMO SPEZZAFERRO	1989-1991	Feb. 16, 1989 to Mar. 26, 1991
ACT. CHIEF WALTER M. BOYER	1991-1992	June 11, 1991 to Nov. 25, 1992
CHIEF GERALD M. LEE	1992-1997	Nov 25, 1992 to Jan.3,1997
CHIEF ANTHONY J. RIELLO	1997-2007	Jan. 4, 1997 to Dec.1, 2007
CAPT-IN-CHARGE MICHAEL J. WYNN	2007-2009	Dec 1,2007 to Jan. 22,2009

Seventy-three years of personal knowledge of the Pittsfield Police Dept.

Deceased Members
Retired Members
Active Members
Officer Francis Honk Connor
Officer John E. Gogan
Officer Royal McGuirt
Detective Francis D. O'Neil
Captain John T. O'Neil
Officer Merton Vincent
No one ever went Thirsty in Pittsfield
Prohibition Era
William Jetty, 99, of Pittsfield
Sam B.Knew of raid in advance
Steve Salvini-Chief Killeen
Joe R. Touring card to Canada

The Berkshire County Eagle
June 1, 3, 1898, July 1, 24, 1916, August 2, 1916
July 17, September 4, December 2, 1901
July 19, 21, 28, 29, 30, 1920
September 13, 1934

April, 1937
April 12, 1939
April 21, 1939
January 24, 27, 1940
January 29, 1940
July 19, 1943
November 10, 1943
January 6, 1945
May 29, 1946
October 9, 1946
January 15, February 11. 12, 13, March 21, August 6,
October 21, 1947
July 24, 1947
August 26, 1947
June 2, 1948
December 18, 1948
July 2, 1952
September 21, 1955
Berkshire Evening Eagle
January 23, July 12, 1911
July 24, August 2, 1916, July 19, 21, 28, 29, 1920
April 20, July 11, 1917, April 7, 10, 15, 1919
February 13, 1924
September 14, 1935
April 24, 29, 1936
December 16, 1939
December 4, 1942
November 10, 1943
September 26,27,28,29, October 1, 22,29,1943 February, 22, 23 24, March 2,
June 9, 1944, July 16, 24, 31, August 7, 8, 1946 October 16, 1947
May 10, 14, 16, 1946
February 11, 1952
December 16, 1953
November 22, 1954
December 20, 1954, February 2, 1955
July 2, 1955
January 9, May 3, 1956
February 8, 11, 1956-Tatro
June 18, 1956
August 4, 18, 1958, April 8, 14, 1959
July 2, 1956
February, 1959
October 14, 15, 20, 1959 March 15, April 8, November 26, 29,
December 8, 9,12,13,19,21,1960
November 28, December 2, 1960, Dec.1, 5, 6, 1961

The Berkshire Eagle
November 11, 12, 23, 1966 - July 23, 1968
October 9, November 1,4,7,1968, April 3, July 7. October 9, 1969
February 10, 16, 26, March 27, April15, 16, 1969
July 3, 1969
October 24, 1969
August 22, November 11, 1969, November 18, 1974
December 23 and 24 1969 March 26, October 8, 1970
July 17, 17, 1969, January 25, March 9, 11, 13, 1971
Spring 1971
June 28, 1971
July 24, 1972, August 3, 1972, March 6, 7, 9, 13, 1973
January 15, 1974
December 3, 1974 November 13, 197
December 24, 1974, January 3, 1975, September 15, 1980
April 11, 1975, February 4, 1978
September 16, 17, 18, 19, 20, 22, 1975
June 8, 1976
May 19, 20, 22,1978 November 15, 17, 1979
December 5, 7, 1978 May 29, 1973
June 24, 26, July 7, 1979, September 23, 1980, March 24, 1984
September 13, 24, 1979, May 27, 1983
September 11, 1980
January 29, 1981
February 6, 1981
February 19, October 18, 1981, October 30, 1985
November 1, 1982 March 31, 1983
December 2 and 3, 1982
December 17, 1983, January 7, May 5, 1984
June 9, 1984
April 22, October 26, 1985
September 16, 17, 18, 1985
September 10, 1986, March 4, 1987
September 8, 11, 1988, May 27, June 16, 20, 1989
September 23, November7, 8, 1988
November 14,15,1988, August 15, 1989
November 15, 1988
July 3, 1990, February 8, 1991
July 13, 1990
October 2, 3, 10, 29, 1990, May 25, 1991
November 29, 1990
December 12, 1990
April 10, 1991, June 9, 1993, July 20, October 7, September 21,
December 15, 29, 1994, January 14, April 21, September 29, 1995
April 25, 26, October 19, 1991
December 14, 1991

July 3.13, 1992
September 7, 8,23,1992 May 22, 25, 1993
November 25, 1992
March 2, 1993
January 11, 12,13,14,15,16,17,19,20,25,28, February
8, 9, 10, 21, 23, 24, March 10, April 1,6,30,
May 5, July 16, October 4,6,8,13,26, 1994, June 4, October 6, 7,
November 2, December 26, 1996, February 7, April 12, 1997
February 21, 1994
August 13, 1994, October 27, December 7, 2001, March 13, 2002.
January 23, 1996
March 2, 1996
September 16, 1997
July 15, 1998
November 16, 1998
November 14, 1998 May 8, 1999, February 12, 2000
September 1, 2, 2000, December 6, 2001
November 16 October 27, 2001
August 8, 9, October 10, 2001
January19, 21, 26, February 12, 2001
March 13, 2002
August 18, 22, 1923,, 2002, October 9. 2004
December 27, 2002, February 1, 2003
January 21, 2003, January 13, 2004
June 8, July 8, 2003, July 31, August 3, November 4, December 2,
2004
July 16 and 17,2003
December 25, 26, 2003
January 13, 2004
January 27, 2004
March 6, 2004
May 1, 2004
September 29, 2004
November 4, 2004
November 4, 2004
November 24, 25, 2004, March 30, 2006
December 23 and 24,2004, February 16, June 1, 2, May 25,31,2006
January 20 21, 22, February 19, August 18, 2005
April 9, May 17, 18, 19, 20, 21, 25, July 6, 2005
August 20, 23, 2005 August 10, September 7. 12, 13, 15, 20, October, 3, 5,7,21,
November 2, 17, 2006 April 5, 24, 2007
March 7,8, 2006, May 16,18, 2007
May 25, 26, 2006
June 18, 2006
November 12, 2006
January 10, 2007

February 16, 2013
Springfield Union Newspaper
Some facts about the department
By G. H. Harris-1903
March 25, 1934
September 9, 1945
September 18, 19, 1975
October 6, 1988
Springfield Republican News Paper
August 1, 1940
July 16, 1944
September 18, 1975
Sun Newspaper
July 30, 1944
Pittsfield Gazette Newspaper
July 16, 1998
January 13, 1994
National Law Enforcement Review Sept. 1946
Union-News
September 23, November 27, 1988
The North Adams Evening Transcript
December 14, 1927
Berkshire Superior Court
Clerk's Office
Criminal Records
East Street, Pittsfield, Mass.

Inquest into Death of Captain Michael Leonard
Central District Court of Berkshire County

Commonwealth vs. Brian Matchett-386 Mass. 492
Commonwealth vs. John F. Noxon- 319 Mass   495
Commonwealth vs. Baggett, Michael – BECR2003-00015
Commonwealth vs. Leone, Nancy-BECR2003-0017
Commonwealth vs. Petrozziello, Ralph - 22 Mass. App. Ct. 71
Commonwealth vs. Donahue, Michael-396 Mass. 590

Photos by
C&S Video
Dondi, Henry, PPD
Garver, Ben, Eagle Photo Editor

Henzel, George, Photography
Librizzi, Joel, Eagle Staff
Mason, William, Police Investigator
Noyes, Leslie, Eagle Staff
Ploffe, William, Photography
Walker, Craig, Eagle Staff
Wynn, James, Police Investigator

Captain John T. O'Neil (Ret.)

Lifelong resident of Pittsfield
Married with three children and seven grandchildren

GRADUATED
Pittsfield High School
Berkshire Community College- Associate Degree in Police Science
North Adams State College-Bachelor of Art
American International College-Master Degree Criminal Justice
Commonwealth of Mass. Municipal Police Training Council
N. E. Institute of Law Enforcement Management
40 Year member Pittsfield Police Department
Receiver of 18 Department Awards:
Exceptional Duty, Life Savings, Certificate of Commendation, Honorable
Service, Gallantry Star,
Unit Citation Award, Special Operations Bureau.
Letter of Commendation from the
Department of the Treasury, US Secret Service.

OFFICES HELD
President MyCom Credit Union
Chairman MyCom Credit Union Credit Committee
Board of Directors Pittsfield Municipal Credit Union
Pittsfield Municipal Credit Union- Security Officer
President IBPO 447S
Treasurer IBPO-447 & 447S
Treasurer Pittsfield Police Association for 38 years
Treasurer Kiwanis Club of Pittsfield
Notary Public for 20 years

National EMT
Massachusetts EMT-A
Massachusetts EMT- Examiner
Massachusetts EMT Instructor/Coordinator
MCJT Council-1St Responder Instructor
City of Pittsfield-Traffic Commission for15 years
Board of Directors EMSCO
Board of Directors American Red Cross
3rd Degree Knights of Columbus, Council No. 103 Pittsfield, Ma.
4th Degree Knights of Columbus, Assembly No. 395, Pittsfield, Ma.
Member Retired State, County and Municipal Employees Association

AUTHORS NOTE

In 2014, Lewis S. Lent JR. confessed to murdering James Lusher of West-field, but to this day (September 21, 2015) his remains have not been recovered. Original details of this murder are on page 285. Joe R. and Sam B. did not want their last names used in the story.

AUTHOR

Captain John T. O'Neil (Ret.)

ACKNOWLEDGEMENT

I want to thank the countless people, who supplied information and provided suggestions during the writing of this book, particularly Tony Demick. Nicole O'Neil for help designing and publishing the book. Matt White and Doreen Magnano for help with edits for without them this book would not have been possible. Listening to senior citizens tell their intriguing stories about prohibition. These stories encouraged me to interview fifty seniors. I was only able to include a few of the many fascinating stories in the book, but have kept notes on each interview.

A Special thanks goes to the retired officers and their families for their many stories and pictures they have shared with me, a collection of over one thousand photos of which only a limited number could be placed in the book.

To the Berkshire Athenaeum, Pittsfield Public Library, Local History Department, Senior Technician Ann-Marie Harris for all her help.

To the Berkshire Eagle for permission in letting me use different articles and photos in this book. Special thanks to Librarian, Jeannie Maschino, for her help in locating different articles.

To the Clerks at Berkshire Superior Court House for their help in researching different cases records.